The Story of Religion in America

The Story of Religion in America

AN INTRODUCTION

James P. Byrd
James Hudnut-Beumler

WESTMINSTER JOHN KNOX PRESS
LOUISVILLE · KENTUCKY

First edition
Published by Westminster John Knox Press
Louisville, Kentucky

21 22 23 24 25 26 27 28 29 30—10 9 8 7 6 5 4 3 2 1

Book design by Drew Stevens
Cover design by Marc Whitaker/MTWdesign.net
Cover photo: The civil rights march from Selma to Montgomery, Alabama, in 1965. Photo by Peter Pettus.

Library of Congress Cataloging-in-Publication Data
Names: Byrd, James P., 1965- author. | Hudnut-Beumler, James David, author.
Title: The story of religion in America : an introduction / James P. Byrd,
    James Hudnut-Beumler.
Description: First edition. | Louisville, Kentucky : Westminster John Knox
    Press, 2021. | Includes index. | Summary: "Written primarily for
    undergraduate classes in American religious history and organized
    chronologically, this new textbook presents the broad scope of the story
    of religion in the American colonies and the United States, paying
    careful attention to balancing the story of Christianity with the
    central contributions of other religions"-- Provided by publisher.
Identifiers: LCCN 2021042040 (print) | LCCN 2021042041 (ebook) | ISBN
    9780664264666 (paperback) | ISBN 9781646982226 (ebook)
Subjects: LCSH: United States--Religion--History.
Classification: LCC BL2525 .B97 2021 (print) | LCC BL2525 (ebook) | DDC
    200.973--dc23
LC record available at https://lccn.loc.gov/2021042040
LC ebook record available at https://lccn.loc.gov/2021042041

Most Westminster John Knox Press books are available at special quantity discounts when purchased in bulk by corporations, organizations, and special-interest groups. For more information, please e-mail SpecialSales@wjkbooks.com.

Contents

List of Figures

Introduction

Christopher Columbus saw what he wanted to see. On October 12, 1492, he landed on an island in the Caribbean he believed was off the mainland of Southeast Asia, then called India. There he and his entourage met a native people who identified themselves with the word "Taíno," by which they meant both "people" and especially "good people," in contrast to their more aggressive neighbors the Caribs. All of this was lost on Columbus. He reported later to King Ferdinand of Spain that the natives on this and other islands were of childlike innocence, eager to give the Spaniards valuables, including gold. The Taíno should be easy to convert, thought Columbus, as he later wrote the king: "They do not hold any creed nor are they idolaters; but they all believe that power and good are in the heavens and were very firmly convinced that I, with these ships and men, came from the heavens, and in this belief they everywhere received me after they had mastered their fear."[1] Columbus captured twenty-four Taíno natives on his first voyage to take them back to Spain and have them trained to be forced missionaries to their own people. Six would survive to join the second voyage.

Those Taíno left on the island of San Salvador (as Columbus renamed it) were treated little better than those on nearby Hispaniola, where, during the visit of his second voyage, Columbus began to require tribute. Each male over 14 years of age was expected to mine and deliver a hawk's bell full of gold (about ¼ ounce) every 3 months, or lacking this, 25 pounds of spun cotton. If this tribute was not paid, the Spanish cut off the delinquent Taínos' hands, letting them to bleed to death. And why did Columbus need the gold? Because, influenced by the Spiritual Franciscans, he believed that he and his contemporaries were living in the last 150 years before the end of time and the gold was desperately needed to help Spain recapture Jerusalem from Islam, part of the same plan that saw the expulsion of the Moors from Spain and, in the year 1492, led Spain to execute 30,000 Jews for not converting to Christianity. Even before his first voyage, Columbus was reminding Ferdinand and Isabella of his gold-for-crusade plan: "I urged Your Highnesses to spend all the profits of this my enterprise on the conquest of Jerusalem and Your Highnesses laughed and said that it would please them and that even without this profit they had that desire."[2] Christopher Columbus was a religious zealot.

Perhaps it was for the best that Columbus proved so poor in inquiring into the religious beliefs of the Taíno, for their religion was polytheistic, featuring worship of zemis, or spirits. Yúcahu, a male spirit, was god of their main crop, yucca, and the sea. His mother, Atabey, was the goddess of the moon, fresh waters, and fertility. Lesser spirits accounted for every other aspect of life, including why hurricanes sometimes came and where people went when they died. Between disease, enslavement, and cultural annihilation, the Taíno would be destroyed nearly everywhere except present-day Puerto Rico, where a remnant of their DNA and tribal ways are still preserved, nurtured, and celebrated. The way religion was involved in the conflict between Spaniards and indigenous people in the 1490s is not an isolated event. American religious history is replete with clashes of cultures and beliefs, often with lives at stake.

———————————————

Five hundred and nine autumns later, on the North American mainland at New York's Yankee Stadium, an extraordinary religious gathering took place to mourn the deaths of 2,606 people in the September 11, 2001, attacks on the twin towers of the World Trade Center. Gathered there were the families of victims, with police, firefighters, celebrities, politicians, and musicians in abundance. The event, introduced by James Earl Jones and emceed by Oprah Winfey, ran for well over two hours. It featured rabbis of every branch of Judaism, Catholic priests and bishops, archbishops—Catholic, Greek, and Armenian Orthodox—Sikh and Hindu leaders, Muslim leaders (male and female), and Protestant leaders from the black church, mainline, and evangelical wings. Police officers and firefighters read Scriptures, the shofar was blown, children sang, and tears were shed.

American religious history had come a long way in five centuries: people were able to openly offer their religious prayers of lament and for healing across faith lines. New York's religious leaders were also on their best behavior that autumn day, aware that the attacks—on the World Trade Center, on the Pentagon, and an aborted one that ended in a plane crash in a Pennsylvania field, presumed to be targeting the White House—were themselves motivated by a violent brand of religious interpretation of Wahhabism Islam emanating from Saudi Arabia. Those gathered at Yankee Stadium to sing, chant, recite Scripture, and pray all sought to fight violent religion with their own brands of peaceful wisdom of the ages. If one were to analyze what the individual faith representatives said that day, one would notice that they were leaning hard in the direction of inclusion—offering the most open-minded things that their traditions had to say to neighbors and strangers, versus the "our way to ultimate reality is the right way" kind of messages that account for there being so many different religious groups in the first place. One clear exception was one Protestant representative of the Lutheran Church–Missouri Synod, Rev. David Benke, President of its Atlantic Division, who used pointedly Christian language throughout his prayer. The first of his three petitions went like this:

> Oh, Lord our God, we're leaning on you today. You are our tower of strength and we're leaning on you. You are our mighty fortress, our God who is a rock. In you do we stand. Those of us who bear the name of Christ know that you stood so tall when you stooped down to send a Son through death and life to bring us back together. And we lean on you today, oh, Tower of Strength. Be with those who mourn the loss of loved ones. Bring them closer to them—to us day by day.[3]

Benke's prayer included allusions to Martin Luther's "A Mighty Fortress" and was as evangelical as anything said that day. He even ended his prayer "in Jesus' name," thus making the rest of the audience Christian, at least by implication. It was surprising to some, therefore, that of all of the people who participated in the interfaith service televised nationally from Yankee Stadium, it was Pastor Benke who was sanctioned by his church for participating. For this participation, he was accused by other pastors in his denomination with six sets of ecclesiastical violations, including syncretism (mixing religions), unionism (worshiping with non-LCMS Christian clergy), and violating the Bible's commandment against worship of other gods. Hence David Benke was suspended from that denomination's roll of pastors. He never apologized for his action and was restored to the ministry on appeal the next year. During the interim he was asked about his decision to step forward as a spiritual leader, and he told reporters, "The religious impulse is extremely strong and vital in the human heart, and will lead people to places they would not go on their own. . . . It is not only a high and altruistic thing; it is a dangerous thing."[4]

This history of religion in America from pre-Columbian times to the present century is a history of contraries—of inclusion and exclusion, of abiding piety that leads to wisdom and reform, and passionate righteousness that leads to schism, dissent, and even more.

A Word for Students

If you have taken an American history course, especially in high school, you might reflect on when religion came up in the course of a typical 500-year-long story. Certain episodes are deemed religious: Pilgrims, Puritans, Prohibition, the election of Jimmy Carter, the faith of George W. Bush. Others have religious dimensions: immigration and nativism, abolitionism, Abraham Lincoln's Second Inaugural Address, Martin Luther King Jr.'s "I Have a

Dream" speech, and protests against abortion. Yet most of the great events of American history are taught with as little reference to religion as possible, for perhaps no other reason so strongly held as the separation of church and state in its customary interpretation in U.S. public schools and consequently the textbooks they buy: to be on the safe side, the less said about religion, the better. Religion-free American history turns out to be incomplete history—a bit like learning chemistry without attention to oxygen and carbon: just as these elements are constituent of so much of physical life, so also religious ideas, organizations, motivations, and conflicts turn out to be central to a large amount of the story of America and its people. So consider this an invitation to learn American history with a new set of lenses, the ones your teachers, school boards, and politicians have conspired to keep from you.

Let us suppose you are one of the growing numbers of the so-called Nones, people who when asked for their religious preference reply "none." What is the payoff in a religious history of America for you? Or, let us suppose you are very religiously committed to your own group and have little initial interest in learning about someone else's religion. What do you have to gain by learning about American religion, what Henry May called "the mode, even the language, in which most Americans, during most of American history, did their thinking about human nature and destiny"? What everyone gains through this kind of study is insight into the ways Americans—Native American, black, white, Asian, Catholic, Protestant, Jewish, Hindu, Buddhist, Baha'i, and so many others—thought about the meaning and the conduct of their lives. All of us live in an American culture shaped by those who went before us. Many of our fellow citizens—though also living in a world of vaccines, the Internet, television, and 24/7 cable news—also think in ways that are highly inflected religiously. So whether you are not very religious, or are very committed to a particular faith, or are somewhere in between, the history you encounter in these pages is one to which you are a recipient. These people, ideas, and groups shaped American culture for better and worse. So this is a good place to warn you that you will meet religious heroes and heroines and villains, good and bad ideas, and inconsistent people in the following pages. Learning about them will help us avoid being too solemn about religion, which after all is a *human* phenomenon; it is about *human beings* seeking and worshiping divine things more than it is about what or whom they seek and worship. Moreover, one cannot be perfectly objective, since that makes one boring (and bloodless) when it comes to people and groups who use their religions to impress and oppress, though we shall endeavor to be fair. There are no "both sides" to religiously inspired enslavement of human beings, or to forced suicides in Jim Jones's Jonestown, for instance, though we shall try to be fair in conveying the evidence about the bleaker sides of history.

Difficult Definitions: America, Religion, and History

It hardly makes sense to begin studying the history of religion in America without defining the key terms. Thus here we provide a brief discussion and delimitation of how this text understands and will use these three important terms, each of which are the subjects of countless books on their own.

America

America was not so much discovered as invented. That is, there was a great contiguous land mass running from the Arctic Circle in the north to the Southern Ocean circling Antarctica, with a great many people living on both of its major continents and many islands. But the land mass had no name until a rich financier and adventurer named Amerigo Vespucci visited parts of present-day Venezuela, Brazil, and Argentina in 1499–1504; he made and signed a map of the continent, showing that what Europeans were sailing to was not Asia. Early in the sixteenth century two subsequent cartographers—Martin Waldseemüler in 1507 and Mercator in 1538—would feminize his name into "America" and put it on their maps, first for South America, and then used it for all of the Western Hemisphere. America, therefore, is a story of invention and application to unknowing peoples who had been on both continents for perhaps 30,000 years. As a concept it also began to fire the imagination of colonizing Europeans who decided that they needed to be there—in America. In this book we will begin with the religious aspects of this invasion of America by the Spanish and Portuguese, the French, the Dutch, and finally the English. Then, as America itself begins to be more and more associated with the people and nation that became the United States, we will follow that thread of the American story most closely. Readers, however, should be alert to the places and times after 1776 where the story of American religion is characterized by geographic expanse and ethnic enrichment.

In a religious history of America, sometimes America goes from being the place *where* the history takes place to being the religious *object of devotion itself*, as in the memorial service at Yankee Stadium we referenced earlier, where the gathered sang hymns to "America, the Beautiful," "The Battle Hymn of the Republic," "The Star-Spangled Banner," and above all, the brassy request/demand of the Deity, "God Bless America," that became a second national anthem of reassurance at sporting events nationwide for most of the next decade. At moments like these, scholars like to talk about a civil religion existing in America: a set of fundamental values, rituals, and beliefs that bind Americans to their nation and to one another, independent of their other particular religious commitments. Both America's many religions and America *as* religion figure into our story.

Religion

In a study of American religious history, it is useful to have a definition of religion that can guide us. Throughout this book we will take religion to mean "belief in and resort to superhuman powers, sometimes beings." Readers will note that this definition, borrowed from our fellow historian Jon Butler, is capacious enough to include religious people and practices that do not presuppose a personal deity, as in the case of many Buddhists and practioners of nature religion, along with the Muslims, Jews, and Christians who are theistic (focused on a divine or supreme being). Our definition also avoids those "religion is good faith, everything else is bad" kind of definitions that plagued religious historians and even anthropologists of the past, who liked to set up distinctions between religion on the one hand and magic, or superstition, on the other. In our view, religion is not on one side of the spectrum, with magic and superstition on the other side. Since it is critical for the sake of learning, we ask readers to stay open to the possibility that if people believed or practiced something seriously, it stands as religion. Indeed, adopting this perspective may open us up to the possibility that Americans before us (and among us still) may have occupied several serious religious stances at once. Great grandpa may have been a Freemason and a Methodist with equal seriousness. Great grandma might have been a faithful Catholic and a practitioner of Santeria. Part of the religious diversity story of America takes place in individual lives. Mother may pray to Saint Jude for healing and wear a New Age copper amulet on the same aching wrist she prays about. Religion in America? It's complicated—and fascinating.

Americans customarily express a belief in God or a supreme, transcendent being in the upper 90 percent range in public opinion polls, even into the early twenty-first century. If this is so, others ask, why are religious congregations not packed each weekend? Are Americans religious hypocrites, or does their belief in transcendence operate both within and beyond ecclesiastical forms? We think a broader definition of religion allows us to explain something about religion in America and to remain alert to subtle signs of religion in America throughout its long history.

History

Though the events of the past are forever fixed, their meaning and significance shifts by virtue of later interpretations, assessments, and questions put to this historical record. In this sense, it is not unfair to say that *questions create history* (in the sense of the history one learns about later). One way most contemporary courses in the history of religion in America differ from those of the middle of the past century is that attention has shifted from traditional religious groups, such as mainline Protestant denominations and Catholicism, to examining the religious dimensions of racism, gender, and social reform in America that are more clearly seen now than in the past. Was religion for or against the forces of justice in America? Did religion defend or decry slavery, for example? Did religious leaders promote women's rights or seek to limit them? As we shall see, often the answer is both. But which religious ideas and practices won and lost the day, and which stayed on the sidelines—these happenings often turn out to have explanatory force for things we care about in our time.

Since all history can be defined as *change over time*, our study of American religious history will look closely for those things that have changed in the historical record. Yet the narratives that are composed about those changes, including this one and the ones readers will form for themselves, are the products of the questions brought to the historical record about what changed and about who mattered when. Thus history, what happened, has a dynamic relationship with historiography, the written accounts given of what happened. The questions we ask can sometimes bring to light new, previously unexplored dimensions of the past. For example, students in the past learned much about the two-hour-long sermons preached by early American male ministers. These students' questions "Where are the women in this story?" and "What did people listening to these sermons think?" led to exciting discoveries about female piety, church membership, and lay disobedience even in the most pious towns; these learnings figure into the way this book relates the story of early American piety. Likewise, questions about enslaved persons constantly subjected to the biblical text "Slaves, obey your earthly masters" (Ephesians 6:5 NIV) led to historians' discovery of neglected primary sources about the "invisible institution" of so-called slave religion and revised the historiography reflected in this textbook.

Where to Begin: A New World for Everyone

Much of the popular and scholarly debate in American history in recent decades surrounds the question of where to begin. Does one begin American history with Jamestown, with Plymouth, with the Spanish and French, or with the indigenous peoples who were already living in the Americas? Or does one try to avoid the vexatious question of beginnings by pursuing a thematic approach instead? American religious history is not exempt from this debate, but we have chosen to tell the story with a chronological frame since it is the one most familiar to students already schooled in American history. Consequently, we begin with large-scale contact in the Americas between Europeans, native peoples called "Indians," first by mistake (in this book we prefer tribal group names when known, but use Native American, Indian, and indigenous as appropriate to the context because these are all widely used by the descendants of indigenous people to positively refer to themselves).[5] Next we move very quickly to regard Africans from more than three dozen different linguistic and ethnic groups, brought here in slavery. For all of these people, this became a new and transformed world, however much they sought to hold on to or transplant the ways of their homelands.

This had profound consequences for the religious and cultural history of the Americas and particularly the nation that would emerge as the United States.

America is a land of many beginnings when it comes to religion: what we call Alaska, Florida, Arizona, Virginia, Massachusetts, and what was once called Huronia are all good places to begin the tale. Yet every religious group and religious person thought, in some measure, that their beliefs and practices were coming with them as religion with a capital *R* (the only and right Religion). Thus they approached the New World as a place where their religion would be continued—a fresh beginning of their own, if you will. As it turned out, the religious story of America became how much the new context transformed the old faith, because in the end process was as important as place. Some of the great successes and failures—even for the dominant Europeans, as we shall see—came by virtue of being remade in the process of indigenization or creolization (mixing). They were not just Europeans abroad since they tried to re-create London in Boston, Charleston, and other cities over time. For Africans the adaptations were complex. The middle passage, the division of families, and even separation from people of one's native tongue on the auction block meant that North America was for some an utter disconnect from previous life. Others found places and people with whom to continue to practice Muslim prayers, plant food familiar from West Africa, and even continue such familiar religious practices as Conjur under conditions of plantation slavery. After 1492, Native Americans also dealt with a new world: they were confronted by disease and Europeans who wanted to trade, take their land, or "save" their souls—the one path unavailable was remaining unchanged.

The religious consequences of peopling North America from so many stocks did not end in the sixteenth and seventeenth centuries, however. An extraordinary dimension of the religious story of America is that people kept coming, bringing their religions with them, and changing American culture in the process. That is as true for the early Quakers coming to New England and Pennsylvania as it is for recent Yazidi refugees coming to America in the wake of the Islamic State's attack on their homeland in Iraq (beginning in 2014).

People and their faiths drive our story, so American religious history is not just about the Pilgrims, who yet are interesting; we will tell their story early on and add more and more fascinating people to the history along the way. Amid the astonishing diversity readers will encounter—the authors warn you—are mostly different kinds of Christians who did not recognize one another as being as similar to each other as we would today. It would be unfaithful to the people who populated America in earlier times to paint a more interfaith picture than existed, but we shall be certain to notice religious diversity as it arrives in our story (thus drawing your attention to how much the diversity story begins as an intra-Christian set of struggles and competitions). We will focus on Christian parts of the story more because there were more Christians. But we will also attend to other parts of the story of religion in America as they arise, especially since the numbers of other religions' adherents mean that they achieve a greater historical impact.

The Action: Exclusion and Conflict; Inclusion and Consensus

Readers hearing that a mostly Christian cast of characters will appear in these pages need not fear that the plot will lack for action. It does not take many people (religious or otherwise) to stir up the question of whether civil society should be influenced more by faith or whether government should be free of religious influences. Historically, Americans like their own particular brands of religion and do not like anyone else imposing theirs upon them. The so-called French and Indian War was, after all, a seven-year-long war about the Catholic or Protestant destiny of North America. Native Americans themselves had religious conflicts leading to war long before Columbus arrived. Conflict is an old story. A related theme throughout our history is who is to be included and excluded in American society when it comes to religion and myriad other matters. It may come as a surprise to think of Baptists and Catholics as at one time among the excluded, but they were. Inclusion is a moving goal.

Even when we learn someone is, say, a Methodist, that can mean very different things at different points in time. There have been times when that religious identification would have clearly required differentiating oneself from society, as in the case of eighteenth-century Methodists banned from wearing metal buttons or any other display of finery, and other times when such a religious identity fit in well with what it meant to be an average middle-class suburbanite in the 1950s.

Religion, therefore, is not just believed; it is also performed, by behaving in ways the adherent finds fitting, or not. Finally, if one is looking for action, watch how many times religion raises the stakes in conflicts in American history. If someone believes God is on their side in a war, or its supposed moral equivalent, woe be to those who take the opposite position. And yet, at times of great national crisis, Americans of the same and different faiths have found themselves drawing on their religions to provide solace in the face of loss or purpose in the face of a seemingly insurmountable challenge.

American religion is to be found in weekend congregations' worship, to be sure, but it is also to be found in the diaries of frightened Civil War soldiers, in civil rights marchers' determined faces, in presidential rhetoric, and in the caretaking rituals that kick in when a neighborhood child is struck with cancer. Religion binds people together, drives them apart, occupies their inward thoughts, and plays all day and night on cable television. Religion is present even in the midst of the worst of American history, serving as a chaplain to slavery *and* providing the motivation to resist it. It was the source for patriotic love of God and country, and the fundamental basis for resisting the war in Vietnam as an unjust war. To comprehend these phenomena we must embrace their breadth.

Primary Documents: A Special Feature of This Book

The authors want to make it possible for readers to examine the evidence for themselves and so have included with this book access to *several dozen* primary documents from the history of religion in America. Together, they might easily double the length of this historiographical account of the history of American religion; yet used in classroom discussions or for personal research, they can not only give a vital flavor of a religious actor or movement in the past, but also allow twenty-first-century people to engage in a kind of time travel, pondering how the past is truly a different country. Many of these documents are briefly introduced in the text at a point where it is relevant to the narrative, and links to these documents are located on the Westminster John Knox Press website for this book (www.wjkbooks.com/TheStoryOfReligionInAmerica). This feature helps instructors and students minimize the cost and hassles of obtaining, clearing, and posting collateral readings.

1. Catholic Missions, European Conquests

Over time, Protestantism ascended to a dominant position in the United States. It did not begin that way, however. First on the scene in the Americas were indigenous peoples, who had religious systems of their own. Then explorers and conquistadors dashed on the scene to win the land for European empires—and for the Roman Catholic Church. This chapter examines this troubling history, especially the often-violent association of mission and conquest.

Religions of the Land

Religious diversity is nothing new in American history. From the beginnings of civilization in North America, various peoples practiced many different religions. Much of what we know about these religions comes from the work of anthropologists and archaeologists, who study many different kinds of evidence, including material sources like pottery, tools, and architecture. In addition, experts in "ethnohistory," an approach to history that combines historical and anthropological methods, have made great strides in understanding indigenous peoples and their religions.

Historians and anthropologists tell us that the original Americans whom the Europeans later encountered may have journeyed across a land bridge (flooded by the rising sea 13,000 years ago) from Siberia to Alaska. But there is much debate about how North America was originally settled. Did people come from Asia or from Europe, or perhaps both? And when did they first arrive? Likely up to thirty thousand years ago, according to the latest estimates. As these peoples spread throughout what we know as the North American continent, they shaped new cultures, and they also shaped the land, building structures that amaze us today, including ceremonial mounds as large as—and often older than—the Egyptian pyramids.[1]

Native American religions were diverse and like many other religions, including Christianity, had views of sacred beings, powers, and objects. We see this diversity reflected in the many languages they spoke. There were several main linguistic families, including Algonquian along the Eastern Seaboard and Northeast, extending as far as the Midwest; Hokan-Sioux, extending from the Southeast all the way to southern California; Uto Aztecan in much of the Southwest; and Eskimo-Aleut in Alaska. This diversity is significant to note because, as Catherine Albanese wrote, "For Native Americans, culture was tradition was religion; so there were as many American Indian religions as there were separate people and societies."[2]

Native American religions reflected their way of life. Some were hunters, like the Oglala Sioux, who moved from today's Minnesota to the Great Plains. They hunted buffalo and practiced the ritual of Sun Dance, a summer celebration of the hunts that brought many tribes together for a four-day ceremony. The Sioux would build a lodge, place a pole in the middle, cover it with symbols, mainly of the buffalo, and have Sioux warriors attach themselves to the pole, usually with bands that painfully dug into their skin. The warriors would then dance around the pole, focusing on the sun for the entire day or until they fell from exhaustion. This was a rite of sacrifice, with the dancers symbolically sacrificing themselves in return for the life-giving nourishment of the buffalo. The point was for hunters to endure pain in appreciation for the gifts of buffalo in the hunt.[3]

In contrast, the Hopi did not hunt buffalo on the plains. They were a Pueblo people, so named because they, like several other tribes in the Southwest, lived in apartment-type dwellings constructed from stone or adobe. Unlike the hunters of the Oglala Sioux, the Hopi farmed, growing beans, squash, and corn. They performed many of their religious rituals in pits called kivas. Because they were farmers, the Hopi followed the pattern of the seasons. And because they farmed in dry, desert lands, their rites focused on water, their most precious resource, much like the buffalo was for the Oglala Sioux.[4]

Whether they were buffalo hunters on the plains or farmers in the Southwest, indigenous peoples shaped religious traditions and rituals around the practical details of their lives. Not all religions were like this, however. Many religions—like Buddhism, Islam, Christianity, and Judaism—are "world religions" in that they exist throughout the world and are not tied to one particular region. In contrast, many Native American religions connected to the land in a more intimate way. It would be difficult to export the religion of the Hopi people from the American Southwest, for example. Missionary zeal was not a mark of most Native American religions because the land played such an important part in their religion. The land was a spiritual guide: it was sacred, directing the people, showing them how to live.[5]

Myths

Central to most religions are "myths," stories about a people and their values, some of which are origin stories, describing how the world and/or a people came to be. Historians label these stories "etiological" myths (from the word "etiology," which means "cause"). We also see stories like these in the Bible, as when the story of Noah's ark explained the origin of the rainbow (Genesis 9:14–15).

According to one Cherokee myth, animals had lived in Galunati, a vault in the sky, until they needed more room, forcing them to venture below into the primordial waters. Leading the way was a water beetle named Dayunisi, who plunged into these waters and brought up mud that later expanded to form the dry land now covering much of the earth. Another figure, the Buzzard, carved the Cherokee's homeland out of the dry land, shaping it into great mountains. This was just one of many stories of creation; most peoples had them, and they often involved mythic figures who shaped the land and the cultures that developed on it.[6]

Native American myths often featured tricksters, who, as the name indicates, lived by deception, tricking others to get what they wanted. Tricksters lived by their wits; they were clever heroes, but not always kind or even moral, not to mention reverent. Tricksters were notorious for their embarrassing sexual and bawdy antics, and they often changed their appearances, assuming various animal disguises. One trickster well known in the Northwest, the Raven, brought the Sun's light to earth by stealing it in a box owned by the Sky Grandfather. This was another etiological myth, explaining how sunlight came to be. Another common trickster was the Coyote. In a myth told by the Nimiipuu people of the Pacific Northwest, the Coyote traveled to the place of the dead to retrieve his deceased wife. He found her but was warned against any contact with the dead, a rule Coyote ignored. He embraced his wife, an act that carried a curse with it. From that time onward, any being who lived would also die. As with the story of the Raven, we see here a story that is both a trickster story and an etiology myth. It shows a trickster acting impulsively, breaking the rules, and it explains why death is universal.[7]

Tricksters did not only cause trouble; they also performed acts of service, such as when the Raven brought light to earth. Most often tricksters were heroes, although flawed and often entertaining. Some of these trickster legends even originated with real people and real events.[8]

Rituals

When many people think of religion, they think less about theology and ideas and more about rituals, especially practices and ceremonies. For Native Americans, rituals allowed people to interact with gods or other holy beings, commemorate rites of passage (rituals that mark changes in life such as from adolescence to adulthood), and celebrate important seasons (such as harvest). Rituals often sought to make things right with the world. When the world seemed out of sorts, such as during a long drought—perhaps the people suffered the drought because of a damaged relationship to sacred beings—rituals could heal the relationship, allowing the people to prosper again.[9]

Rituals tell us a lot about the people who practiced them. Some Native American people hunted to survive, so they had thanksgiving rituals, allowing people to give thanks for a good hunt. We saw an example of this with the Sun Dance of the Oglala Sioux, who danced to give thanks to the buffalo for a hunt. Other hunting peoples had similar practices. The Inuit believed that all living things had *inua*, an essence or spiritual nature that made them unique and survived even after the body had died. If all beings, including animals, had a sacred inner nature, then hunters could not treat animals as mere objects for slaughter. If hunters killed a bear, for example, they had to value the bear's inua, which meant thanking the bear for giving its life for the hunt. If hunters failed to perform this ritual, the bear's inua would inform other bears, who may retaliate by refusing to cooperate with hunts in the future. No bears for hunts meant less food for the people, which led to starvation. Ritual, therefore, could be invaluable to the food supply.[10]

Europeans of colonial times did not typically believe that all beings had a sacred inner nature, so they could not always understand why Native Americans dealt with animals as they did. A Moravian missionary in colonial America was puzzled when he saw a Delaware hunter shoot a bear and then talk to the bear while it writhed in pain: "Hark ye! Bear; you are a coward, and no warrior as you pretend to be. Were you a warrior, you would show it by your firmness and not cry and whimper like an old woman." The hunter continued, "Our tribes are at war with each other, and . . . yours was the aggressor." Then he accused the bear of stealing his people's hogs. Note the language of two "tribes": the Delaware tribe versus the bear tribe. We can see why the Delaware people respected bears. Not only could bears walk upright like humans, but bears also were not just helpless victims; they could also be predators, turning human hunters into prey. Bears were worthy adversaries. The bear needed to understand, therefore, why the hunter shot him: the Delaware and the bears were at war, so the bear should not hold it against the hunter. He hoped the bear would not seek spiritual payback against the Delaware people, cursing them and their future hunts. These rituals dumfounded Europeans, who could not understand why anyone would talk to an animal and expect to be understood. Native Americans disagreed, believing that conversation between hunter and hunted was important, as was respect for the carcass of the slain animal.[11]

As these examples demonstrate, some of the earliest written sources about Native Americans were from Europeans, often missionaries, who wrote about the people they encountered in the "New World." While we learn much from these sources, we must do what we should do with any source—understand its agendas and contexts. Just as there are no completely neutral, unbiased people, there can be no completely neutral, unbiased sources. This doesn't make such sources useless or inferior, but we need to keep their agendas in mind as we evaluate the sources.

Most of these Europeans assumed they were culturally superior to any other people in the world. That is, European culture—a broad term that includes beliefs, values, social practices, education, and technology—was superior to that of any other people, many of whom were considered to be primitive and sometimes even barbaric.

As Christians, these missionaries also believed that Christianity was the world's one true faith, superior to all others. These two related assumptions—European cultural superiority and Christian religious superiority—affected how the missionaries viewed Native Americans and their religions, which affected how they described what they encountered with these peoples. We should also remember that most missionaries came to the Americas with the permission of European monarchs who were more interested in American lands and riches than in American souls. From the beginning, therefore, missions and conquest went hand in hand.

Divided Christianity, Mission and Empire

An important phase of the European encounter with Native Americans began when Christopher Columbus (1451–1506) first sailed in 1492. A few months before Columbus set sail, the Muslims in Granada surrendered to Christian Spain, ending the Reconquista (Reconquest), in which the Spanish Empire completed a "reconquest" of territory that Muslims had controlled since the 700s. This was a triumph for the Catholic Church and the Spanish Empire. Also, 1492 was near the beginning of the Spanish Inquisition (1478–1834), which Spanish rulers devised to centralize their power while fighting what they considered to be false belief or "heresy." Those condemned as "heretics" (believers in false doctrine) were often tortured to death. This was a violent age, when European monarchs, like Spain's Ferdinand II and Queen Isabella I, sealed an alliance of empire and church as they sought to expand their reach in the New World.[12]

For Columbus and other Europeans, Christianity and civilization went together. About three decades after Columbus sailed to the Americas, the Protestant Reformation erupted in Europe, separating upstart protesters, or "Protestants," from the Roman Catholic Church. As the Reformation revitalized and fragmented Christianity, new political and religious structures formed. France, Spain, and England each wedded itself to a different form of Christianity, resulting in a rivalry of empires combined with a rivalry of religions, pitting French Catholics, Spanish Catholics, and British Protestants against one another.[13] All had plans for the land—including exploration, settlement, and acquiring wealth—and all had plans for the people already living in the Americas, including conversion to Christianity and, if they resisted, conquering them by military force. Missions were not just religious efforts; they were also imperial efforts, tied to empires.

Native Americans believed they were constantly surrounded by spiritual forces in animals, plants, and the land. In contrast, many European Christians found most spiritual insights in Scripture. We see the influence of the

Bible almost everywhere, including in the career of Columbus. Although he was far from an expert on the Bible, he perceived his voyages from within a biblical perspective. "God made me messenger of the new heaven and the new earth of which he spoke in the Apocalypse of St. John after having spoken of it through the mouth of Isaiah; and he showed me where to find it," Columbus wrote.[14]

Isabella and Ferdinand, according to Columbus, promoted "the Christian faith, and are enemies to the doctrine of Mahomet [Muhammad], and of all idolatry and heresy." At stake was not only the New World, but also the global conflict between Islam and Christianity. Columbus intended to explore the East Indies, convert the people he encountered to Catholicism, and strengthen an eastern opposition to the Muslims who, much to the horror of the Christian world, still controlled Jerusalem (the Holy Land). New World conversions would also bring riches under the control of the Catholic Church, yet another way to strengthen the Spanish Empire. All these ambitions for conquest, conversion, and exploration were understood through a biblical perspective, as Columbus described in his *Libro de las Profecias* (Book of Prophecies).[15] "Neither reason nor mathematics," Columbus wrote, "nor world maps were profitable to me; rather the prophecy of Isaiah was completely fulfilled," referencing Isaiah 46:11: "the man that executeth my counsel from a far country."[16]

Although the Bible was Columbus's map of the future, he could have used a better map of the Atlantic Ocean in his present. Granted, Columbus knew more than many today give him credit for. He knew the world was not flat, but he still chased the dream many Europeans had of finding an easier way to the Far East by sailing west. Columbus believed he could find this route, but he did not know how far it was to China and Japan. So, when he arrived near the present-day Dominican Republic, only about 3,500 miles away, he thought he had reached India. Columbus landed, founded a community, and named the island Hispaniola. There Columbus met thousands of Taínos, who would soon wish they had never seen Columbus or his ships. As more Spaniards followed Columbus to the New World, the majority of Taínos died in droves while others would work the rest of their lives in slavery.[17]

COLUMBUS'S TROUBLED LEGACY

Christopher Columbus, for all his religious motivations and justifications, was a conqueror and enslaver of indigenous peoples. Columbus did not care much for converting the native peoples to Christianity, despite his claims otherwise. In 2006 some previously undiscovered texts came to light, revealing the full extent of the horrible cruelties that Columbus inflicted on the native peoples under his control.*

*See David Treuer, *The Heartbeat of Wounded Knee: Native America from 1890 to the Present* (New York: Riverhead Books, 2019), 23–24.

It is worthwhile to pause here to consider the horrific influence of diseases on Native Americans. Although war and genocide took unnumbered lives, diseases killed more people than swords. Europeans knew about catastrophic diseases. Perhaps 100 million Europeans died of the plague in the 1300s and later. Another "Black Death" on a similar scale devastated indigenous peoples who came in contact with Europeans but had no immunity to European illnesses like smallpox. Some, like the Puritan governor of Massachusetts, John Winthrop, had a chilling take on such deaths: "For the natives, they are neere all dead of small Poxe, so as the Lord hathe cleared our title to what we possess."[18]

Founding a New Spain in the "New World"

Europeans tried to replicate their old-world empires in the Americas. Even the names of the places they founded show us this desire: they wanted a New Spain, a New France, and a New England. Early on, the contest for dominance among empires was no contest at all because the Spanish took the lead. Thirty years after Columbus first arrived in the New World, the Spanish had begun a conquest of the Americas, with Conquistador Hernán Cortés (1485–1547) moving into Mexico to challenge the Aztecs. Cortés,

FIGURE 1-1. Hernán Cortés, portrait by José Salomé Pina, circa 1879 (Wikimedia Commons, P003430)

like Columbus, believed that the Bible justified his conquest. In the Old Testament, the Israelites conquered the Canaanites to seize the Promised Land. Likewise, Cortés would conquer the Aztecs to claim Mexico for the church and for Spain.[19]

These mixed motives for conquest were clear in Cortés's letter to the king of Spain, Charles V, recently crowned as the Holy Roman emperor: "We were in a position to win the greatest kingdoms and dominions in the world for Your Majesty. . . . We were only doing what we were obliged to do as Christians, by fighting against the enemies of our faith." Earthly riches and glory blended with religious duty. God would fight on behalf of God's chosen people, who, according to Cortés, were the Spanish.[20]

The letters of Cortés included dramatic narratives of deliverances in battle, including one case in which he and his men were trapped by "an hundred thousand warriors, who surrounded us on all sides." Despite the long odds, "it truly appeared that it was God who battled for us, because amongst such a multitude of people, so courageous, and skilled in fighting, and with so many kinds of offensive arms, we came out unhurt."[21]

At the time the undisputed conqueror of Central Mexico was Montezuma II (1466–1520), who ruled from Tenochtitlán, the Americas' greatest city in the sixteenth century and the site of modern-day Mexico City. Tenochtitlán must have been a sight to behold for Cortés as he approached. Spain had no city as large as Tenochtitlán, which even rivaled Paris in size. Cortés likely marveled at Tenochtitlán's stone pyramid, the site of Aztec rituals, including human sacrifice.[22]

The meeting between Montezuma and Cortés was monumental, a scene of two conquerors from rival civilizations, greeting one another. It also was a monumental confusion. As any dignified Spaniard would, Cortés walked up to embrace Montezuma, not knowing that it was forbidden to touch the great leader. The embarrassment of that first meeting aside, they did exchange necklaces, and Montezuma honored Cortés by allowing him to stay at his father's palace. But there are usually two sides to every story, and the fact that neither side recognized the other's language did not help. According to Cortés, Montezuma presided over a ceremony where he willingly submitted to the Spanish king and pledged allegiance to Spain. Montezuma likely did no such thing; Cortés probably misinterpreted or misrepresented what the Aztec ruler said.[23]

Later Montezuma did submit to Cortés—by force, as the conquistador captured Montezuma and "transferred" the Aztec Empire from Montezuma to Emperor Charles V. Despite what Montezuma really said in the ceremony, Cortés did not need much justification to conquer the Aztecs because, as he saw it, he was a Christian and an agent of the Holy Roman emperor, while Montezuma was an uncivilized pagan ruler. Cortés thought it was his civic and religious duty to replace Aztec paganism with Spanish Catholicism.

Cortés and his men sacked the Aztecs, removing and destroying their items of worship, which the Spanish called idols, and replacing them with Catholic icons. This infuriated the Aztecs, as did Cortés's capture of Montezuma. They eventually revolted and expelled Cortés and his men from the city. It was a short reprieve, however, as Cortés regrouped and seized control of the city in 1521.[24]

About 18 years later another Spanish explorer, Hernando de Soto, sailed into Florida, along with an army of about 600 Spaniards. They had heard of the challenges indigenous peoples presented, and they were ready with chains and collars in hand to capture and enslave them. De Soto's devastation in the American Southeast matched that of Cortés in Mexico. Native Americans either submitted to Spanish rule or faced dire consequences. Some were dismembered; others were burned at the stake.[25]

As with Columbus, perhaps more devastating to indigenous peoples were the diseases de Soto, his men, and their pigs brought with them. Native Americans sometimes understood these diseases as a mighty supernatural power possessed by the Europeans. If Europeans could bring death, perhaps they could also employ their power for good, some reasoned. After de Soto crossed into present-day Arkansas, the Casqui people asked de Soto

FIGURE 1-2. Montezuma receiving Ferdinand Cortez (Hernán Cortés). www.loc.gov/item/2018756664/, LC-DIG-ppmsca-58839 (Library of Congress)

to cure the sick and perhaps to cause rain to fall and relieve their drought. De Soto gave them a cross instead, demanding that they kneel before it and worship Christ, the Son of the only God, and the giver of eternal life. This talk of "eternal life" gave some indigenous people the idea that Christians would never die. Yet de Soto died. To maintain the ruse of invincibility, de Soto's successor hid his body, burying it in the Mississippi River. As far as the Native Americans were concerned, however, de Soto had risen to the heavens. Some, however, doubted that de Soto was in heaven, and one of those doubters was a fellow Spaniard, Bartolomé de Las Casas (1484?–1566), who figured that de Soto had been damned for eternity for his atrocities against the Native Americans.[26]

From a young age, Las Casas had been fascinated by the Americas. He had seen Christopher Columbus in a parade in Seville, celebrating his return from the New World. No doubt Columbus impressed the crowds with real-life Native Americans (Taínos), along with other exciting souvenirs from his adventures. By 1502, Las Casas was in Hispaniola, working as a Dominican religious teacher. His position gave him a clear view of the atrocities indigenous peoples suffered at the hands of Europeans, including slavery and murder, experiences that turned him into a fierce opponent of European enslavers. That compassion did not extend to Africans, however, as he suggested that Europeans enslave Africans instead of Native Americans, although he came to regret this horrific scheme.[27]

Las Casas stirred controversy by publishing *An Account, Much Abbreviated, of the Destruction of the Indies*, an attack on Spanish mistreatment of Native Americans. The critiques of Las Casas and others got the pope's attention, who in response issued *Sublimis Deus* in 1537, stating, "Indians and all other people who may later be discovered by Christians, are by no means to be deprived of their liberty or the possession of their property, even though they be outside the faith of Jesus Christ; and that they may and should, freely and legitimately, enjoy their liberty and the possession of their property; nor should they be in any way enslaved; should the contrary happen, it shall be null and have no effect."[28]

It was clear to many at the time, therefore, that the conquest of the Americas shaped a toxic alliance of violence and religion. This was never more evident than in the relations between the Pueblo tribes and the Spanish in New Mexico. There, Pueblo peoples resisted Spanish domination with an explosive revolt in 1680. For twenty prior years, Pueblos had suffered through droughts that damaged crops and fended off attacks by invading Apaches and Navajos. All these hardships proved to the Pueblos that Spanish Christians had no special relation with divine powers that could either improve the weather or protect their people. What good, then, was Christianity? It brought only trouble. More Pueblos thus rejected Christianity in favor of their traditional religions, and this revival of Pueblo religions offended Spaniards, rousing them to attack Native American priests and ceremonies. In response, many Pueblos vowed that the Spanish had to go; it was the only way for Native Americans to return to their way of life and, hopefully, to prosper.[29]

But how? The Pueblo tribes had attempted revolts before, but these uprisings had faced impossible odds due to a lack of organization and planning. How could nearly 20,000 Pueblo, living in about 25 scattered villages, organize a revolt, especially since they spoke half a dozen languages? The answer came with Popé, a Tewa Pueblo and medicine man whom the Spanish had whipped and imprisoned for practicing "sorcery." By 1679, however, Popé was free, hiding from Spanish authorities, and planning a massive rebellion.

FIGURE 1-3. Statue of Po'Pay (Popé), New Mexico Marble by Cliff Fragua, given in 2005, Capitol Visitor Center, Emancipation Hall, U.S. Capitol (Wikimedia Commons)

The Spanish did not see it coming until it was too late. Led by Popé, the Pueblos hit hard and fast, killing hundreds of Spanish and destroying their buildings and fields. This was partly a religious war as the Pueblo laid waste to churches, destroyed Catholic images, and tortured and executed 21 missionaries.[30]

After winning their independence, the Pueblo held it for thirteen years. The Spanish, meanwhile, remained in El Paso, looking for the opportunity to reconquer the land. In 1693, Spanish governor Diego Vargas, supported with an army of a hundred Spanish soldiers and some Pueblo allies, defeated the Pueblo at Santa Fe. This time Spanish rule held, even though the Pueblo tried to revolt again in 1696.[31]

After the Spanish reconquered New Mexico, the Franciscans (missionaries and members of a Catholic religious order named after Saint Francis of Assisi) lost much of their stature in Pueblo communities. In previous years, these missionaries had been the main mediators between the Spanish and the Native Americans. No longer. Native Americans relied less on Franciscan friars to negotiate with Spanish officials. By this time, the Franciscans were not as important to a Spanish crown that was less concerned with missionary work and worried more about the French, who had closed in on Spanish territory, carving their way through the Mississippi River Valley.[32]

Many Pueblo welcomed this decline in the Franciscans' power, believing the missionaries had done more harm than good. Between 1600 and 1750, when the friars had wielded authority, the Pueblo had seen their people decimated, perhaps losing 90 percent of their population. So much for Christian "salvation," many Pueblo believed. Though many Pueblos converted to Catholicism, most were probably Christians in name only.[33]

Spanish missions, and controversy over their methods, expanded in the eighteenth century as Friar Junipero Serra led missions into California. Serra, a professor from Mallorca, traveled to Mexico City to take a position at the Franciscan College of San Fernando. After two decades there, Serra moved west and founded Mission San Diego in July 1769, the first mission in the territory that would become California. He went on to found eight additional missions, including San Francisco, founded in 1776, just as Thomas Jefferson and his colleagues were declaring independence from the British Empire. These missions had two main goals: convert Native Americans to Christianity, and help Spain hold its claim to the Pacific coast, an important objective because others, including Russian explorers, had their sights set on the region.[34]

In his efforts for missions, Serra worked tirelessly, although much of that work included abuse of Native Americans. Missionary work could be harsh, Serra believed, and he had no qualms about beating indigenous peoples into submission. He would whip them, lock them in stocks, and mete out other punishments so severe that a governor in the area complained of his methods. (Usually the friars were the ones complaining that the governors were too hard on the Native Americans.) This was an issue in 2015, when Serra became Roman Catholicism's first saint to be canonized in the United States. While advocates pointed to the merits of this "Apostle of California," others pointed to his brutal treatment of the Native Americans. Serra's canonization is yet another reminder that church and crown comprised the Spanish Empire in North America. Many Spanish missionaries, although limited by the Eurocentric bias of their time, wanted to convert the Native Americans so that they would live and die as sincere Christians and thus be saved. Yet missionaries answered to Spanish governors, who had authority over the church in mission territories, a right given by the popes. This hampered missions, mainly because Native Americans could not separate the Christian faith from the imperialistic oppression that came with it.[35]

THE JUDGMENTS OF HISTORY

The debate over Serra reminds us that the judgments of history change over time. Different times have different values, and we see this especially when we consider honoring people from the past. Serra's conflicted canonization process also reminds us that people from the past, like people from the present, rarely fit into tidy categories of "hero" or "villain." Few human beings can be judged that simply. Even those who accomplished great acts of justice probably also committed atrocious acts as well, and even those who committed the worst of atrocities probably also did some good things in their lives. This does not give people from the past a pass on judgment—far from it. Historians have a responsibility to reveal the past honestly, based on the best evidence, and that means calling out injustices and holding accountable those who were responsible. History should not degenerate into nostalgia, a sentimental or romantic view of a past that never was.*

*See Gordon S. Wood, *The Purpose of the Past* (New York: Penguin Press, 2008), "Introduction"; Russell Johnson, "Imagining History without Heroes and Villains," in *Sightings: Reflections on Religion in Public Life*, September 14, 2020, https://mailchi.mp/uchicago/sightings-217225?e=980cc6e621.

Finally, we should correct the common view that Europeans, like the Spanish, overpowered native peoples with little opposition. The truth is much different; it was not just a story of the Spanish running roughshod over Native Americans. For example, from the beginning of the eighteenth century, the Spanish faced new enemies on the horizon, the Comanches, who launched an empire of their own that more than matched the Spanish Empire in North America. Until the late 1800s, the Comanches controlled more of the Southwest than any European power.[36]

A New France in Canada and the Midwest

Aside from the Comanches, another of Spain's competitors for dominance in the Americas was France, Europe's other great Catholic empire. While the Spanish focused on the Southeast and the Southwest, the French moved into Canada and territory that later became the American Midwest, exploring these lands in the sixteenth century. In the early seventeenth century, the English joined the race for colonization by founding Jamestown in 1607. The French followed the next year with the founding of Québec (city). French colonists, led by Samuel de Champlain, pursued profits through fishing and fur trading and, like many others, hoped to find the legendary "Northwest Passage," an easier way to the Far East by sailing west.[37]

Like the Spanish, French explorers traveled with Catholic missionaries, hoping to win Native Americans for church and empire. Unlike the Spanish, most French missionaries were not Franciscans; they were of a different religious order: the Jesuits, the Society of Jesus, founded by Ignatius of Loyola in 1540. The Jesuits differed from the Franciscans in their approach to Native American cultures. In contrast to the Spanish Franciscans, the Jesuits benefited from previous missionary experience in China, which taught them much about relating to non-Western peoples. Jesuits took seriously St. Thomas Aquinas's belief that God empowered all humans with reason, so all had some sense of morality and God, even if they had neither seen a Bible nor heard a word about Christianity. [38]

Jean de Brébeuf, who came to America in 1625, was a Jesuit missionary among the Huron (Wendat) peoples who worked to learn Huron cultures and languages, even if it meant suppressing the European revulsion to Native American cultures. As Brébeuf wrote to would-be missionaries, eat the Hurons' food "in the way they prepare it, although it may be dirty, half-cooked, and very tasteless. As to the other numerous things which may be unpleasant, they must be endured for the love of God, without saying anything or appearing to notice them." Above all, missionaries should "have sincere affection for the Savages," Brébeuf advised, "looking upon them as ransomed by the blood of God, and as our Brethren."[39]

Jesuits had success among the Hurons, in part because of their more culturally sensitive missionary practices, but also because the Hurons needed the French to help them against the Iroquois.[40] No Native American people had a more intimidating reputation than the Iroquois confederacy, comprised of the Five Nations of the Mohawk, Oneida, Onondaga, Cayuga, and Seneca. "The character of all these [Iroquois] Nations is warlike and cruel," said Paul Le Jeune, a Jesuit missionary. "The chief virtue of these poor Pagans being Cruelty, just as mildness is that of Christians, they teach it to their children from their very cradles, and accustom them to the most atrocious carnage and the most barbarous spectacles," Le Jeune wrote in 1657.[41] Many Native Americans would rightly dispute this claim for the "mildness of Christians."

War had great cultural value for the Iroquois. When they lost loved ones, the Iroquois would often channel that grief and anger into an attack on their enemies, a practice that came to be known as a "Mourning War." Usually the female relatives of the dead called for a raiding party. Any captives could be adopted, repairing the spiritual void of the dead, or the mourners could assuage their anger by torturing the captives. These rituals involved ripping fingernails out, slowly burning parts of the body, scalping, and beheading. After killing the captive, the Iroquois would cook and eat the flesh. Through it all, the Native Americans respected captives who could face death and torture bravely and without emotion; in contrast, they despised cowards who pled for their lives. In war, therefore, the Iroquois celebrated and unified their people, proved their martial power, and taught their young men to face death without fear.[42]

Stories of the Iroquois' torture of Jesuit missionaries have received a lot of attention, especially the killing of Jean de Brébeuf in 1649. Brébeuf faced torture and death bravely, earning the respect of the Iroquois. After Brébeuf died, his torturers paid him the ultimate tribute by eating his heart, hoping it could give them some of his courage.[43] Brébeuf's death became legendary in Christian history. Catholics lifted him up as a martyred saint while Protestants described him as one who accepted the dangerous challenge of Christianizing a frontier. For the Iroquois, however, his death was likely a ritualistic killing.[44]

We see, then, that Native Americans' religious views differed greatly from each other, although there were some characteristics that seemed prominent across many traditions. For the most part, they were local religions, each specific to a particular people who inhabited a certain place and lifestyle. As Europeans worked among them, Catholic missionaries from France and Spain rarely understood religious views of the people they were trying to convert. Along with misunderstandings based on cultural differences and language barriers, missionary work also suffered because of the missionaries' often violent methods as they worked with explorers to Christianize and exploit the "New World."

2. Puritanism in New England

As the Catholic nations of France and Spain launched conquests and missions in the Americas, England also experienced vitality and growth. Adventures on the high seas had brought unprecedented pride to the English people, peaking with the English defeat of the Spanish Armada in 1588. A few years later, as English colonists founded Jamestown, Virginia, in 1607, William Shakespeare was enjoying the prime of his career, having recently written *King Lear* and *Macbeth*. There seemed to be nothing the English people could not do.[1] In 1534 the king of England had even defied the Roman Catholic Church. Henry VIII (1491–1547) wanted a son who would follow him on the throne, and he was convinced that he could never have a male child with his (current) wife, Catherine of Aragon (1485–1536). Henry sought to annul his marriage to Catherine so that he could marry Anne Boleyn (1507?–36), but Pope Clement VII had no intention of granting an annulment, especially since Catherine's nephew was Charles V, the king of Spain and the Holy Roman emperor. This crisis could not be solved legally; it called for a restructuring, Henry believed, and he dissolved the relationship between the English church and the pope. The Church of England no longer stood under the authority of the pope, but under the authority of the crown.

History is often a story of unintended consequences. Henry got what he wanted, a church that invalidated his marriage to Catherine of Aragon, but he also got something he did not want, an English church that was neither fully Catholic nor fully Protestant. Some wanted England to join the Protestant Reformation, but Henry did not want to follow Martin Luther (1483–1546), John Calvin (1509–64), and others in reforming the church. Likewise, Henry got his desired marriage to Anne Boleyn; but just as with his first marriage, he received no son, only a daughter, Elizabeth, much to Henry's frustration. Eventually the king rejected Boleyn. A group of Henry's advisers brought charges against her for adultery and other crimes, eventually leading to her execution by beheading. Next he married Jane Seymour, and that marriage finally produced a son, Edward (1537–53), who succeeded Henry on the throne. Edward, only nine years old when he became king, ruled through adult advisers, many of whom were Protestants. One of these advisers, Thomas Cranmer (1489–1556), used his positions as royal adviser and as the Archbishop of Canterbury to reform the liturgy and doctrine of the church, moving it farther away from Catholicism and putting it more in line with the Protestant movements of Luther and Calvin.

This English move toward Protestantism, however, halted when Edward died in 1553. He was succeeded by his half sister, Mary Tudor (1516–58), daughter of Henry and Catherine of Aragon. A staunch Catholic, Mary tried to restore the English church to its Catholic beginnings, which meant cleansing the church of Protestant liturgy, doctrine, and especially Protestant ministers. Mary earned her name "bloody Mary" by having 288 Protestants burned at the stake, including Cranmer. Not all Protestants succumbed to Mary's fiery furnace, however. Many of them fled to the European continent, where they took refuge with other Protestants in Switzerland, especially in Geneva, and in southwestern Germany. Geneva was home to the reformer John Calvin, and many of these other areas were home to people who shared similar views—often called the "Reformed tradition" to distinguish this approach to the Reformation from other views, including those of Martin Luther.[2]

Mary Tudor's persecution of Protestants did not last long. She died in 1558, and many English men and women who had taken refuge in Europe returned home to find a new queen, Elizabeth I (1533–1603), daughter of Henry and Anne Boleyn. Protestants had high hopes for Elizabeth. She placed the English church on a more firmly Protestant footing, ending Mary's persecution, and many Protestants hoped that she would complete the reformation of the church, ridding it of its remaining Catholic elements in doctrine and liturgy.

Others in England were tired of all the turmoil over religion. In just a few years, the church had changed from Catholic to Protestant, then turned back to a more Catholic direction, and then reversed course again, moving back to a stronger Protestant position. This was lunacy, many believed. Religious affiliations were deeply meaningful for many people, and they could not simply change their religious views every time a new monarch took the throne.

Elizabeth did not want to get entangled in religious divisions and debates. She tried to avoid religious extremes, an approach that troubled some Protestants, especially those who had spent Mary's reign exiled in Europe. These Protestants wanted a stricter reform of the Church of England, a reform that was needed because the English church had been tainted with Catholicism, they thought. Many of them equated Catholicism with the authority of the antichrist, the evil power who would make war on the church, as they believed was foretold in the book of Revelation and other scriptures. These strict Protestants earned the nickname "Puritans" because they wanted to purify the church.

Elizabeth reigned for a long forty-five years (1558–1603), and the Puritans worried for much of that time, dissatisfied with her lack of interest in reforming the church as they wanted it done. Her successor, James I

(1603–25), was even worse, in the Puritans' view. He gave England a new Bible, the Authorized Version of 1611, later famously known as "the King James Version"; but the Puritans preferred the Geneva Bible, which had marginal notes reflecting Reformed theology and somewhat radical politics. By the time Charles I (1600–49) came to the throne in 1625, many Puritans were looking for another place to raise their children. Not only did Charles sympathize with Catholicism, but he also offended Parliament (where Puritans had supporters), and he even tried to rule without Parliament. Under Charles's command, William Laud, Archbishop of Canterbury, opposed Puritans, viewing them as enemies of the Church of England. About this time, Puritans and their families began moving to North America, hoping for the freedom to live as they believed the Bible dictated. As we shall see, their search for freedom for themselves did not carry with it a desire to allow freedom to those who disagreed with them.[3]

Separatist "Pilgrims" and Non-Separatist "Puritans"

Puritans were not the first English people to set sail for the New World. We have already mentioned the English settlement of Jamestown, Virginia, in 1607, about which we will share more later. In addition, another group of English people moved to New England in 1620, and these were the famous "Pilgrims" who landed in Plymouth. Previously, many of these people had left England for Holland, where they could have the freedom to worship as they wanted. But they wanted to raise their children in an English, not Dutch, culture. This was one of the main reasons they migrated to North America, to form a "New England." One of their leaders, William Bradford, described the move: "They left the godly and pleasant city which had been their resting place; . . . but they knew they were pilgrims and looked not much on those things but lifted their eyes to the heavens, their dearest country, and quieted their spirits." In September 1620, Bradford was among those who boarded the *Mayflower* and sailed for North America.[4]

Their charter had been granted by the Virginia Company, and they planned to put down their anchor in the Virginia region, which at that time was larger than the present state of Virginia and included part of the Hudson River in today's New York. But stormy seas drove them over two hundred miles northward, and they settled near Cape Cod in November. Since they were not within the jurisdiction of the Virginia Company, as they had planned, they drafted a document so that all could agree on the government and structure of their community. Aboard ship, William Bradford and William Brewster joined other leaders in adopting the Mayflower Compact, which was a religious and a political document. These Pilgrims shared many beliefs with the Puritans, which is why many of the major points of Puritan theology, especially the idea of covenant, marked the Mayflower Compact.[5]

Not all these English settlers counted themselves among the Pilgrims, but those who did made it clear that they wanted to construct a godly community free from the corruptions of the English church. These Pilgrims were "separatists," meaning that they believed the English church was so corrupt that it was not possible to purify it from within. They instead separated from the Church of England, believing it was no longer a true church. This belief set the Pilgrims apart from the Puritans who migrated to America a decade later. About a thousand Puritans arrived in Massachusetts Bay around the year 1630; within ten years, an additional twenty thousand joined them. These settlers still thought the English church was a valid church, even though they believed it to be corrupt and in need of reform. In short, the Pilgrims of Plymouth (famous for the legendary tales of the first Thanksgiving) separated from the English church, while the Puritans of Massachusetts Bay believed the English church could still be "purified" of its errors. Other than this key difference, the Pilgrims and the Puritans shared similar beliefs and lifestyles.[6]

Leading the settlers of Massachusetts Bay was their first governor, John Winthrop (1588–1649), a lawyer with a Cambridge education. While aboard a ship named the *Arbella*, Winthrop delivered one of the most famous speeches in North American history, "A Model of Christian Charity," which was a motivational speech with a warning. As Winthrop said, they had all bonded together to leave England, "to seek out a place of cohabitation . . . under a due form of government both civil and ecclesiastical." In both state and church, they strove "to improve our lives to do more service to the Lord," which would be possible because they had found a place where they could avoid "the common corruptions of this evil world," and they could "serve the Lord and work out our salvation under the power and purity of His holy ordinances." This was key: they wanted to follow a proper worship, a biblical worship, cleansed from the non-biblical, Catholic-influenced practices of the Church of England. They committed to each other and to God, vowing to honor a "covenant": "Thus stands the cause between God and us: we are entered into covenant with Him for his work," Winthrop said. They had the opportunity to be a beacon to the world, but then here was the warning: if they failed, they would be a disgrace to God.[7]

JOHN WINTHROP: THE CITY ON A HILL

"We must consider that we shall be as a city upon a hill, the eyes of all people are upon us. So that if we shall deal falsely with our God in this work we have undertaken, and so cause Him to withdraw His present help from us, we shall be made a story and a by-word through the world."*

*John Winthrop, "Model of Christian Charity," in *American Religions: A Documentary History*, ed. R. Marie Griffith (New York: Oxford University Press, 2008), 18–19.

Presidents and other leaders throughout the centuries have echoed Winthrop's words, referring to the United States as a "city upon a hill" (cf. Matthew 5:14), enlightening the world as a beacon of freedom. Winthrop had nothing like that in mind. He wanted to motivate his fellow settlers to follow their covenant with God, to be faithful and band together to make the colony a success. If their experiment with church purity and civil government failed, they would face God's retribution; if it worked, they would be an example for others to follow, which was their hope. Winthrop envisioned an English, Protestant empire in the New World, a people who would stand in the face of what they saw as a wilderness, just as they would be a bulwark against both French and Spanish Catholicism.

"To Live Ancient Lives"

Several features of Puritan life are worth remembering because of their influence on American religious history, and one of these was the Puritan view of Scripture. For Puritans, the Bible was not only a devotional guide for spiritual life; it was also a guide for all of life, including church, family, and state. Puritans received this view of Scripture from many sources, including Reformers Theodore Beza, Martin Bucer, John Calvin, and others in the Reformed tradition. This tradition believed that sin, beginning with the "fall" of Adam and Eve, had damaged human reason enough that people could not comprehend much about God. In response, God accommodated this human weakness by providing the Bible. Other sources of knowledge were helpful, including reason and church tradition, but no authority rivaled the Scriptures. While some Protestants, including many in the Church of England and Lutherans, believed that people should avoid doing anything the Bible prohibited, Puritans were stricter, saying that people could only do what Scripture explicitly commanded.[8]

Historians have called Puritans "primitivists" because they focused on the "primitive" church as revealed in the the Bible, which they believed was pure, before the church was corrupted through its long history. A main problem with the Catholic Church, they believed, was that priests and popes had damaged Christianity by adding doctrines, worship practices, and layers of ecclesial hierarchy that had no biblical support. Naturally, they believed that many of these non-biblical elements also corrupted the Church of England because its roots were in Catholicism. Puritans despised these "new traditions" and "human inventions," seeking instead to "walk in the old way" described in the Bible. With Bible in hand, they sought "to live ancient lives" by following the pattern of the primitive church.[9]

As was often the case with Scripture, the devil was in the details—literally, some Puritans would say. It was one thing to lift up the Scriptures as the ultimate authority, but what, specifically, did the Bible teach? People disagreed. For example, church organization was a major sticking point. Most Puritans agreed that Scripture condemned the Catholic Church and the idea of a pope. Other than that, Puritans disagreed on church polity. Did the Bible command a "presbyterian" polity, with church members electing "elders" who then ran local churches, which in turn had to answer to regional meetings of ministers called "synods"? Or did the Bible endorse a congregational polity, with each church organized separately by the people of that local church, who then chose their leaders and ran their congregations without interference from synods?

Most Puritans who traveled from England to New England believed in congregational polity, and they stated these convictions in the Cambridge Platform (1648). As is the case with many statements, this one responded to a specific problem. Although most colonists in Massachusetts Bay believed in congregational polity, some favored presbyterianism, and this prompted the legislature to make it clear that "the New England Way" was a congregationalist system. The Platform adopted the Westminster Confession, a statement of Reformed doctrines recently accepted but never implemented by the Church of England. Yet New England Puritans disagreed with the presbyterian nature of the Westminster Confession, as they made clear in the Cambridge Platform. Each local church had the autonomy to do its business without outside interference. Also, the Platform required magistrates to advise churches, and churches were to call on magistrates to punish heresy.[10]

Both "Congregationalist" and "Presbyterian" later became names for specific denominations. But the names themselves refer to the forms of church organization described here. When we capitalize "Congregationalist" or "Presbyterian," we mean the specific denominations. Otherwise we are referring to the polity. This is important because not all churches that adopted a congregationalist polity were part of a denomination called "Congregationalist." Baptists, for instance, have typically been congregationalist in polity.

Election, Predestination, and Salvation

As noted earlier, Puritans believed in covenants, as seen in documents such as Winthrop's "Model of Christian Charity" and the Cambridge Platform. The Bible, as many Puritans read it, centered on covenants, sacred contracts between God and God's people. "Covenant," English Puritan William Ames said, was "God's special way of governing rational creatures."[11] God, although sovereign and high above all of humanity, accommodated to human weakness and entered into covenants with people. Scripture itself was the story of an Old Testament, or "covenant," followed by a New Testament, or "covenant." Puritans drew this "covenant theology" not only from John Calvin but also from German theologians, such as Zacharias Ursinus (1534–83), who distinguished between a "covenant of works" and a "covenant of grace." God entered into a "covenant of works" with Adam and Eve, which required them to obey God's commands in order to receive life. They failed, disobeying God, breaking the covenant, and falling into a state of sin from which they could not escape. In response, God established a new "covenant of grace," as especially seen in the story of Abraham, which offered salvation in return for faith, not works. For Christians, Christ fulfilled the demands of the covenant of works, perfectly obeying God's demands and then sacrificing himself for the elect, paying the price for their sins and enabling them to have faith.[12]

Despite God's covenant of grace, most people never attained a true knowledge of God, Puritans believed. These people died without salvation and suffered eternal punishment in hell. Puritans explained this through the common Reformed belief in predestination, the view that salvation is a work of God alone, independent of any human action. That is, God chose some to receive grace, leading to salvation, and left others in sin, leading to their damnation. This belief had its critics, and one of its most prominent was Jacobus Arminius (1560–1609), a professor at the University of Leiden in Holland. For Arminius, predestination offended human reason and turned God into a tyrant who condemned people to damnation before they were born. Arminius agreed that sin, which began with Adam and Eve, tainted all people, so no one could turn to Christ and have faith unless God's grace helped them. But God gave this grace to everyone, not only to certain "elect" people. And individuals had the power to refuse God's grace; they could reject God's offer of salvation, live sinful lives, and it would be their own fault if they spent eternity in hell.

These ideas provoked religious and political upheaval, leading to an international meeting of Reformed ministers and theologians at the Synod of Dort, which took place in the Dutch city of Dordrecht from 1618 to 1619, a little more than a year before the Pilgrims sailed for New England. The final decision condemned Arminius's teachings and asserted several ideas, which we can remember with the acronym TULIP: "Total depravity" (sin tainted and corrupted all aspects of life); "unconditional election" (God elected certain people for salvation, and did so unconditionally); "limited atonement" (Christ's sacrifice only applied to the elect); "irresistible grace" (if God offered grace to individuals, they could not resist: a human did not have the power or desire to reject God); and "perseverance of the saints" (if God elected individuals, they would not ultimately fall away from the faith; if people seemed to turn away from God after first appearing to be devout Christians, they were never really saved in their hearts).

Puritans accepted these views and rejected "Arminianism," which was the name for Arminius's teaching. In their view, God had elected some to salvation and allowed others to be eternally damned for their sins. Election had nothing to do with human actions. This was a hard teaching to accept, but for Puritans it was a biblical teaching. We can cite several examples that to the Puritans made sense of these ideas. In the Exodus story, "The LORD hardened the heart of Pharaoh" (Exodus 9:12), and he refused to let the enslaved Israelites go free, despite the plagues that God sent to warn him. In the New Testament, the apostle Paul used the image of the potter and the clay: God was the potter, and humans were the clay, and God had the power to shape us in any way God desired. "Hath not the potter power over the clay, of the same lump to make one vessel unto honour, and another unto dishonour?" (Romans 9:21). Likewise, in Ephesians, Paul wrote, "As he hath chosen us in him before the foundation of the world, that we should be holy and without blame before him in love: Having predestinated us unto the adoption of children by Jesus Christ to himself, according to the good pleasure of his will, To the praise of the glory of his grace, wherein he hath made us accepted in the beloved" (Ephesians 1:4–6).[13]

Critics of predestination attacked the idea with many questions. Where in this teaching was human free will? Were people machines, predestined to salvation or damnation against their wills, regardless of what they did? The Reformed, including Puritans, replied that God never violated an individual's will or intellect. God worked salvation out in a way that respected individuals' hearts and minds. For example, God always used "means of grace" to move people in ways they could understand. These means of grace were tangible practices, like listening to sermons and taking Communion in a worship service. Bible reading was certainly another method in which God worked with people in ways they could understand. Again, it was not enough for people to have an intellectual knowledge of God and salvation; their religious experience must penetrate to the soul, involving the will and emotions.[14]

This meant that predestination did not violate human free will. God did not force people to act. If people did not want to be saved, God did not force them into salvation, nor did God force them to read Scripture, go to church, pray, and do good works. Instead of compelling people to act against what they wanted to do (their "inclinations"), God changed their inclinations. God transformed people so that they *wanted* to go to church, read Scripture, and use all the other means of grace. God "converted" people, changing them from people who loved sin into people who loved God. People were free to do what they wanted, but after God changed their hearts, they wanted to love God and to follow God's will.[15]

Church, State, and Religious Liberty

The covenant motif was not just important for understanding salvation; it also guided how the Puritans viewed other areas of their lives. For congregationalists, each church was based on a covenant between God and the people in that congregation. God also formed covenants with nations, as

God did with Israel, the chosen people described in the Hebrew Bible (or the Old Testament, as Christians call it). God's relationship with Israel served as important lessons for other nations that entered into covenants with God, and the Puritans paid attention to Israel's experience. As we have seen with John Winthrop's speech "A Model of Christian Charity," these Puritans, too, wanted to form a godly commonwealth in covenant with God. Although they knew that no nation would ever be as special as God's chosen nation in ancient Israel, they believed other nations could live faithfully to God as "New Israels" in more modern times. No matter whether they were presbyterian or congregational, most Puritans agreed that the state should support the church (financially and otherwise), and that the church should advise the state. They believed in the separation of church and state only in the sense that pastors were not also magistrates, but the state should fine, imprison, and even execute citizens for religious crimes. The Ten Commandments, after all, included both civil crimes (like murder) and religious offenses (like idolatry), so it was the duty of the church and the state to work together to punish both kinds of violations.

THE PURITANS AND RELIGIOUS LIBERTY

Contrary to popular belief, the Puritans did not believe in religious liberty for everyone, but they wanted it for themselves. They felt persecuted in England, so they sailed to America, hoping to create a colony that they could control. Yet they did not hesitate to discipline any who disagreed with their political and religious views. The prime example was Roger Williams (1603–83). The cooperation of church and state, which most Puritans saw as key to both religious purity and civil peace, Roger Williams saw as the opposite—a dangerous idea that threatened both the church and the state.

Roger Williams, like many Puritan clergy, started out as a minister in the Church of England—and an educated one at that, finishing at Pembroke College, Cambridge, a school with many Puritan-leaning students. In 1630, he and his wife, Mary Barnard Williams, traveled to Massachusetts Bay. Williams's arrival was a godsend, settlers in the colony believed. He was educated. He was devout, as serious about his faith as anyone could be. And he probably had a winning personality; even some folks who were appalled by his views seemed to like him personally. Soon after he reached New England, therefore, Puritan leaders offered Williams a job as teacher at the Boston church. Yet Williams always seemed full of surprises, and he dropped a big one on them by turning down the job. It would not be right to accept the position, Williams said, because the church in Boston had not declared its separation from the Church of England. This was surprising because, as far as anyone knew, Williams had been like other Puritans: he wanted to *reform* the Church of England, not *separate* from it. Surely Williams had not turned into a radical Separatist, who, like the Pilgrims, declared that the English church was so corrupt that it was no longer a church at all, had he? But that was exactly what Williams had done. Somewhere along the way, perhaps while crossing the Atlantic, he had become a Separatist.[16]

It did not get any smoother for Williams in Massachusetts Bay. Over the next few years, he disputed with Puritans to the point that they banished him from the colony on October 9, 1635. The General Court of Massachusetts Bay listed four charges against him: First, he rejected the validity of the colony's patent, which they received from King Charles I. This was truly radical: Williams not only told the Puritans they had no right to the land they lived on; he also defied the king, saying that Charles had no right to grant the land, arguing instead that "the Natives are the true owners of it."

FIGURE 2-1 (LEFT). Roger Williams statue by Franklin Simmons, given 1872, Senate Wing, 2nd Floor U.S. Capitol (Wikimedia Commons)

FIGURE 2-2 (BELOW). Title page of Roger Williams's *Bloudy Tenent of Persecution*, 1644, The Seventeenth Century, Part 2. Religion and the Founding of the American Republic. Rare Book & Special Collections Division (Library of Congress)

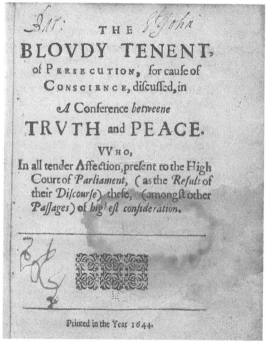

Few Europeans fathomed the idea that Native Americans could own land, believing they were savages who had no concept of ownership, at least none that could rival the claims of an English monarch. Williams disagreed. Second, Williams insisted that civil courts had no right to force non-Christians to swear oaths or pray. These were activities of worship; they belonged in church, not in the courtroom. The third offense was his "separatist" claim that the Church of England was irredeemable. The fourth charge was perhaps most alarming: he claimed that civil officers had no authority in religious matters. It would be hard to see how Williams could have offended the Puritans more.[17]

After the General Court banished him, Puritan leaders allowed Williams to stay in the colony through the winter as long as he did not teach his radical views to others. Williams violated that order—no surprise there—by preaching to anyone who would listen. Colonial leaders tried to arrest him, but he escaped and headed south. He finally settled at Narragansett Bay, where he purchased land from the indigenous peoples there and established a community that he called "Providence," which, in contrast to Massachusetts Bay, would allow religious liberty for all. While in Providence, Williams founded America's first Baptist church (1638), but he did not remain a Baptist for long. Within a few months he rejected all forms of organized religion because he had come to believe that no church was truly faithful to the New Testament. He would wait for Christ to return to reestablish the true church.

Meanwhile, Williams rarely rested. Fortunately for historians, he spent much of his time writing, and he published his writings during trips to England. Not only did he publish books on religious liberty, including his famous *The Bloudy Tenent, of Persecution, for cause of Conscience* (1644), but he also published writings on Native Americans, based largely on his interactions with the Narragansetts. His *Key into the Language of America*, a study of dialect, also included information on culture and beliefs.[18] Most often, Williams defended Native Americans against Europeans who called them savages and heathens. In his *Christenings Make Not Christians or A Briefe Discourse concerning that name Heathen, commonly given to the Indians*, Williams railed against Europeans who mistreated indigenous peoples while claiming to convert them to Christianity. Many such "conversions," Williams believed, were merely coerced baptisms, and he wanted no part of this kind of so-called missionary work. Of the Spanish conversions of native peoples, Williams wrote: "If the reports . . . be true, what monstrous and most inhumane conversions have they made; baptizing thousands, yea ten thousands of the poore Natives, sometimes by wiles and subtle devices, sometimes by force compelling them to submit to that which they understood not, neither before nor after such their monstrous Christning of them."[19]

On the use of the term "Heathen" to refer to the Native Americans, Williams wrote:

How oft have I heard both the English and Dutch . . . say, These *Heathen* Dogges, better kill a thousand of them then that we *Christians* should be indangered or troubled with them; Better they were all cut off, & then we shall be no more troubled with them: They have spilt our *Christian* bloud, the best way to make riddance of them, cut them all off, and so make way for Christians. I shall therefore humbly intreat my country-men of all sorts to consider, that although men have used to apply this word *Heathen* to the Indians that go naked, and have not heard of that One-God, yet this word *Heathen* is most improperly sinfully, and unchristianly so used in this sense.[20]

In Williams's definition, "Heathen" described all who oppose the "People of God," and that included "All People, *civilized* as well as *uncivilized*, even the most famous States, Cities, and the Kingdomes of the World." So the fact that indigenous peoples of the Americas did not fit the European definition of "civilized" did not make them any more "Heathen" or opposed to God than those "civilized" Europeans who departed from God. "There is no respect of Persons with him [i.e., God], for we are all the worke of his hands," and that included the Native Americans. Also, if one considers the native peoples' "sins, they are far short of *European* sinners: They neither abuse such corporall mercies for they have them not; not sin they against the Gospell light, (which shines not amongst them) as the men of *Europe* do," Williams wrote.[21]

The Banishment of Anne Hutchinson

If the leaders of Massachusetts Bay hoped that the ruckus with Williams would be the last disturbance of their peace, they were soon disappointed. More banishments and even executions would come, and most of these had religious issues at the core of the dispute. The next major disruption concerned some of the most cherished of Puritan convictions: salvation and holy living.

Given Puritan views on election and predestination, each Puritan faced a troubling question: Am I among the elect? Unfortunately, there was no way to know for sure whether they were elect and bound for heaven, or damned and bound for hell. Even a person who went to church every time it opened, read Scripture daily, and tried their hardest to live a Christian life could not know for certain if they were elect. Perhaps they were doing these good works out of fear, to avoid hell, and not because they really wanted to do them, motivated by love for God in their hearts. Understandably, Puritans worried a lot about salvation.[22]

This anxiety over salvation created pastoral problems as people fretted over whether they were of the elect. Ministers tried to help by charting the "order of salvation" (*ordo salutis*), believing that God chose a method in converting people and that they could investigate their hearts to determine which "stage" of salvation they may be in.[23] English Puritans like William Perkins had dealt with this in the late 1500s, concentrating on the order of salvation as a way to give people a road map to God's progress in the soul. In Puritan New England, Thomas Hooker (1586–1647) took up this task and wrote a lot about the steps along the way to salvation, including an early stage called "preparation." For many ministers, in this first stage of salvation, God prepared the heart for Christ, a preparation that usually involved some kind of humiliation: people had to give up on their own goodness and depend solely on God's grace. Humiliation does not sound like a good thing, but it was for Puritans because it convinced people to release their own sense of control over their hearts, recognizing that they could not save themselves. In preaching this way, Puritan ministers often presented "the law," the hard rules of Scripture, including God's high expectations for righteousness—expectations that people could not possibly satisfy on their own. One Puritan minister, Thomas Shepard, was said by some congregants "to pound our hearts all to pieces."[24] This was seen as a means to drive one to seek the repentance in Christ, sometimes called "the first use of the law."

This anxiety over salvation contributed to a crisis that disrupted Puritan New England early on. Anne Hutchinson (1591–1643) had emigrated to New England partly out of loyalty to her pastor, John Cotton, a respected Puritan minister. Hutchinson took theology seriously, to the point that she met weekly with several women to discuss the previous Sunday's sermon. This was not unusual, neither in the colonies nor in England. Women typically met to discuss theology, the church, and to tend to tasks that helped maintain the community. Yet Hutchinson's meetings departed from the norm; they developed from a standard weekly meeting to a controversial hot point that grew to envelop the colony.

Hutchinson, several ministers feared, had moved away from orthodox theology to teach "antinomianism," a heresy that said the elect no longer needed to obey biblical laws or church rules to be a Christian. To be clear, all New England ministers denied that people could work their way into salvation by obeying the rules. Only God could save, out of sheer grace, through the gift of faith to the elect. But God did not do it all. Along the process of salvation, the *ordo salutis*, redeemed persons showed evidence of "sanctification," that Christ had changed the person in a way that others could see in their good works. Sanctification, most people believed, was evidence of "justification," meaning evidence that a person had been redeemed by God. In all this talk of good works, preparation, and sanctification, Hutchison feared that most Puritan ministers preached works righteousness, believing that people could save themselves by good works. John Cotton, she argued, was one of the few ministers who had stayed true to orthodox belief that God saved only by grace, not works.[25]

The main issue in the controversy, as a leading historian puts it, was "whether or not you had to know that God loved you before you could trust the signs that you loved" God. Hutchinson's opponents, which included most ministers in the colony, said one could look to their souls and their actions and find evidence that God had given them grace, whether they had sensed it or not. Again, the issue was assurance: since God had elected only a few to salvation, people understandably wanted to know if they would be saved from eternal punishment. Ministers dealt with this pastoral problem by telling people to look for signs in their hearts, referred to as the practical syllogism: if they saw good signs of God's grace in their souls, then they could trust these signs as possible evidence of election. Not so, said Hutchinson—one could take no comfort in good works. Just because people found it easy to follow God's rules did not mean God had given them grace. The only true evidence was a personal experience of God's grace acting directly within the soul. All else was just works righteousness, which was dangerous.[26]

From the perspective of most Puritan ministers, however, it was Hutchinson and her followers who were dangerous. Not only had Hutchinson launched an attack on the ministry of New England, but many also believed that she had attacked law and order in the colony. As we have pointed out, this was a colony based on covenants, and it depended on citizens obeying the laws of the land just as they obeyed the laws of God. But Hutchinson seemed to disrespect the law. She denied that mere obedience to the law was evidence that an individual was truly a Christian in their heart. What would happen if enough people decided that laws were useless, even dangerous? It could spell anarchy. Also, antinomianism was not new; it had appeared elsewhere, especially in England, and the results could be catastrophic, some people thought.

If Hutchinson had been a man, the controversy would have been explosive enough. But her gender increased the intensity of the conflict. As a woman speaking out so convincingly, and so radically, she rocked this patriarchal society to its core. The colony demanded that she answer for her ideas in court, and she did so in 1638.

The court transcripts revealed Hutchinson to be a remarkable theologian, which worked against her in the view of men who did not believe it proper for a woman to have such a command of theological intricacies. Many were looking for a reason to condemn her, and she gave it to them by claiming she had received communication directly from the Holy Spirit, without the confirmation of Scripture. This was one of the most radical statements one could make in Puritan New England. God communicated only through Scripture, they believed. The Holy Spirit could inspire and reaffirm truths revealed in the Bible. But God did not speak directly to people anymore, not since biblical times. In effect, some thought she was claiming to have a line of communication with God similar to Moses, or apostles like Saint Paul. Even a man who made such a claim would be in trouble; the fact that Hutchinson was a woman only made matters worse and confirmed the misogynist suspicions of men that women, since the time of Eve, often were the main culprits in defying God and spreading heretical teachings. The tragedy only intensified after Hutchinson's "revelation." The court banished Hutchinson and her followers, who then moved to Rhode Island and finally settled in New York. She was killed when her settlement was attacked by members of the Siwanoy people, who were involved in an ongoing conflict with the Dutch leaders of the colony.[27]

As important as Anne Hutchinson was to the controversy, it did not center totally on her. Other prominent colonists also had sympathies with "antinomianism," including Henry Vane, who had been an adviser to Charles I, as well as John Wheelwright and John Cotton. All the uproar put Cotton in an awkward position, to say the least, but he was not alone. The controversy divided many preachers in New England, and they produced many writings in trying to settle the controversy and come to terms with the theological issues involved.

Spiritual and Military Warfare

The Anne Hutchinson controversy demonstrated how fragile both civil and religious authority were in the colony. This was a cause for anxiety for both ministers and magistrates. They had read the Old Testament; they knew that God judged a wicked people and favored an obedient people. Which would their people be? They envisioned a colony comprised of "visible saints," filled with settlers who not only attended church (which was the law), but who had also joined the church by giving a reliable description of their conversion experience. This was a high standard, and only those who satisfied it were members of the church, only they could take the Lord's Supper, and only they could have their children baptized in the church.

Troubles arose in the 1650s as ministers noticed a decrease in the number of people who sought membership in the church. Fewer people could, or would, relate a conversion experience, which meant fewer people could take Communion, and most important, fewer people could have their children baptized. This was a crisis, many believed, because their plan for the colony depended on a population of Christian people. What if they had a whole generation of children who grew to adulthood without ever receiving baptism? The crisis provoked disagreement among clergy. Some said the colony should stand by its principles. If fewer people joined the church, they just had to keep praying and preaching and hope that God would send revival. Others wanted to devise a solution, and this side won out. In 1662, they drew up a compromise called the Halfway Covenant, a plan that allowed adults who had been baptized as infants, but had never joined the church through their own profession of faith, to have their children baptized. These adults would not be full church members, yet they were not completely out of the church. They had received baptism, but they could not receive Communion. They were "halfway members." To supporters, this plan enabled the dream of a Christian colony to continue. Without this move, they argued, much of the population would fall outside the church's influence. To opponents, the Halfway Covenant compromised their principles. It watered down the faith and would lead to lukewarm churches.[28]

Added to this spiritual warfare between ministers over church membership, New Englanders faced an even more serious challenge in military warfare. In 1675, five years before the previously discussed Pueblo revolt in New Mexico, a conflict often called "King Philip's War" erupted in New England. This complicated war involved English colonists, with some Mohegan, Mohawk, and Pequot allies, fighting against Nipmucks, Pocumtucks,

FIGURE 2-3. Phillip [sic] alias Metacomet of Pokanoket, engraving by Benjamin Church, LC-USZ62-96234 (Library of Congress)

Wampanoags, Abenakis, and especially Narragansetts. This was a massive confrontation, a war that devastated the land and killed thousands on all sides. "In proportion to population," Jill Lepore noted, King Philip's War "inflicted greater casualties than any other war in American history."[29]

Eventually the English colonists won the war, and that gave them the privilege of telling their side of the story. As is often the case, the winners of wars most often are those alive to define the war's meaning. They wrote hundreds of letters, dozens of accounts of the war, and filled many diaries with their reflections on it. This was not only a war over land, Puritans wrote, but it was part of the larger warfare between good and evil. In writing about this war, New Englanders carved out an identity. "Out of the chaos of war," Jill Lepore wrote, New Englanders "proclaimed themselves to be neither cruel colonizers like the Spanish nor savage natives like the Indians."[30]

Despite the massive loss of blood in this conflict, some Puritans refused to call it a "war." When the Puritan minister Increase Mather published his account, *A Brief History of the Warr with the Indians in New-England*, others resented Mather's title, claiming that this conflict did not deserve to be called a war. When Rev. William Hubbard published his account, therefore, he gave it what he believed was a more fitting title: *Narrative of the Troubles with the Indians in New-England*. This had not been a war, Hubbard said, because the Native Americans had no understanding of the rules of fighting a just war as Europeans understood them. The events of this conflict were better described as "Massacres, barbarous inhumane Outrages," Hubbard wrote. Not only was this not a war, but a description of it did not deserve the name of a "history." So Hubbard thought it best to title his account a "narrative" (not a "history") of "troubles" (not a "war").[31]

No matter what they called it, King Philip's War devastated New England and provided an ominous indicator of bad times to come. Ten years after this war began, New Englanders faced challenges from England's new king, James II (1633–1701), who was, to the Puritans' horror, Roman Catholic. James took away Massachusetts Bay's autonomy, placing the colony under the jurisdiction of the newly formed "Dominion of New England," which included New Jersey and New York. Much to the Puritans' relief, the "Dominion" lasted only three years, ending when Protestants William and Mary took the throne in 1688. This was, for English Protestants, a "Glorious Revolution," a bloodless end to Roman Catholic tyranny once and for all in England. As thrilling as this news initially was for New Englanders, new policies dampened the mood. In 1691, Massachusetts Bay had to accept a new charter that allowed the king to select the colony's governor. Not only did New Englanders lose some of their control over their leaders, but their churches also lost some of their influence in the colony. Previously, only church members had the right to vote in the colony, but the new charter based the right to vote on land ownership. The dream of a colony run by visible saints seemed to be fading.[32]

Salem Witch Trials

This was a time of disillusionment for many residents of the Bay Colony. Their world seemed to be changing at a rapid pace, and not for the better. Some residents felt that their way of life was under attack, not just from enemies in the English government, but perhaps from Satan, who seemed to have directed his attention to Salem, Massachusetts, in 1692.

Many historians have seen the Salem witch trials as a characteristically Puritan event. Puritans ignited the hysteria over witchcraft; Puritans organized and officiated at the trials; and Puritans executed the so-called witches. Yet Puritans were not the only people caught up in the hysteria over witchcraft. Consider the case of Joseph and Bathsheba Pope, who were Quakers, not Puritans. In fact, Quakers were a group that Puritans had persecuted earlier in the century, even sending some to the gallows. But in 1692, Bathsheba Pope felt another form of persecution. According to her testimony, she had been haunted by the specters of three individuals later executed as witches. Fourteen years after the trials ended, Bathsheba's sister, Abiah, gave

FIGURE 2-4. Trial of George Jacobs of Salem for witchcraft, by Tompkins Harrison Matteson, LC-USZ62-94432 (Library of Congress)

birth to Benjamin Franklin, one of the future nation's founders and a leading figure in the American Enlightenment, the ultimate man of science, far from a believer in witchcraft. Yet these two worlds, the world of witchcraft in Salem and the world of Benjamin Franklin, were just a few years apart.[33]

Accusations of witchcraft were nothing new in 1692. Europeans had reported witch attacks for centuries, and an estimated fifty thousand were executed as witches between 1400 and 1775. The witch hunts at Salem were small when compared to some European witch hunts. Witchcraft came in diverse forms, however, and each situation seemed to be different. In Salem, the uprising of witchcraft accusations occurred mostly among young women, almost always referred to as "girls" at the time, and that was unusual. Prior to this, most accusers of witches had been men. Also unusual was the nature of the hauntings in Salem. They were almost always "spectral attacks," meaning that only the people under attack could see the specter or ghost that tormented them. Usually, before Salem, witches cast their spells without the help of ghostly specters to do their bidding.[34]

The attacks began in 1692. Girls in Salem Village began having fits, which were diagnosed as the effects of witchcraft. Accusations of witchcraft ensued and escalated, with some of the accused witches responding by accusing others.

As the accusations increased, so did doubts about them. By October, over 150 colonists faced accusations of witchcraft, including some who had been pillars of the community. More people expressed skepticism about "spectral evidence," including Rev. Increase Mather, who urged that the court stop the trials. Governor William Phipps agreed and dismissed the court. Five years after the trials ended, Boston's judge Samuel Sewall, who had ruled in the trials, called them a gross error and repented. In 1714, the colony reversed the rulings in the witch trials and proclaimed that the colony must repent of the whole affair. Apologies and proclamations aside, no one could deny the travesty of over 150 false accusations and 20 people unjustly executed.[35]

Historians have found a lot of factors at play in the trials. A few of the men accused of witchcraft owned land that others coveted, and many of the women accused were social outcasts. Also fueling the accusations was the tension between residents of Salem Village and those of the more prosperous Salem Town. Perhaps the most decisive factor in explaining witchcraft accusations was gender. Of all people accused of witchcraft in Europe and America, the vast majority were women, indicating that witchcraft accusations expressed a pattern of misogyny and violence against women that had persisted for centuries. Regardless of the contributing factors, the witch trials wreaked havoc in the colony. The reputation of Puritanism never fully recovered after 1692. In the minds of many Americans, Puritans would be remembered as self-righteous fanatics and hysterical witch hunters who executed innocent victims.[36]

Puritanism had a unique and enduring presence in American history. "The puritan vision of America figured importantly in the construction of American culture," writes Amanda Porterfield. Additionally, the Puritans "influenced the development of many other religious traditions in this country." Porterfield lists four major concerns pervading American religions that began with Puritanism: "religious freedom, individual experience, family life, and social reform."[37] Many deny that Puritans had any concern for religious freedom (Roger Williams and Anne Hutchinson would have agreed). But, as Porterfield points out, the Puritans did suffer persecution for their religious convictions in England, and that persecution influenced their move to North America. Once in New England, Puritans banished Williams and Hutchinson, and that treatment opened them up to charges of hypocrisy. They wanted religious freedom, but they refused to extend it to those who disagreed with them. Yet, as Porterfield writes, if the Puritans "had been shameless tyrants, they never would have been accused of hypocrisy." The Puritans supported the principle of religious freedom, but they disagreed with others on its definition and scope. This is not unlike many Americans throughout history who have voiced agreement with religious freedom, but define it in various, even contradictory, ways.[38]

Thus Puritans defended religious freedom (as they understood it); they also valued individual experience. Before men or women could join the church, they had to give a convincing account of their individual experience with God, demonstrating how God was working out salvation in their souls. This was a high standard for church membership, and that was the point for Puritans. They valued the individual's spiritual experience because it was essential to their witness in both church and state. That said, individualism only went so far, and Puritans stressed the family's role in raising pious and responsible individuals. Like all aspects of Puritan social life, covenant was the key: the family, like the church and the state, was a covenant relationship between parents, children, and God. This emphasis on the spiritual and moral value of the family would have a long legacy in American religious history.

The Puritans' focus on the Bible brought with it a focus on literacy and education. They were adamant that people learn to read, not only because it made good sense for their everyday lives, but also because it was vital that they be able to read the Scriptures. This passion for education led the Puritans to become leaders in American education. It is no accident that Harvard and Yale are in New England, just as it is no accident that these universities were led by ministers for many years after they were founded.

Above all, Puritans believed in a holy and just society. That was their mission, with church and state pulling together to bring it to reality in New

England. From Winthrop's "Model of Christian Charity" and its vision of a "city upon a hill," through the challenges of the Halfway Covenant and Native American warfare, Puritans looked to their Bibles and found their experience reflected there, especially in ancient Israel, God's chosen nation. Puritans were not so bold as to declare that they could be as precious in God's eyes as Israel. But they could aspire to be a new Israel in New England. That hope gave even their failures a promising accent. God would punish them for their sins, which came in the form of wars, revolts, and even witchcraft. But they were confident that God would not abandon them.[39]

3. Early American Religious Diversity

The Caribbean, the Middle Colonies, and the South

Colonial America was a mosaic, featuring transatlantic rivalries involving Britain, France, and Spain, rivalries that frequently broke out in violence involving Narragansetts, Pequots, Pueblos, Hurons, Iroquois, and other peoples. Amid all these nationalities and rivalries, religion was a constant presence, though in complex ways. Unlike Puritan New England, religion in the Middle Colonies (New York, New Jersey, Delaware, Pennsylvania), the Caribbean, and the South (Maryland, Virginia, the Carolinas, and Georgia) was more diverse. Even when people in these colonies opposed this diversity, religious toleration resulted out of practical necessity because no single religious tradition had enough power to enforce uniformity for long.

Rivalries and Religion

English Protestants often saw the Atlantic world as a world of war, a battle between them and their enemies. Some English ministers called Catholics the new Amalekites, a people in the Old Testament who were related to the Jews, but who betrayed them and tried to kill them. In a similar way, Catholics claimed to be Christian, and so were related to Protestants, but they worked for Satan, many Protestants believed. "*Rome* is that *Amalek*, with whom God will never make peace," wrote John Flavel (ca. 1628–91), an English Presbyterian. As he saw it, Catholicism "is a FALSE: BLOODY: BLASPHEMOUS: UNCOMFORTABLE: AND DAMNABLE RELIGION." A harsh statement, to be sure, but many Protestants agreed with it.[1]

The English wanted to stake their claim on the New World before Catholic rivals from France and Spain could conquer it. Some of the same leaders who planned the Virginia settlements had supported England's takeover of Ireland, a Catholic country, and they hoped for similar victories in North America. This was a primary motive for colonization, as seen in many writings of the time, including *Discourse concerning the Western Planting*, which Richard Hakluyt (1552?–1616) dedicated to Queen Elizabeth I in 1584. Hakluyt, an Oxford graduate and student of theology and geography, inspired Elizabeth with his visions of exploration and conquest.[2] He had a reputation as England's top expert on America, even though he never set foot on American shores. What he lacked in hands-on experience he tried to make up for with research. He gathered lots of information, much of it true, some of it not. Like many of his contemporaries, he believed that sea monsters lurked deep within the Atlantic and that native peoples, many of them cannibals, threatened any foreigners who dared cast ashore. Yet such danger was worth the risk, he told the queen, because at stake was the cause of Christianity—and enormous profits, of course.[3]

In making his case for colonization, Hakluyt led with religion. Think of the Native Americans' souls, he urged, and think of the Bible. He cited Paul, who wrote in Romans 10 that any who called on Christ would be saved, "but how shall they call on him in whom they have not believed? And how shall they believe in him of whom they have not heard? And how shall they hear without a preacher? And how shall they preach except they be sent?" The Native Americans needed preachers to be sent to them, and who better to do that than Queen Elizabeth? "The Kings and Queens of England have the name of Defenders of the Faith," Hakluyt wrote. English monarchs had to *defend* the Protestant faith. It needed a strong defense in a spiritual warfare against Catholicism, Islam, and paganism, and the battleground for that defense included North America.[4]

INDIGENOUS PEOPLES AS A RELIGIOUS PROBLEM

The ancestry of the Native Americans presented a quandary for Europeans: from whom did they descend? Many believed they were descendants of the "Ten Lost Tribes" of Israel, who had dispersed all over the world in biblical times. According to this logic, the Native Americans were part of God's chosen people, but they had forgotten their heritage. The fact that indigenous peoples often rejected Christianity angered missionaries, who saw them as betrayers of the faith, just like the Amalekites. This led many English to believe they could treat the Native Americans as harshly as Israel treated the Amalekites. This reading of Scripture, in the view of some English Protestants, justified genocide.*

*See John Corrigan and Winthrop S. Hudson, *Religion in America*, 9th ed. (New York: Routledge, Taylor & Francis Group, 2018), 72–73.

The rivalry between Catholic Spain and Protestant England served Hakluyt well in trying to arouse interest in America. Although he despised Catholicism, Hakluyt quoted the Spanish Catholic priest Bartolomé de Las Casas (1484?–1566), who described how cruelly the Spanish treated the Native Americans. "So many and so monstrous have been the Spanish cruelties, such strange slaughters and murders of those peaceable, lowly, mild, and gentle people," Hakluyt stated. Leaving out few details, Hakluyt followed Las Casas's account, detailing how "the Spaniards with their horses, spears, and lances" devastated Native American towns, sparing none, not even pregnant women as they "ripped their bellies and cut them in pieces."

They seized children from their mothers "and crushed their heads against the cliffs." They would bind Native Americans in groups of thirteen, "in the honor and worship of our Saviour and his twelve apostles," and set fire to them. Only the English, with the strong support of their monarchs, could rescue the indigenous peoples, defeat the Catholics, especially Spanish Catholics, and plant the Protestant faith in the New World, Hakluyt believed. In describing these Spanish atrocities, Hakluyt and other English writers overlooked how viciously the English treated the Irish in the sixteenth century, killing indiscriminately, including children. They also decapitated some of them and displayed their heads in public to forewarn any who dared resist the English invasion. (This practice of displaying the severed heads of one's enemies was not that unusual at the time, yet another indication of the brutality of the age.)[5]

Hakluyt's dreams seemed to come true when Walter Ralegh (often spelled "Raleigh"; 1554?–1618) answered Elizabeth's call to explore the mid-Atlantic coast. There was no better man for the job. Elizabeth had knighted Ralegh, in part because he had fought admirably against the Irish.[6] In 1585, Ralegh's venture launched, stocked with approximately one hundred colonists, setting sail and eventually landing in Virginia territory, which is now part of North Carolina's Outer Banks. Once they settled on Roanoke Island, these colonists failed quickly, unable to get a foothold on farming the land, and running afoul of local indigenous peoples. Soon these colonists abandoned America, but Ralegh, not to be denied, sent another group in 1587, led by Governor John White. Again, they landed on Roanoke, and again they struggled, leading White to head back to England for provisions and advice. White stayed in England longer than he expected, delayed by fighting between England and Spain, including the dramatic defeat of the Spanish Armada in 1588. When he finally arrived back at Roanoke, he found only a mystery: the colonists were gone. He and those who traveled with him found a tree with "CROATOAN" carved on it, causing some to speculate that the colonists had moved to a nearby island of that name. But none was found on the island. The fate of these colonists is still unknown.[7]

Virginia

Within two decades, the English tried again, founding a colony in Jamestown, Virginia, in April of 1607, approximately twenty-three years before the Puritans landed in Massachusetts Bay. Much of what we know of Jamestown comes from descriptions of the colony's leader, Captain John Smith (1580–1631), especially his letter *A True Relation of Such Occurrances and Accidents of Noate as hath hapned in Virginia* (1608), *A Map of Virgina* (1612) by Smith, and from other published works, including his *The True Travels, Adventures, and Observations of Captaine John Smith, in Europe, Asia, Affrica, and America* (1630). This latter work has challenged historians to separate exaggerations (or outright lies) from truth. As Jill Lepore notes, a reader of the book will "expect that when the Captain, wearing full armor, has his stallion shot out from under him he'll mount a dead man's horse before his own has hit the ground, and reload his musket while he's at it." Surely, "nobody could have survived so many sea fights, shipwrecks, mutinies, deserted islands, musket wounds, betrayals, captivities, and gashes received while jousting except a man whose coat of arms depicted the severed, turbaned heads of three Turkish champions he defeated in back-to-back duels in Transylvania, and whose motto, emblazoned on his shield, sounds like the title of a James Bond film set in Elizabethan England: *Vincere est vivere.* 'To conquer is to live.'"[8]

For centuries many doubted Smith's account of his exploits, though recent historians have verified much of what he wrote. By any measure, he had seen more than his share of adventures before he arrived in Virginia. By age 16, he had left England for war, first against Catholic Spain, and then against Muslims in Hungary. During these campaigns he suffered battle

FIGURE 3-1. Statue of Captain John Smith on Jamestown Island, part of the Colonial National Historical Park in Jamestown, Virginia. Photo by Carol M. Highsmith, LC-HS503-3302 (Library of Congress)

wounds, fought a duel, and was sold into slavery and shipped off to Istanbul. After escaping, he returned to England, but not before stops in Poland, Russia, and Morocco. Finally, he pursued yet another adventure in Jamestown, where he joined at least two other Englishmen with their own experiences in the Middle East. "To these men," Lepore writes, "the New World beckoned as but another battlefield for the Old World's religious wars; they went, mainly, to hunt for gold to fund wars to defeat Muslims in Europe."[9]

These colonists also wanted what most colonists wanted: to make money, and to explore the New World. Despite high hopes, they met hard times, in part due to ill preparation.[10] The struggles began immediately, as newcomers to Jamestown suffered through famine, disease, and death in their early years. The winter of 1609–10 was brutal, with the colony's population decreasing from 500 to 60. George Percy, the lieutenant governor, described the starvation the people endured, which led to cannibalism. "One of our Colline murdered his wife Ripped the Childe outt of her woambe and threwe it into the River and after Chopped the Mother in pieces and salted her for his food."[11]

Naturally, Jamestown's settlers turned to God for help in hard times. They prayed and preached, led by Robert Hunt, a clergyman whom John Smith called "our honest, religious and courageous divine."[12] Hunt admired Richard Hakluyt and shared his zeal to colonize America and to convert indigenous peoples to Protestant Christianity. Through his leadership, Jamestown's settlers quickly built a worship space, even if it was humble and homely. It was more barn than chapel, John Smith said. When it burned down less than a year later, colonists engineered a massive upgrade, a much larger building: measuring "64 feet by 24 feet, it was an architectural marvel for its time," according to an article on it in the *New York Times* in 2011. The writer with the *Times* knew these dimensions because archeologists had discovered the remains of the chapel, perhaps the oldest remains of any Protestant church in North America. In 1614, this was likely the place where Pocahontas (1596–1617), the famous Powhatan princess, married the Englishman John Rolfe (1585–1622).[13]

Centuries before the story of Pocahontas inspired a blockbuster film with Disney, it inspired English people from Virginia to London. Pocahontas, whose original name was likely Matoaka, was the daughter of Wahunsenacah (d. 1618), leader of the Powhatan peoples. Despite dicey relations between her people and the English, she befriended the English settlers, even warning them of an attack in 1609. John Smith reported that she saved his life when the Powhatans tried to execute him, although many doubted that Smith knew what was really going on in that episode. Other turmoil followed. In 1613, the English captured Pocahontas and tried to exchange her for some Englishmen the Powhatans had imprisoned. While living (imprisoned?) with the English, Pocahontas converted to Christianity, received baptism, and took yet another name, an English name: Rebecca.

Pocahontas's marriage to John Rolfe helped to make peace between the English and the Powhatans, but that was not the only reason for the marriage. Rolfe wrote to the governor of Virginia about his relationship with Pocahontas, and he clarified one point from the outset: Their connection was not about "the unbridled desire of carnal affection." Instead, it was "for the good of this plantation, for the honor of our country, for the glory of God, for my own salvation, and for the converting to the true knowledge of God and Jesus Christ, an unbelieving creature, namely Pokahuntas." In Rolfe's mind these were good motivations, practical and sound. But Rolfe had more to say about his feelings: "my hearty and best thoughts are, and have a long time been, so entangled, and enthralled in so intricate a labyrinth, that I was even awearied to unwind myself thereout." In other words, his feelings for "Pokahuntas" were conflicted and complex.[14]

Despite his affection for Pocahontas, Rolfe worried over what the Bible said about interracial and intercultural marriages. Rolfe wrote that he was not "ignorant of the heavy displeasure which almighty God conceived against the sons of Levi and Israel for marrying strange wives." Here Rolfe referred to a biblical warning, recorded in the book of Ezra. God's people of Israel had lost everything. The Babylonians had defeated them, sacked Jerusalem, destroyed their temple, and forced them into exile. Centuries later, when the exile was over, some Jews returned to their homeland, hoping to

FIGURE 3-2. Portrait of Pocahontas, in the Capitol, Richmond, Virginia. Photo by William Henry Jackson, c. 1902, LC-D416-14207 (Library of Congress)

rebuild the temple and to get on with their lives. But the people had angered God by intermarrying with foreign wives and thereby polluting "the holy seed" by mixing "with the peoples of the lands" (Ezra 9:2). Rolfe worried that his marriage to Pocahontas would fit into that category. As was the case with most English and European whites of the time, Rolfe's reading of the Bible was affected by their assumptions of white racial and cultural superiority to all other races and peoples. Accordingly, he worried that it would anger God if he, a white Christian man, were to wed a Powhatan woman. He admitted that the match did not make much sense, and he pondered what "should provoke me to be in love with one whose education hath bin rude, her manners barbarous, her generation accursed." But he was wrong to think this way, he concluded, deciding that these doubts were the taunts of the devil. God had called him to marry her, Rolfe believed; it was a missionary duty. He was not trying to satisfy his lust. If he wanted to do that, he could do so "with Christians more pleasing to the eye"; he was not "so desperate" that he had to take a Native American wife.[15]

Even if Jamestown's colonists did not embark on a Puritan mission like the people who settled Massachusetts Bay over two decades later, religion was important to them. We see it in John Rolfe's musings on the Bible and his marriage to Pocahontas, and we see it in the priority they placed on a worship space. In Jamestown, the law required church attendance and enforced strict rules for Sabbath observance. The Virginia Company's charter claimed that missionary work was a top priority, calling on colonists to convert indigenous peoples to Protestant Christianity. This missionary endeavor involved a spiritual warfare between good and evil, colonists believed, because the Native Americans, as a tract advertising the colony described, had to be rescued "out of the arms of the Devil," where they were "wrapped up unto death, in almost invincible ignorance."[16]

Eventually this fledgling, starving colony prospered. The main reason was tobacco. Native Americans near Jamestown grew it. Within a decade of their settlement, Jamestown colonists realized the market potential of this leafy gold. Tobacco smoking was a huge hit in Europe, where many believed it was a healthy habit. Tobacco farming brought more money to Virginia, but it also brought more animosity between English colonists and the Powhatans. Profits from tobacco increased the colonists' avarice for more land, just as it also increased the colonists' dependence on the Powhatans for food. (It did not help the food supply that colonists were growing more tobacco and less corn).[17]

Tensions between English and the Powhatans erupted in 1622, when the Powhatans unleashed an attack on the colonists. The turmoil convinced the English government to take over the colony from the Virginia Company in 1624, making Virginia a royal colony, which meant more organization, more brutal treatment of American Indians, above all more indentured servants, and then enslaved Africans beginning in 1619.[18]

Despite its legal authority in Virginia, the Church of England struggled. There was too much land to cover and too few clergy to serve the expanding population. The church did not plan its congregations well, and people who wanted to attend services often could not do so because there was no congregation in their area. Organization was a problem, but so was personnel. Virginia settlers often complained of inept and lazy ministers, many of whom spent more time in taverns than in churches.[19]

These struggles in Virginia revealed a harsh reality: the parish system, which worked so well in England, struggled from the beginning in colonial America. This system, as it existed for nearly a millennium in parts of Europe, took for granted that all citizens must be church members. People lived in geographical regions called parishes, and all members of the parish attended the same church, and that church received the support of the state. In North America, only New England and Virginia had any success in implementing the parish system, and even their efforts eventually failed. Part of the problem was land. There was so much of it, and people often lived far from one another, which made it almost impossible to divide areas into localized parishes that ministers could manage. In addition, as we have seen, religious diversity trumped religious uniformity in North America. People came from various places—England, Germany, the Netherlands, Africa, France, Spain, and more—and they professed many different beliefs. It became nearly impossible to compel everyone in a particular area to embrace only one established church. For these reasons and others, the winner in North America was not the parish system, but the voluntary church. Religion was optional, not mandatory. If they attended church at all, colonists attended the church of their choice, which meant that churches had to compete for members with other religious communities. Churches could not rest secure, supported by the state and by all people in a given area. Churches had to persuade people to follow them, which put much emphasis on persuasive preaching to draw people in.[20]

Maryland

Both churches and clergy struggled in Virginia, therefore, and they struggled in Maryland as well, but for different reasons. Although English Protestants disagreed on much, many of them united in their fear and loathing of Roman Catholicism, which made the going difficult for Maryland, a colony owned by a Catholic. The colony was a gift from King Charles I to George Calvert, Lord Baltimore (1578/79–1632), making Maryland America's first "proprietary colony," meaning that the land belonged to an individual, not a company. The land passed to George Calvert's son, Cecil (the second Lord Baltimore, 1605–75), who settled the colony. The Calverts dreamed of a safe haven for Catholics, especially English Catholics who could not practice their faith in England. They proclaimed their loyalty to England and to the Catholic Church—an impossibility, many English believed. Unlike today, many English people in the seventeenth century did not distinguish between loyalty to the state and loyalty to the Church of England. The Calverts wanted to change people's minds on this point, showing how Protestants and Catholics could live together and, perhaps most importantly, profit together. The place that made this possible was Maryland.[21]

In England, some Protestants detested this Catholic colony. To them, it seemed ridiculous and even dangerous to give Catholics control of American lands. Not to worry, replied defenders of the colony, because Maryland was no paradise; it was "a wilderness," where Catholics would scrape by to survive, surrounded by "savages and wild beasts." It was a punishment to send Catholics to America, they said, adding that some criminals "have chosen rather to be hanged than to go to Virginia."[22]

Besides, there was no way Catholics could establish a major power base in Maryland because, as Lord Baltimore knew, Protestants greatly outnumbered them. Catholic leaders in Maryland knew they were Catholics in an anti-Catholic land. They would always need to reckon with Protestants who feared and distrusted them. But if the colony made money, would its residents care less about religious differences? Cecil Calvert hoped so. He invited all to come to Maryland, Protestant and Catholic alike, and two ships sailed to Maryland in 1634. From the beginning, Calvert worried that religious disputes would wreck his colony. He cautioned Catholics not to argue with Protestants. "Preserve unity and peace among all the passengers" on shipboard, he said. He also warned Catholics against public displays and ceremonies at sea. They should worship privately, and they should "be silent upon all occasions of discourse concerning matters of religion."[23]

Not long after the first settlers arrived in Maryland, their homeland entered a time of chaos, with England occupied by a civil war (1642–51) between the forces of Charles I and the soldiers of Parliament, ending when the king was beheaded. After that, the English endured the uncertainties of life without a king or queen, living under the Protectorate of Oliver Cromwell (1653–58), which ended with the restoration of the monarchy and the return of Charles II (1660). Not only did a king return to the throne, but Anglican bishops also returned to Parliament, giving a boost to the Church of England. When Charles II died in 1685, his brother, James II, became king. James II had pedigree and a background of military service, both in the French army and as Lord High Admiral of the English navy. Yet, as noted earlier, James II was a Catholic, and for that reason many English people had dreaded his reign for years. Through a series of maneuvers, James II was deposed and replaced on the throne by the Dutch Protestant ruler William III of Orange (1650–1702) and his wife, Mary II (James's daughter) (1662–94). With their rise to power, Parliament issued a Bill of Rights that forbade a Roman Catholic from ever ruling England again. English Protestants called the deposition of James II and the ascension of William and Mary the "Glorious Revolution" because it secured the alliance between Protestantism and England without bloodshed.[24]

For Maryland's Catholics, the Glorious Revolution was not so glorious. Anti-Catholic sentiments intensified, and Maryland shifted from a proprietary colony, controlled by a Catholic owner, to a royal colony, controlled by Protestant rulers. From that point onward, Maryland became a Protestant colony, and the Anglican Church became the colony's official church. That may have been so, but ink on paper did not completely change reality. The Anglican Church would wield much power in Maryland, but so would Catholicism because many Catholics lived there, and many others would find a home there in the future.[25]

**From
New Amsterdam
to New York**

In their focus on the English colonies, Americans often forget the Dutch, another band of European immigrants who arrived in the New World in the seventeenth century. Sponsored by the West India Company, the Dutch crossed the Atlantic in 1626, with aims to extend Holland's profits as a maritime power. Sandwiched between the English settlements in New England and Virginia, the Dutch carved their way through lands that Americans would later call New York, New Jersey, Delaware, and Pennsylvania.

The Dutch were used to religious diversity. One needed to look no further than Amsterdam to see one of Europe's most progressive cities in its acceptance of people from around the world. There was a reason the famous "Pilgrims" who fled England first moved to Holland: they knew they would find toleration there. The problem was that in Holland they found too much toleration, too much diversity of cultures and religions. So they changed their minds and their location, boarding the *Mayflower* to sail for the New World, where they could establish a *new* England, where they could control the church and establish an English society in America.

When the Dutch sailed to North America, they took with them no Puritan dream of a "city upon a hill." Instead, their colony would match the diversity of their homeland. At least half of those who lived in the Dutch-founded island of New Amsterdam, later named "Manhattan," were not Dutch; like the Amsterdam of the old world, they came from Norway, Italy, Germany, Africa, and elsewhere. Many of them were original settlers of the land. As one historian described it, this island became home to "the first multiethnic, upwardly mobile society on America's shores, a prototype of the kind of society that would be duplicated throughout the country and around the world."[26]

THE PRACTICAL ROOTS OF RELIGIOUS DIVERSITY

New Amsterdam's religious diversity resulted from the practical nature of the colony. The purpose was profit. As one of the great Dutch poets of the era wrote, "We Amsterdammers travel wherever profit drives us." Dutch colonists were not any more focused on profits than others, but they had seen that fewer religious restrictions could strengthen commerce. Accordingly, this colony attracted a variety of people with a variety of religious identities, with little agreement on religion but much agreement on the need to make money. Profits followed the Dutch as they established a thriving fur trade.*

*See George L. Procter-Smith, *Religion and Trade in New Netherland* (Ithaca: Cornell University Press, 2010), 1; Edwin S. Gaustad and Leigh E. Schmidt, *The Religious History of America*, rev. ed. (New York: HarperSanFrancisco, 2002), 74–75.

New Amsterdam's enterprise was led by merchants, but ministers were present as well. First to arrive was Dutch Reformed minister Jonas Michaelius, who came in 1628 and faced hardship from the beginning. His wife died, leaving him and their three children alone to make it in a new ministry in a new land. Michaelius tried to take comfort in his providential view of the world. "The Lord himself has done this, against whom no one can oppose. . . . And why should I even wish to, knowing that all things must work together for good to them that love God?" (cf. Romans 8:28).[27]

Along with his personal tragedy, Michaelius struggled in his ministry. The European settlers, in his view, seemed "rough and unrestrained"; the indigenous peoples were "entirely savage and wild," and "proficient in all wickedness and godlessness." They were "devilish men, who serve nobody but the Devil," he wrote. Further, they "have so much witchcraft, divination, sorcery and wicked arts, that they can hardly be held in by any bands or locks." With these words, Michaelius expressed the racist views of many Europeans about Native Americans. "They are thievish and treacherous," he wrote, "altogether inhuman, more than barbarous, far exceeding the Africans."[28]

Not surprisingly, Michaelius did not last long in North America; he was back in Holland within four years. Within that time, New Netherland adopted the Dutch Reformed Church as the legal religion of the colony. Officially, the Dutch Reformed Church would be the colony's only religion; unofficially, colonial leaders knew better than to try enforcing religious conformity. Life in diverse Holland had taught them that. Too much religious enforcement led to too much strife and thus too much distraction from the economic pursuits of the people.[29]

But was there a limit to toleration? As the colony grew, the diversity of its people expanded, and the variety of cultures worried Peter Stuyvesant, who assumed the role of the colony's director in 1647. He wanted a uniform, disciplined colony, not a confused mixture of religions and cultures. It was bad enough, in his view, that he had to put up with Presbyterians, Lutherans, and even Catholics; yet in 1654 he saw a group of poor Jewish refugees arrive, and he promptly asked them to leave. This took some Jews by surprise. Had the leaders of New Amsterdam abandoned the tolerant policies of their homeland? Apparently so. Dutch Reformed minister and missionary Johannes Megapolensis complained that these Jews "have no other God than the unrighteous Mammon, and no other aim than to get possession of christian property, and to win all other merchants by drawing all trade towards themselves."[30]

New Amsterdam's Jews took up their case with the West India Company and received confirmation that they would be able to "travel and trade to and in New Netherland and live and remain there, provided that the poor among them shall not become a burden to the company or to the community." Thus Jews found a home in New Netherland worshiping together in homes from the 1650s and built one of the first synagogues in America, Congregation Shearith Israel.[31]

Just a few years after these Jews started worshiping together, the colony's major settlement changed its name from New Amsterdam to New York. The Dutch had lost the colony in 1664, when England took control and renamed the settlement to honor King Charles II's brother James, the Duke of York. The English targeted New Netherland for conquest, mainly because it was sandwiched between the English colonies of Maryland and Connecticut. It was all part of the effort to strengthen England's power in the Middle Colonies. Just as the English took control of the New Netherland, they also established the colony of New Jersey.[32]

In the western side of New Jersey, English Quakers were in control. "Quaker" was a name given to the Society of Friends because they often "quaked" or shook in worship (cf. "tremble" in Isaiah 66:2, 5). They believed that each person had an "inner light" or connection with the divine, a belief that some others thought disrespected biblical authority. In addition, Quakers opposed all violence and war; this pacifism offended most of the people around them. Understandably, then, Quakers had endured persecution since they appeared on the scene in England, led by their founder, George Fox (1624–91). Most Protestants deemed Quakers too radical for polite society. And yet that was exactly what the Quakers were capable of producing: a well-ordered and peaceful society in America. Much of the credit for this reality goes to William Penn (1644–1718), a Quaker who supported West Jersey before making history by establishing Pennsylvania, a colony devoted to liberty of conscience.[33]

Pennsylvania

Pennsylvania had the advantage of time. William Penn founded the colony in 1682, decades later than the other English colonies of Jamestown (1607), Plymouth (1620), and Massachusetts Bay (1630), which meant that he had time to learn from the mistakes of these colonies. Penn was selective about the people he invited to emigrate to Pennsylvania, and he warned everyone who dared venture to the New World that it would be tough going from the start. It was not for those who wanted riches without struggle.[34]

Struggle had been nothing new to William Penn—he was a Quaker, after all, and used to mistreatment. After finding Quakers guilty of various charges, including blasphemy, New England Puritans hanged four of them between 1659 and 1691, after which they shifted from hanging Quakers to hanging accused witches. Back in England, William Penn studied at Oxford and converted to the Society of Friends in 1667. Shortly afterward he landed in prison for criticizing the Church of England, an experience that led him to write *No Cross, No Crown*, a major devotional work that remains in print. Shortly afterward he published another classic, *The Great Case of Liberty of Conscience*, perhaps the most thorough defense of religious liberty since Roger Williams's lengthy treatises several decades earlier. In this book, Penn defended the Quakers' religion (they were the true followers of Christ) and their politics (they posed no radical threat to the state).[35] For Penn, the conscience belonged in God's domain, not under the control of civil authorities. The courts had no business making religious decisions.

Penn hoped his argument for liberty of conscience would convince English rulers and bishops to at least tolerate Quakers and other minority groups. But toleration was not in their plan, at least not for nearly two decades, when England finally adopted the Toleration Act of 1688 (approved by the king in 1689). Meanwhile, Penn's ideas found a more agreeable home in North America. King Charles II gave Penn the land for the colony as repayment of a debt Charles owed to Penn's father. William Penn subsequently put his ideas into practice in "Penn's Woods." The government, as he framed it, protected the conscience as the ultimate treasure. The state would allow people to worship as they pleased, including Quakers, who would find a refuge in this colony. Toleration did have its limits. Everyone living there had to worship the one God, creator of the world, and they had to obey the many moral rules that Penn made law of the land. Within these strictures, people could seek God's truth without civil interference or intimidation.

Worship would be available and free to all, and this religious diversity would support civil peace, not endanger it.[36]

Penn's tolerant colony did not only entice Quakers; other groups moved there as well, including Mennonites, Amish, and Moravians, along with Presbyterians from Scotland. But Quakers dominated, which affected how the colony dealt with conflict. Given that Quakers were typically pacifist, Penn naturally wanted to avoid war, particularly war with Native Americans, which had wreaked havoc in other colonies. The first step for him was to secure an understanding with the Delaware people before embarking on his adventure in the new colony. Penn was proactive, sending representatives to meet with the Delaware, telling them that he wanted to settle the area, but only with their blessing. The Delaware knew as well as Penn the recent history of wars between the English and indigenous peoples in colonial America, and Penn said he wanted no such conflict in Pennsylvania. Colonists had been ruthless and unjust, he told them, and things would be different with him. There would be a fair treaty, he promised, and he delivered in 1701. It was not a perfect situation, but relations between the English and the Native Americans fared better in Penn's colony than in its predecessors.[37]

Pennsylvania was, as Penn called it, a "holy experiment" and "an example . . . to the nations," a phrase that resembled John Winthrop's statement that the Puritans in Massachusetts would be a "city set upon a hill." Penn's "experiment" was far different from the Puritan vision for religious uniformity. Yet both statements show that many people saw hope in North America. There was promise in these British colonies, and America had a providential purpose to fulfill. That idea changed radically over the years, with many conflicting views of it, but the idea itself never died.[38]

The Caribbean, Bermuda, and the South

By the 1670s, English colonization had become a full-blown economic success story, with profits surging from sugar production, mainly due to slavery. But the center of this bustling activity was not in the mainland colonies of North America; it was in the Caribbean, especially the island of Barbados, which the English had settled in 1627. During the 1600s, sugar became Barbados's gold, the most profitable crop on the island, displacing tobacco. As planters in Barbados shifted from tobacco to sugar, they also shifted from indentured servants, most from Ireland, to enslaved Africans. The sugar empire shaped a slavery empire.

Could enslaved people be Christian people, even members of the Church of England? In principle, most English people said yes. As we have seen, missionary work and colonization went hand in hand: the English sought to win the New World for the church and for the crown. In reality, however, most planters in Barbados had little interest in converting Africans to Christianity. For planters and colonial leaders, the Africans' work mattered more than their souls, and there was the vexed question of whether it was acceptable to enslave a Christian brother or sister. This was not just a quandary in Barbados; it also occupied colonists and missionaries throughout the Atlantic world. Planters and colonists worried about slave conversions. Would enslaved people naturally feel empowered by conversion? Would they confuse Christian freedom of the soul with civil freedom?[39]

When Charles II ascended the throne in 1660, England tried to restore order, and the church tried to set the record straight on conversions of enslaved people. Parliament ordered the governor of Barbados to convert enslaved Africans to Christianity, and by 1663 the governor put forward a bill that recommended this missionary effort. Still, the planters, who held much of the power in Barbados, stalled on these efforts.[40]

In the 1650s, Quakers stepped in to do the missionary work the planters ignored. Many Quakers moved to Barbados, and some Barbadians converted to the Quaker faith. The Society of Friends was less than ten years old, but already they were coming under fire for their radical beliefs, both in England and Barbados. At this point, Quakers had not rejected slavery; many Quakers in Barbados were slaveholders, but when Quaker founder George Fox visited the island in 1671, his encounter with slavery disturbed him. He called for enslaved people to be educated and converted: "[Christ] died for Tawnes and for the Blacks, as well as for you that are called Whites." After leaving Barbados, Fox printed his reflections in *To the ministers, teachers and priests (so-called and so stiling your-selves) in Barbadoes*, attacking ministers for not trying to convert the Africans, even while acknowledging that the Quakers were doing this work.[41]

Missionary work in Barbados changed abruptly in the wake of an attempted slave rebellion in 1675. This was the planters' nightmare, a nightmare they had planned for by strengthening the island's militia. The rebellion was to take place in June. Enslaved African men plotted to murder their masters, seize control of the government, and crown an African man named Cuffy the new king of Barbados. The plot did not materialize: word leaked out, prompting the planters to launch a preemptive strike, accusing 107 enslaved Africans of conspiracy, and executing 42 of them. Another repercussion was legal: The Council of Barbados strengthened their laws regulating enslaved people, limiting their activities and calling for stricter punishment for violations. In addition, the new laws included "an Act to prevent the People called Quakers, from bringing Negroes to their Meeting." Clearly missions, particularly those led by Quakers, undermined the slave system, the planters believed. This caused a backlash, both against Quakers, whom planters blamed for inciting the revolt, and against missionary work among enslaved Africans altogether. Although the Church of England continued to support missions to enslaved people, they met resistance from slaveholders, who believed that slave missions led to slave rebellions, and they cited Barbados as a prime example. In this and other ways, Barbados influenced other islands in the West Indies, including Jamaica and Antigua. The case was similar in the American South, where many slaveholders resisted religious instruction for enslaved people, in part due to fear that it would undermine slavery.[42]

Over 800 miles northeast of the West Indies, Bermuda, a group of seven larger islands and approximately 170 smaller islands, was England's smallest colony in the New World. Soon after colonizing Bermuda in 1612, the English began construction of a church, St. Peter's, which remains the oldest Anglican congregation outside of Britain. As expected, most Bermudans were loyal to the Church of England, but many of them leaned toward Puritanism, and several ministers in Bermuda exchanged letters with Puritans in Massachusetts Bay. Early on, pressure from the Church of England, especially from the anti-Puritan William Laud, Archbishop of Canterbury, tried to keep Bermuda's ministers in line. Even if Christians in Bermuda were not as zealously Puritan as settlers of New England, they came close.[43]

As the conflict between Parliament and Charles I intensified in England, so did tensions among Bermudans. Near the end of 1641, Bermudans heard the shocking news from England: The Long Parliament, led by Puritans, had imprisoned Archbishop Laud. Puritan power in England was reflected in Bermuda, with Puritan-leaning ministers gaining more authority. As things went from bad to worse in England, with Charles I and Parliament fighting a civil war, several Puritan ministers in Bermuda denounced the Church of England and declared their independence from it. Before long, a power struggle erupted between Puritans and those loyal to the Church of England and the crown.[44]

Bermuda was small, but this conflict had large consequences. Back in England, the Long Parliament (1640–60) heard the protests of Bermuda's Puritans and called for all governors in all English colonies in the New World to grant religious freedom to their inhabitants. This was good news for Puritans in Bermuda, but it was bad news for Puritans in Massachusetts Bay. These Bay Colony Puritans ruled New England, their "city upon a hill," and the last thing they wanted was to grant religious freedom to all, as they made clear by running Roger Williams out of the colony.[45]

The next few years in Bermuda were years of dissension, both political and religious, culminating in accusations of witchcraft. Bermudans heard what was happening in England, where civil war and unrest had led to witch-hunting. In 1645–47, as many as 300 people were accused of witchcraft, and officials hanged more than 100 of them. During this decade, several books on witchcraft appeared in London, with titles such as *A true and exact Relation Of the Severall Informations, Examinations, and Confessions of the late Witches* (1645), *Select Cases of Conscience Touching Witches and*

Witchcrafts (1646), and *The Discovery of Witches* (1647). Many people read these works, along with older, more familiar works such as *A Discourse of the Damned Art of Witchcraft* (1608), written by the influential Puritan William Perkins. Bermudans likely read these or other books and found in them guidance on the proper way to identify a witch.[46]

In May of 1651, witch-hunting was underway in Bermuda, and by 1655 a total of twelve people were accused of witchcraft. Several of the accused faced the standard tests for witchcraft, including physical exams in which their bodies were inspected for a "little teate," or perhaps a "blewish spot" that would "not bleede" when stuck. Another accepted way to identify a witch involved throwing accused witches in the water to see if they would sink. A witch, they believed, would never sink (nor would anyone else in the salty Atlantic waters of Bermuda). As expected, a woman named Jeane Gardiner failed this test and died by hanging on May 26, 1651. Also failing the water test was one John Middleton, a middle-aged man who also had suspicious marks on his body and, according to one accuser, had "a Black creature . . . in the shape of a catt but farre Bigger, with eyes like fier" lurking around his house. After Middleton's wife gave a conflicted testimony—maybe her husband was a witch, maybe not—Middleton admitted that he was a witch, then named other witches. He died by hanging on May 9, 1653. These events, which occurred nearly fifty years before the witchcraft trials in Salem, show how widespread and devastating the terrors over witchcraft were in the Atlantic world.[47]

Bermuda was not the only non-New England Puritan outpost in the Americas. For some of the leading Puritan gentlemen in London, the future lay not in New England, but in the West Indies. Supported by slavery, they could produce profitable crops that could never grow in New England, and it was there that the English could beat the Spanish at their own game. The Spanish had led the way on colonizing the Latin world, and the English needed to gain the upper hand. Only then could the profits boost the English economy, and only then could English Protestantism, with a Puritan tinge to it, combat the rising tide of Roman Catholicism in the Americas. To reach these goals, English Puritans, working through the Providence Island Company, founded an island colony just off Nicaragua's coast. The year was 1630, the same year that John Winthrop's band of Puritans set sail to settle the Massachusetts Bay Colony. Unlike these New England settlers, the founders of this Puritan outpost on the Costa de Mosquitos did not want a "city upon a hill" so much as the seed of a future English empire in the Caribbean.[48]

They named the island "Providence," but the colony did not seem to be blessed by providence, at least not at first. Early on, settlers argued over which crops to grow, how best to defend the colony, and other issues. Yet providence did seem to smile on them in 1634, when they fended off an attack by the Spanish. Surely God had delivered them, they believed. By defeating the Spanish, they had opened the way to profit from state-endorsed piracy (privateering), and they had an excellent location for it. As an English official stated, Providence Island "lieth in the high way of the Spanish fleets that come from Cartagena, . . . from Porto Bellow, . . . also from the Bay of Nicoraga," so ships carrying riches passed within easy reach. This led some historians to argue that the so-called Puritan commitments of the colony were just a ruse; the true goal of the colony was profit through privateering. Not so, say most historians. Many settlers of Providence Island held genuine Puritan convictions. This was piracy for God: it was, as a Providence Island committee reported, a way of "annoying the Spaniard and intercepting his treasure whereby he hath troubled and endangered most of the States of Christendom and doth foment the wars against the professors of the reformed Religion."[49]

By the early 1640s, island leaders tried to convince Puritans to abandon New England and move south to Providence Island. This promoted an argument by letter exchange, between Lord Saye, an island supporter, and Governor John Winthrop of Massachusetts Bay. Winthrop criticized Lord Saye for putting down New England. Saye, in turn, wrote that Winthrop and the Bay Colony Puritans misinterpreted the Bible in a self-serving way, claiming that New England was like the fertile land of Canaan. In reality, New England was no Canaan; it was more like a barren desert that made wealthy people poor. Was it so wrong, Governor Winthrop, to invite Puritans to "a warmer clymate and in a more frutefull soyle," Lord Saye asked. "Why are you angry with me for this?" A short time later, Winthrop was only too happy to report the news that Providence Island had fallen to the Spanish in 1641, a final stroke that ended this Puritan experiment in the Caribbean Sea.[50]

Unlike in Providence Island, Jamaica was no Puritan outpost—far from it. Jamaica, which the English captured from the Spanish in 1655, was a complex colony of planters and pirates, Jews and Quakers. Port Royal was a pirate's paradise, filled with merchants, taverns, and houses of ill repute. As a leading historian wrote, "Port Royal became known as the Sodom of the Indies." The most accurate image of Jamaica, as shown on a map printed in England, displayed a duel between two men, firing their pistols.[51]

Planting and piracy both thrived in Jamaica. The land was fertile, and the English imported enslaved Africans by the thousands and set them to work on sugar plantations. Planters and pirates did not always coexist well, mainly because pirates scared off the planters' customers: ship captains, whether they carried merchandise or enslaved people, avoided areas where pirates lurked. Some planters gave up and climbed aboard pirate ships because the money was better. The legendary buccaneer Henry Morgan enjoyed so much success that the governor sent him to attack Spanish cites in Nicaragua, Cuba, Panama, and Venezuela. When his raid on Panama caught the attention of Charles II, the king called Morgan to London, ostensibly to punish him. Instead, the king knighted Morgan for his courageous attacks on the Spanish. When planting finally replaced piracy as Jamaica's main pursuit, planters saturated the colony with slavery. In 1689, approximately 30,000 enslaved Africans lived in Jamaica. By 1713, that number had grown to 55,000, giving Jamaica more enslaved people than Barbados, with eight enslaved people to every one slaveholder.[52]

In Jamaica's religions, as in politics and society overall, disorder reigned. No single religious group dominated, but the colony became a refuge for outcasts. Sephardic Jews moved to Jamaica from Brazil and other areas, mainly to work as merchants. They segregated themselves in town and built a synagogue. Some Jews were poor, but others prospered and tried to find ways to avoid the tax on Jews. In Port Royal, Jews worshiped alongside Quakers, Anglicans, and Presbyterians.[53]

On June 7, 1692, disaster struck. An earthquake demolished half of Port Royal in less than five minutes, pulling hundreds of people and buildings into the ocean. In the seventeenth century, such devastating natural disasters seemed to be acts of God that required interpretation. One Quaker expressed the views of many: God had punished the people for their sins. This Quaker was especially concerned to describe the horrifying scene of bodies floating on the water after the disaster. This, to him, was a visual sermon against pride. "If thou didst see those great persons that are now dead upon the water thou couldst never forget it. Great men who were so swallowed up with pride" had faced God's wrath in the quake, and "now lie stinking upon the water, and are made meat for fish and fowles of the air." Religious interpretations of the event made headline news back in England. Several pamphlets, printed in London, included such titles as *Earthquakes explained and practically improved: . . . Jamaica's miseries shew London's mercies* (1693). As some saw it, God had focused his earthshaking vitriol on the pirates, punishing Jamaica for their crimes. This colony was no longer a battleground for supremacy between pirates and planters; God had spoken, and the planters had won.[54]

Carolina

Business had been so good that the English wanted more land to expand their empire, and they found it by establishing a new colony in 1670. They called it Charles Town, naming it after King Charles II, and they located it strategically between English-controlled Virginia and Spanish-controlled Florida.[55] Not only did they name the town after Charles, but the entire region they named in a Latin variant for Charles, "Carolina." And why not honor the king? After the Restoration of Charles II, many English people breathed a sigh of relief. The strife-filled years of the civil war, followed by the unruly religious situation during Oliver Cromwell's rule, made the monarchy look good. A king would bring stability, they believed, a return to life as it should be, which meant a king in charge and a strong Church of

England. Radicalism, both political and religious, had to go. Yet they found that this was easier said than done, at least in the colonies. After he gained the throne, Charles II had favors to give out to men who had supported him; as we have seen, he handed out some of these favors in the form of land, given through proprietary charters.

The first order of business for men who received these lands was to fill them with people, preferably from England. This was especially urgent in Carolina: because of its risky location just north of French and Spanish territories, the colony's leaders wanted to get as many English people to Carolina as possible so that they could defend the colony. Yet most of the English who wanted to go to America were not Anglicans but dissenters, those who belonged to churches other than the official Church of England, which was endorsed by the government. These dissenters wanted to live in a place where they could worship without interference. In these post-Restoration colonies, therefore, dissenters outnumbered Anglicans, making it hard for the Church of England to force the people to conform.[56]

We see the religious situation reflected in "The Fundamental Constitutions of Carolina," written by Lord Anthony Ashley Cooper and his assistant, a young man named John Locke. They envisioned a colony with plenty of land, plenty of enslaved Africans, and a hands-off policy on religion, within certain limits. The Church of England would be established because it was "the only true and orthodox and the national religion of all the King's dominions." But the colony could not thrive if it required everyone to be members of the Church of England. Besides, "civil peace may be maintained amidst diversity of opinions" as long as all agreed "that there is a God" and that they should worship God "publicly." In addition, all churches had to show "the external way whereby they witness a truth as in the presence of God, whether it be by laying hands on or kissing the bible, as in the Church of England, or by holding up the hand, or any other sensible way." Individuals over age 17 had to be church members; otherwise they could not "have any benefit or protection of the law, or be capable of any place of profit or honor." The rules forbade any attacks on the government, or any attacks on religious views, because this was a sure way to disturb the peace.[57]

Not surprisingly, several religious groups populated Carolina. By the beginning of the eighteenth century, about 1,700 Anglicans lived in the colony, where they had to make room for an assortment of Presbyterians, the second largest group at about 1,300 members, along with Huguenots, Baptists, and Quakers. The Fundamental Constitution specifically invited Jewish settlers. As colonial leaders figured it, Jews had suffered during the Spanish Inquisition, so they would likely despise the Spanish. This would make them strong defenders of the colony against the Spaniards in Florida. Jews, Protestants, and even Quakers were welcome in Carolina, but not Roman Catholics.[58]

The profit-making goals of the colony meant that religion would be friendly with slavery. According to the Fundamental Constitution, any slaveholder had "absolute power and authority over his negro slaves, of what opinion or religion soever." Most important for slaveholders, religion did not change one's "civil estate or right," so enslaved people could join any church they pleased, but it did not change their situation; they remained enslaved, with no higher standing than before.[59]

"Carolina" officially divided into North and South Carolina in 1712. Christianity would support slavery in the Carolinas for years to come, and the support paid dividends for slaveholders. By the 1820s, enslaved people comprised the majority of South Carolinians. The Lowcountry of the state had approximately 123,000 enslaved people and about 33,000 whites. Enslaved workers built the state of South Carolina, literally constructing canals, various buildings, forts, and more. Transportation was critical, and enslaved workers expedited it by building numerous roads. While constructing one of these roads, enslaved workers near the Stono River (a tidal channel) got the idea for a revolt. Road construction was the best preparation for rebellion these workers could ask for, giving them good knowledge of the land and the people who lived on it. When the Stono rebellion erupted in 1739, South Carolinians saw the worst slave revolt in their history. Ironically, working on building the state infrastructure gave enslaved people the information they needed to attack it.[60]

Georgia

In Georgia, as in the Carolinas, officials tolerated many religions, not because they liked it, but because the need to attract a lot of settlers outranked the desire for religious uniformity. Founded in 1732 and named for King George II, Georgia was governed by trustees who banned slavery and alcohol from the colony (neither of these restrictions lasted more than a few years). Key to the founding of Georgia was Thomas Bray (1658–1730), an Oxford graduate and one of most critical supporters of the Anglican Church in North America. Bray was innovative and organized. In 1695 he had drawn up "Proposals for Encouraging Learning and Religion in the Foreign Plantations," and he devoted his life to educating clergy and supporting missions. Unlike many Anglican leaders, Bray actually came to America, so he witnessed the problems in the colonies and devised realistic ideas for addressing them. He founded the Society for Promoting Christian Knowledge (1699), devoted to publishing books to educate clergy. Two years later he founded the Society for the Propagation of the Gospel in Foreign Parts, devoted to hiring missionaries and sending them to the colonies. Later in life, Bray founded "Dr. Bray's Associates," which led in the founding of the colony of Georgia, which became a refuge for England's poor and a missionary outpost.[61]

Early on, the colony attracted Scottish Presbyterians, Huguenots, and German Lutherans, all of whom worshiped with little interference. But there were limits to toleration. If Carolina was in a precarious location, dangerously close to the Spanish in Florida, Georgia was even closer, making it even more important that Georgia's settlers be willing to fight the Spanish if called on for that. Georgia's trustees, therefore, did not so much care for what its colonists thought about worship or doctrine, but they had no use for pacifists, like the sizable group of Moravians who had found a home there. In 1738, therefore, colonial officials ejected many of the Moravians from Georgia. Also unwelcome, of course, were Catholics, who could not be trusted to remain loyal to British Georgia if a confrontation erupted with Spanish Catholics.[62]

Jews posed a tougher case. Just as colonial trustees were discussing whether to let Jews into Georgia, some forty of them showed up in Savannah. Some trustees wanted to banish them, but others, including Governor James Oglethorpe, allowed the Jews to stay. As officials in Carolina had pointed out, Jews were no friends to Spanish Catholics, so they would likely be loyal British colonists. Besides, Georgia needed physicians, and one of the Jewish settlers was Dr. Samuel Nunez, who gave invaluable service by treating the sick. In a short time, Nunez became one of Georgia's most respected colonists. Respect for Nunez and other Jews led Georgians to welcome even more Jewish settlers, and religious diversity grew to a point that the Church of England was not even officially established in this English colony until 1758. Even then, the colony remained tolerant of Jews and all Protestants, but not Roman Catholics.[63]

In the eyes of many English, Georgia was a dangerous wilderness. Only adventurers dared to go there, and some of those adventurers had religious agendas. Perhaps the most famous was John Wesley (1703–91), leader of an English society that later became the Methodist Church. While at Oxford, Wesley and his brother, Charles Wesley (1707–88), had formed a group of fellow students who devoted themselves to religious training and strict moral discipline. Nicknamed the "Holy Club," or "Methodists," these students attracted jokes and ridicule, but they were serious and organized, and soon they gained a following.

Wesley suffered from anxiety about his soul even though he was an Anglican priest. When he heard about Georgia and the need for missionaries there, he signed on as a volunteer, commissioned by Thomas Bray's Society for the Propagation of the Gospel in Foreign Parts. Along with his brother, Charles, newly ordained as a priest himself, John set sail for Georgia in 1735. Wesley had high hopes for his mission in the New World. This, he hoped, would be his chance to serve the Lord under the most extreme conditions, braving the American frontier, ministering to white settlers and Native Americans alike. Maybe his ministry in Georgia would help him grow in his faith. As he put it before he left, "My chief motive . . . is the hope of saving my own soul."[64]

FIGURE 3-3. John Wesley, by John Faber, 1730–56, LC-USZ72-154 (Library of Congress)

The soul-saving began aboard the ship bound for America. This was John Wesley's first time at sea, and he was already intimidated by the prospect of a hard voyage across the dark Atlantic in winter. His worst fears came true when his ship navigated rough waters. At the height of one storm, with the ship tossed on the waves and almost crushed, Wesley came to a chilling realization: He was not ready to die, and it terrified him. If he were as faithful a Christian as he should have been, he would have assurance, he thought, and he would welcome death as an entry into paradise. This fear revealed just how lost he was. To make matters worse, he saw a group of German Moravians on the ship who showed no fear of the storm. As he attended one of their services, the waves rose so high that water drenched the ship, damaged the mainsail, and it appeared "as if the great deep had already swallowed us up." Terror gripped everyone aboard, except these Moravians. They did not even lose their place in the psalm they were singing. Wesley had never seen anything like it. He wanted that kind of assurance, and it would be his goal to receive it.[65]

Miraculously to him, Wesley survived the voyage and reached the dry land of Georgia in February of 1736. Later, he would call his time in Georgia "the second rise of Methodism." He valued the Georgia experience, but he never wanted to repeat it. Since the Moravians had so impressed him aboard ship, he sought the advice of one of Georgia's Moravian leaders, August

Spangenberg, and the Moravian influence would be critical to his spiritual development.

The Wesley brothers tried to witness to the Creek Native Americans, but they made little progress, and the experience sobered them on missionary work in the American South. Most of Wesley's work focused on the Methodist societies in Savannah and Frederica, along with work with the indigenous people, whom he referred to mostly as "gluttons, drunkards, thieves, dissemblers, liars"—and that was just the beginning. He had more favorable views of the enslaved people he met, though the experience depressed him, leading him to develop a plan for approaching the planters with the need to instruct enslaved people in religion. A high point of the Wesleys' ministry was worship, which attracted healthy numbers in Savannah. In 1737, the Wesleys published *A Collection of Psalms and Hymns*, America's first book of hymns in English. A century earlier Puritans had published *The Bay Psalm Book*, a metrical Psalter; but by the time of the Wesleys, hymns were coming to replace metrical psalms. Many of the hymns in the Wesleys' *Collection* were existing songs, and they were central to Methodist worship. That importance was reflected in the work of Charles Wesley, who would earn great renown as the author of thousands of hymns.[66]

John Wesley's ministry in Georgia came to an abrupt end in 1737. Sophy Hopkey, a woman Wesley had been romantically involved with, married another man. A spurned and angry Wesley retaliated by refusing to serve her Communion on the grounds that she had neglected to publish the banns of marriage, the legal notice of an upcoming wedding, required so that anyone could come forward if they knew of a reason why the couple should not marry. Hopkey's husband struck back by filing charges against Wesley, and the grand jury in Savannah agreed to indict Wesley on ten formal charges (it did not hurt that Hopkey's guardian was the chief magistrate). This would not go well for Wesley, and he knew it. He skipped bail, slipped out of town, boarded a ship, and fled back to England.[67] Wesley's time in America ended unceremoniously, therefore. He never returned, and he spoke out against the American "patriots" in the Revolutionary War. Few could have predicted that the movement he founded would later grow to become one of the largest Protestant denominations in the United States.

Throughout the colonial period, religious diversity expanded in the Caribbean and in the southern and middle colonies. For most of the seventeenth century, nine out of ten congregations in colonial America were either Puritan (Congregationalist) or Church of England. By the eve of the American Revolution, that ratio changed significantly: Puritan Congregationalists and Anglicans made up only a combined 35 percent of congregations. By that time Presbyterians, mainly from Scottish and Irish backgrounds, accounted for 18 percent of congregations, while Baptists made up 15 percent. Also numerically significant by this time were Lutheran and Reformed churches with German and Dutch backgrounds, and Quakers; each of these groups accounted for 5–10 percent of churches. The days of Puritan and Anglican dominance had ended by the Revolution (1775). Religious diversity expanded, aided by increased European immigration, the growth of some religious groups, and nontraditional religious views, including practices of the occult and magic. Perhaps the most important factors in these religious shifts were the revivals, later called the Great Awakening, that sprang up in various regions in the eighteenth century—a subject to which we turn in the next chapter.[68]

4. The Great Awakening

Revivals ignited a new kind of religious zeal in the eighteenth century, but the idea of revival was nothing new. Christianity, it seemed, was constantly in need of renewal. In the 1500s, Protestant Reformers, like Martin Luther and John Calvin, sought to renew a Catholic Church that they believed had gone astray, departing from its biblical roots. By the 1600s, German Pietists like Philip Jacob Spener tried to revitalize Lutheranism, just as the Puritans were trying to usher the Church of England back to its biblical foundations. In Scotland, Presbyterians celebrated "holy fairs" in preparation for Communion services, often four days long and a combination of revival and holiday, which Presbyterians from Northern Ireland and Scotland brought with them when they moved to North America and settled mainly in the Middle Colonies. Aided by these and other influences, revival surged through colonial America by the 1740s, led by George Whitefield (1714–70), who became an international celebrity, supported in part by his friend and printer Benjamin Franklin (1706–90). In England, Whitefield had been one of the Oxford Methodists, along with John and Charles Wesley, and like the Wesleys he was an Anglican priest. At about the same time John Wesley was fleeing from Georgia, returning to England to avoid arrest, Whitefield was heading from England to Georgia, where he enjoyed much more success than Wesley, eventually making seven preaching tours through colonial America.[1]

In parts of the colonies, revivals transformed the religious landscape, creating excitement but also dissension. Itinerant preachers like James Davenport and Gilbert Tennent mixed calls for revival with harsh criticisms of their fellow ministers. In New England, Jonathan Edwards (1703–58) defended the revivals and crafted a theological legacy that had a wide-ranging influence. With all of its diversity and its controversy, the Great Awakening gave rise to evangelicalism, a Protestant movement stressing that all people were sinners and needed to undergo the "new birth," a conversion experience, which radically altered the direction of one's life.[2]

"My Heart Was Broken"

Through the Eyes of Nathan Cole, Connecticut Farmer

On October 23, 1740, Nathan Cole was working on his farm in Connecticut when a visitor told him that George Whitefield would be preaching later that morning in Middletown, twelve miles away. He immediately dropped his tools and called his wife. Within minutes they were riding as fast as their horse could go. Before long, their horse tired, and Cole's wife rode alone while Nathan ran behind, moving, as he later wrote, "as if we were fleeing for our lives." They were not alone. As they passed other farms, they found them deserted; it seemed that everyone had left to see Whitefield. As they approached within a few miles of Middletown, they saw a great cloud of dust, churned up by riders on horses, galloping at a frantic pace, trying to make it to see the famous evangelist in time. Cole saw so many horses, hundreds of them, one "behind another, all of a Lather and foam with sweat, their breath rolling out of their nostrils every Jump; every horse seemed to go with all his might to carry his rider to hear news from heaven for the saving of Souls."[3]

When the Coles arrived, they found somewhere between 3,000 and 4,000 people crowded together, waiting for Whitefield. Finally, the moment arrived when the "Grand Itinerant" stepped up to preach. "He Lookt almost angelical," Cole wrote, "a young, Slim, slender, youth before some thousands of people," Whitefield "looked as if he was Cloathed with authority from the Great God." Then Whitefield seemed to prove it when he began preaching. His sermon affected Cole deeply, giving him "a heart wound," convincing him that much of what he had thought about God and salvation was wrong. Cole had believed he could "be saved by my own works such as prayers and good deeds." But Whitefield convinced Cole that his righteousness was rubbish; as Cole wrote, "I was convinced of the doctrine of Election." Now Cole knew "that all I could do would not save me; and" that God "had decreed from Eternity who should be saved and who not."[4]

This belief did not comfort Cole—far from it, he figured that God had not chosen him, that he was one of the lost, bound for hell. "I was made to be damned," he thought. This was no temporary conviction; it lasted for two years, with Cole living in anxiety and guilt, expecting to fall into hell at any moment. He thought about hell a lot, almost obsessing over it. When he smoked, he would stick his fingers in the pipe, just so he would get a sense of how hell would feel, imagining his entire body burning "in Hell fire for ever and ever."[5]

Eventually, Cole experienced God's deliverance from his torments. "In my mind God appeared unto me," Cole wrote, describing a vision in which he "seemed to hang in open Air before God, and he seemed to Speak to me in an angry and Sovereign way," admonishing him for his lack of faith. Then, lightning quick, God "vanished," leaving Cole, but also taking away Cole's distress about his soul. "My heart was broken," Cole wrote, but he meant it in a good way: "my burden was fallen of[f] my mind; I was set free, my distress was gone, and I was filled with a pining desire to see Christs own words in the bible."[6]

Cole's vision fascinates historians, not only because he was a typical farmer and not an educated minister, but also because his narrative unveils several important features of the revivals that historians call the Great Awakening (or First Great Awakening, to distinguish it from another massive movement of revivals in the nineteenth century). First, Cole shifted from an Arminian to a Calvinist, believing that God elected only a certain number of people for salvation. At first he found election distressing, but after a period of struggle he found the idea comforting. This surprised some at that time and even some today, who wonder how belief in election could flourish amid revivals. If all have been elected to heaven or hell before they were born, why preach? In reality, however, many of the major revival preachers were Calvinists, including George Whitefield and Jonathan Edwards. They preached to everyone because no one knew for sure who was elect. Also, they denied that God ever converted people against their will.

Second, as Cole and many others experienced it, the "new birth" could be sudden, an instant change of heart and mind. In the revivals, preachers fixated on the instant when a person made the decision to submit to Christ, a decision that brought about the rebirth to which Jesus referred when he said to a Pharisee named Nicodemus, "Except a man be born again, he cannot see the kingdom of God" (John 3:3). This idea of a "new birth" confused Nicodemus, and it also puzzled many in colonial America. How did you know if you were born again? This question confused some and agonized others, as many questioned themselves—and often their ministers; they struggled to find assurance that they had been saved from the terrors of hell, just as Cole worried about his eternal destiny. For him, and for many at the time, this life was much less important than the next life, because in the next life one would spend eternity in either heaven or hell. This heightened sense of anxiety permeated the revivals, leading many people to contemplate the nature of the mind, body, and soul and how they interacted in religious experience.

Third, the revivals, which preachers hoped would unite their churches into a mighty force to evangelize the world, divided as much as they united. Revivals infused excitement into churches and provoked some people to reassess their religious experience, their churches, and their clergy. After their spiritual deliverance in the revivals, some laypeople left the churches they grew up in, believing their churches had fallen from the true gospel, and attended other churches that seemed more redeemed. Nathan Cole was an example. Although his narrative describes an event from 1740, he wrote it down over twenty years later, when it was part of his argument for leaving the Congregational churches, the Puritan-founded and established churches of New England.[7]

"The Most Famous Man in America"

George Whitefield, Traveling Evangelist and International Celebrity

At the time that Nathan Cole was galloping down a dusty road to catch a glimpse of George Whitefield, few people had heard of Benjamin Franklin, but Franklin had heard a lot about Whitefield. Franklin the printer always had his eye out for news, especially marketable news that people would want to read about in the *Pennsylvania Gazette*. Whitefield *was* news, and the best kind, because he was both famous and controversial, partly because the revivals were controversial. Some believed the evangelists were God's tool for saving souls; others believed they were the devil's tool for deceiving people and distorting their faith. Whitefield drew crowds like no other person of his time. As historian Thomas Kidd stated, Whitefield was "the most famous man in America" by 1740, and he "was probably the most famous man in Britain, too, or at least the most famous aside from King George II."[8]

Franklin scoured London newspapers for stories about Whitefield, and he reprinted them. These stories seemed impossible to believe, with accounts of the great preacher speaking before twenty thousand people or more, amazing in a world without microphones or loudspeakers. Franklin doubted these stories, but he printed them anyway. Whitefield also aroused Franklin's curiosity. Ever the scientist, he had to investigate for himself this phenomenon of Whitefield. In 1739, Franklin got his chance when Whitefield came to Philadelphia.

Franklin, religious skeptic that he was, liked the fact that Whitefield had upset some of the elite ministers in the area, offending them to the point that they refused to allow him to speak in their churches. No problem for Whitefield: he responded by preaching outdoors, which was his specialty anyway. Outdoor preaching allowed Whitefield to reach a broader audience, not just folks of a specific denomination, but this also stirred controversy. When John Wesley heard that his friend (and sometimes nemesis) was preaching outside, he condemned "this strange way of preaching in the fields." Preaching outside a church seemed indecent and disorderly. Wesley wrote that he was "so tenacious of every point relating to decency and order that I should have thought the saving of souls almost a sin if it had not been done in a church." He changed his mind when he saw Whitefield preach to a crowd of some thirty thousand in England. After that, Wesley "submitted to 'be more vile'" and started preaching outdoors as well.[9]

Preaching in the fields worked for Whitefield, and Ben Franklin could attest to that. "The multitudes of all sects and denominations that attended his sermons were enormous, and it was a matter of speculation to me, who was one of the number, to observe the extraordinary influence of his oratory on his hearers," Franklin wrote in his *Autobiography*. What was it about Whitefield that drew such crowds? It puzzled Franklin that so many people wanted to attend Whitefield's services, to hear "his common abuse of them, by assuring them they were naturally *half beasts and half devils*."[10]

MR. FRANKLIN ENCOUNTERS THE REVEREND WHITEFIELD

In spite of his objections to Whitefield's message, Benjamin Franklin's curiosity about evangelist got the better of him, and eventually the printer/philosopher had to hear for himself. "He had a loud and clear voice, and articulated his words and sentences so perfectly, that he might be heard and understood at a great distance," Franklin wrote. He also remarked at how silent such a large audience was when Whitefield spoke. Just how many could hear Whitefield? Franklin wondered, so he decided to measure the distance and count the crowd. One evening when Whitefield preached from the steps of the courthouse, Franklin moved backward to determine how far away Whitefield's voice carried. The results amazed him. "I computed that he might well be heard by more than thirty thousand." Now the outlandish reports in the London newspapers did not seem so preposterous: clearly, Whitefield had preached to crowds that large.*

Not only did Franklin evaluate Whitefield's multitudes, but he also gauged the evangelist's effectiveness. How good a preacher was he? Franklin found out after hearing Whitefield preach a sermon in part to raise money for an orphanage he wanted to build in Georgia. Franklin approved of the project but disapproved of the site—there were many better places than Georgia, including Philadelphia—so Franklin refused to contribute. Franklin attended the sermon, knowing that Whitefield would "finish with a collection, and I silently resolved he should get nothing from me."† This was the frugal Franklin, author of *Poor Richard's Almanac*, which included the quip, "a penny saved is two pence clear."‡ Yet Franklin went to the sermon with money in his pocket, specifically "a handful of copper money, three or four silver dollars, and five pistoles in gold." As Whitefield preached, Franklin "began to soften, and concluded to give the coppers. Another stroke of his oratory made me asham'd of that, and determin'd me to give the silver; and he finish'd so admirably, that I empty'd my pocket wholly into the collector's dish, gold and all." One of Franklin's friends took precautionary measures against the collection by not bringing any money with him. Yet Whitefield preached so well he tried to borrow money from another of their friends who was standing nearby. Whitefield must have been an exceptional preacher if he could preach well enough to convince Franklin to contribute to a cause he did not fully agree with, using a theology that he detested.§

*Benjamin Franklin, *The Autobiography of Benjamin Franklin*, ed. Peter Conn (Philadelphia: University of Pennsylvania Press, 2005), 85–86. †Franklin, *Autobiography*, 84–85. ‡Benjamin Franklin, *Poor Richard's Almanac for 1850*, ed. J. Doggett (New York: J. Doggett Jr., 1849), 29. §Franklin, *Autobiography*, 84–85.

Whitefield's preaching was unlike anything most people had seen or heard. He had the volume, as Franklin attested, but he also had the style.

FIGURE 4-1. George Whitefield, half-length portrait with hands raised, preaching in a church, engraving by Elisha Gallaudet, New York, 1774. LC-USZ62-45506 (Library of Congress)

FIGURE 4-2. Benjamin Franklin by J. Pelicier, 1782. LC-USZ62-45334 (Library of Congress)

Before he joined the ministry, Whitefield had been an actor on stage in England, and his acting skills enhanced his preaching. In a world in which most preachers read directly from manuscripts, Whitefield memorized his sermons so he could focus on the people, not a sheet of paper. Unlike most preachers of his day, who preached formal sermons heavy on doctrine, Whitefield preached more informal sermons, appealing to people in plain talk, imploring them to seek the "new birth." It helped that Whitefield was young and handsome, and it helped that he was cross-eyed, as some associated that feature with spiritual power.[11]

Franklin and Whitefield, the skeptic and the evangelist, disagreed on many things, but they became friends and business associates. In Franklin, Whitefield found a media-savvy printer who would publish his writings and publicize his preaching tours. In Whitefield, Franklin found a celebrity, someone people wanted to read about, which translated into profits for Franklin's printing business. "In the early 1740s," Thomas Kidd wrote, "more than half of the books that Franklin published were related to Whitefield."[12]

Whitefield knew the value of publishing for drawing attention to the revivals. During his tours of the colonies, he brought along hundreds of pamphlets and books, including his own, which he distributed widely. Whitefield may have been preaching an old message from the Bible, but he marketed it in new ways, using modern techniques to advertise the revivals. Whitefield was a religious innovator in his methods, and he has been called "an entrepreneur, an impresario" who influenced later evangelists.[13] Armed with the resources of this time, Whitefield publicized the revivals, and he was not alone. Other preachers and publishers in England, Scotland, and the colonies published books, pamphlets, and newspaper articles to generate enthusiasm about the revivals.

Jonathan Edwards, Theologian of Revival

If George Whitefield was the foremost preacher of revivals, Jonathan Edwards was their greatest theologian. Edwards was a pastor in Northampton, Massachusetts, where he succeeded his grandfather, Solomon "Pope" Stoddard, who had held the pastorate for fifty-seven years. Stoddard was an exceptional minister, adored by his congregation, an outstanding preacher, and an innovator in church management. He was preaching revivals before most folks were talking about a transatlantic "awakening." When Stoddard died, Edwards continued his grandfather's tradition of revival preaching. Many historians trace the beginning of the Great Awakening not to Whitefield's arrival in the colonies, but to a revival that broke out in Jonathan Edwards's Northampton church in 1735, the same year that Whitefield experienced conversion at Oxford.

Edwards published an account of this revival in his *Faithful Narrative of the Surprising Work of God* (1737), which became a classic in revival literature. John Wesley, who detested Edwards's Calvinism, admired *Faithful Narrative* and published an edition of it, hoping Methodists would take it to heart.[14] With his *Faithful Narrative*, Edwards hoped to excite those in the colonies, England, and Europe who were looking for signs that God was sending a worldwide revival that would convert thousands of people to Christianity. The Holy Spirit was moving among the people, Edwards believed, and he filled the *Faithful Narrative* with evidence of the Spirit's work, including dramatic scenes of people struggling with their faith before turning from sinful lives to embrace God's love. As Edwards saw it, the statistics spoke for themselves: over three hundred people experienced the new birth in six months, both men and women in almost equal numbers, unusual since women often outnumbered men in the churches. The movement was racially diverse, with some African Americans converting during the whirl-wind of revival that spread through the area.[15]

Aside from reporting on the impressive numbers, Edwards investigated the psychology of conversion, describing in detail how individuals experienced the revivals, and two of those conversion stories became classics in evangelical circles. First, Abigail Hutchinson, a quiet and reserved woman, experienced conversion late in life. At first, thought of death terrified her, especially after she became aware that her sin had opened a gulf between her and God that she could never bridge. Then came the breakthrough, when God touched her soul and gave her a "sense of the glory of God's truth" and a desire for the "sweetness" of God. After this, she moved from one extreme to another: death no longer terrified her; it attracted her, and she described her yearning for death in morbid terms. When someone read the text from Job (19:26), describing worms eating a corpse, she smiled and "said it was sweet to her to think of her being in such circumstances." Eventually she got her wish. She died peacefully, Edwards reported, "as a person that went to sleep, without any struggling."[16]

Second, Phoebe Bartlett was a four-year-old girl who was terrified of hell because of her many sins, and her fears of eternal torment caused her to adjourn to her closet five or six times a day to pray for salvation. Finally she experienced deliverance from her torments and felt assured that God had saved her. This child's faith fascinated Edwards and convinced him that God could bless anyone with a mature faith, even a four-year-old. For many people today, it is appalling to think of a child who was tortured by thoughts of hell, feeling guilty for her horrific sins. (How bad could her sins be, anyway? we may ask: she was four!) Edwards would disagree. In his world, hell was a constant threat, especially for children, because children were more likely to die in Edwards's time than today. It was healthy to worry about hell, therefore, because it could motivate people to seek God's deliverance, which was their only eternal hope.[17]

Quite possibly young Phoebe Bartlett's terrors came from witnessing a lot of hellfire preaching, similar to Edwards's most famous sermon, "Sinners in the Hands of an Angry God." This sermon, preached in 1741, was reprinted countless times, often included in anthologies of American literature, where even today it is required reading in many high school English literature classes. Although most people today may cringe at Edwards's images of hellfire, these descriptions make the sermon worth reading after all these years. "Sinners" is "arguably America's greatest sermon," wrote Harry S. Stout, for it is a masterpiece of rhetorical effectiveness and vivid imagery.[18] Consider the following unforgettable lines:

> The wrath of God burns against [sinners], their damnation does not slumber, the pit is prepared, the fire is made ready, the furnace is now hot, ready to receive them, the flames do now rage and glow. The glit-

tering sword is whet, and held over them, and the pit hath opened her mouth under them. . . . The devil stands ready to fall upon them and seize them as his own, at what moment God shall permit him. . . . The devils watch them; they are ever by them, at their right hand; they stand waiting for them, like greedy hungry lions that see their prey, and expect to have it, but are for the present kept back; if God should withdraw his hand, by which they are restrained, they would in one moment fly upon their poor souls. The old serpent is gaping for them; hell opens its mouth wide to receive them; and if God should permit it, they would be hastily swallowed up and lost. . . . The God that holds you over the pit of Hell, much as one holds a spider, or some loathsome insect over the fire, abhors you, and is dreadfully provoked: his wrath towards you burns like fire; he looks upon you as worthy of nothing else, but to be cast into the fire; he is of purer eyes than to bear to have you in his sight; you are ten thousand times more abominable in his eyes than the most hateful venomous serpent is in ours. . . . 'Tis nothing but his hand that holds you from falling into the fire every moment.[19]

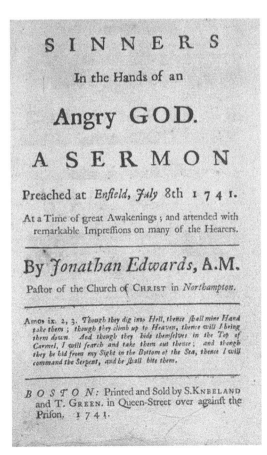

FIGURE 4-3. Title page from Jonathan Edwards's famous and terrifying sermon, "Sinners in the Hands of an Angry God," 1741 (Wikimedia Commons)

The intensity of the sermon built to a fevered pitch, as Edwards warned people that once they were in hell, there would be no hope:

> If you cry to God to pity you, he will be so far from pitying you in your doleful case, or showing you the least regard or favor, that instead of that he'll only tread you under foot: and though he will know that you can't bear the weight of omnipotence treading upon you, yet he won't regard that, but he will crush you under his feet without mercy; he'll crush out your blood, and make it fly, and it shall be sprinkled on his garments, so as to stain all his raiment. He will not only hate you, but he will [also] have you in the utmost contempt; no place shall be thought fit for you, but under his feet, to be trodden down as the mire of the streets.[20]

Edwards wanted his congregation to sense the threat of hell, almost to the point of feeling the heat. But he did not think that made him sadistic; in his view, it made him realistic. Edwards's hearers believed in hell—many people did in the 1700s—but few believed they would end up there. Edwards worried that his congregation did not feel the threat of hell. Many people had a false sense of security, Edwards believed, and he used sensible images in his sermon to awaken people to their predicament. It worked. Although Edwards was not an emotional preacher, this sermon terrified the congregation to the point that Edwards could not finish delivering it.[21]

Just as many people in Edwards's world believed in a real hell, they also believed in a real Satan, who lurked among the people, watching for every opportunity to hijack the gospel and to entrap people in sin and eventually into eternal torment. Satan hated the revivals, Edwards believed, and looked for ways to disrupt them.[22] Yet some people took the opposite opinion, claiming that Satan did not threaten the revivals; he supported them, because the revivals were doing his diabolical work. God did not send revivals to unite the churches; Satan sent the revivals to divide them. Some of the most fervent anti-revivalists were ministers, many of whom saw revivals as a threat to their authority. When Whitefield came to town, ministers saw their congregations flock to see a preacher who put their preaching to shame. Local ministers had reason to be concerned. Intentional or not, traveling evangelists often caused Christians to question their pastors, even to evaluate the state of their pastors' souls. This was an insult, many ministers believed. After all, they were elites, respected and often more educated than anyone else in their towns, and they were the ones who had the expertise to evaluate the spiritual lives of their congregations, not the other way around. To them, the world seemed to have turned upside down when revivalists like Presbyterian Gilbert Tennent warned Christians of *The Danger of an Unconverted Ministry* (1740).

"An ungodly Ministry is a great Curse and Judgment," Tennent said in this controversial sermon, which he preached in Nottingham, Pennsylvania, and then later published. Ungodly ministers were often highly educated and impressively ordained, but they lacked what mattered most: "true Love to Christ and the Souls of their Fellow-Creatures." So their sermons "are cold and sapless," and their words seemed to "freeze between their Lips!" These ministers were "dead Dogs, that can't bark," and they had "no Experience of a special Work of the Holy Ghost, upon their own Souls," meaning they were like the Pharisees who pestered Jesus: they had the intellectual knowledge of the law, but no experience of the Spirit. Since God had not blessed these ministers with his Spirit, the people should not bless them with their presence. Tennent's recommendation was simple yet radical: stay away from these unconverted ministers and their churches. Instead, go, find godly ministers who had experienced the new birth, and then attend their churches. Suddenly the people, not the ministers, were in charge of their spiritual lives. And the people, uneducated as many of them were, believed they could judge between ministers, declaring some of them true and others false. This was a radical idea in a world more accustomed to settled parishes, where people had to go to the church they had been assigned to in their areas.[23]

Although the revivals provoked controversy from the start, it was not an either/or issue, with all Christians either for or against the revivals. For years, historians spoke of a widespread disagreement between "New Lights," who loved the revivals, and "Old Lights," who hated them. More recently, as Thomas Kidd pointed out, historians recognize at least three groups.

First, "anti-revivalists," like famed Boston minister Charles Chauncy (1705–87), believed revivals were religion run berserk, a dangerous perversion of true religion, which was rational and orderly, not chaotic and fanatical. In his *Seasonable Thoughts on the State of Religion in New England* (1743), Chauncy launched a massive assault on the new revivals. Once people caught the fever of revival, they lost all sense of religious authority, Chauncy believed. They became judgmental, believing the Spirit gave them the ability to judge whether one was among the elect, knowledge known only to God. They embraced the old but dangerous idea that God spoke directly to individuals, "without any Respect to, or Concurrence with the Word" (that is, the Scriptures). They even believed that "the immediate Revelation of my good Estate [assurance of salvation], without any Respect to the Scriptures, is as clear to me as the Voice of God from Heaven to Paul." They attacked the idea that sanctification, including good works, was "Evidence of Justification" because, again, evidence of salvation came directly as a revelation from God.[24] These are just a few accusations that Chauncy and other anti-revivalists hurled against the revivals, which they identified with especially outlandish preachers like James Davenport, who burned books—and his clothes—to proclaim their rejection of worldly things.

Second, on the other extreme, "radical evangelicals" like Davenport saw revivals as an outburst of divine energy, infusing converts with the power to shatter the old, cold religious ideas and even churches that had lost their spiritual vitality. Some of them did champion the radical ideas that Chauncy and others attacked, although few adopted all of them.

Third, "moderate evangelicals" thought the revivals were from God, but that Satan tried to spoil them with radical preachers who used the revivals as an excuse for unseemly behavior. They winced at bad actors like Davenport, who caused people to reject the revivals. Edwards was one of this moderate group, and he joined with other ministers in reprimanding Davenport and other radicals. Edwards agreed with many of Chauncy's attacks on more extreme evangelicals but claimed that these false beliefs and practices did not discredit the revivals overall.[25]

A PREACHER STIRS UP TROUBLE

The escapades of radical preachers continued to rile up the revival's opponents and embarrass its defenders. Laws were passed aimed at curtailing those like James Davenport, including a Connecticut statute that forbade traveling preachers from encroaching on the territory unless they had the permission of pastors in the area. The law did what it was designed to do when officials arrested Davenport in Hartford, Connecticut, on May 27, 1742.

In its account of the arrest, the *Boston News-Letter* reported that Davenport told people to flee from the *"unconverted ministers"* who dominated the pulpits of the area. He tried "to *terrify* and *affect* his hearers," by telling them "the end of the world" was near—a fact he knew because he claimed a special communication from God. He also attacked his opponents, "vehemently crying out, That *he saw hell-flames flashing in their faces*; and that *they were now! Now! Dropping down to hell*; and also added, *Lord! Thou knowest that there are many in that gallery and in these seats, that are now dropping down to Hell!*" When the sheriff tried to restrain Davenport, "by speaking and gently taking him by the sleeve," Davenport cried, *"Lord! Thou knowest somebody's got hold of my sleeve[;] strike them! Lord, strike them!"*

God did not strike the sheriff, but many of Davenport's followers tried to. They charged "in violently [and] interposed to prevent and resist the sheriff; while others refused their assistance when commanded, saying, *they were serving the devil.*" Chaos ensued. "In the mean time, almost all night, in other parts of the town, were such shocking scenes of horror and confusion, under the name and pretext of religious devotion, as language can't describe." Finally, officials forced Davenport out of the colony.*

*See Thomas S. Kidd, *The Great Awakening: A Brief History with Documents*, Bedford Series in History and Culture (Boston: Bedford/St. Martin's, 2008), 14, 98–102.

As controversy swirled over the revivals, Edwards accepted an invitation to preach at Yale College and titled his sermon, "The Distinguishing

Marks of a Work of the Spirit of God," which was his attempt to separate the good from the bad in the revivals.[26] This was one of several of Edward's evaluations of revivals, culminating five years later in his *Treatise concerning Religious Affections*. In this important book, Edwards addressed what he believed were the central questions provoked by the revivals: what is true religious experience, and how do people know their religious experience is valid?[27]

Edwards had no use for radical preachers who let their passions run wild, to the point that they rejected all religious authority and social decorum. Passions were all heat (emotion) and no light (intellect), but that was not what the revivals were about. As Edwards put it, "There must be light in the understanding, as well as an affected fervent heart[;] where there is heat without light, there can be nothing divine or heavenly in that heart." Yet "light without heat, a head stored with notions and speculations, with a cold and unaffected heart" is also useless because if divine truths are "rightly understood, they will affect the heart."[28]

The revivals, at their best, were holistic, embracing both heart and mind, invigorating the entire person with the Holy Spirit. True religion could not just be an intellectual faith; it needed to move beyond our intellectual knowledge of God to an "inclination" toward God, and not just a slight inclination for God. The key term for Edwards was the "affections," which he defined as the "more vigorous and sensible exercises" of the inclinations. The affections moved people beyond cold calculation to heartfelt inclination. Affections stirred people up, excited them, and inspired them to divine thoughts and good works. True religion was not "weak, dull and lifeless" but instead involved "fervent exercises of the heart."[29]

Yet there were so many questions, so much anxiety bound up with these issues. How much "affective" religion was too much? How could the people be sure that their experience of the "new birth" was real? Christians in Edwards's time often obsessed over the question of assurance; they wanted to know that they were among the elect, saved by God from eternal damnation. This was an intellectual issue, debated by ministers who were both for and against the revivals, but mostly it was a pastoral issue. In addressing this question, Edwards was at his analytical best. He collated the evidence to defend what was good about revivals while being critical of their misuse. In the end, "Gracious and holy affections," Edwards wrote, "have their exercise and fruit in Christian practice." People who are empowered by holy affections would behave like good Christians: they would live morally, worship faithfully, and practice humility and generosity, not because they should, but because they wanted to. As Jesus said, "Ye shall know them by their fruits" (Matthew 7:16), not by what they say, by their holy conversations about religion, but by their actions. As Edwards put it, "Hypocrites may much more easily be brought to talk like saints, than to act like saints."[30]

The Great Awakening and the Growth of the Baptists

After experiencing the "new birth" in the revivals, many converts became dissatisfied with their ministers, either because they rejected the revivals, or because they did not support them fervently enough. In addition, revivals inspired some people to desire greater church purity, believing that all church members should have experienced conversion. These concerns led many Christians to take a bold step: they left their state-supported Congregational churches and formed "Separate" congregations, led by revivalist ministers and populated by people who craved church purity. This does not seem like a big deal today, when people often switch churches, sometimes on a whim. Yet this was a crisis in colonial America, where people believed that churches supported the society, and an upheaval in the churches could incite chaos in a colony. Despite these cautions, many converts to revivals made that bold move, stepping out of their home churches, taking the chance on an unauthorized congregation. Some evangelicals did not stop there. In their goal to find a purer church, composed only of serious Christians who had experienced the new birth, they became Baptists. That is, they eventually rejected infant baptism, deciding to restrict baptism and membership to professed believers. So many people made this move that the number of Separate Baptist churches soared after 1750.[31]

A key figure in this transition from Congregationalist to Separate to Baptist was Isaac Backus (1724–1806). Born and baptized in 1724 at Norwich, Connecticut, Backus dated his conversion to August 22, 1741, during a time of revivalist fervor in the area. Benjamin Lord, the pastor of his home church, celebrated the revivals when they swept through the area in the early 1740s, but he started to back off his endorsement of them once he saw lay exhorters who seemed too radical and too emotional in their excitements for the gospel. They were possessed by a spirit, no doubt, but Lord questioned whether it was the Holy Spirit. If Lord began to cool on the revivals, many in his congregation were still hot for them and questioned Lord's leadership. At about the same time, Lord expressed reluctance to limit full membership to those who had given a convincing testimony of their conversion experience. That was enough for some of his congregation, who left in 1745 and formed a new congregation farther west in Norwich. Backus was among those who left the state-endorsed church, and he never looked back. He later justified separation, calling on many Scriptures, including 2 Corinthians (6:14, 17), where Paul wrote, "Be ye not unequally yoked together with unbelievers: for what fellowship hath righteousness with unrighteousness? and what communion hath light with darkness? . . . Come out from among them, and be ye separate, saith the Lord, and touch not the unclean thing; and I will receive you." It was one thing to worship with sinners: all are sinners, after all. But it was another to worship with "manifest unbelievers," those who openly reject sound doctrine. A church that tolerated that kind of error was a place to avoid, Backus wrote.[32]

These reasons were good enough for Backus, and they were good enough for many other New England Congregationalists as they left the legally established, tax-supported churches and formed hundreds of Separate congregations. They gathered and worshiped, which disturbed both ministers and magistrates in their areas, and they networked with each other to spread the gospel. Backus became one of the most effective networkers among Separates: he traveled, preached, and witnessed to the revival. In 1748 he was in Titicut, Massachusetts, where he joined with a group of Separates to start a new church. He agreed to be their pastor, despite his lack of education and ordination. No matter, they said; he had the Holy Spirit with him, and that was qualification enough. They arranged for his ordination with the help of other Separate pastors nearby, and Backus led the church through a period of rapid growth, from sixteen members when they began to sixty-one members in about a year.[33]

The more the Separate congregations grew, the more attention they drew from magistrates, who often loaded members down with fines and even jail time for refusing to pay the taxes that supported the legally established churches. During this period, Backus and others who joined Separate churches began to see just how much their convictions would cost them. While they faced these struggles from outside their churches, they also dealt with dissension within them. If true church purity was the goal, several of their members said, then why were they baptizing infants? This was a problem, especially since the New Testament described a lot of adult baptisms but no infant baptisms. Besides, if church purity were the goal, it made the most sense to baptize only those who confessed to a conversion experience. Backus and others followed this logic, and it led them to join the Baptist movement. In 1756, Backus helped to organize a Baptist church in Middleboro, Massachusetts, with him as pastor, a position he held for fifty years.

During his lifetime, and partly due to his efforts, Baptists grew dramatically in New England: "from only 25 congregations in 1740 to nearly 24,000 members in 312 churches and 13 regional associations by 1804," Mark Noll reported.[34] Baptists were not new to North America; they had been around since the seventeenth century, when Roger Williams founded the first Baptist church in Providence. Although Williams soon left the Baptists, others remained loyal to Baptist convictions, although they remained a persecuted minority. All that changed with the Great Awakening.

The success of Baptists in the wake of the revivals brings up one of the most controversial questions about the Great Awakening: Did the revivals promote a democratic religion, perhaps even a democratic vision for society? No, say some historians. The revivals' leaders were mainly white and male, and they did more to support existing churches and denominations than they did to empower religious upstarts. Other historians disagree and point to the Baptist movement as one of the major examples of a more democratic form of Christianity that thrived because of the revivals.

The revivals may have been democratic in some ways and antidemocratic in others. There is no question that some people who experienced the revivals discovered a newfound freedom. People in the pews started challenging their ministers' views, claiming their own ability to read the Bible and understand God's messages to them. Sometimes the results provoked controversy. In Plainfield, Connecticut, a handicapped woman named Mercy Wheeler called on Christ's power to enable her to walk. Ministers had told her not to expect Christ to heal her: miracles, they believed, had not appeared since the early church. Yet her Bible told her differently, and she experienced Christ's healing power during a revival service in 1743, enabling her to walk. Some called it a fake and attacked her for her deception; others praised God and gloried in this modern miracle.[35]

Consider also Bathsheba Kingsley ([?]–1748), who lived near Westfield, Massachusetts. In 1741, as the revivals reached their peak, she had to stand before her minister and her church and face a serious charge: she had "stolen" a horse (borrowed it from her husband), and on the Sabbath, no less. Yet horse stealing was a minor problem compared with why she needed the horse: to launch her career as a traveling preacher, despite the obvious facts that she was unordained, uneducated, and most troubling of all, a woman.

Within two years Kingsley found herself in trouble again. This time her pastor called in experts to reprimand her, including Jonathan Edwards and other well-known ministers. They met at her house for a couple of days, listening with much interest (and horror) to Kingsley talk about her communications with God—which had come to her in dreams, she reported—and in "impressions," convincing her of a calling to the ministry. She took it upon herself to pursue that calling; she had no choice, since ordination of a woman was out of the question. But then, other itinerant male ministers had taken it upon themselves to respond to revival by traveling and preaching. Why not Kingsley? So she traveled, exhorted, and inspired all kinds of ridicule. If Gilbert Tennent had warned of the "danger of an unconverted ministry," so did Bathsheba Kingsley, calling out ministers for their sins and ineptitude, speaking to them as one who had the right to do so. It was no wonder that Kingsley shocked Edwards and his colleagues. It would have been radical for an unordained and uneducated man to do the things she had done. For a woman, it was unthinkable. The council of the church threw down its ruling: she had "almost wholly cast off that modesty, shamefacedness, and sobriety and meekness, diligence and submission, that becomes a Christian woman in her place." The ministers had no problems with Kingsley speaking about her own experiences, but she could not preach, and she could not travel around as an itinerant evangelist.[36]

Bathsheba Kingsley was not an isolated case. Historians have analyzed how revivals influenced society and politics, but "the most momentous development of all," as Catherine Brekus wrote, was "the unprecedented appearance of women's voices in the churches."[37] Before the revivals, as

Brekus notes, "the Anglicans, the Puritans, the Presbyterians, and the Dutch Reformed were united in their attitude toward female speech: they all demanded that women must obey Paul's command to 'keep silence in the churches.'"[38] The revivals came, however, and so did challenges to religious authority: those challenges often came from women. One of the key messages of the revival, as many people heard it, was that an experience of the new birth transformed individuals from all races, genders, and social classes. It was this experience of true conversion, and not ordination or education, that qualified a person to understand spiritual realities.[39]

Although they did not intend to do so, revival preachers encouraged nonelites to challenge authority. Revival preachers almost bragged about how many African Americans and uneducated white men and women converted during the revivals. Jonathan Edwards made a point of this in his *Faithful Narrative*, and George Whitefield made similar comments, as when he said, "The Lord chooses the foolish things of this world to confound the wise."[40] These preachers did not think that conversion would empower women and African Americans, giving them a greater sense of their own spiritual authority. They thought conversion would lead to self-denial, a desire to sacrifice themselves for God's will. Yet the new-birth experience empowered individuals to trust their own views on spiritual matters, even leading them to judge their ministers.[41]

In his attacks on the revival, Charles Chauncy complained that the revivals stirred up women and young people to act inappropriately. It is "among *Children, young People* and *Women*, whose Passions are soft and tender, and more easily thrown into a Commotion, that these things *chiefly* prevail." Chauncy, Boston's leading young conservative, was not wrong: revivals did inspire women to traverse traditional gender roles. Not only did women speak enthusiastically about their conversion experiences; some women also became "exhorters," or lay speakers. Technically, they did not preach sermons on biblical texts, and they had no ministerial status. But they spoke from the heart, and many of their hearers believed that the Holy Spirit inspired them. Several of these women spoke only a few times, as the Spirit led them, while others exhorted on an ongoing basis.[42]

Many Separatist churches allowed women exhorters and even encouraged them for a time. This endorsement found its way into print when Ebenezer Frothingham, a Separate pastor in Middletown, Connecticut, published *Articles of Faith and Practice, with the Covenant That is Confessed by the Separate Churches of Christ*. True, Paul did command women to be silent in the churches, Frothingham admitted. But what about Jesus? Frothingham pointed to Luke 11, which describes an occasion in which a woman interrupts Jesus while he is speaking, saying, "Blessed is the womb that bare thee." Jesus does not rebuke the woman: he engages her, saying, "Yea rather, blessed are they that hear the word of God, and keep it" (11:27–28). This was proof that women had a right to speak in church, Frothingham concluded, although neither he nor any other Separate minister approved of women preachers or pastors.[43]

This qualified endorsement of women's voices in the churches did not last. Most evangelical ministers began to agree with Chauncy and other revival critics, concerned that female exhorters provoked too much contention and disorder. Behind some of this concern lay a larger worry about the decline of male authority. Colonists had built a patriarchal culture, where men headed their households, ruling over submissive wives and obedient children. Yet things changed as the 1700s progressed. With population increases, land was harder to purchase, and fewer men owned enough property to pass on to their sons. The sons left home, therefore, looking for better opportunities. As fathers watched their sons move away, they saw their influence over them diminish. At the same time, these men saw women speaking more in churches, and they feared that as yet another sign that they had lost control. They needed to reassert their authority in the home and in their local churches. Starting at about 1750, many Separate and Baptist churches, even some that had been open to women's speech in church, began to restrict church speech to men.[44]

While the revivals began to subside in New England and the Middle Colonies, they picked up momentum in the South. In New England, the prime time for revivals was the early 1740s; in the southern colonies most revivals did not begin until later in that decade, and they spread sporadically through the 1760s. In the South, the main early beneficiaries of revivals were the Separate Baptists, who saw their numbers skyrocket. In Virginia, for example, their congregations increased from seven in 1769 to fifty-four by the beginning of the Revolutionary War (1775).[45]

Influential among Separate Baptists were Martha Stearns Marshall (1726–ca. 1793); her brother, Shubal Stearns (1706–71); and her husband, Daniel Marshall (1706–84): these New Englanders took the revival to the South in 1755. They wound up in North Carolina, where they established the Sandy Creek Baptist Church and used it as a launching point for more than forty additional churches in North and South Carolina and Virginia. The leadership of Martha Stearns Marshall demonstrated that these Separate Baptists supported women in the ministry, but this became a point of contention with more conservative "Regular Baptists," who looked down on revivalism and preferred a more dignified worship style and a professional, educated, and exclusively male voice in the churches.[46]

In the end, most Baptists followed other denominations in forbidding women to speak in churches. The influential Philadelphia Baptist Association ruled in 1765 that churches should forbid "all women whomsoever from all degrees of teaching, ruling, governing, dictating, and leading in the Church of God." Other Baptist associations followed suit. "In a pattern that would appear over and over again in American history," Catherine Brekus noted, "evangelical women lost their public voice as a struggling, marginal sect matured into a prosperous denomination with all of the trappings of respectability, including a well-educated male clergy."[47]

African Americans, Slavery, and the Great Awakening

Just as revival critic Charles Chauncy attacked the revivals for inspiring women to step outside their place, he attacked the revivals for doing the same for African Americans. Under the influence of revivals, Chauncy wrote, "Women and Girls; yea, Negroes, have taken upon them to do the Business of Preachers."[48] Chauncy need not have worried too much, at least not yet. True, revivals did inspire some women to speak in church and even to preach. But, as we have seen, the male ministers and churches that first encouraged them soon turned against women's voices in the churches. Similarly, revival preachers rarely encouraged African Americans to preach, and some of these ministers accepted slavery and owned enslaved people.[49]

Whitefield, Edwards, and other revival preachers wanted African Americans to experience true conversion, so they were happy to see them attending revival services. In his *Faithful Narrative*, Edwards noted that "several Negroes . . . appear to have been truly born again," and nine African Americans joined his church while he was pastoring in Northampton. Edwards looked forward to the millennium, when he believed "many of the Negroes and Indians will be divines, and . . . excellent books will be published in Africa, in Ethiopia, [and] in Turkey." But those were millennial dreams for Edwards, not realities that he envisioned in his lifetime. Whitefield believed much the same. He spoke out against slaveholders' abuse of enslaved people (as if slavery itself were not abuse) and supported slave conversions. Enslaved people could experience the freedom of Christ in the "new birth," and they should, but neither they nor their masters should think salvation would lead to emancipation. Whitefield's hope for the conversions of enslaved people did not convince him to reject slavery.[50]

Freedom was a volatile idea, however. Even if Whitefield saw no relation between spiritual freedom and freedom from slavery, some of his converts did. We see this in the case of Hugh Bryan, a slaveholder and planter in South Carolina. After hearing Whitefield preach in 1740, Bryan experienced conversion, along with a crisis that led him to embrace the social effects of the gospel as he saw them. Worldly goods, he realized, had little spiritual value and often actually interfered with the gospel. Whitefield thought it would be a good idea for Hugh Bryan and his brother, Jonathan, to start a school for enslaved people. But Hugh Bryan did more than that: he rejected slavery altogether and began to envision himself as a prophet who would deliver God's word to Charleston. When fire struck the city in November 1740, Bryan called it God's punishment for the city's sins and especially those of ministers. Not long afterward, Charleston officials heard that Bryan and others had encouraged enslaved people to meet in large groups, a suspicious development in a slaveholding society. Even more alarming, officials heard that Bryan envisaged the city's destruction, "by fire and sword, to be executed by the Negroes before the first day of next month." When officials came to arrest Bryan, he backed off his claims, asked for forgiveness, and blamed all his delusions on Satan's influence. Bryan made right with white society by paying his fine and returning to his slaveholding ways. Later he and his brother assisted Whitefield in procuring a plantation, together with enslaved people to work it. Although Bryan repented of his radical views, he gave Anglicans all the ammunition they needed to brand evangelicalism a threat to slaveholding. Evangelicals denied this, claiming that revival preaching reinforced the social order, so masters should encourage their enslaved people to embrace the new birth.[51] That compromise between the gospel and slavery prevented many enslaved people from converting to Christianity. Mass conversions of African Americans to evangelical Protestantism did come, but not until the late eighteenth century and later.

The Great Awakening has fascinated historians for over two centuries, and there seems to be no end to the questions they have posed. Just how widespread were the revivals? Were they really that influential and ubiquitous, or did their advertisers exaggerate the revivals and their influence? In an influential essay from 1982, Jon Butler called the Great Awakening (1735–ca. 1755) a "fiction," created almost a century later by ministers who wanted to cite precedents to support their own revivals. Revivalists in Whitefield's time almost never referred to the revivals as a "Great Awakening"; the term only gained popularity with Joseph Tracy's book *The Great Awakening*, published in 1842, about a century after the revivals peaked. Of course, revivals did occur in the colonies, Butler admitted, but he believed historians had overstated their breadth and their influence. Butler's groundbreaking argument did not end studies of the Great Awakening; it improved them by forcing historians to be more careful of overgeneralizing about the revivals. In response to Butler, Frank Lambert agreed that the Great Awakening was, to some extent, an "interpretative fiction," but it was not a creation of the nineteenth century. Instead, Whitefield, Edwards, and other preachers and promoters in the eighteenth century "constructed the idea of a great and general awakening," and the reputation endured. Again, it is not that the revivals never existed, but they were not as unified as historians previously argued. Revivals did occur at different times and places, but they varied in theologies and in their attitudes toward politics and society, with some more radical than others.[52]

In the 1740s, revivals appeared mostly in the Middle Colonies and especially in New England. The Great Awakening helped to shape a new American evangelicalism. Those who supported the revivals did not call themselves "evangelicals," although historians often do. Instead of "evangelicals," a term more frequently used at the time was "Whitfeldarians." Although today's evangelical movement has changed significantly over time, it owes much of its character to the Great Awakening.[53]

By the 1760s the new evangelical movement was in full swing: the revivals had overturned many older views of conversion, ministerial authority, and church membership. But the revivals did not only change the religious situation; they also influenced politics and society.[54] Did that mean there was a relationship between the revivals and the American Revolution (1775–83)? Historians have pondered this question for decades. And what about the connection between the revivals and the Enlightenment, the intellectual movement that transformed the way many people thought in the eighteenth century? We will deal with these important questions in the next two chapters.

5. The Enlightenment in America

The Enlightenment, an intellectual movement that originated on the European continent and the British Isles and flourished in North America, had so many facets that it was not really one movement; it was an assortment of ideas, some of them contradictory, that overall promoted science and reason. For years, historians thought of the Enlightenment as a unified, secular movement. More recently, historians have argued that the Enlightenment was neither unified nor secular; instead, it was diverse movement, to which religion was central.[1] Even so, many leading French and British intellectuals did see their time as an "Age of Reason," a new era that would right the wrongs of the past and pave the way for a brighter intellectual future. For two decades several French thinkers worked on the *Encyclopédie*, which would bring the latest intellectual discoveries to the common reader. In this work intellectuals saw great promise; but many others, including government officials and religious leaders, feared the *Encyclopédie* and tried to quash it, though it saw print in 1751–72, with later supplements, editions, and translations.[2]

Although the Enlightenment flourished in the eighteenth century, it began in seventeenth-century England. Francis Bacon (1561–1626) led the way. He was one of many thinkers who advocated inductive reasoning, which he preferred to the "syllogistic" logic most associated with medieval thought.

Isaac Newton (1642–1727) examined the physical world, concluding that the universe resembled a machine because it operated according to natural laws, like gravity, that were universal and omnipresent. In *Philosophiae naturalis principia mathematica* (1687), Newton argued that natural events had natural causes, that nature operated according to natural laws, without divine interference. As English poet Alexander Pope expressed it,

> Nature and Nature's laws lay hid in sight;
> God said, Let Newton be, and all was light.[3]

Newton was no modern secularist, however. He was a religious thinker and spent many hours studying the Scriptures. So, neat divisions between religious and secular thought are problematic, even in the Enlightenment period.

We find another example in John Locke (1632–1704). Many thinkers of the time were aware that "experience" was a key word of the age. In *Essay concerning Human Understanding* (1690), Locke argued that all human understanding rested on experience. Our knowledge comes first from observation, the data we receive from our senses, and these sights, sounds, sensations, tastes, and smells shape the ideas that we comprehend in our minds. Many disagreed with Locke, but his ideas influenced intellectuals, including many religious thinkers. If Locke were right, there were no innate ideas, no truths given apart from the truths perceived from experience. That meant there was no natural sinfulness (called "original sin") inherited by infants at birth, nor was there any natural goodness. Infants came into the world with no previous knowledge, but they soon began learning from their senses as they observed the world around them. Given that experience was the basis for all reason, some thinkers elevated experience above any other access to reality, including revelation from God. Few thinkers cast off Scripture or divine revelation altogether—even Locke did not make this move—but they stressed that divine revelation had to be reasonable. Some thinkers began to criticize overly metaphysical reasoning that seemed disconnected from human experience.[4] Alexander Pope expressed well the views of some of the more radical thinkers:

> Know then thyself, presume not God to scan,
> The proper study of Mankind is Man.[5]

Even if "the proper study of" humanity is humans, this focus on human experience and human happiness changed how some people thought about God. The Enlightenment energized a religious movement called "deism," advocated by thinkers like Henry St. John (the Viscount Bolingbroke, 1678–1751) in England, and later Elihu Palmer (1764–1806) and Thomas Paine (1737–1809) in America. Deism was a diverse movement, but in general those who called themselves deists wanted to excise from Christianity any beliefs that seemed out of sync with the modern world. Some turned to John Locke's aptly titled book *The reasonableness of Christianity as delivered in the Scriptures* (1695), where Locke, who did not call himself a deist, made a case for the reasonableness of Christianity's fundamental beliefs while also contending that much of Scripture was unreasonable and unnecessary for the Christian faith. Locke expressed a common opinion that the church had corrupted the simple, sensible gospel of the New Testament, complicating it with theological abstractions and unnecessary ideas that most people could not accept. It was unreasonable, deists argued, to ask modern people to believe in doctrines like original sin, for instance. As Locke wrote, "Can the righteous God be supposed, as a punishment of one sin, wherewith he is displeased, to put man under the necessity of sinning continually, and so multiplying the provocation[?]"[6]

A special focus of deist vitriol was the Roman Catholic Church. In France, François-Marie Arouet Voltaire (1694–1778) took on the Catholic Church with a vengeance, seeing in it much of what was wrong with the world, including political, ethical, and intellectual perversion. In their attacks on Catholicism, deists found common ground with Protestants in Britain and North America, who were overwhelmingly anti-Catholic.

Deists were not atheists. They believed God existed, but mainly as the creator of reason and a reasonable universe that operated according to natural laws. Since natural laws were God's creation and worked as God designed, God did not need to tinker with them, nor did God need to violate these natural laws with supernatural events like miracles.[7]

The Enlightenment and the Nation's Founders

Long before the American Revolution, these new ideas had made their way to the American colonies, and some of the more avid proponents of these ideas were the nation's founders. Any consideration of the founders should start by admitting that Americans honor their founders in a unique way. According to Gordon Wood, "No other major nation honors its past historical characters, especially characters who existed two centuries ago, in quite the same manner we Americans do. We want to know what Thomas Jefferson would think of affirmative action, or George Washington of the invasion of Iraq." Americans continue to look back on the founders in part because this is a relatively new nation, especially when compared with France, Germany, England, and many other nations. Also, the founders made ideas and values the center of the nation's identity, rather than the population's ancestry or its religious traditions. These beliefs, as articulated by these elite white men from the revolutionary generation, framed the Constitution of the United States (effective from 1789) and set the parameters of the nation. It makes sense, then, that Americans continue to look back on them—not only to praise them, but also to critique them and their failings (especially slaveholding).[8] Many of these ideas and values, which the founders sealed into the fabric of the nation, were mainly drawn from the Enlightenment, but other sources, including the Bible, were important as well.

The founders grew up and reached maturity just at the time Enlightenment ideas were arriving in America. In 1714, Jeremiah Dummer gifted Yale with a number of books by John Locke, Francis Bacon, and Isaac Newton. By the middle of the century, not only were Yale, Princeton, and Harvard students reading all about the New Learning, but so were many educated people throughout the colonies. Especially popular in America was *The Spectator*, an English magazine published 1711–14 and headed by Joseph Addison (1672–1719) and his partner, Richard Steele (1672–1729). *The*

Spectator was an Enlightenment gem. It featured an assortment of writings about the New Learning, in both nonfiction and fiction. Addison and Steele did not so much break new intellectual ground as popularize cutting-edge ideas in an entertaining and easy-to-understand format that was accessible to a broad readership. Avid readers of *The Spectator* included Benjamin Franklin, Thomas Jefferson, and James Madison.[9]

Benjamin Franklin

When Americans hear the name "Benjamin Franklin" (1706–90), they often picture a man of rare genius, whose experiments with electricity and many other inventions made him famous: a self-made man, who lived the stereotypical rags-to-riches story of a man from Puritan stock who lacked the money to attend Harvard but turned his printing business into a profitable enterprise, which allowed him to retire wealthy. But did he ever really retire? This was also the man who threw in with the American Revolution even though he was well into his senior years. By 1776, Franklin was seventy: how many seventy-year-olds join revolutions? Think about the comparison with other founders: Franklin was "twenty-six years older than Washington, twenty-nine years older than John Adams, thirty-seven years older than Jefferson, and nearly a half century older than Madison and Hamilton." Not only was he older than these other founders; he was already famous in the Atlantic world while most people of the time had never heard of the other founders, including Jefferson and Washington.[10] And yet there was Ben Franklin, following his convictions, even when they led him to revolt against a nation he loved so deeply that some revolutionary patriots could hardly believe he had joined them.

Franklin was born to a Puritan, working-class family in Boston and baptized in Old South Church, a congregation with deep Puritan roots. Franklin sprang far from those roots. By the time he was a teenager, he had rejected the Calvinism of his father, but he did not replace the faith of his childhood with another creed or church.[11] Franklin adopted a "chameleon-like religion," one historian argued; John Adams agreed: "The Catholics thought him almost a Catholic. The Church of England claimed him as one of them. The Presbyterians thought him half a Presbyterian, and the Friends believed him a wet Quaker."[12]

Franklin, it seems, always had something to hide behind those inquisitive eyes. He called himself a deist, but this label does not capture his religion because he accepted some opinions that most deists rejected, like the idea that God providentially intervened in human affairs. He only rarely attended church, and he doubted the Trinity and the deity of Christ. He knew his Bible, however. Franklin's knowledge of Scripture rivaled that of eighteenth-century preachers, many of whom knew the Bible almost by

FIGURE 5-1. Benjamin Franklin by Joseph Duplessis, 1778, Wikimedia Commons

heart, and far surpassed that of most people today. Sometimes he showed off his biblical acumen with hilarious results, as when he wrote a phony story that claimed to be from the Old Testament. He printed it, inserted it into his Bible, and then read it to others as a joke, hoping that they would believe it was really from Scripture. He played with the Bible, therefore, as he played with almost everything, finding even the most serious topics free game for a witty satire. Not that Franklin was never serious about religion; he was. But he kept his religious views mostly to himself, probably because he knew that many would attack them. "Talking against Religion is unchaining a Tyger," he said, and most of the time he preferred to keep his tigers bound up and muzzled.[13] When Franklin did address religion, he almost always related it to practical, human concerns. Theology left him cold, so he only rarely speculated about abstract notions of the divine. Humanity, however, was another story. He never ceased to speculate about human morality.[14]

Franklin displayed his insights on humanity when he assumed his many personas, including women like "Silence Dogood" and "Cecilia Shortface," and men like his bestselling almanac writer Richard Saunders (*Poor Richard's Almanack*).[15] One of many Franklin sayings is

If you wou'd not be forgotten
as soon as you are dead and rotten,
either write things worth reading,
or do things worth writing.

In the voice of Poor Richard, Franklin focused many of his proverbial teachings toward what he thought mattered about religion: actions, not words; specifically morality and virtue, not doctrines. As he declared, "Serving God is Doing good to Man, but Praying is thought an easier Service, and therefore more generally chosen." Franklin did not write all of Poor Richard's sayings, but even the ones he borrowed he often revised and improved. Not always, but usually Poor Richard's sayings represented Franklin's views, as when Poor Richard preached humility and egalitarianism: "The greatest monarch on the proudest throne, is obligd to sit upon his own arse." He railed against hypocrites: "He that is conscious of a Stink in his Breeches, is jealous of every Wrinkle in another's Nose." Poor Richard remarked that the greatest fools were those who fooled themselves: "He that lives upon Hope, dies farting." Franklin really meant to write "fasting," some historians claim, attributing "farting" to a printing mistake. "But I ask you," writes Jill Lepore, "who was the printer?"[16]

Jonathan Edwards, who was three years old when Franklin was born, warned of hellfire if people did not turn from sin; Franklin also grappled with temptations, constantly inventing rules of behavior to hold them in check. "He is a Governor that governs his passions, and he a Servant that serves them."[17]

Franklin's religious views are a puzzle that historians are still trying to solve. One of the latest to accept the challenge is Thomas Kidd, who found "the key" to Franklin's faith in "the contrast between the skepticism of his adult life and the indelible imprint of his childhood Calvinism. The intense faith of his parents acted as a tether, restraining Franklin's skepticism." In Franklin, Kidd finds "a pioneer of a distinctly American kind of religion," what he calls "*doctrineless, moralized Christianity.*" Just as Franklin experimented with lightning rods, bifocals, stoves, and many more things, so Franklin experimented with Christianity, finally embracing a practical faith in morality and activity, not doctrine. As Kidd notes, "Doctrineless Christianity, and doctrineless religion, is utterly pervasive today in America," seen "in major media figures of self-help, spirituality, and success, such as Oprah Winfrey" and "Houston megachurch pastor Joel Osteen," among others. The basic "message of these authors (and their countless followers) is that a life of love, service, and significance is the best life of all." According to this faith, tolerance of other beliefs is a must. In Franklin's day, this kind of morality-based, non-doctrinal faith would end the religious conflicts, even wars, that had raged between religious groups, especially Protestants and Catholics.[18] This was an Enlightenment-based solution to religious discord and violence. Today those concerns remain, as are concerns to encourage pluralism and acceptance in a world of religious and cultural diversity.

Franklin was nothing if not tolerant in his religious beliefs. When his parents once wrote to him, concerned that Ben had adopted radical opinions on religion, he wrote, "You both seem concern'd" that "I have imbib'd some erroneous Opinions." He had; he did not deny it. Yet he was open to being proved wrong:

> I imagine a Man must have a good deal of Vanity who believes, and a good deal of Boldness who affirms, that all the Doctrines he holds, are true; and all he rejects, are false. And perhaps the same may be justly said of every Sect, Church and Society of men when they assume to themselves that Infallibility which they deny to the Popes and Councils. I think Opinions should be judg'd of by their Influences and Effects; and if a Man holds none that tend to make him less Virtuous or more vicious, it may be concluded he holds none that are dangerous; which I hope is the Case with me. I am sorry you should have any Uneasiness on my Account, and if it were a thing possible for one to alter his Opinions in order to please others, I know none whom I ought more willingly to oblige in that respect than your selves: But since it is no more in a Man's Power to think than to look like another, methinks all that should be expected from me is to keep my Mind open to Conviction, to hear patiently and examine attentively whatever is offered me for that end; and if after all I continue in the same Errors, I believe your usual Charity will induce you rather to pity and excuse than blame me. In the mean time your Care and Concern for me is what I am very thankful for.[19]

Franklin must have known how bewildering his religious beliefs were, which is why he asked for understanding, patience, and an open mind from his parents, just as he was happy to extend the same to others. We will never fully know the details of his convictions, because he never fully expressed them. Almost certainly his beliefs changed over the course of his long life. Historians have compared his religious beliefs to Abraham Lincoln's: both departed from the Calvinism of their upbringing to embrace skeptical views, but neither fully released the beliefs they grew up with, especially the belief in divine providence, at least in some form. Lincoln said and wrote a lot about providence, especially during the Civil War (1861–65). Franklin said and wrote much less, but his experience through the American Revolution seemed to convince him that God was not just the God of the deists, a creator God who had no other direct interaction with the creation; instead, God, mysterious as God was, still guided history in some way, toward some conclusion.[20]

Thomas Jefferson

Of all the facets of the Enlightenment, none was more important than its legal and political influence. Enlightenment ideas shaped the founding of the United States, and the person most responsible for planting these ideas into the nation's government was Thomas Jefferson (1743–1826).[21]

Jefferson was a person of the Enlightenment, not only in politics but in religion as well. He shared the doubts and the questions of other thinkers of his time. He asked: Does the world really need religion? The answer, Jefferson wrote in a letter to John Adams, depends on what we mean by "religion." If we mean "sectarian dogmas, in which no two of them agree," the answer is easy: the world would be better off without it. But if we mean the universal moral principles and "the sublime doctrines of philanthropism and deism taught us by Jesus of Nazareth," then life would be hell on earth without it.[22]

Born and raised Anglican, Jefferson, like Franklin, disliked institutional religion. In the mid-1780s, he recommended a list of books on religion to his nephew and advised him to use his reason to study religion, calling into question "every fact, every opinion. Question with boldness even the existence of a god; because, if there be one, he must more approve of the homage of reason, than that of blindfolded [fear]." Bible reading was important, he said, but he advised him to read Scripture as he would any other book, "as you would read Livy or Tacitus," using reason to evaluate the Bible.[23]

In the decade following the Revolutionary War, he spent a good deal of time studying Jesus' life and teachings, guided by writers such as Joseph Priestley, a Unitarian minister whom Jefferson first met in London. Priestley's books, including *History of Early Opinions concerning Jesus Christ*, fed Jefferson's fascination with Jesus. As Jefferson saw it, Jesus agreed with the Jews' belief in one God, but he improved their ethical teachings, mainly by stressing human equality. This was a purely humanitarian gospel. As Jefferson wrote, "The doctrines of Jesus are simple, and tend all to the happiness of man." Yet Jesus' simplest teachings proved too hard for religious and political authorities to accept because he threatened their power. So, authorities executed Jesus and then distorted his teachings, perverting them "into an engine for enslaving mankind." This was a great tragedy: Jesus' teachings, "the purest system of morals ever before preached," were "adulterated and sophisticated by artificial constructions, into a mere contrivance to filch wealth and power" to those who claimed to be Christians. Thus was the sad history of Christianity, Jefferson believed, a story of monarchs and ministers who distorted Jesus' clear teachings of morality into a complicated religion that served the powerful and persecuted any who questioned it.[24]

While he was President of the United States, Jefferson pondered his faith in private writings, including "Syllabus of an Estimate of the Merit of the Doctrines of Jesus, Compared with those of Others," and most famously his "The Life and Morals of Jesus of Nazareth" (referred to as "The Jefferson Bible"). In this second work, Jefferson edited the Gospels, trying to separate what he thought were Jesus' actual teachings from errors that were added later. It was an exercise, as he put it, of picking "out diamonds from dunghills." This was Jefferson's own brand of biblical criticism. If something in the Gospels did not seem reasonable to him, Jefferson edited it out. Overall, Jesus' moral teachings made the cut, but his miracles did not. Eventually Jefferson's faith resembled Unitarianism, and he summarized Jesus' key teachings into

three points: "1. That there is only one God, and he all-perfect. 2. That there is a future state of rewards and punishments. 3. That to love God with all thy heart and thy neighbor as thyself, is the sum of religion."[25]

When it came to sharing his religious ideas in public, Jefferson was about as cagey as Franklin. Faith is a personal matter, Jefferson believed, a conversation best had between God and one's conscience. "I never told my own religion, nor scrutinized that of another," Jefferson said. This helps us to understand Jefferson's famous conviction about "a wall of separation" that should stand guard between church and state. Religion is a matter of conscience, and not under the domain of the state; because one's religious beliefs do not harm anyone else, they are none of the state's business.[26]

Yet Jefferson did not eliminate God from all conversations about rights: far from it. As he wrote in the Declaration of Independence, all people "are endowed by their Creator with certain unalienable Rights," a major statement that launched the argument for a new nation. People needed to know that their rights and their liberties had a solid foundation, not in some individual's opinion, but in God. As he wrote elsewhere, "Can the liberties of a nation be thought secure when we have removed their only firm basis, a conviction in the minds of the people that these liberties are the gift of God? That they are not to be violated but with his wrath?" People could believe whatever they wanted about God or gods—one's religious beliefs were a matter of conscience—but a nation's liberties need to be secured in God, the most solid and sacred foundation possible.[27]

Jefferson fleshed some of this out in the Virginia Statute for Religious Freedom (1786). "Almighty God hath created the mind free," Jefferson wrote, and because of that the mind cannot be forced. "All attempts to influence [the mind] by temporal punishments, or burthens, or by civil incapacitations, tend only to beget habits of hypocrisy and meanness, and are a departure from the plan of the holy author of our religion, who being lord both of body and mind, yet chose not to propagate it by coercions on either, as was in his Almighty power to do, but to extend it by its influence on reason alone." The attempt to force orthodoxy onto people has led only to false religion and hypocrisy. Taxes for religion were corrupt, therefore, because they force people to give their money to support churches they do not attend. This was "sinful and tyrannical," Jefferson wrote. It was equally wrong to require civil officers to submit to religious tests as a requirement to hold office. "Our civil rights have no dependence on our religious opinions, any more than our opinions in physics or geometry."

THE VIRGINIA STATUTE FOR RELIGIOUS FREEDOM

"We the General Assembly of Virginia do enact that no man shall be compelled to frequent or support any religious worship, place, or ministry whatsoever, nor shall be enforced, restrained, molested, or burthened in his body or goods, nor shall otherwise suffer, on account of his religious opinions or belief; but that all men shall be free to profess, and by argument to maintain, their opinions in matters of religion, and that the same shall in no wise diminish, enlarge, or affect their civil capacities."*

*"A Bill for Establishing Religious Freedom, 18 June 1779," Founders Online, National Archives, https://founders.archives.gov/documents/Jefferson/01-02-02-0132-0004-0082.

One of Jefferson's classic statements of religious liberty is from his *Notes on the State of Virginia*: "The rights of conscience we never submitted, we could not submit. We are answerable for them to our God. The legitimate powers of government extend to such acts only as are injurious to others. But it does me no injury for my neighbour to say there are twenty gods, or no god. It neither picks my pocket nor breaks my leg."[28] We often credit the Enlightenment-era thinkers for "inventing" such ideas of religious liberty. It is true that Enlightenment thinkers emphasized religious liberty, in part because they had seen too much religious intolerance and violence in religious wars and persecution. But these concepts of religious liberty were widespread in Christianity, even in the early church, and Jefferson knew it. While paging through Jefferson's own copy of his *Notes on the State of Virginia*, historian Robert Louis Wilken looked at the quote above and found that underneath it Jefferson "had written in Latin [a] passage from the early Christian theologian Tertullian," which translated said: "It is only just and a privilege inherent in human nature that every person should be able to worship according to his own convictions. For one person's religion neither harms nor hurts another. Coercion has no place in religious devotion, for it is by free choice not coercion that we should be led to religion." The similarities between this statement and Jefferson's are remarkable.[29]

White Supremacy and Slavery

In some ways, Thomas Jefferson *was* the Enlightenment; he personified the movement in all its lofty, intellectual heights, yet also in all its vast contradictions. Americans have called Jefferson "the Apostle of Liberty," mainly because he wrote the Declaration of Independence, including those immortal lines, "We hold these truths to be self-evident, that all men are created equal, that they are endowed by their Creator with certain unalienable Rights." Yet this "Apostle of Liberty" also endorsed slavery, not just theoretically but in real life as a slaveholder who enslaved hundreds of people on his plantation at Monticello. In preaching liberty and practicing slavery, Jefferson personified "America's foundational contradiction," a hypocrisy that later spiraled the nation into Civil War and still haunts the nation today.[30] Although we can fault all the founders, on some level, as shapers of "America's foundational contradiction," Jefferson's hypocrisy took on a more personal tone after DNA evidence confirmed a rumor that has persisted since at least 1802—that Jefferson had a sexual relationship with Sally Hemings, a woman he enslaved at Monticello, and that this relationship produced at least one child and most likely up to six children.[31]

Jefferson claimed to hate slavery, but he depended on enslaved people all his life and never made any serious efforts to emancipate all of them. Instead, more than any other founder, Jefferson dodged responsibility for slavery. There was always someone else to blame for the horrid institution. In part of a draft of the Declaration of Independence (later edited out), Jefferson blamed King George III, who "has waged cruel war against human nature itself, violating [its] most sacred rights of life & liberty in the persons of a distant people who never offended him, captivating & carrying them into slavery in another hemisphere, or to incur miserable death in their transportation thither."[32] Jefferson neglected to mention the responsibility of slaveholders like himself who created the market demand for enslaved people. This was not an isolated case. Early on in his political career, Jefferson claimed that more experienced leaders should end slavery. Years later, after he had stepped down from the presidency, Jefferson took the opposite view, claiming it was the job of "the younger generation" to emancipate enslaved people.[33]

Jefferson expressed some of his clearest views on race and slavery in *Notes on the State of Virginia*, which he completed in 1781. In it, he floated a plan to end slavery gradually in Virginia. All enslaved people born on January

1, 1801, or later would be freed, but they would have to leave Virginia and colonize another land. Free blacks and whites could not live together, Jefferson argued, because of white racism and black resentment over racism and slavery. "Deep-rooted prejudices entertained by the whites," wrote Jefferson, along with "ten thousand recollections, by the blacks, of the injuries they have sustained"—all these made separation the only option.[34]

Unlike Native Americans, who demonstrated artistic ability and "strokes of the most sublime oratory" that "prove their reason and sentiment strong, their imagination glowing and elevated," Jefferson could not "find that a black had uttered a thought above the level of plain narration," and he had not seen "even an elementary trait of painting or sculpture." Suffering often inspired creative expression, but not in the case of Africans, Jefferson believed. "Misery is often the parent of the most affecting touches in poetry. —Among the blacks is misery enough, God knows, but no poetry. Love is the peculiar œstrum of the poet. Their love is ardent, but it kindles the senses only, not the imagination. Religion indeed has produced a Phyllis Whately [Wheatley]; but it could not produce a poet. The compositions published under her name are below the dignity of criticism."[35] Jefferson tried to discredit Wheatley's work, first by casting some doubt on whether she actually wrote "the compositions published under her name,"

FIGURE 5-3. Image of Phillis Wheatley from 1773 by Scipio Moorhead, engraving on paper, LC-USZC4-5316

and second by discounting their quality. This was a self-serving move for Jefferson, because Wheatley's abilities as a writer threatened his argument for white superiority.

Jefferson's racist comments were not offhand remarks; he carefully formulated and defended these views. Nor can we pretend that all whites of Jefferson's day shared such opinions. When Jefferson made his case for white superiority, he saw several of his revolutionary colleagues refute his claim that blacks were naturally inferior to whites. No less a revolutionary than Benjamin Rush stated in 1795 that slavery was the reason why there were not more great African American intellectuals. "By educating [blacks] in the higher branches of science, and in all the useful parts of learning," Rush wrote, "we shall . . . confound the enemies of truth by evincing that the unhappy sons of Africa, in spite of the degrading influence of slavery, are in no wise inferior to the more fortunate inhabitants of Europe and America." Despite his other great achievements as a thinker and statesman, Jefferson was among what Rush called "the enemies of truth" on the issue of white superiority and slavery.[36]

WHITE SUPERIORITY IN AN "ENLIGHTENED" AGE

The opposition of Rush and others notwithstanding, Jefferson's argument for white superiority was not some antiquated relic, out of place in a modern world. Instead, white superiority, along with other views of race and ethnicity, formed central elements of Enlightenment thought. Their studies of humanity led thinkers to classify peoples into categories of race and region. The Scottish philosopher David Hume, who leveled one of the most vicious attacks on Christianity, also articulated one of the sharpest examples of white superiority verbiage of any leading thinker:

"I am apt to suspect the Negroes to be naturally inferior to the Whites. There scarcely ever was a civilized nation of that complexion, nor even any individual, eminent either in action or speculation. No ingenious manufactures amongst them, no arts, no sciences. On the other hand, the most rude and barbarous of the Whites, such as the ancient Germans, the present Tartars, have still something eminent about them, in their valour, form of government, or some other particular. . . . There are Negro slaves dispersed all over Europe, of whom none ever discovered any symptoms of ingenuity; though low people, without education, will start up amongst us, and distinguish themselves in every profession. In Jamaica, indeed, they talk of one Negro as a man of parts and learning; but it is likely he is admired for slender accomplishments, like a parrot who speaks a few words plainly."*

*David Hume, *The Philosophical Works of David Hume* (Edinburgh: Adam Black & William Tait, 1826), 3:236.

Along with Jefferson's statements in *Notes on the State of Virginia*, this quotation from Hume is one of the most-cited examples of racism from an "enlightened" thinker in the eighteenth century. Hume added this statement as a footnote in his "Of National Characters," a book he first published in 1748, although he did not add this note until five years later. Hume's argument for white superiority was part of an ongoing debate over the history and nature of humanity.

Hume's views are morally repugnant today, yet even in his own day many thinkers disagreed with him. A Scottish philosophical society, which included faculty from the University of Aberdeen, took Hume to task on this subject. Among the critics was Scottish poet and philosopher James Beattie, who questioned Hume's position on Europeans' superiority to all other peoples. Beattie and his colleagues wrote, "Learn, Mr. Hume, to prize the blessings of Liberty and Education, for I will venture to assure you that had you been born and bred a slave, your Genius, whatever you may think of it, would never have been heard of." The conviction about white superiority had major implications for the slave trade, which was thriving in the British Empire and beyond. Some defenders of slavery cited Hume's quote to justify enslaving Africans, but Hume did not; in fact, he opposed slavery.[37]

An Evangelical Enlightenment

It was no coincidence that the Great Awakening broke out during the Enlightenment. Just as empiricists like John Locke focused on experience as the key to knowledge, Jonathan Edwards (who read Locke) and other ministers studied religious experience, focusing specifically on the ways in which revivals affected people. They asked: How can we know that God, not Satan, inspired the revivals? How do we know that our assurance of salvation is real?

These were questions posed by people experiencing revivals, and they were also the kinds of questions about experience that people of the Enlightenment era could be expected to ask. Continually evangelicals looked within themselves, probing for evidence that God was working in their hearts, hoping for some sign of assurance that they were saved. "How do I know this God is mine; and that I myself am not deceived?" asked Sarah Osborn, an evangelical who lived in Newport, Rhode Island. She would know, as she put it, "By the evidences of a *work of grace* wrought in my Soul." We know much about Osborn because she wrote a lot, filling page after page, over two thousand of which survived: prayers, a diary, and letters.[38]

She had a lot to write about. Raised in a home with "severe" parents, she contemplated suicide when she was young. At age seventeen, she married a sailor, with whom she had a son; after he died, she married a tailor. It was a hard life. Her second husband, Henry Osborn, had some sort of ailment that prevented him from supporting the family, which included three of his children from a previous marriage. Out of necessity, then, Sarah Osborn worked hard, mostly as a teacher, though she never made much money and lived her life in poverty. Through all her struggles, Osborn left a view of her life, and she demonstrated that well-read ministers like Edwards and philosophers like Locke were not the only ones who scrutinized experience during the eighteenth century. As Catherine Brekus writes, "Evangelicals defended their faith against the skeptical and liberal strains of the Enlightenment by appropriating an enlightened language of experience, certainty, evidence, and sensation as their own." For centuries, Christians had rarely said they were certain of their salvation: that smacked of pride, the worst of all sins. But these Enlightenment-era evangelicals "claimed that they could empirically feel and know whether they had been spiritually reborn."[39]

On one level, then, evangelicals were just as engaged with the Enlightenment as intellectuals like Jefferson and Franklin. One aspect of the Enlightenment was its skepticism, not only its criticism of Christianity, but also its questions about knowledge itself. Some worried about Locke's claim that all knowledge arises from the senses and that all our ideas derived from impressions in our minds of what we see, hear, touch, smell, and feel. How do we know that ideas in our minds correspond to the real world and are not just concepts we have made up in our minds?

David Hume and others posed this disturbing question. In attempting to answer it, many turned to the Scottish Philosophy of Common Sense, a facet of Enlightenment thought that was especially influential on evangelicalism. Most historians trace this philosophy to Scottish philosopher Thomas Reid (1710–96), but his students were more influential on evangelicals, including James Beattie (1735–1803) and Dugald Stewart (1735–1828). From these thinkers, evangelicals took several main ideas that shaped their convictions. First was the idea that everyone had "common sense," an ability to understand reality. The senses revealed the world as it was, and people had the common sense to understand it.

Second, this common sense also applied to morality, so humans naturally knew the difference between right and wrong, just as they knew some basic principles of reality. As Thomas Jefferson wrote in the Declaration of Independence, some "truths" are "self-evident," or "common sense," including "life, liberty, and the pursuit of happiness."

Third, Scottish commonsense theorists taught evangelicals that all reasoning, including theology, should follow the same rules. As Presbyterian theologian Charles Hodge later put it, "The Bible is to the theologian what nature is to the man of science. It is his storehouse of facts; and his method of ascertaining what the Bible teaches is the same as that which the natural philosopher adopts to ascertain what nature teaches." Early evangelicals, like most Protestants before them, assumed that the Bible was true, but commonsense philosophy influenced "the way evangelicals have construed the nature of the Bible's truthfulness," as Mark Noll wrote. Evangelicals began speaking "as if the Bible's saving truthfulness rested on its factual truthfulness, instead of assuming—with both the reformers and the Protestant dogmaticians until the eighteenth century—the reverse." So "it is not in the conviction *that* the Bible is true that reveals the greatest evangelical debt to Common Sense, but *how* it is true."[40]

The relationship between the Enlightenment and religion was complicated, in part because the Enlightenment was a complex movement with various phases and characteristics. The focus on empiricism and evidence caused some intellectuals to attack Christianity as an unreasonable religion. But this newfound interest in empirical knowledge led non-elites like Sarah Osborn to trust their own experience of the Holy Spirit, even more than they trusted educated ministers and doctrines. What mattered was the "new birth," and one who had that experience could speak with authority, no matter if they were Native Americans, women, or enslaved Christians. As David Bebbington wrote, "The activism of the Evangelical movement sprang from its strong teaching on assurance. That, in turn, was a product of the confidence of the new age about the validity of experience. The Evangelical version of Protestantism was created by the Enlightenment."[41] So, the Enlightenment influenced Christianity in contrasting ways. Although one facet of the Enlightenment ushered in new attacks on Christianity, another facet of the Enlightenment gave Christians new defenses against these attacks.

6. *The American Revolution*

The American Revolution was not primarily about religion, but religious influences were never far from it, both inspiring patriots to revolt and cautioning them to remain loyal to Britain. Many colonists, including the founders, used the Bible and religious arguments to support the Revolution and to construct the new nation. Not only did religious ideas influence the Revolutionary War (1775–83); they also set the stage for future wars. As Harry S. Stout has stated, one of the features of American history is the "symbiotic" relationship between religion and war. This was a nation founded in war; as Stout argues, "American wars are *sacred* wars and American religion, with some notable exceptions, is martial at the very core of its being." This relationship between religion and war has persisted for over two centuries, with wide-ranging influence on Americans' understanding of their nation, religion, war, and patriotism.[1]

From Revivals to Revolution?

Although the American Revolution centered on ideas of equality and liberty, colonial society at the time was dominated by white men in positions of power. Among the most powerful colonists were ministers, who were among the highest paid, most educated, and most respected men in society. They advised political leaders and held prestigious positions. The founder of Harvard was a minister, and ministers typically held the highest leadership positions at Harvard, Yale, and Princeton.

As discussed in a previous chapter, ministers had led the Great Awakening, one of the most pervasive and most disruptive events prior to the Revolution. What, if any, was the relationship between the revivals of the "Great Awakening" in the 1740s and the American Revolution three decades later? This question has fascinated historians because it involves politics and religion, and particularly evangelicalism, an international movement that traces its American beginnings to the Great Awakening. Today "evangelical" is almost a political term in the United States, where many evangelicals consider themselves patriotic Americans, especially in wartime.[2] Did this strong connection between evangelicalism and patriotism begin with the Great Awakening and the American Revolution?

Perhaps. But the relationship between the revivals and the Revolution has puzzled historians. Some evangelicals did become patriots, but not all patriots were evangelicals—far from it, especially if we think of founders like Franklin, Jefferson, Adams, Washington, and Paine. The Great Awakening did not cause the Revolution, but the revivals may have exerted a more subtle, rhetorical influence. Revival preachers, led by George Whitefield, innovated with new ways of drawing huge crowds of people and persuading these people to follow Christ. It is not difficult to see how this kind of rhetorical innovation could be put to political use.[3]

There is no question that evangelicals often saw a close relationship between their spiritual zeal for the gospel and their patriotic zeal for the Revolution. Many evangelicals also assumed that any great preacher would expound patriotic ideas. One of the most remarkable scenes took place in September 1775. George Whitefield had been dead for five years, and the Revolutionary War had been raging for five months. A band of officers from the Continental Army uncovered Whitefield's tomb in Newburyport, Massachusetts. They had his coffin opened, then they swiped the collar and wristbands from Whitefield's skeleton so that they could take these relics with them to battle. Surely these relics from the great man of God would bring God's military power with them, they hoped. Whitefield would have wanted them to do it, they no doubt believed, because they considered him to be a man of the people, a patriot, who spoke for God even in opposition to people in power.[4]

If the revivals somehow influenced the Revolution, it brings up another important question: How much has religion shaped American wars? The reverse question is also relevant: How have American wars shaped religion? Christianity played a role in previous wars that influenced the revolutionary crisis, especially the Seven Years' War (1754–63), which began just after the Great Awakening. This was a colossal war, much more massive than the Revolutionary War, and the last in a series of conflicts that pitted Protestant England against Catholic France, with both nations fighting for dominance in northeastern America. This war raged through the colonies and Europe, even involving West Africa, the Philippines, India, and the Caribbean. In North America, the Seven Years' War involved three empires: England, France, and the Iroquois Confederacy, which was a powerful alliance of the Mohawk, Oneida, Onondaga, Cayuga, and Seneca peoples.[5] Colonists often called the Seven Years' War "The French and Indian War," named for the alliance of French and Native Americans that threatened them at every turn. As they fought, colonialists saw themselves as the armies of God's Protestant nation against French and Native American enemies. For many British colonists, victory in the Seven Years' War fused religious conviction and national patriotism into a potent combination, with consequences for the Revolution and beyond.[6]

"No Taxation without Representation"

In more ways than one, the price of victory in the Seven Years' War was the Revolutionary War. Wars cost money, and the Seven Years' War left Britain strapped with debt. When the British tried to increase revenue by imposing taxes on their American colonies, many colonists believed that something diabolical was going on, something more serious than taxes alone. For Parliament back in London, taxation was only sensible; the colonists should help pay for the cost of their own defense.

The tax that accelerated the crisis was the Stamp Act, issued in 1765. Previously, Britain had imposed duties on imports to the colonies, but the Stamp Act was a direct tax on all paper goods, a tax that colonists paid when

FIGURE 6-1. "The massacre perpetrated in King Street Boston on March 5th 1770," frontispiece in *A short narrative of the horrid massacre in Boston, . . . observations on the state of things prior to that catastrophe*, printed by order of the town of Boston, 1770. LC-USZ62-45554 (Library of Congress)

they purchased various items. Many colonists believed it infringed on their rights. The complaint, repeated constantly by colonists, was "No taxation without representation." The colonists had no representatives in Parliament, so the British government had no business imposing taxes. The resistance to the Stamp Act caught Britain off guard, as colonists banded together into patriotic groups and protested, often with the support of ministers who preached against the Stamp Act.[7]

Parliament heard the colonists' cry, at least temporarily, and repealed the Stamp Act. Celebration ensued in the colonies, but this proved to be just the beginning of their troubles with Britain. The repeal lifted the colonists' spirits, convincing them that they had so much power when they banded together that they could defy king and Parliament. At the same time, the repeal alienated British officials, provoking them to clamp down on the colonists.

The next major crisis came with the famous "Boston Massacre" on March 5, 1770. Tensions between British soldiers and citizens of Boston had escalated until the soldiers fired muskets on a mob of people, leaving five colonists dead. This was an attack on their people, many New Englanders believed, proof positive that the British had turned into tyrants. Although the crisis calmed down for a couple of years, ministers never forgot this event, and they held annual commemorations of it, with sermons to commemorate the tragedy.[8]

After the Boston Massacre, the next major eruption, again in Boston, was the infamous "Tea Party," on December 16, 1773. It was years later before anyone called it the "Boston Tea Party," but everyone knew about this dramatic protest of the Tea Act. Colonists, like the British, were serious about their tea: they drank over a million pounds of it per year, and they resented the fact that the British insisted on taxing it. To strike back, many colonists stopped buying the tea sold by the East India Company, which was sold and taxed by the British, and started buying untaxed tea shipped in by smugglers such as John Hancock. In retaliation, the British imposed the Tea Act in May 1773, which gave major advantages to the tea sold by the East India Company, including dropping the price, all in an attempt to induce colonists to buy the taxed tea instead of the smuggled (and untaxed) tea. Several colonists, especially tea smugglers, were furious and saw this as another unfair tax imposed by the tyrants in Britain. They decided on a creative way to take action and make a statement. When they dressed as Mohawks and threw a shipload full of tea into the Boston Harbor, many knew the stakes of the crisis had risen yet again, and some wondered if the colonies would soon be at war.[9]

The British Empire struck back, imposing new acts to show colonists that neither King George III nor Parliament would tolerate such rebellion. The British passed more acts, and the crisis escalated. Ministers fed the patriotic fire, persuading colonists of the seriousness of the situation. Often political acts had religious implications. When colonists learned that Anglican officials wanted to appoint a bishop in the colonies, they saw it as a diabolical plan to undermine them. Decades after the Revolution, John Adams recalled how the threat of a bishop in America alarmed many colonists. If Parliament could appoint a bishop, people reasoned, then what was to prevent Britain from imposing all kinds of religious polices: they could "establish tithes, forbid marriages and funerals, establish religions, forbid dissenters, make schism heresy, impose penalties extending to life and limb as well as to liberty and property." No wonder colonists wanted nothing to do with a bishop from the Church of England in the colonies.[10]

Religious Arsenals: Fighting the War

It is no coincidence that New England, the most militant region during the Revolutionary War, was also the region with the most sermons. New England, as we discussed earlier, was a region settled by Puritans, who saturated their society with sermons. Over a century after the Puritans arrived, New England society was still brimming with sermons, delivered not only on Sundays but on other occasions as well, including political occasions. The year that colonists declared their independence from Britain was 1776; that was also the year that more sermons than ever were preached in New England.[11]

Once the war had begun at Lexington and Concord in April 1775 (in the Province of Massachusetts Bay), ministers supported the war from the pulpit. To hear some ministers preach about it, this was the most crucial war in world history, a war with a providential purpose. In 1776, Connecticut minister Samuel Sherwood proclaimed that the patriots were not only fighting for themselves against the tyrannical British; they were also fighting for Christ against the tyrannical forces of antichrist. "God Almighty, with all the powers of heaven, are on our side," Sherwood insisted. "Great numbers of angels, no doubt, are encamping round our coast, for our defense and protection. Michael [a mighty angel of God] stands ready; with all the artillery of heaven, to encounter the [British] dragon, and to vanquish this black host."[12]

Chaplains played an important role in the Revolutionary War effort. General George Washington believed in the value of good chaplains: not only could they help him to keep his army in order morally, but maybe a more devout army would help to ensure victory. Like so many people of the time, Washington believed in divine providence, so the outcome of the war was under God's control. According to the army's General Orders of July 4, 1775:

RELIGION AND THE CONTINENTAL ARMY

"The General most earnestly requires, and expects, a due obser-vance of those articles of war, established for the Government of the army, which forbid profane cursing, swearing & drunkeness; And in like manner requires & expects, of all Officers, and Soldiers, not engaged on actual duty, a punctual attendance on divine service, to implore the blessings of heaven upon the means used for our safety and defence."*

"I have Long had it on my mind to mention to Congress, that fre-quent applications had been made to me, respecting the Chaplains pay—which is too Small to encourage men of Abilities—Some of them who have Left their flocks, are obliged to pay the parson act-ing for them, more than they receive—I need not point out the great utility of Gentlemen whose Lives & Conversation are unexception-able, being employed for that Service, in this Army, there are two ways of makeing it worth the attention of Such—one is, an advance-ment of their pay, the other, that one Chaplain be appointed to two Regiments, this Last I think may be done without inconvenience I beg Leave to recommend this matter to Congress whose Senti-ments hereon, I Shall impatiently expect."†

*George Washington, "General Orders, 4 July 1775," *Founders Online*, National Archives, https://founders.archives.gov/documents/Washington/03-01-02-0027. †"From George Washington to John Hancock, 31 December 1775," *Founders Online*, National Archives, https://founders.archives.gov/documents/Washington/03-02-02-0579.

When addressing soldiers, preachers tried to inspire bravery in the face of battle while condemning cowardice as one of the greatest of sins. The ideal patriot was willing to die for the cause.[13] Long before the war, Protes-tantism had prepared colonists to value sacrifice to the death as the ultimate act of devotion. For generations they had heard about martyrs for Christ, including those courageous Protestants whose deaths were described in John Foxe's *Actes and Monuments*, often called Foxe's *Book of Martyrs*.[14]

During the Revolutionary War, ministers constantly delivered sermons about sacrifice, often calling men who died in battle "martyrs." In a sermon preached after the war, titled *America Saved, or Divine Glory displayed, in the late War with Great Britain*, Thomas Brockway of Connecticut praised those patriotic colonists who had "nobly died martyrs to liberty." Those "offi-cers and brave soldiers" had "spilt their blood in the cause of liberty." He wished that the cost, "the price of their blood, be ever treated as sacred." This language of martyrdom and sacred sacrifice, which patriots learned from Scripture and Christian tradition, appeared throughout the war. American revolutionaries did not claim their war was only about religion; it was a war about rights and liberties, a just war, they believed. But they also often described the war as blessed by God.[15]

Not everyone was carried away with patriotic fervor, and that included Christians in pulpits and pews. A minority of Christians, like Quakers, were pacifists who opposed all wars, while others supported war in principle but not *this* war. John Wesley, whom we discussed earlier as the founder of the Methodist movement in England, opposed the Revolution, and so did many others.[16]

The Bible as Common Sense

By far the most important publication in support of the American Revolution was the best-selling *Common Sense*, popular because it did not look like a high-brow political pamphlet; it looked more like a sermon, aimed at a broad readership.[17] This was, as Jill Lepore writes, "an anonymous, fanatical, and brilliant forty-six-page pamphlet that would convince the American people of what more than a decade of taxes and nearly a year of war had not: that it was nothing less than their destiny to declare independence from Britain." But who wrote it? When the pamphlet first appeared, it did not list an author, and that mystery led to rumor upon rumor. Could it have been Ben Franklin, America's most famous colonist? Thomas Jefferson, maybe? Or perhaps John Adams? Hardly. "I could not have written any Thing in so manly and striking a style," John Adams said to his wife, Abigail Adams. Who, then, was this "manly and striking" stylist? "His Name is Paine," John Adams reported: Thomas Paine, to be exact.[18]

But who was Thomas Paine (1737–1809)? "Nobody," some said—or at least not anyone whom people in high society knew before *Common Sense* swept through the colonies. He only arrived in America near the end of 1774, a 37-year-old washout with virtually no belongings.[19] Soon everyone would know him, for had it not been for his *Common Sense*, which appeared in January of 1776, there may not have been a Declaration of Independence in July of that year. Colonists were fighting a war against England, but they were far from united around the idea of declaring independence from the homeland. They were not united, that is, until *Common Sense* helped to convince them that it was foolish to trust King George III, or any other king, for that matter. As John Adams wrote, "Without the pen of the author of *Common Sense*, the sword of Washington would have been raised in vain." Adams did not like Paine, to put it mildly, but he gave credit where it was due, grumbling to Thomas Jefferson, "History is to ascribe the American Revolution to Thomas Paine."[20]

Common Sense seized people's attention and aroused patriotic fervor with stirring lines: "The cause of America is in a great measure the cause of all mankind," Paine wrote, because the cause of America was the cause of liberty against tyranny. This was a battle of good versus evil, a battle everyone should care about. And the evil in need of destruction was monarchy, because monarchy was an unnatural institution that turned people into their worst selves, converting them into tyrants, obsessed with power. As Paine put it, "A thirst for absolute power is the natural disease of monarchy." Monarchy defied human liberty and equality. Particularly galling to Paine was hereditary succession: rulers ruled not because they deserved their positions, but because they were born into them. As he wrote, there is a great "distinction for which no truly natural or religious reason can be assigned, and that is the distinction of men into KINGS and SUBJECTS." To prove his point, he turned to the Bible: "In the early ages of the world, according to the Scripture chronology, there were no kings; the consequence of which was, there were no wars; it is the pride of kings which throws mankind into confusion." "Government by kings," Paine declared, "was the most prosperous invention the Devil ever set on foot for the promotion of idolatry." On this issue, Paine wrote, nature and the Bible spoke with one voice. The Bible, Paine insisted, supported republican government, not monarchy:

> Near three thousand years passed away, from the Mosaic account of the creation, till the Jews under a national delusion requested a king. Till then their form of government . . . was a kind of Republic, administered by a judge and the elders of the tribes. Kings they had none, and it was held sinful to acknowledge any being under that title but the Lord of Hosts. . . . Monarchy is ranked in scripture as one of the sins of the Jews, for which a curse in reserve is denounced against them.[21]

Paine's main biblical argument came from the story of how Israel finally did get a king, even over the opposition of God and Samuel, one of God's greatest prophets:

> [The Jews] came in an abrupt and clamorous manner to Samuel, saying, . . . make us a king to judge us like all the other nations. And here we cannot but observe that their motives were bad, viz. that they might be like unto other nations, i.e. the Heathens, whereas their true glory lay in being as much unlike them as possible. But the thing displeased Samuel when they said, give us a King to judge us; and Samuel prayed unto the Lord, and the Lord said unto Samuel, hearken unto the voice of the people in all that they say unto thee, for they have not rejected thee, but they have rejected me, THAT I SHOULD NOT REIGN OVER THEM. [1 Samuel 8][22]

In demanding a king, the Israelites rejected God. Monarchy was evil from the beginning, Paine insisted, and the fact that a "few good kings" have reigned did not make that great wrong a right. To those who would cite David as a great king, Paine noted that Scripture never praised him because he was a king, "but only as a Man after God's own heart." Finally Paine nailed home his point: "These portions of scripture are direct and positive. They

FIGURE 6-2. Thomas Paine, Engraving of a 1794 painting by George Romney, LC-USZ62-8238 (Library of Congress)

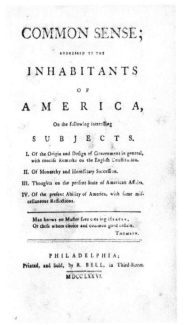

FIGURE 6-3. Title page of Thomas Paine's *Common Sense*, 1776, LC-USZ62-10658 (Library of Congress)

admit of no equivocal construction. That the Almighty hath here entered his protest against monarchical government is true, or the scripture is false."[23]

Paine's use of the Old Testament in *Common Sense* was brilliant, savvy, and above all successful. But Paine probably did not believe a word of the Bible, or not many of them anyway. Consider this report from John Adams about a conversation he had with Paine about *Common Sense*: "I told him . . . that his Reasoning from the Old Testament was ridiculous, and I could hardly think him sincere. At this he laughed, and said he had taken his Ideas in that part from Milton: and then expressed a Contempt of the Old Testament and indeed of the Bible at large, which surprized me."[24]

Adams made two important statements here. First, Paine "laughed" when Adams referred to his use of the Old Testament. This was probably true. After the Revolution was won, Paine published *The Age of Reason*, in which he ridiculed the Bible for its "obscene stories, . . . voluptuous debaucheries, the cruel and torturous executions, the unrelenting vindictiveness," concluding that "it would be more consistent" to call the Bible "the word of a Demon, than the word of God. It is a history of wickedness, that has served to corrupt and brutalize mankind; and, for my own part, I sincerely detest it as I detest every thing that is cruel." And yet there was Paine in 1776, quoting Scripture like a revival preacher in *Common Sense*, because he knew that a convincing argument for independence from Britain needed biblical support. Paine may not have believed the Bible, but he believed in the Bible's religious and political gravitas in revolutionary America.[25]

Second, Paine told Adams that he got his biblical ideas from John Milton (1608–74). This, also, was probably true. In the previous century, Milton, the renowned English poet and author of *Paradise Lost*, had also turned to the Bible to support his political views. He helped to shape a tradition of "Hebraic republicanism," an anti-monarchial interpretation of the Old Testament almost identical to Paine's in *Common Sense*. So when Paine argued from the Old Testament that God ordained republican government and that monarchy was a sin demanded by the people, he was using an idea that Milton had employed to support English opposition to kings near the time of the English Civil War and the execution of Charles I.[26]

By the time Paine wrote *Common Sense*, therefore, some English writers like John Milton had already been using the Bible to support republicanism, which we can define as a set of political beliefs modeled on ancient classical republics, especially Rome. As one who visits Washington, D.C., today can see, the influence of the classical world is displayed in the architecture, including the Capitol building. Republican ideas inspired the founders to revolt against Britain, and republican views have been central to American politics ever since. Alongside the classical world and its ancient republics, many people in the founding generation also revered the Bible, not just for spiritual direction but for political guidance as well. John Adams, for example, called the Bible "the most Republican Book in the World."[27]

A republican government was the best kind of government, the founders believed, because a republic valued the liberty of its citizens, and it did so by protecting them from rulers who exploited their people. In a republic, no leader or branch of government had too much authority, and for good reason, because people were naturally motivated by self-interest, and too much power tempted even good rulers to be tyrants. According to republican thought, two evils threatened liberty and good government above all else: immorality and tyranny. The bad news was that immorality and tyranny had plagued human existence for all time: both the Bible and classical history taught this lesson. Almost everyone knew the basic history of Rome and Greece; they knew that these once-mighty empires fell because their leaders abandoned virtuous patriotism for selfish ambition and tyranny. Citizens needed to be on guard, therefore, always keeping an eye out for self-serving leaders and tyrannical governments that might violate their rights.[28]

In a republic, the people governed themselves—through elected representatives, of course—so a republic was only as good as its citizens. Good government depended on virtuous citizens who would sacrifice themselves for the greater good, just as it depended on virtuous leaders who would do what was best for all the people without using political influence to fill their own pockets. In short, good government depended on virtue, a word that meant moral character and self-sacrificial courage. Whoever lacked virtue could not be a true patriot. Patriots were willing to die for the nation: what could be more virtuous than that? This was one reason why so many colonists believed that Christianity supported patriotism, because Christianity supported virtue and self-sacrificial love.

Slavery, Religion, and the Revolution

All the talk of morality, virtue, and republicanism in revolutionary America often took place with some reference to the great moral travesty of American history, slavery. "All men are created equal," Thomas Jefferson wrote. How, then, could he support slavery, even cling to slaveholding, and be dependent on enslaved people throughout his life? Americans have asked that question since the United States began, and they continue to ask it. Questions surround what Jefferson must have meant by "men." Did he use "men" to refer to all people, male and female? Even if he did so, that did not mean he believed men and women should be social and political equals. And surely he did not mean all "men," certainly not African men, or else he could not have supported slavery. Perhaps the main question is what he meant by "equal." Did he mean political equality? Or was he speaking of some metaphysical way in which God looked upon all people of equal spiritual value, regardless of their social or political standing in life?

In addressing these questions, it helps to remember that Jefferson lived in a world based on human inequality. Monarchy, the main system of government for most nations, assumed that people were far from equal. Some people were kings, others were enslaved, and between them were many levels. Just because Jefferson and other American patriots revolted against the British monarchy in 1776 did not mean they opposed all hierarchical structures. When Jefferson wrote, "All men are created equal," he was denying some elements of that world of inequality, but not all of it.[29]

Ironically, the founders and other patriots constantly spoke of the evils of slavery, but not usually with reference to the slavery of Africans. A key example is in Thomas Jefferson's 1774 pamphlet *A Summary View of the Rights of British America*, in which Jefferson described the tyranny of King George III and Parliament as "a deliberate and systematical plan of reducing us to slavery."[30] Jefferson said this, as many others did, even while they forced human beings into slavery. It was outrageous for Jefferson and other white elites to compare their political trials to slavery, even while they themselves were slaveholders and profiting from slavery, and many British did not miss the irony. Samuel Johnson said it best in his attack on the Revolution, *Taxation No Tyranny*, "How is it that we hear the loudest yelps for liberty among the drivers of negroes?"[31]

"IMPATIENT OF OPPRESSION"

In 1774, the famous poet Phillis Wheatley, who had known slavery firsthand, wrote to Samson Occom, a Mohegan pastor, "In every human Breast, God has implanted a Principle, which we call Love of Freedom; it is impatient of Oppression, and pants for Deliverance." Occom, a Native American, had been stung by white racism nearly his entire career in the ministry and had spoken up for the plight of the African Americans, which impressed Wheatley. She called slaveholders "our Modern Egyptians," referring to the Exodus narrative, in which Egyptians enslaved the Israelites till God set them free. "God grants Deliverance in his own way and Time," Wheatley wrote, and she pointed out the great contradiction of the era: "How well the Cry for Liberty, and the reverse Disposition for the Exercise of oppressive Power over others agree,—I humbly think it does not require the Penetration of a Philosopher to determine."*

*Phillis Wheatley, *The Collected Works of Phillis Wheatley*, ed. John C. Shields (New York: Oxford University Press, 1988), 176–77.

Phillis Wheatley was an early evangelical, a believer in revivalist Christianity in the wake of the Great Awakening. (One of her most famous writings was her poem "On the Death of George Whitefield.") Not all

FIGURE 6-4. Portrait of Samson Occom by Mason Chamberlin, 1766, Wikimedia Commons

evangelicals opposed slavery, but some did, including several who revered Jonathan Edwards and his theology. Among these was Lemuel Haynes of Massachusetts, a Calvinist minister and admirer of Edwards who also fought in the Revolutionary War, first in the militia and then in the Continental Army. Haynes was biracial: his father was African American, and his mother was white. He attacked slavery in his "Liberty Further Extended: Or Free Thoughts on the Illegality of Slave-keeping," which he wrote in 1776. In this work, which he shared with other ministers but never published, Haynes quoted from the Declaration of Independence and from the Bible, including the often-cited Acts 17:26, "[God] hath made of one blood all nations of men," and he directly linked the revolutionary cause with opposition to slavery. As Haynes wrote, patriots needed to oppose both the British tyranny and also tyrannical slavery to "be *consistently* Engaged in the Cause of Liberty!"[32]

Almost a decade after the war, Jonathan Edwards Jr., son of the famous revivalist preacher, attacked slavery in *The Injustice and Impolicy of the Slave Trade, and of the Slavery of the Africans*. Edwards's point was as simple as it was devastating: Slavery violated the Golden Rule, Jesus' command, "All things whatsoever ye would that men should do to you, do ye even so to them" (Matthew 7:12). "Should we be willing, that the Africans or any other nation should purchase us, our wives and children, transport us into Africa and there sell us into perpetual and absolute slavery?" It was a rhetorical question, to be sure, yet it was also hard to dispute. Why was it acceptable to enslave Africans because their skin was black? As Edwards exclaimed, "Their colour indeed is different from ours. But does this give us a right to enslave them?"[33]

And that was a key question: Did Africans' black skin give whites "a right to enslave" Africans? It all came down to rights, and it all recalled the language of Jefferson's Declaration: What of equality? What of rights?

Regardless of what Jefferson's thoughts were when he wrote, "All men are created equal," Americans from 1776 onward would cite his words and then give their own meaning to them. And for many people the American Revolution conflicted with slavery, making the presence of slavery in the United States an example of hypocrisy on a massive scale. That hypocrisy itself was a legacy of the Revolution. For all its talk of (and fighting for) freedom, the American Revolution did not put an end to slavery: this was, as many historians point out, the Revolution's fatal flaw. That said, the Revolution did, as Gordon Wood points out, create "for the first time in American history the cultural atmosphere that made African American slavery abhorrent to many Americans."[34]

With all their successes and failures, the ideas of the American Revolution aroused the desire for a new nation, a desire that burned bright enough for many that they took on the British Empire and eventually won. They did not fight for God alone—this was not exclusively a religious war—but the Revolutionary War taught Americans that Christianity could be a martial force, a powerful motivator to war, and a moral defender of its causes and consequences. This war made the new nation possible, but it did not create it. That work was left to the founders who channeled revolutionary ideas, many of them contradictory, into a new republic that would propel religion in new and often bewildering directions.

7. The New Nation

When determined colonists living on the edge of the frontier defeated the British Empire, their world changed. Many of them started believing that ordinary people had extraordinary potential. No longer did they need to tip their hats to social elites. They were as good as anybody. They had the chance to usher in a new era for a new nation, but what kind of nation would it be? Would it be ruled by a strong, centralized government, or would it be led by a loose confederation of states? And what role would religion play in the new nation?

Whatever else happened, it was clear that American religion would be more diverse and more democratic than it had been in the colonial period. Democratic ideas inspired people, changed their outlook on life, and changed their religious views. In a nation that had no official religion, denominations competed with one another, turning religious life into a marketplace of ideas and practices, and it quickly became apparent that evangelicals had a decisive edge.[1]

The Constitution and Religion

After the Revolutionary War had been won, colonists went about the business of founding a nation, and one of the most pressing issues was the need (or not) for a Constitution, a question that had not been decided by the time the Constitutional Convention was held in Philadelphia in 1787.

Supporters of the Constitution, called "Federalists," wanted a stronger federal government to revise the Articles of Confederation (1781), which had established a confederation of states that came together temporarily for common interests, like fighting wars, but left most of the power in the states.[2] Although the Revolution had empowered more people to vote and even to hold public office, some wondered if this was a good idea. Would the common people be able to rule themselves? Or, more precisely, would the common people have the moral virtue and good sense necessary to elect able and virtuous leaders? By the 1780s some founders, including James Madison (1751–1836), had begun to worry. If average Americans lacked "virtue and intelligence to select men of virtue and wisdom," then, Madison wrote, "no theoretical checks, no form of government, can render us secure."[3]

This was mainly a problem in state legislatures, where ordinary people, many of them from rural areas, won elections and sat in places of power. Madison feared that they would vote their own interests only and create chaos, a form of democratic tyranny as bad as the tyranny of King George III. This was democracy run amuck, and it needed to be tempered. One of the reasons for the Constitution, according to some of the founders, was the belief that the nation needed a virtuous leadership, empowered through a stronger federal government, guided by elite white men of good character. This would not be a democratic "rule by the mob," but a sensible rule by elected officials, mostly well-off financially, who did not need the government's money. Such men could see past their own selfish needs and act for the good of the nation.[4]

At least that was the theory. Not everyone bought this argument, including the nation's Anti-federalists. For them, national virtue was best safeguarded not by a strong federal government, headed by elites in Washington, but through a more distributed model of power in the states. They were suspicious of a Constitution that would centralize more of the nation's power and take it away from the states. Among the Americans who were suspicious of the Constitution was Patrick Henry (1736–99) of Virginia. The Constitution, Henry reasoned, "presupposes that the chosen few who go to Congress will have more upright hearts, and more enlightened minds, than those who are members of the individual legislatures." If the nation wanted to centralize authority, then why the Revolution? Why not just have a king? Temptations to tyranny do not diminish by putting more power in a centralized system ruled by fewer people; the opposite was true. Best to share the power along a more decentralized model, divvied out among the states.[5]

We can find this line of thinking throughout the revolutionary period. In his *Common Sense*, Thomas Paine had written, "Society is produced by our wants, and government by our wickedness; the former promotes our happiness positively by uniting our affections, the latter negatively by restraining our vices. The one encourages intercourse, the other creates distinctions. The first is a patron, the last a punisher. Society in every state is a blessing, but Government, even in its best state, is but a necessary evil; in its worst state an intolerable one."[6] The best government was the smallest, with less intrusive government, said more liberal republican thinkers like Paine. With some minor differences, Thomas Jefferson also fit in that category. In short, Federalists and Anti-federalists agreed on many of the same principles, calling for a balance of powers and warning of dangerous tyranny at the top. But they disagreed on how best to put these principles into practice.[7]

Also undecided was the place of religion in the new nation, an issue so controversial that most delegates did not want to address it. Benjamin Franklin was an exception, as he most always seemed to be. As we have seen, Franklin was hardly an orthodox Christian. Yet the convention needed

God, he said. "In this situation of this assembly," Franklin said, "groping, as it were, in the dark, to find political truth, and scarce able to distinguish it when presented to us, how has it happened, sir, that we have not hitherto once thought of humbly applying to the Father of Lights to illuminate our understandings?" Franklin could not forget the Revolutionary War, the miraculous victory it was, and the role of God in it:

> In the Beginning of the Contest with Britain, when we were sensible of Danger, we had daily Prayers in this Room for the Divine Protection! Our Prayers, Sir, were heard; and they were graciously answered. All of us, who were engag'd in the Struggle, must have observ'd frequent Instances of a Superintending Providence in our Favour. To that kind Providence we owe this happy Opportunity of Consulting in Peace on the Means of establishing our future national Felicity. And have we now forgotten that powerful Friend? or do we imagine we no longer need its Assistance?

Franklin reminded everyone that he was old. Sort of the founding father of the founding fathers, Franklin was about a generation older than several other leading founders. And his experience had taught him not to ignore God's role in human affairs: "I have lived, Sir, a long time; and the longer I live, the more convincing Proofs I see of this Truth, That GOD governs in the Affairs of Men! . . . We have been assured, Sir, in the Sacred Writings, that 'except the Lord build the House, they labor in vain that build it.' I firmly believe this; and I also believe that without his concurring Aid, we shall succeed in this political Building no better than the Builders of Babel."[8]

What Americans needed most was unity, but unity, it seemed, was a most rare commodity; only God could help, Franklin believed. Without God, people would care only for their "local Interests," with no regard for the greater good of the nation. Lest these representatives forget, the world was watching, looking to see if a new republic could shape itself into a viable nation with no king. If this nation failed, Franklin said, the world may give up on "establishing Government by human Wisdom, and leave it to Chance, War and Conquest. I therefore beg leave to move, That henceforth Prayers, imploring the Assistance of Heaven, and its Blessing on our Deliberations, be held in this Assembly every Morning before we proceed to Business; and that one or more of the Clergy of this City be requested to officiate in that Service."[9]

No one could deny Franklin's eloquence, nor could they deny his fame or the respect he garnered. But the delegates rejected his proposal to open sessions with prayer. It raised too many issues: Who would be asked to pray? Would the request show favoritism to one denomination over others? This scene shows just how fraught the topic of religion was during the Constitutional Convention—and in any conversation about American national identity ever since.[10]

When it was finally printed, the Constitution said almost nothing about religion, other than a prohibition of religious tests for office holders: "No religious Test shall ever be required as a Qualification to any Office or public Trust under the United States."[11] How should we interpret this relative silence? Does it mean that the founders cared little about religion? The answer depends on what we mean by "religion." If we mean doctrine and deep concepts of theology, the answer is likely a resounding "yes" for some of the founders. But if we mean religious influences on morality and character, the answer is probably "no."

The founders wanted religion to exert a strong influence on morality because they were founding a *republic,* and republics relied on public virtue more than most types of government. In a monarchy, for example, a king or queen could force people to do what they demanded. People would be good citizens out of fear, if for no other reason. Not so in a republic: there was no king or queen. Leaders were not born into power; they were *elected* by the people, so republics relied more on the goodwill of their citizens to do the right thing for their nation.

The key term to describe virtuous leadership is "disinterestedness," willingness to sacrifice selfish interests for the sake of the nation, forsaking one's own wants for the needs of the many. Recall again Ben Franklin's worry that Americans would become too caught up in their local interests to care about the needs of others. Others worried about this, too. The nation needed virtue; it was critical for a republic to survive, which is why there were so few republics: they usually did not last because people were not often virtuous enough to sustain them.[12] Most people acted out of self-interest, and George Washington never tired of pointing this out. "The few" people "who act upon Principles of disinterestedness," Washington wrote, "are, comparatively speaking, no more than a drop in the Ocean."[13]

That was a major reason why religion was so important to the first president. Washington's famous "Farewell Address," published widely in 1796, argued for religion's critical role in the nation: "Of all the dispositions and habits which lead to political prosperity, religion and morality are indispensable supports. In vain would that man claim the tribute of patriotism, who should labor to subvert these great pillars of human happiness, these firmest props of the duties of men and citizens. The mere politician, equally with the pious man, ought to respect and to cherish them."[14]

As soon as he put these thoughts to paper, Washington knew that some intellectuals and religious skeptics would question this firm connection between religion and morality. He was ready with a response: "Let us with caution indulge the supposition that morality can be maintained without religion." Education is great, but it is not enough: "Reason and experience both forbid us to expect that national morality can prevail in exclusion of religious principle." It would be enough if Washington had been alone in this opinion, but these were not just Washington's words: James Madison, Alexander Hamilton, and John Jay all helped him write the address. Clearly this view of religion was not an isolated opinion but one shared by many near the turn of that century.[15]

Religious Establishment and Religious Liberty

The Constitution had no easy road to ratification in the states, and churches took sides. Some Anti-federalist Christians feared the Constitution's centralized model of power, and they also feared what the Constitution lacked: a Bill of Rights that would guarantee religious liberty, an issue that had been debated for years.

But what did "religious liberty" mean? People disagreed. Just after the Revolutionary War ended, there was no consensus on what the relationships between church and state should be in these newly "united states." As each state worked toward its own solution, all eyes focused on Virginia. The colony's official, tax-supported church had been the Church of England, the Anglican Church. But after the Revolution the name "Anglican" was a liability because of its association with England. In 1789 the Anglican Church in America wisely chose a new name, the Protestant Episcopal Church in the USA. It helped, but other problems remained. Whether they called it "Anglican" or "Episcopalian," this church faced opposition from Virginians who worshiped in other churches, Virginians who did not want their tax money to go to fund a church they did not otherwise support.

This idea seemed too radical to Patrick Henry, who worried about a state that did not have the support of a church. As we have seen, republican political thought stressed the importance of a virtuous citizenship, and religion was the most powerful motivation to virtue among the people. Henry's solution was a "general assessment" plan, which would allow people to select the church that would receive their tax money. This strategy, as Henry surmised, would support religion, and virtue, without violating citizens' religious liberty by forcing them to pay for a church they did not attend. This view had robust support, including the backing of George Washington, which was the strongest endorsement of all.[16]

Yet the "general assessment" plan did not win the day, mainly because of Thomas Jefferson and James Madison. In June 1785, Madison wrote his *Memorial and Remonstrance against Religious Assessments*. The "general assessment" plan was a slippery slope, Madison argued. If you give government the power to "establish Christianity, in exclusion of all other Religions," then what is to stop the government from establishing a denomination? The question was not *which* religion was established; it was the question of religious establishments itself.[17]

Besides, religion did not need the protection of government, said Madison. Any glance at Christian history showed that the church had survived just fine without government help. In fact, Christianity had even thrived in the face of opposition and torment. Despite persecution, despite martyrdom, despite attacks from all sides, Christianity endured. Most ominously, when states attempted to enforce religious views, the results ended up tragic and violent. "Torrents of blood have been spilt in the old world, by vain attempts of the secular arm, to extinguish Religious discord, by proscribing all difference in Religious opinion."[18]

Arguments like these defeated the assessment plan in Virginia. This victory then gave Madison the opportunity to put forward Jefferson's Bill No. 82, "A Bill for establishing religious freedom," known as the Virginia Statute for Religious Freedom. It became law in 1786, thanks mainly to Madison's tireless work in navigating the bill through the legislature.[19] This bill, which ended Anglican establishment in Virginia, was a classic statement of religious liberty: parts of it are worth quoting:

> Almighty God hath created the mind free, and manifested his supreme will that free it shall remain by making it altogether insusceptible of restraint; that all attempts to influence it by temporal punishments, or burthens, or by civil incapacitations, tend only to beget habits of hypocrisy and meanness, and are a departure from the plan of the holy author of our religion, who being lord both of body and mind, yet chose not to propagate it by coercions on either, as was in his Almighty power to do, but to extend it by its influence on reason alone.

Jesus preached the gospel but never forced it on anyone. In contrast, state-supported churches and civil rulers kept all the power to themselves, legitimized each other, and the result was tyranny in body and soul. As Jefferson wrote, "To compel a man to furnish contributions of money for the propagation of opinions which he disbelieves and abhors, is sinful and tyrannical."[20]

This statement reaffirmed the widely held belief that God authored freedom and rights, sentiments most famously enunciated in the Declaration of 1776. The God of liberty, the God of the Revolution, could not abide tyranny; the conscience was its own authority, and the state had no right to interfere with it.[21]

Given all this writing and fretting over religious liberty, some Americans expected a statement on the issue to be included in the Constitution. Yet they were disappointed. When the Constitution came up for ratification, therefore, questions circulated about why this critical founding document said nothing about religious liberty. This was a sensitive issue for Baptists. Recall that Roger Williams, founder of the first Baptist church in America, was the most vocal proponent of religious liberty in the 1600s, and it cost him severely as Puritan authorities banished him from the Bay Colony. One of Roger Williams's great admirers was Isaac Backus (1724–1806), leader of Baptists in New England who led the way in promoting religious liberty in the wake of the Revolution. Backus adopted the republican, political language of freedom, so prominent in revolutionary America, and used it to argue for religious freedom. With Baptists like Backus paying close attention, the Constitution had little chance of ratification unless it included some guarantee of religious liberty.[22]

If James Madison did not already know this, he soon would. In early 1788, he received a letter from Captain Joseph Spencer, who reported that Baptists were making trouble for the Constitution in Virginia, especially in Orange County, where Baptist ministers "are much alarm'd fearing Religious Liberty is not Sufficiently secur'd." Madison should meet with the Baptists, Captain Spencer advised, but not just any Baptist. The man to deal with was John Leland (1754–1841), a colorful and renowned evangelist from Massachusetts who had defended religious liberty from Virginia to Connecticut.[23]

According to Baptist lore, Madison met with Leland and assured him that if the Constitution were successfully ratified, a Bill of Rights would be issued and would guarantee religious liberty. This meeting supposedly satisfied Leland and secured his support. If Madison did persuade Leland to deliver the Baptist vote to ratify the Constitution, this was a monumental meeting with wide-ranging consequences. We do not know if the meeting actually took place, but we do know that the rumor was circulating in the early nineteenth century. We also know Leland changed his mind on the Constitution and recruited Baptists to support it. With support of Baptists, like Leland in Virginia and Backus in Massachusetts, these two states ratified the Constitution, but just barely. We also know that Leland wrote to Madison in February 1789, congratulating him on his appointment to Congress and asking Madison to keep him informed of various matters. "One Thing I shall expect," Leland wrote, "that if religious Liberty is anywise threatened, that I shall receive the earliest Intelligence."[24] In 1791, Madison delivered on his promise for a Bill of Rights, including a statement on religious liberty.

THE FIRST AMENDMENT ON FREEDOM OF RELIGION

"Congress shall make no law respecting an establishment of religion, or prohibiting the free exercise thereof; or abridging the freedom of speech, or of the press; or the right of the people peaceably to assemble, and to petition the Government for a redress of grievances."*

*United States Courts, "First Amendment Activities," www.uscourts.gov/about-federal -courts/educational-resources/educational-activities/first-amendment-activities.

No church or denomination would receive federal endorsement, nor would the nation's government interfere with anyone's right to worship. This did not stop states from holding on to their established churches, which they did for a time in New England (Massachusetts did not end its establishment of the Congregational Church until 1833).

The same year that Americans were pondering the First Amendment, John Leland deployed a full arsenal of biblical arguments and Jeffersonian language in his attack on religious establishments in Connecticut: *The Rights of Conscience Inalienable, and Therefore, Religious Opinions Not Cognizable by Law; or, The High-Flying Church-Man, Stripped of His Legal Robe, Appears a Yaho.* "Religion is a matter between God and individuals," Leland argued, "the religious opinions of men not being the objects of civil government, nor in any way under its control."[25]

Even though this was still a hotly debated issue in the states, the First Amendment ensured that the federal government would not establish an official, national church. This strong sentiment for religious liberty eventually led to the end of tax support for churches in the states. With the leadership of Jefferson and Madison, and the support of countless evangelicals like Leland, the new nation abandoned tax support for churches—one of the most important results of the American Revolution.

Although the First Amendment prevented the United States from establishing a national religion or church, this did not mean that the national government would be completely secular, with no use for religious influences in politics. There were and are many different opinions on that issue. Even with the drive for disestablishment in revolutionary America and beyond, states typically mandated some theological requirements of office holders, such as belief in God and/or the Scriptures.[26] Citizens continued to have some religious expectations of their leaders, and this expectation has continued. To this day an admitted atheist has never been elected President of the United States.

Opposites Attack: Evangelicals and Rationalists

For Enlightened thinkers like Jefferson and Madison, the First Amendment was pure gold. But it was just as valuable for evangelicals, especially Baptists. Jefferson and other enlightened thinkers wanted religious liberty because they wanted to protect the state from religious interference and sectarian squabbles; Baptists wanted religious liberty because they wanted to protect their churches from the corruption resulting from political involvement in their affairs. Consequently, enlightened thinkers and evangelicals shaped a potent alliance with dramatic ramifications for American religious and political history.

We find a great illustration of this odd alliance in the relationship between John Leland and Thomas Jefferson. Most famously, Leland presented to President Jefferson a "Mammoth Cheese," weighing 1,235 pounds, on January 1, 1802. This must have been quite a sight: it attracted crowds of people from all around. Reportedly, it took nearly 1,000 cows to supply the milk for this great cheese, which had engraved on it: "Rebellion to tyrants is obedience to God." It was a gift from Leland and the citizens of Cheshire, Massachusetts, to Jefferson.[27]

While Leland was in town, Jefferson invited him to preach a sermon before Congress, which he did, drawing ridicule from Federalists, who called him "the cheesemonger," labeling him "poor ignorant, illiterate," and a "clownish creature." Consider the sources, Leland and Jefferson probably thought, as neither was a fan of Federalists.[28]

Although Jefferson and Leland could hardly have disagreed more in their religious views, Leland believed that Jefferson was a gift from God to the nation. "Kind Providence, which produced a Washington to deliver us from the invading foe, presented a Jefferson," Leland wrote in 1813. It was Jefferson "who snatched the constitution from the talons of its enemies, and turned the government into its natural channel." Americans should "celebrate the virtues of Jefferson, which secured to you the blessings that Washington achieved."[29]

Beyond national politics, both Jefferson and Leland distrusted ministers who yearned for power, prestige, and money. This was an age of missions and fundraising; churches increased support for missionary work on the

FIGURE 7-1. Plaque of John Leland on the Cheshire Mammoth Cheese monument in Cheshire, MA. The monument commemorates the press that shaped the "Mammoth Cheese" presented to Jefferson. Photo by Makeitalready, Wikimedia Commons. Licensed under the Creative Commons Attribution-Share Alike 3.0 Unported license

expanding frontier. In 1801, the Presbyterian Church in the U.S.A. formed a "Plan of Union" with New England-based Congregationalists, pooling their resources to promote missions and revivals. Not to be outdone, Baptists formed a denomination in 1814, calling it the General Missionary Convention of the Baptist Denomination in the United States of America for Foreign Missions. Leland wanted nothing to do with it. This was a power move, Leland thought, an attempt to turn the Baptist churches into an empire so that Baptists could climb the social ladder and be more like the "respectable" denominations such as the Congregationalists, Episcopalians, and Presbyterians. This was a trap, Leland believed, a mixture of power, prestige, and money that would lead Baptists astray from simple, biblical Christianity.

The trouble was, too many ministers wanted respectability and a cushy job, Leland feared. He took aim at them with his satirical poem "The Modern Priest," which tells us much about how religion had become transformed by ideas of democracy in Leland's time. The fictitious object of Leland's ridicule is "Ignatius" (a perfectly Catholic name, Leland probably thought), who trained at a university but got little from it. He thought about becoming a doctor, but realized most doctors were quacks. The legal profession interested him, but the only lawyers who made money were the crooked ones. Then he considered the ministry—there was a profession with possibilities for easy money, he thought.

> Preaching is now a science and a trade,
> And by it many grand estates are made.

Ignatius could pray long prayers and preach short sermons, neither of which would be extemporaneous (as evangelicals preferred). Instead, he would memorize his prayers and read his sermons from a manuscript. Best of all was the light workload and the steady flow of money.

> While others labor six days, I but one,
> For that day's work I'll gain a pretty sum.[30]

This "Modern Priest" also took a modern view of the Scriptures, a view that Leland and most other evangelicals detested. For them, the Bible was best understood by common sense, and its meaning was available to any sincere reader. "Is the Bible written . . . so intricate and high, that none but the letter learned . . . can read it?"[31] No, according to Leland. God intended for individuals to read the Bible for themselves, without interference from a pope, bishop, or some high-flown theologian. And people did not need anything other than the Bible to understand what God needed them to know.

Leland would have agreed with the statement of Phoebe Palmer, an influential Methodist writer and speaker: "The Bible is a wonderfully simple book; and, if you had taken the naked word of God as . . . your counsel, instead of taking the opinions of men in regard to that *Word*, you might have been a more enlightened, simple, happy and useful Christian."[32] Palmer was no lone voice on this topic; she spoke for countless evangelicals in the nineteenth century.

Not the "Modern Priest," however. In his view, the Bible was hard to understand, so it was better to rely on theologians:

> The Bible was so dark, the style so poor,
> He gain'd but little from the sacred store;
> Pool, Whitby, Burchett, Henry, Yorick, Gill,
> He read, to find what was Jehovah's will.[33]

It was the saving experience of God, not theological knowledge, that mattered to Leland and most evangelicals. "Orthodoxy, heterodoxy, or any other doxy, without the love of a holy God in the heart, is a miserable doxy for me," Leland stated. "If the greatest reasoner is the greatest saint, philosophers excel Christians, and the Devil goes beyond them all." As for Leland, "When I hear a long harangue of metaphysical reasoning on abstruse questions, I feel more like calling for my night-cap than anything else."[34]

The French Revolution and the "Age of Reason"

Just as Leland and many other evangelicals rejected the metaphysical speculations of theology, so did enlightened thinkers like Thomas Paine. Like Leland, Paine believed much of traditional theology had been corrupted by medieval speculations that were more philosophical gibberish than the commonsense teachings of Jesus. Yet whereas evangelicals desired a return to a plain reading of the Bible, Paine was ready to reject most of the Bible altogether.

When last we met Paine, he had dashed onto the scene in 1776 with *Common Sense*, the most influential pamphlet of the American Revolution. Paine had nowhere near the notoriety of other well-known founders, not to mention the money. He even refused to profit from *Common Sense*, giving his royalty money to equip the Continental Army. He fought in the war and wrote for the cause, publishing essays in pamphlets titled *The American Crisis*, inspiring troops with such lines as "These are the times that try men's souls. The summer solider and the sunshine patriot will, in this crisis, shrink from the service of their country. . . . Tyranny, like hell, is not easily conquered; yet . . . the harder the conflict, the more glorious the triumph." These were the lines Washington wanted his men to hear before they braved a blizzard to cross the iced-over Delaware River to attack Trenton. Likely the men listened to Paine because he was one of them, a soldier in the Continental Army. In fact, he wrote part of *The American Crisis* while sitting in the cold among Washington's troops. His devotion to the cause knew no bounds.[35]

The Revolution ended in 1783; but in a way, it never ended for Paine. He kept fighting for revolutionary ideas, only changing the location. When

Americans heard about the French Revolution in 1789, they cheered the storming of the Bastille, seeing in it the influence of the American Revolution, and many Protestants rejoiced in the attack on the Catholic Church. Once again tyranny was being struck down, as it was in the American Revolution, many Americans believed. Could this even be a sign of the approaching millennium? Hopes soared among American Christians as they looked for more news from France. Soon, however, they watched those developments take an alarming turn: revolutionaries in France attacked the monarchy, executed priests, and beheaded King Louis XVI in 1793.

By then Thomas Paine was in France and had witnessed the chaos firsthand. He had been welcomed to Paris in 1792, even elected to the National Assembly for his celebrated book *The Rights of Man* (1791 [part 1] and 1792 [part 2]). Yet Paine fell out of favor in France, in part because he opposed the execution of Louis XVI. That was the nature of the French Revolution: fortunes could turn at a moment's notice, and they certainly changed for Paine. Before long, he found himself in prison.[36]

While in his cell, Paine watched hundreds of other prisoners march to their executions during those bloody days. But Paine did not just watch and wait; he thought and wrote, producing another book—and certainly it ignited controversy. This time his topic was not only revolution but also religion; this book, *The Age of Reason*, would cause a revolution, or close to it: his ideas were beyond radical for most Americans. No matter for Paine. This was his chance—likely he thought it was his *last* chance—to attack religion, which he had come to see as the root of much evil.[37]

Near the beginning of *The Age of Reason*, Paine stated his "profession of faith," including belief in "one God, and no more; and" his "hope for happiness beyond this life." Next Paine stated his confidence in "the quality of man" and his opinion "that religious duties consist in doing justice, loving mercy, and endeavoring to make our fellow creatures happy." As far as the creeds of any church, Paine rejected them: "My own mind is my own church," he wrote. All other "national institutions of churches"—including "Jewish, Christian, or Turkish"—were "human inventions, set up to terrify and enslave mankind, and monopolize power and profit."[38]

Paine explained his reasoning: "Soon after I had published the pamphlet *Common Sense* in America," he wrote, "I saw the exceeding probability that a revolution in the system of government would be followed by a revolution in the system of religion." In *Common Sense*, he launched the first Revolution; in *Age of Reason*, he hoped to launch the second.[39]

His "revolution" featured an attack on Scriptures, not only the Old and New Testaments, but the Qur'an as well. Paine did not attack Jesus, a historical figure who "preached most excellent morality, and the equality of man"; but, typical of other thinkers in the age of Enlightenment, Paine attacked the religious traditions built up around Christ. Paine aimed his assaults on the Bible, even though, as we noted previously, he had cited Scripture extensively to argue for American independence in *Common Sense*. No longer. Paine had cited Scripture when he needed it to inspire revolution. Now that the war had been won, Paine turned on Scripture, telling the people what he really thought. "What is it the Bible teaches us?—Rapine, cruelty, and murder." Specifically, the New Testament asks people "to believe that the Almighty committed debauchery with a woman, engaged to be married! And the belief of this debauchery is called faith." Beyond his swipes at Scripture, Paine's attack on Christianity was vicious. "Of all the systems of religion that ever were invented, there is none more derogatory to the Almighty, more unedifying to man, more repugnant to reason, and more contradictory in itself, than this thing called Christianity."[40]

THOMAS PAINE AND THE REASONED CRITIQUE OF RELIGION

The always-quotable Mark Twain observed, "It took a brave man before the Civil War to confess he had read the *Age of Reason*."[*] Yet people did read it, thousands of them. From Paine, Americans heard a convincing argument that Christianity, like all state-supported religions, had been more about power and tyranny than spirituality and morality. "It has been the scheme of the Christian Church, and of all other invented systems of religion, to hold man in ignorance of the Creator, as it is of Governments to hold man in ignorance of his rights," Paine wrote. Nations and churches had propped one another up for centuries, with churches endowing nations with sacred authority, and nations endowing churches with money and political clout. Americans opposed to tyranny, Paine argued, should oppose Christianity as fiercely as they would oppose any despot.[†] *The Age of Reason* found a wide readership among folks who wanted a radical democracy, with little to no interference from government, and this included Americans who streamed into frontier areas like Kentucky.[‡]

*Jill Lepore, *The Story of America: Essays on Origins* (Princeton: Princeton University Press, 2012), Kindle ed., 67. †Lepore, *Story of America*, 68–69. ‡See Amanda Porterfield, *Conceived in Doubt: Religion and Politics in the New American Nation* (Chicago: University of Chicago Press, 2012), Kindle ed., chap. 1.

The fallout from *Age of Reason* was extreme. Paine was no longer an American hero, the stirring patriot of *Common Sense* and *American Crisis*; now Paine was an infidel, public enemy number one for many Christians. "Do you think that your pen, or the pen of any other man, can unchristianize the mass of our citizens?" asked Samuel Adams. The clear answer, for Adams and countless Christians, was no.[41]

Attacks on *Age of Reason* mischaracterized Paine and his work, calling him an atheist, even though he had clearly stated a belief in God and the morality of Jesus. Regardless, few politicians wanted to be associated with

Paine, not even the Democratic-Republicans who were sympathetic to his politics.

There was another important result of the backlash against Paine's *Age of Reason*. From that point onward, it was more politically dangerous than ever to attack the Bible. Skepticism of Christianity became political poison. In contrast, faithfulness to Scripture and Christianity became even more important for any politician who wanted to get elected. For many Americans, any expression of doubt about Scripture or Christianity recalled the bloody radicalism of the French Revolution, and Tom Paine, whom Teddy Roosevelt would later (incorrectly) ridicule as that "filthy little atheist."[42]

Republican Religion in New Forms

During the revolutionary era, Americans began to think of their new nation in religious terms. Various scholars have identified American forms of "civil religion," a term popularized by sociologist Robert Bellah in the 1960s. This "civil religion" has a complex definition yet points to Americans' views of the United States as a divinely chosen nation, with a religious destiny unique in world history. Often, Americans' patriotic ideas and feelings have blended with spiritual beliefs, and this phenomenon grew stronger after the

FIGURE 7-2. The reverse of the Great Seal of the United States, James Trenchard, 1747–, engraver [1786], LC-USZ62-45509 (Library of Congress)

American Revolution and reached high points, especially as the nation went to war.[43]

Civil religion in the United States was republican religion, a divine endorsement of the nation and its destiny. As we have discussed, "republican" was not just a political term. It referred to a new way of looking at the world, a reform of older ways of thinking about authority, tradition, and virtue—all ideas that involved religion.

Americans experienced republican-influenced religion in various ways, and one of the most prominent influences was Freemasonry, a fraternity that fused republican and religious values in a way that made sense to scores of men in the Early Republic and even today. We see the imprint of Masonry in national symbols, including the nation's Great Seal, with its images of the pyramid and the "eye of Providence," which remains on the nation's currency.

Freemasonry, as Americans experienced it, started in London, where a lodge opened in 1717. The movement spread quickly in revolutionary America, where members included George Washington, Alexander Hamilton, and Benjamin Franklin. These men, many of whom rejected traditional Christianity, found in Freemasonry a proxy religion, complete with many spiritual features. In Freemasonry, men of the Enlightenment could experience secret rituals and community bonding without hellfire preaching and the constant bickering over theology that they saw in many churches. They preferred the lodges over the churches because among fellow Masons they found a republican brotherhood, allowing them to cultivate friendships across social and political lines, training them how to live free and enlightened lives. George Washington called it "a lodge for the virtues."[44]

Just as the new nation was a new experiment in republican government, so was it a new experiment with religion. Gone was age-old alignment of church and state, in which the state endorsed and supported one church for the nation, while marginalizing or even banishing all others. Yet the new nation did not cast off the old ways totally. Even if the nation would not endorse a single church, that did not mean that the nation abandoned religion or its supports. New ways of being religious were working their ways through the United States, including varieties of civil religion, in which American patriotism became very much like a religious conviction. The next chapter considers how the nineteenth century became a competitive religious marketplace, a survival of the fittest in which some churches and religious movements adapted to the republican ethos of the nation and surged in popularity, while others were uneasy in the new nation.

8. New Revivals and New Faiths

The American Revolution ushered in a whirlwind of change like colonists had never seen. In a few years, colonial Americans had been catapulted from fighting a Revolution into adopting a Constitution and founding a new nation, all the while looking on as the French Revolution erupted in Europe. New religious movements formed, including the Mormons, who brought new scriptures and new beliefs that challenged other denominations in radical ways. Despite slavery, African American churches flourished. Revivals reignited in the cities and along the frontier, inspiring evangelical growth throughout a young nation that was expanding its boundaries. There was so much movement, so many transformations, that Americans struggled to come to terms with them.

Rip Van Winkle and Religion in American Society

No story better captured the bewilderment Americans felt than Rip Van Winkle.[1] When Washington Irving published this rewritten version of an old German story, he knew that Americans would relate to Rip, a rather lazy chap and "obedient henpecked husband" who drank magical liquor before the Revolution and awakened twenty years later.[2] At first, Rip thought he had only slept a few hours. He ambled down to the village, perplexed that he could find neither his dog nor his gun, and was confounded to see strangers everywhere, even though he was sure he knew most everyone who lived there. Everyone dressed differently. Rows of new houses had been built, and he saw a flag he had never seen before, bearing an "assemblage of stars and stripes," fully "strange and incomprehensible." As he looked toward the hotel, he expected to see a sign with "the ruby face of King George," but in its place he saw that "the red coat was changed for one of blue and buff, a sword was held in the hand instead of a scepter, the head was decorated with a cocked hat, and underneath was painted in large characters, GENERAL WASHINGTON." What disturbed Rip most was the change in "the very character of the people": "There was a busy, bustling, disputatious tone about it, instead of the accustomed phlegm and drowsy tranquility." Immediately then he saw an orator shouting "about rights of citizens—election—members of Congress—liberty" and such, all "perfect Babylonish jargon to the bewildered

Van Winkle." When the man asked Rip "on which side he voted," wondering "whether he was a Federal or Democrat," Rip could only stare back at him "in vacant stupidity." Finally, Rip was "at his wit's end" and exclaimed, "Every thing's changed, and I'm changed, and I can't tell what's my name, or who I am!"[3]

Indeed, everything had changed, it seemed. Americans had seen their world transformed seemingly overnight. When Thomas Jefferson assumed the office of president, the nation he would oversee had a population of over 5.2 million people, about 20 percent of them were enslaved. The population was expanding rapidly, growing at double the rate of European nations, in part because this was a young nation: "in 1810 [some] 36 percent of the white population was under the age of ten, and nearly 70 percent was under the age of twenty-five," Gordon Wood reported.[4]

Not only were many Americans young; they were also leaving home at remarkable rates, heading out to claim their own land and make their own futures. Tennessee, which became a state in 1796, saw its population multiply ten times over by 1820. During the first decade of the nineteenth century, New York's population expanded by 374,000 people. Ohio saw its

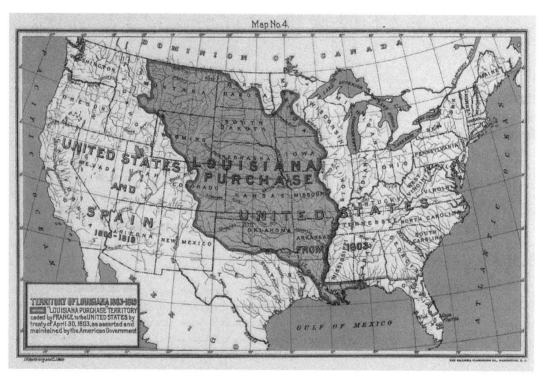

FIGURE 8-1. Louisiana Purchase. National Archives 594889

white population skyrocket from 45,000 to more than 230,000 in a decade. In 1803, Thomas Jefferson made a colossal land deal with France: the Louisiana Purchase, which doubled the nation's size.[5]

Transportation was a nightmare. The roads that existed were unpaved and useless in bad weather, so most Americans could not travel long distances except over water, which is why Americans built cities along coastlines or rivers. Transporting a ton of supplies thirty miles on land was expensive, about the same as it cost to ship the same load across the Atlantic.[6]

The typical American could not afford to buy many clothes, so most wore only what they could stitch together at home. Store-bought shoes were a luxury, and many rural people lived most of their lives in bare feet. Hygiene was hardly what we would expect today. Most Americans wore the same clothes repeatedly. Weekly bathing was rare, since it was inconvenient to fetch water, carry it into the house, and heat it over the fireplace. Many people took a bath in the springtime, and that was it for the year, though some did not bathe even that often. Most baths did not include soap because the soap they made was often too abrasive to be used on skin; people just used it to wash their clothes.[7]

Although life was hard, increasing numbers of Americans were enterprising and would allow nothing to hold them back, certainly not traditional social hierarchies. One foreign visitor said of Americans, "The lowest here . . . stand erect and crouch not before any man." In postrevolutionary America, white men in Boston all expected to be called "Mr." even though previously that title had been reserved for elites.[8]

A Second Great Awakening

This was the world of American evangelicalism, a movement spurred on by the American Revolution, which empowered ordinary people to relish freedom, and the Second Great Awakening, an eclectic mix of revivals that spanned from cities through the frontier. As the nation expanded and Americans moved West, revivals proved to be an effective means of converting people to Christianity. The denominations that embraced revivals, mainly Baptists and Methodists, grew rapidly; denominations that did not, including Episcopalians and Lutherans, grew more slowly. In the middle were Presbyterians and Congregationalists, denominations that practiced revivalism in certain regions and saw increases in membership in those areas.[9]

Revivals were not all the same. Some centered in cities; others flourished in rural outposts. Some were more intellectual and refined; others were more radical and emotional. Frontier revivals were often planned events scheduled outside church walls, specifically in camp meetings, which were social and religious events that drew thousands of people of various races and denominations and featured an array of evangelical preaching, along with less spiritual activities. These camp meetings had deep roots, extending to the sixteenth-century Scottish "holy fairs," sacramental festivals that combined ritual devotion with a festive celebration. This tradition influenced Scots-Irish Presbyterian minister James McGready when he preached camp meeting revivals in Logan County, Kentucky, at the turn of the nineteenth century.

CANE RIDGE

The nation's most famous camp meeting was held in Cane Ridge, Kentucky, in 1801. Leading the event was Presbyterian minister Barton Stone (1772–1844), who organized a massive festival with over 10,000 attendees to hear sermons from Methodist, Presbyterian, and Baptist preachers throughout the week. This was a revival that, to many observers, looked more like chaos than worship: people fell on the ground, moaned, jerked, danced, and made animal noises, including barking and growling. All signs of the Holy Spirit, said some; proof positive of religion gone mad, said others.*

*See Daniel Walker Howe, *What Hath God Wrought: The Transformation of America, 1815–1848* (New York: Oxford University Press, 2007), Kindle ed., 177. For the Scottish Presbyterian influence on the camp meetings, see Leigh Eric Schmidt, *Holy Fairs: Scotland and the Making of American Revivalism*, 2nd ed. (Grand Rapids: Wm. B. Eerdmans Publishing Co., 1989), 11–12; Paul Keith Conkin, *Cane Ridge, America's Pentecost*, The Curti Lectures, 1989 (Madison: University of Wisconsin Press, 1990).

At about the same time that enthusiastic converts were worshiping at Cane Ridge and elsewhere, a different kind of revival emerged at Yale College, led by college president Timothy Dwight; as a grandson of Jonathan Edwards, Dwight had impeccable revivalist credentials. The revivals did not end at Yale but spread throughout churches in the area and beyond, spurred on by some of Dwight's students, including Nathaniel William Taylor, who taught at the new Yale Divinity School and led in adapting a new theological perspective, the "New Haven Theology," which revised major themes of Calvinism.

Taylor wanted a new kind of Calvinism for new times. Like scores of other Americans, he rejected the doctrine of "original sin," which taught that Adam and Eve's sin had infected all generations of people with guilt and a sinful nature until Christ redeemed them. Taylor did not deny that everybody sinned: the evidence was hard to deny. But sin is not some inherited trait, Taylor said. Sin is a choice. "Sin is in the sinning," he insisted, and claimed that everyone had the *ability to resist sinning*. People had freedom; they were not strapped with an inability to make a choice to accept or to reject God's offer of salvation, a theology that fit well with the times in this freedom-loving new nation.[10]

Religion became above all a matter of choices, therefore, and God had empowered people to make choices. Leaders of the Second Great Awakening urged people to make their own decisions for Christ, and nobody did more urging than Charles G. Finney (1792–1875). Finney's legal career was essentially over in October 1821, when he experienced a new stirring in his soul, convicting him to devote his life to spreading the gospel. From that point onward, he had "a retainer from the Lord Jesus Christ to plead his cause," as he put it.[11]

Although primarily an evangelist, Finney was also an innovator, a combination of scientist and entrepreneur of revivalism. Unlike the brilliant Jonathan Edwards, the fiery George Whitefield, and other famous preachers of the past, Finney and some other evangelists of his day denied that revivals were mysterious blessings delivered from heaven. "A revival of religion is not a miracle," Finney wrote. "A revival is the result of the *right* use of the appropriate means."[12] Revival was a science; like all sciences, it depended on using the right methods to achieve results. To explain, Finney used an analogy many folks could understand: there were methods to revival just as there were methods in farming. A farmer who did no work in the field could not expect God miraculously to grow a crop of wheat. The same was true for preachers who did not use the methods of revivalism: they could not expect God to bring revival. "A revival is the work of God, and so is a crop of wheat; and God is as much dependent on the use of means in one case as the other."[13]

These revival methods, which Finney called "New Measures," included the "Anxious Bench," a seat near the preacher where folks who were "anxious" about their salvation sat within view of all. The "New Measures" provoked new controversies. The "Anxious Bench," some said, was a manipulative ploy, a gimmick that pressured people into making a decision that had nothing to do with true conversion. Authentic religious experience developed over time, through prayer and spiritual discipline, and could not be concocted by a charismatic preacher who hustled emotionalism disguised as spirituality.[14]

Despite criticisms, complaints, and outright attacks, Finney's "measures" worked. He preached to packed revival services in major cities: Rochester, Boston, Philadelphia, and more. When he was not preaching, he wrote. His controversial *Lectures on Revivals of Religion*, published in 1835, inspired preachers to adopt the "new measures," which could produce revivals at will. For ministers who wanted to win in the religious free market in the United States, Finney was an expert guide.[15]

Evangelicals of Finney's day started calling their revivals "the Second Great Awakening" as a way of comparing them to what they called "the First Great Awakening," which had been spearheaded by Whitefield and Edwards. This labeling of the "awakenings" was new. The first history of the initial "Great Awakening" was not published until 1845, when the Second

Great Awakening was winding down; even then, the book was partially a response to Finney's "new measures."[16]

These were revivals for a new, vigorous nation of confident individuals who refused any limitations imposed by the past. Common people and uneducated ministers had the upper hand, feeling spirited and free to challenge all elites, especially elitist ministers. These revivals were bewildering in their diversity, flourishing on the frontier and in the cites, pulsing in fits and starts, beginning in the 1790s and finally fading in the 1840s.

The "Benevolent Empire"

Although the Second Great Awakening aimed at converting lost individuals, its leaders also wanted to reform society. When Americans looked around at the state of the nation, many of them believed religion was needed more than ever. We have discussed how Americans were young, enterprising, and on the move, many of them heading west to better themselves. In addition, American society was competitive and violent, with scores of fistfights, riots, and duels. Although this behavior seems barbarous by our standards today, it was widely accepted at the time.

To cite one prominent example, nobody loved a cockfight or horse race more than Andrew Jackson. More than twenty years before he was elected President of the United States and after he represented Tennessee in the Senate, Jackson and a man named Charles Dickinson argued over a horse-race bet. Evidently Dickinson accused Jackson of cheating on the wager while also insulting his wife. Jackson and Dickinson decided to settle the matter in a duel. Jackson shot Dickinson, and Dickinson shot Jackson. Dickinson died; Jackson recovered, though he kept the bullet in his chest for the rest of his life. Jackson participated in many more duels. No one knows the exact number, though some estimate as many as one hundred.[17]

Although some preachers blasted duels as unchristian and barbaric, dueling had its own rules of etiquette (the Code Duello), and it was considered a gentlemanly way to settle disputes and preserve honor. Remember that in 1804 Alexander Hamilton, first Secretary of the Treasury, was killed in a duel by Aaron Burr, Vice President of the United States. Compared with much of the violence Americans experienced, duels were almost tame. People on the frontier saw horrific fights, which included eye gouging, hair pulling, and biting.[18]

All this violence concerned many religious leaders, but nothing perplexed them more than the increase in liquor drinking (and doubtless the two were related). It is hard for us to fathom just how much alcohol Americans drank. The statistics are astounding. According to Gordon Wood, "American consumption of distilled spirits" increased "from two and a half gallons per person per year in 1790 to almost five gallons in 1820—an amount nearly triple today's consumption and greater than that of every major European nation at that time." Stills appeared all over, seemingly overnight. Farmers found they could make more money and more easily ship whiskey than grain. "Distilling whiskey was good business because, to the astonishment of foreigners, nearly all Americans—men, women, children, and sometimes even babies—drank whiskey all day long." Workers often drank from morning until night, and people even drank in the courts, where "a bottle of liquor might be passed among the attorneys, spectators, clients, and the judge and jury."[19]

Before this time, most Christians had no problem with moderate drinking, but the huge increase in alcohol consumption alarmed churches and ignited a crusade for temperance that expanded throughout the nation and crossed social, cultural, and racial lines. The temperance movement did more than discourage drinking; it also encouraged Christians to go further in exerting their influence on society. If Christians, primarily evangelicals, could slay the alcohol monster, who knew what other social ills they could vanquish? Faith-based societies popped up everywhere, soliciting (and getting) volunteers to wage war against poverty, mental illness, biblical illiteracy, prostitution, and especially slavery—all creating a "Benevolent Empire" that changed history.

Although Christians in these movements overcame great obstacles and made some positive changes in society, they often carried with them some destructive ideas. Many believed that it was the "manifest destiny" of the United States to transform the continent into God's new chosen nation, which meant a Protestant nation, led by whites.[20]

Leaders of evangelicalism's explosion into social reform included Charles Finney, who advocated temperance and opposed slavery, yet also others, including the famous Beecher family. Lyman Beecher (1775–1863), who had studied with Timothy Dwight at Yale, was the family's patriarch. Born into a family of farming and blacksmithing in Connecticut, Lyman served pastorates from Long Island to Boston to Cincinnati. He latched on to a socially oriented gospel that never divorced spirituality from social results. As he put it, "The great aim of the Christian Church in its relation to the present life is not only to renew the individual man, but also to reform human society."[21]

Perhaps Beecher's greatest influence on history came through his marriage to Roxana Foote, a schoolteacher who focused on educating girls, an effort that ushered in huge results at home. The Beecher children included Harriet Beecher Stowe (a bestselling novelist whom we will examine later), Isabella Beecher Hooker (who fought for suffrage), Catharine Beecher (a writer and advocate for women's education), and Henry Ward Beecher (1813–87), who became the nation's most famous preacher.[22]

The Beecher family proved that Christianity could influence the nation even if that nation did not officially endorse a church. In 1818, when Connecticut was one of the last states to cast away its established church, Lyman

Beecher worried about the future of Christianity in America. Yet he came to see that Christianity could prosper when separated from state endorsement. All religion would be voluntary religion, with no tax support, no official endorsement of the state. During this period voluntary religion exploded like state-supported churches never had. Revivals and voluntary societies that promoted causes like temperance propelled evangelical Christianity through the nation with an intensity that few could have forecast.[23]

Just as the Beechers exemplified social reform, so did they also represent a troubling side of Protestantism: its strong anti-Catholicism. Lyman Beecher published a popular anti-Catholic sermon, *A Plea for the West*, in which he called Catholicism "the most skillful, powerful, dreadful system of corruption to those who wield it and of debasement and slavery to those who live under it, which ever spread darkness and desolation over the earth." Likewise his son Edward published *The Papal Conspiracy Exposed and Protestantism Defended in the Light of Reason, History, and Scripture*.[24]

It was a difficult time to be Catholic or Jewish in the United States: Protestants ruled religious life in many ways because of their numbers and their social influence. Massive immigration in the nineteenth century would change the religious landscape, but immigrant Catholics and Jews quickly recognized the difficulties they would face in this Protestant-dominated land.

Denominations on the Move

Protestants dominated religious life in the United States because evangelical movements grew dramatically in the nineteenth century. No denomination expanded as quickly as the Methodists, who had surged past their reputation as anti-American Tories (in part because founder John Wesley published against the Revolution). In England, the Methodists had not officially formed a church but were a society that functioned within the Church of England. This was a tense issue since the Methodist societies started to act like churches, and many who attended preferred the Methodist society meetings to services in the Church of England. Yet both John Wesley and his brother Charles, the great hymn writer, remained within the Anglican Church.

In America, however, Methodists understandably wanted to separate themselves from the Church of England in these postrevolutionary times. In the 1784 "Christmas Conference," held in Baltimore, Methodists crafted a denomination well suited to thrive in the new nation.

The secret to Methodist success was something like an evangelical pony express: circuit rider preachers who traveled endless miles on horseback, weighed down with few possessions, and inspired with a laser-sharp focus on spreading the gospel far and wide, covering nearly every isolated outpost of the frontier. Backwoods preacher Peter Cartwright (1785–1872) was right: "A Methodist preacher in those days, when he felt that God had called him to preach, instead of hunting up a college or Biblical institute, hunted up a hard pony of a horse," and took little besides a Bible and a book of hymns as he rode "through storms of wind, hail, snow, and rain; climbed hills and mountains, traversed valleys, plunged through swamps, swam swollen streams, lay out all night, wet, weary, and hungry, held his horse by the bridle all night, or tied him to a limb, slept with his saddle blanket for a bed, his saddle or saddle-bags for his pillow, and his old big coat or blanket, if he had any, for a covering."[25]

Intellectuals they were not, for the most part, but their self-sacrificial devotion yielded results. As Cartwright wrote, "literary gentlemen" may have called Methodists "ignorant babblers," and educated Presbyterians may have looked down their noses at them, but "illiterate Methodist preachers actually set the world on fire (the American world at least) while" other denominations "were lighting their matches!"[26]

If the Methodist circuit rider was, as Daniel Walker Howe writes, "a Christian Lone Ranger" and "among America's most heroic western frontiersmen," much of the credit goes to Francis Asbury (1745–1816). Born to a working-class family in England, Asbury never forgot how to relate to common people, a skill that proved invaluable after John Wesley sent him to America in 1771.[27]

As the driving force of Methodism in the United States, Asbury was a bishop who redefined the role. He threw off any claim that Methodists, even bishops, should be elitist power brokers, sitting comfortably in wealthy parishes and cities. Instead, Asbury set the example as a self-sacrificing bishop, a circuit rider who put all others to shame.

Asbury served for 45 years, spending much of that time on horseback, traveling a minimum of 130,000 miles, refusing to either marry or buy a home. In his constant traveling, Asbury set the example for a network of circuit-rider preachers. This Methodist "method" of preachers on traveling circuits, which Wesley engineered in England, Asbury perfected in America, finding it the perfect mechanism for covering the huge landscape and far-flung American population.

Even Asbury could not have anticipated how successful the system would be in growing the Methodist movement in America from fewer than 1,000 members when he arrived in 1771 to over 200,000 when he died 45 years later. But the Methodists were just getting started. Circuit-rider preachers innovated with Wesley's system of "classes," in which clusters of people in a local area would worship and support one another without requiring a minister to be present. Methodists also led in the Sunday school movement and in establishing institutions such as Asbury College, founded in Baltimore in 1816. Although Methodism started in England, it became ethnically diverse fairly early in America. Two denominations founded by

Americans from Germany, the United Brethren in Christ and the Evangelical Association, eventually joined the Methodists. By the midpoint of the nineteenth century, there were over one million Methodists of various types in the United States, double the adherents of the next largest denomination, the Baptists.[28]

Although they could not keep pace with the Methodists in the first half of the nineteenth century, Baptists also grew dramatically, reaching about 600,000 members by 1850.[29] Like Methodists, Baptists embraced revivals from the start. The First Great Awakening in the 1700s had propelled the Baptist movement from New England through the South. Unlike Methodists, who baptized infants, Baptists embraced believer's baptism. This voluntary church membership, requiring people to decide to join the church rather than being born into it, fit well with the nation's ethos of individual freedom and self-reliance. Like Methodists, Baptists did not require an educated clergy, so they opened the way for ordinary people to receive ordination and preach. While Methodists employed circuit rider preachers, the typical Baptist minister was the "farmer-preacher," a bi-vocational minister who had secular employment and preached for little or no money. While Methodists grew through an elaborate system of preaching circuits and class meetings, Baptists benefited from a congregationalist polity, which freed each congregation to run its own affairs. Any group of Baptists could covenant together and form a church, with no interference from a bishop, synod, or other authority. Baptists did form denominations, mainly geared toward missions, and Baptist churches joined local "associations" that oversaw various parts of Baptist life. Yet neither denominations nor associations had any control over individual congregations. Most Baptists guarded local church autonomy as a sacred right.[30]

Baptists often claimed that their church was the closest to the form of the New Testament church. Baptists not only claimed to be the most biblical denomination, but also the most American because of their belief in religious freedom and local church autonomy. Some Baptists took these views to extremes. In the context of religious rivalries in the nineteenth century, a Baptist movement called Landmarkism emerged in the old southwest, centering in Tennessee under the leadership of James Robinson Graves (1820–93), a preacher and journalist. Baptists, Graves claimed, were not only the most biblical church, but the Baptist church was *in* the Bible. The Baptist church had all the major "landmarks" of the New Testament church, especially believer's baptism, and Baptists had endured all through history up to modern times, although they had gone by different names.[31]

The rivalry between Baptists and Methodists sometimes grew heated, almost coming to blows. James Robinson Graves launched a major attack on Methodists with his massive book *The Great Iron Wheel: or, Republicanism Backwards and Christianity Reversed* (1855). The "great iron wheel" was a metaphor a Methodist had used to describe the many interconnected parts of the Methodist bureaucracy, including bishops, elders, deacons, presiding elders, and circuits. Graves seized this metaphor to attack Methodism as a mysterious and interconnected system that worked to deceive the public. He posed the Methodist system as anti-American, closer to Catholicism than Protestantism. Graves dedicated the book "To every American who loves our free institutions and scorns to be degraded or enslaved in church or state," and he described himself as one who had a "love of republicanism, in civil and ecclesiastical government." The Methodist church was no true church, Graves argued, because it could not be traced back to the New Testament church. Instead, John Wesley invented it "in the days of George III." Instead of being rooted in Scripture, Methodism owed its character to Roman Catholicism, Graves said; this was a sharp attack in the largely anti-Catholic United States. Methodism, he wrote, is "the Popery of Protestantism" and "as absolute and all-controlling as Jesuitism."[32]

Striking back at Graves was William G. Brownlow, a Tennessee Methodist and editor of the *Knoxville Whig*, in his *The Great Iron Wheel Examined: or, Its False Spokes Extracted* (1856). Brownlow, who later sided with the North in the Civil War and was appointed governor of Tennessee, held nothing back in his counterattack on Graves. This Nashville Baptist had gone too far in unfair attacks and fabrications against the Methodist Church, Brownlow believed. It was only fair, Brownlow wrote, that "I take the slanderer by the throat, and drag him forth from his hiding-place, and shake him naked over hell, in all his deformity!"[33]

One of the key issues in the debate between Graves and Brownlow was "primitivism." Which denomination, they asked, was most faithful to the primitive pattern set by the first churches, founded by the apostles, and recorded in the New Testament? Primitivism was an American Protestant tradition that extended all the way to the Puritans' arrival in Massachusetts in the 1600s. One of the key points of Puritanism was an attempt to "purify" the Church of England from any non-biblical teachings and practices, an attempt to restore Christianity to its pure, primitive form as described in Scripture.[34] That desire for primitivism became a trademark of American Protestantism, which is why J. R. Graves was so adamant to prove that the Baptist church most closely resembled the New Testament church, while the Methodists had adopted a watered-down version of Catholicism.

Other Protestant groups shared this zeal for primitivism, and several movements are called *restoration* movements precisely because they attempted to restore the original form of the New Testament church. If they could restore the church of the New Testament, they could prove their superiority to all other denominations and help Americans share in the faith that Jesus intended. Because they were sick of denominational rivalries that developed over the years, these restoration movements would simply call themselves "Christians."

Since many folks were thinking along the same lines, restoration movements appeared in various regions, independent of each other. Some groups started out in North Carolina, others in New England, and they cooperated in 1820, calling themselves the "Christian Connection." Farther west, Presbyterian Barton Stone, who led the Cane Ridge camp meeting revival, was alienated from the Kentucky Synod by 1803, and by the next year he had started a union of churches called simply "Christians." Stone had had enough of denominational bureaucracies, doctrines, and creeds; he preferred the Bible alone to be his guide.

Stone had identified something widely appreciated. Less than thirty years later about ten thousand of Stone's "Christians" were distributed throughout the Ohio River Valley. Meanwhile, another restoration movement had taken hold in Pennsylvania, led by other Presbyterians, Scots-Irish pastor Thomas Campbell (1763–1854) and his son, Alexander Campbell (1788–1866). Alexander took the lead in the movement and expanded it. Calling themselves the "Disciples of Christ," they grew rapidly throughout much of the South and Midwest. Campbell's group joined forces with Stone's Christians in 1832, and they took the name of Campbell's group, "Disciples of Christ." Like Baptists, they jealously guarded their local church autonomy, and they attracted many Baptists to their fold, along with Methodists. Eventually they expanded and subdivided into several denominations, including Churches of Christ.[35]

The Rise of Independent African American Churches

Evangelicals, although controversial and despised by many, spread like a prairie fire and along the way did something no other form of Christianity had been able to do: convert African Americans in large numbers. From the beginning, Christianity was a tough sell for most Africans in the Americas because they first encountered Christianity as a slaveholding religion. The nations that captured and enslaved them were predominantly Christian nations, and yet so-called Christian masters enslaved and brutalized Africans.

Contrary to what many slaveholders claimed, Africans had their own religious traditions: they lived within a variety of traditional religions in West Africa. Although there was much diversity among these religions, they often shared a belief in one supreme god, along with various lesser deities and spirits that remained engaged with the everyday world. To cite one prominent example, the Yoruba people, who lived in Nigeria and other areas, called their ultimate god Olodumare, a deity who entrusted much interaction with humans to other gods, collectively called "orisha," but there are many further examples from other religious traditions. African religions typically held great reverence for ancestors, believing they still held power in this life, and in spirit possession.[36]

The variety of traditional African religions made it hard for Africans to continue practicing their religions under slavery, since they were surrounded by Africans from other cultures. This was just one of many impediments to the practice of traditional African religions in the Americas, many of which were deliberately put in their way by slaveholders, who despised African religious practices. Despite slaveholders' attempts to wipe out African religions, they endured, at least in part, although scholars have debated just how much of traditional African religions and cultures survived the slave system. Most recent historians concede that much from these traditional religions was lost, but much remained, transformed under slavery and accommodated to Christianity in many cases. For example, after slaveholders forbade enslaved people from drumming, they adapted similar practices instead, including call-and-response singing and clapping.[37]

The heavily Catholic population in the Caribbean opened avenues for an amalgamation of African and Catholic religions. In the vaudou, or voodoo, tradition, for example, deities from African religions converged with saints from Roman Catholicism, enabling enslaved people to practice their traditional African faiths while seeming to practice Catholicism. Syncretism, or mixing of religious elements, was common in many African religions, so this convergence of religious elements from different traditions was nothing new for enslaved people.[38]

It was a different situation in the United States, where Protestantism dominated and Protestants had no use for saints or the rituals of Catholicism. Yet the Great Awakening opened new pathways for Africans to respond positively to Christianity. Revival-based religion depended less on memorizing doctrines, creeds, and catechisms and more on a personal response to God's offer of grace. As historian Albert Raboteau states, "The camp meeting proved to be a powerful instrument for accelerating the pace of slave conversions." Revivalism, with its focus on individual conversion, "fostered an inclusiveness which could border on egalitarianism."[39]

Theological education was not that important for evangelicals, and many Baptist and Methodist preachers had little or no education themselves. What mattered most was the influence of the Holy Spirit on the heart, transforming the soul, often in an emotional response to a revival service. African Americans, many of them enslaved, could resonate with evangelicalism because it valued spirit over formal learning. "The plain doctrine and heavy emotion of revivalist sermons," Raboteau observed, "appealed as much to the black slave as to the white farmer."[40] The evangelical teaching that the Holy Spirit dwelled within the Christian appeared to be similar to African religions' belief in spirit possession. In the ring shout and other rituals, African Americans adapted the rituals of traditional African religions to the theology of evangelicalism, calling on the Holy Spirit rather than the spirits of traditional African deities.[41]

In Baptist and Methodist churches, white leaders sometimes allowed African Americans to worship with them, but they were usually separated from whites either through seating areas such as galleries or separate services for black attendees. As more African Americans converted to Christianity, the number of black preachers grew. Many of them were enslaved and preached to other enslaved people, often as part of the "invisible institution," the informal church that developed without the knowledge and control of whites. Some black preachers received permission to preach to whites, and eventually independent African American churches were formed, most often under white supervision. Baptists led the way, freed up by the fact that their churches were independent and locally controlled, with no bishop or synod to rule over them.

Likely the first independent African American church was a Baptist congregation formed in Silver Bluff, South Carolina, just before the Revolutionary War (ca. 1773–75). This was not just the first church; it also was an influential church. From Silver Bluff, which sat just on the South Carolina side of the Savannah River, Baptists traveled throughout the region, baptizing and forming new communities.

The church began when a white preacher converted several enslaved people, including David George and Jesse Galphin, who then took leadership of the congregation. As the church was growing in its first few years, the British occupied the area, causing some to flee while others took up with the British. After the British ceded the region to the Americans, several enslaved people believed they would need to leave to gain their freedom. David George headed north, finally settling in Nova Scotia, and founded another Baptist church nearby. Meanwhile George Liele, another preacher and longtime friend of David George, left for Jamaica, where he founded the first Baptist church in Kingston. Taking the lead at Silver Bluff was Jesse Galphin. The church grew so quickly that its members decided to expand by planting the First African Baptist Church in Augusta, Georgia.[42]

Meanwhile, near Savannah, whites and African Americans were gathering to hear the preaching of Andrew Bryan, who had been converted by George Liele. Local whites, many of whom were angry to see enslaved people depart, believed Bryan and his brother, Sampson, were troublemakers. They and around fifty other African Americans were imprisoned and whipped. Bryan, while bleeding profusely from his lashes, told authorities that he would gladly endure whippings, and even death, if Jesus called him to do so. Likely embarrassed by their barbaric treatment of Bryan and others, officials released them and allowed them to worship during daylight only.

Bryan went on to lead a successful congregation at the First African Baptist Church in Savannah, where his church grew to 225 members by 1790. Within two decades there were three African Baptist churches in the area.

This fit the pattern of many African American churches throughout the South: they began under white leadership but grew once African American ministers took control, or at least some measure of it. They also faced repeated cycles of endorsement and persecution from whites, who increasingly saw them as a threat to slavery.[43]

The numbers tell the story: the majority of African Americans who converted to Christianity became evangelicals, and most of them were Baptist or Methodist. By 1820, approximately 20 percent of Methodists were African Americans, many of whom joined Methodist churches after hearing circuit-rider preachers.[44] No Methodist minister exerted more influence on African Americans than Richard Allen (1760–1831), who was born into slavery in Delaware. A Methodist circuit rider led him in converting to Christianity and to Methodism at age seventeen.

Although many slaveholders forbade enslaved people from attending worship services, Allen's master, Stokeley Sturgis, encouraged him and his family to attend services. They were careful to make sure their work was

FIGURE 8-2. Richard Allen and other bishops of the African Methodist Episcopal Church, LC-DIG-pga-03643 (Library of Congress)

done so that whites in the area could not argue that they neglected their duties. Their master noticed. As Allen reported, "Our master said he was convinced that religion made slaves better and not worse, and often boasted of his slaves for their honesty and industry." Allen's ministry began there: he persuaded Sturgis to allow Methodist preachers to hold services on the property, services that later converted Sturgis himself. Perhaps convicted that slavery was sinful, Sturgis allowed Allen to purchase his freedom, which he did in 1783.[45]

Not long afterward, Allen followed his calling to be a traveling preacher, eventually settling at Old St. George's Methodist Church in Philadelphia. Allen took Methodism seriously. In his view, the Methodist church was the best church for African Americans. Not only did Methodist founder John Wesley publish against slavery, but the early Methodists also seemed to follow his lead, condemning slavery in strong terms. As Allen reflected: "The Methodists were the first people that brought glad tidings to the coloured people. I feel thankful that ever I heard a Methodist preach. We are beholden to the Methodists, under God, for the light of the Gospel we enjoy; for all other denominations preached so high-flown that we were not able to comprehend their doctrine. Sure am I that reading sermons will never prove so beneficial to the coloured people as spiritual or extempore preaching. I am well convinced that the Methodist has proved beneficial to thousands and ten times thousands."[46]

At first, it seemed that the Methodists would live up to their promise for African Americans. When the Methodists founded an American church in 1784, they declared that one could not own enslaved people and receive Communion in the church. Slavery, it seemed, had no place in the Methodist Church. Yet even from the beginning, Richard Allen was not so sure that Methodists would stay true to their liberating convictions. The problem, as he saw it, was that white Methodists had their first taste of respectability, and they liked it. Commenting on the Christmas Conference of 1784, Allen wrote: "This was the beginning of the Episcopal Church amongst the Methodists. Many of the ministers were set apart in holy orders at this Conference, and were said to be entitled to the gown; and I have thought religion has been declining in the church ever since. There was a pamphlet published by some person which stated that when the Methodists were no people, then they were a people; and now they have become a people, they were no people, which had often serious weight upon my mind."[47]

White Methodists quickly made it clear that African Americans, if they had a place in white churches at all, would be second-class citizens at best. Allen saw this change in Methodist identity firsthand. At Old St. George's Church, Allen, Absalom Jones, and other African Americans were accosted while praying, literally pulled up while they were kneeling, because they were in an area where whites wanted to sit.[48] Allen, Jones, and others knew from that day forward that white-controlled churches would not be hospitable to them; they needed their own worship space. But what denomination would it be?

The incident at St. George's gave them every reason to reject the Methodists, as Jones and many others in the group wanted to do. But not Allen. Despite the mistreatment, Allen said: "We were in favour of being attached to the Methodist connexion; for I was confident that . . . no religious sect or denomination would suit the capacity of the coloured people as well as the Methodist; for the plain and simple gospel suits best for any people, for the unlearned can understand, and the learned are sure to understand; and the reason that the Methodist is so successful in the awakening and conversion of the coloured people, the plain doctrine and having a good discipline."[49]

Two major churches in Philadelphia started out of this rupture at St. George's: the St. Thomas Protestant Episcopal Church, where Absalom Jones became rector; and Bethel African Methodist Episcopal Church, where Richard Allen became pastor.

Allen's commitment to Methodism never wavered, but his connection with the Methodist Episcopal Church did. He cut ties with the denomination in 1801 and started a new denomination in 1816: The African Methodist Episcopal (AME) Church, the nation's first African American denomination. In his view, this was more than a Methodist church controlled by African Americans; it was an authentic Methodist church, a church that would remain committed to Methodist principles that he believed the white Methodists had compromised: Gospel preaching for all, regardless of race or social condition, the vision he found essential to true Wesleyanism.[50]

Women in the Pulpit

Allen became a stickler for Methodist discipline, to the point that he informed female preacher Jarena Lee (1783–1864) in 1809, "As to women preaching, . . . our Discipline knew nothing at all about it. . . . It did not call for women preachers." That did not stop Lee, however. Born free in Cape May, New Jersey, Lee had been converted under Methodist preaching and felt her own call to preach, which she pursued, preaching wherever and whenever she could. By 1817 she had changed Allen's mind and received his authorization. Allen, by then the first bishop of the AME Church, had heard and seen Lee preach, and he was so impressed that he issued an invitation for her to attend the annual conference meeting. Richard and Sarah Allen also cared for Lee's son when she would go on the road to preach.[51]

Jarena Lee not only preached; she also wrote and published an account of her life and ministry, making her one of the few women evangelists who left a written account of her activities.[52] Her *Religious Experience and Journal of*

FIGURE 8-3. Jarena Lee. Lithograph by P. S. Duval, from life by A. Huffy, Wikimedia Commons

Mrs. Jarena Lee, Giving an Account of Her Call to Preach the Gospel, as the title indicated, was an argument to defend her choice to preach the gospel.[53] Lee read the experience of her calling in light of the prophet Jonah. As Catherine Brekus notes, "By anchoring her narrative in scriptural precedent, [Lee] tried to weave her personal story into the fabric of sacred history, grafting her life onto the Bible. Jonah's story was as timeless as the Bible itself, and according to Lee, it was being recapitulated in her own life. Female preachers quoted so extensively from the Bible that it is sometimes hard to tell which of the words are uniquely their own."[54]

In many ways, Lee's account of her spiritual life resembled that of other evangelicals—it began with strong conviction for sin, often leading to a severe depressed state before the Holy Spirit restored them to faith and assurance of God's mercy. This could be a tumultuous ordeal. Lee's despair over her state was so severe that she went to a nearby brook and considered drowning herself. It seemed "some one" (almost certainly Satan) encouraged her to kill herself, "saying put your head under, it will not distress you." Only "the unseen arm of God," Lee wrote, "saved me from self-murder." Yet still her despair had not lifted entirely. As she contemplated her soul, she lived for a time with a Catholic family, who took a dim view of her Bible reading—fitting the popular stereotype among Protestants that Catholics forbade individuals from reading the Scripture for themselves. As Lee reported, a woman in the Catholic family "took the Bible from me and hid it, giving me a novel in its stead," which Lee "refused to read." Finally, Lee tried a white Methodist church, which she did not appreciate. Just as she had despaired of Methodism along with Catholicism, she heard Richard Allen preach, who convinced her "that this is the people to which my heart unites." Three weeks later she experienced true conversion under Allen's preaching.[55]

But conversion was not the end of the journey for Lee. She, like most Methodists, looked also for sanctification, which for many Methodists meant "perfection," a doctrine with many meanings that aroused much controversy. Perfection, for John Wesley, had not meant that one was free from all sin, but that one had a perfect love for God and one's neighbor. That doctrine had a different meaning for Finney, and Methodist Phoebe Palmer later transformed its meaning even more fully in ways that influenced holiness and pentecostal movements later in the century and beyond.

JARENA LEE AND THE FIRST STIRRINGS OF WOMEN IN THE PULPIT

For Jarena Lee, perfection came as a sudden infusion of God's Spirit. While praying, she heard a voice telling her to "pray for sanctification." When she did, "That very instant, as if lightning had darted through me, I sprang to my feet, and cried, 'The Lord has sanctified my soul!'" No other person witnessed this, except for "the angels who stood around to witness my joy—and Satan, whose malice raged the more."

Lee's calling to preach came in another voice, telling her, "Go preach the Gospel!" She mistook this voice for Satan until she prayed to God, who gave her a vision of a Bible on a pulpit. Lee was not alone. As the early nineteenth century brought new ideas of freedom, with people questioning authority at every turn, female preachers in larger numbers started trusting their call to preach and acting on it, regardless of any obstacles placed in their paths. Not only Methodists, but also the Christian movements, Freewill Baptists, and others started opening up their pulpits to women.*

*See Jarena Lee, *Religious Experience and Journal of Mrs. Jarena Lee, Giving an Account of Her Call to Preach the Gospel* (Philadelphia: Published for the Author, 1849), 10–11.

In the previous century, the few women who dared to preach often admitted that their female identity was a problem, and they saw the need to argue for an exception to normal rules, in a sense to apologize for their gender before taking the pulpit. But the early nineteenth century brought a shift: no longer did female preachers see their gender as a weakness. Now they called on biblical women—like Deborah, the mighty warrior in the book of Judges; and Phoebe, mentioned by Paul in the book of Romans—and used them to justify their calling to the pulpit.[56]

Although the number of women preachers increased, it was still rare to see a woman preach. Typically, women rarely stepped into the pulpit, although they dominated in the pews, outnumbering men by a significant margin in American history.[57] Even so, following the American Revolution women gained more of a public voice. This was partly because women were joining and even leading many voluntary societies and benevolent agencies for causes, such as temperance.

In part because of this increased activity in public, Americans started thinking of women as superior to men, more virtuous and more religious. This was a shift. Prior to the revolutionary era, women had a reputation as the weaker sex, both physically and morally, thus more corruptible than men and more morally suspect. This way of thinking was evident in the male-dominated Western Christian tradition, appearing everywhere from sermons to Milton's *Paradise Lost*, where Satan (disguised as the serpent) tempted Eve because she was an easier target than Adam. This started to change in the nineteenth century, when women gained a more virtuous and religious reputation. In fact, the meaning of the word "virtue" shifted: from masculine connotations during the revolutionary period, when it meant self-denying courage and martial strength; to more feminine connotations in the early 1800s, when it came to mean benevolence and devotion. Yet this shift did not give women more status in society, especially political status. In fact, the largely patriarchal society that called women more virtuous than men used that as a reason for marginalizing them.[58]

The groups that gave women the most chances to preach were most often evangelical churches that prided themselves on their separation from the rest of society, the fallen "world" and its corruptions. One way to demonstrate their separation from the world was to support the lowly, including the poor and women, those whom God favored but society treated as outcasts. There was also an apocalyptic angle to this appeal. Many evangelicals were on the lookout for signs of the end times, when Christ would return and inaugurate his millennial rule. Some reasoned that God was pulling out all the stops to convert the world before it was too late, even empowering women and enslaved people to preach. Evangelicals quoted the prophet Joel (2:28), "I will pour out my spirit upon all flesh; and your sons and your daughters shall prophesy, your old men shall dream dreams, your young men shall see visions." Millennial times called for prophetic measures, including female preaching.[59] That was not the norm, however, as larger Protestant denominations barred women from the pulpit. The women who had the courage and opportunity to preach battled the dominant, male-dominated structures of most forms of Christianity in the United States.[60]

New Religions and Latter-Day Revelations

After the First Amendment cast aside religious establishments, declaring that no denomination would receive official support from the national government, upstart religious groups saw themselves competing on a level playing field with older denominations. Denominational rivalries erupted, as we saw in the heated exchange between Baptist J. R. Graves and Methodist William Brownlow. Beyond squabbles between Baptists and Methodists, other denominations argued over infant baptism, predestination, free will, and more. Universalists, who claimed that eventually all people would be saved, caught fire from Baptists, Methodists, and others. Presbyterians and Episcopalians looked aghast at both Baptists and Methodists for their emotional and often undignified worship styles, the very features that accounted for their appeal with many Americans.

Even with all these squabbles and some significant differences, Protestant groups had a lot in common. In contrast with these groups, many new religious movements burst onto the scene in the nineteenth century. These movements were not completely new: most of them innovated with existing forms of Christianity. Yet they often set themselves apart with practices and ideas that appeared bizarre and even dangerous to more traditional Christians. These new religious movements expected criticism, even persecution, because they openly criticized parts of American society that they opposed.[61]

DIVERSITY AND CONFLICT IN NEW RELIGIOUS MOVEMENTS

New religious movements flourished in part because rapid changes in American society left many questions unanswered. In this land of liberty, would the traditional place of women in society change? What about marriage and gender roles for men and women? What was the best way for people to live together in society? Should people be divided by class, race, wealth, or gender? What was the point of society anyway? There were diverse and conflicting opinions on these questions and more, and religious debate and discord stirred anxiety, leaving Americans to ask, "How do we know which religion is true?" Most people had little room for shades of doubt when it came to religion. Truth was universal, not divided, and neither was God. Chances were that one version of Christianity had it right and all others were more or less wrong, perhaps deadly wrong, a prospect that had dire consequences for people in the pews. Choose the wrong religious belief, and one could wind up in hell, despite all good intentions and faithful attendance at what they thought was a godly church. A lot of Americans were looking for evidence to prove which religious views were authentic.*

*See Jeremy Rapport, "New Religious Movements: Nineteenth Century," *ERA* 3.

Members of the new religious movement led by a young man named Joseph Smith believed they had the best proof of the authenticity of their beliefs. They did not simply have a new perspective on the Bible; they had a new Bible, the Book of Mormon, a written account of God's revelation that backed their claim to be *the* true church. At a time when preachers proliferated, Smith was no preacher; he was a prophet, and a young one at that, in his midtwenties when he dug up a collection of golden plates in upstate New York. This region had earned the name "burned-over district" because it had been scorched by so many preachers warning about hellfire, and also because so many new religious movements sprang up from it. Folks there had seen a lot of unusual religious ideas pop up, but they had never seen anything like Joseph Smith.[62]

He called the golden plates the "Plates of Mormon" because Mormon was the name of the prophet who, Smith said, had written on them in the 300s. Mormon was part author, part editor, and thanks to him the plates contained a new scripture that Joseph translated from "Reformed Egyptian" to English and published as the Book of Mormon. When it was printed, the Book of Mormon looked a lot like the Bible. It was long, but at about six hundred pages, it was not as long as the Bible. Readers found that the Book of Mormon's phrasings and vocabulary resembled the King James Bible, and so did its descriptions of ancient peoples and sacred history.

But the Book of Mormon moved beyond the Bible, focusing on ancient peoples who left biblical lands and moved to America about six hundred years before Christ's birth. The main patriarch of these peoples was a man named Lehi, and the narrative focused on the families of his sons, Laman and Nehi, who fought a war against each other, a war the Lamanites won. These Lamanites struggled, and their descendants may have lived on as Native Americans. (Many people at the time wondered where the Native Americans had come from, and there was much speculation that they descended from Israel's "Ten Lost Tribes.") Mormon, one of the last surviving Nephites, wrote and edited this history and other records and recorded them on the golden plates. Moroni, his son, finished the work and buried them. Hundreds of years later, Moroni materialized as an angel to Joseph Smith, showed him where to find the plates, and announced that Joseph had been selected to reveal God's new plan to the people of America.[63]

Americans who first encountered the Book of Mormon found a fascinating mix of Old Testament–like history with a New Testament–like concentration on Jesus Christ, together with a regional focus on the Americas. As the Book of Mormon gives the story, Jesus came to the Americas after his resurrection, revealed himself to the Nephite people, and showed them his crucifixion wounds to prove it was really he. Jesus then proclaimed the Nephites to be God's chosen people, the authentic remnant from the Israelites.[64]

The Book of Mormon is filled with these kinds of bold scenes and striking claims; it is a massive, authoritative book that purports to fulfill, correct, and extend the biblical record. As historian Daniel Walker Howe describes, "True or not, the Book of Mormon is a powerful epic written on a grand scale with a host of characters, a narrative of human struggle and conflict, of divine intervention, heroic good and atrocious evil, of prophecy, morality, and law." Howe further states that "the Book of Mormon should rank among the great achievements of American literature, but it has never been accorded the status it deserves," mainly because "non-Mormons, dismissing the work as a fraud, have been more likely to ridicule than read it."[65]

The message of Joseph Smith, like that of many other religious zealots of the time, was a millennial message filled with anxiety and hope at the expectation of Christ's imminent second coming. Smith's people were "Latter-day Saints," charged with an urgent message for America. But Smith as a prophet exceeded preachers who drew their message from the Bible because he claimed to be bringing new information from God—a claim that shocked Christians who traditionally believed that revelation had stopped with the biblical writers. There was no new revelation outside of the Bible, they thought. And yet here was young Joseph Smith, who had the audacity to try proving otherwise.

Smith was an unlikely prophet, however. Born in Vermont in 1805, Smith's life was altered by the preliminary trembling and pyroclastic flows (from April 5, 1815) and then massive eruption of the Mount Tambora volcano in Indonesia on April 10, 1815—an eruption far more devastating than the 1980 eruption of Mount St. Helens. The explosion spewed sulfuric gases that blocked the sun's rays enough to lower the earth's temperature, an effect that helped to cause unusual weather activity. New Englanders saw snowfall in July and August, and South Carolinians saw frost in the middle of May. Crops failed, food ran short, and panic gripped farmers, causing speculation that the end of the world was near. It was this desperation that led Joseph Smith's family to move from Vermont to western New York in 1816.[66]

As Joseph Smith relayed it, his visits from the angel Moroni started in 1823, directing him to uncover the golden plates at the nearby Hill Cumorah, the site of the last battle between the Lamanites and Nephites. By 1827 Smith had the plates in his hands and was busy translating them with the help of seer-stones. By 1830, the Book of Mormon was in print. Not surprisingly, this new scripture aroused suspicion and attack, especially from other Bible believers who had their own views about how the world would end. Alexander Campbell, leader of his own movement to restore true Christianity, published *Delusions: An Analysis of the Book of Mormon* (1831); in it he called Joseph Smith "as ignorant and as impudent a knave as ever wrote a book," and he called the Book of Mormon an "impious fraud," among other insults. Campbell also accused Smith of making up solutions to current problems and questions: "This prophet Smith" wrote about "every error and almost every truth discussed in N. York for the last ten years. He decides all the great controversies—infant baptism, ordination, the trinity, regeneration," and more.[67]

Attacks like this multiplied, ridiculing Smith and his "new" scripture. But perhaps the old adage is true—there is no such thing as bad publicity—because scores of people joined Smith in his quest for a new path led by new revelation. By the time Campbell had called out Smith for his fraudulent faith, over two hundred Latter-day Saints were calling him God's prophet. Smith kept up his communications with God, resulting in new scriptures, including the *Doctrine and Covenants.*

Smith and his followers were in Kirtland, Ohio, by 1831, where their numbers had increased to about 2,000, with another 2,000 members elsewhere. Most of Smith's members came from New England Puritan stock, where folks were used to sermons about millennialism and Old Testament Israel's importance as a political pattern for the present. In all, Latter-day Saints drew members from a diverse cross-section of society. Many of them, like Smith, were looking for some authoritative evidence that made one religious community stand out from the many rivaling denominations.[68]

Like so many people in this rapidly changing society, the Latter-day Saints kept moving. By 1831 Smith and Sidney Rigdon, a convert to Mormonism from another millennial group, picked the site for a major temple in Missouri. When the situation for Mormons deteriorated in Ohio, with Smith beleaguered by financial problems, he and some 600 followers moved to Missouri. The situation was even worse in Missouri, a frontier territory where vigilante justice ruled and settlers lashed out against Mormon invaders until they finally expelled most of them. Mormons next moved to an area named Nauvoo, located along the Mississippi River in Illinois. Led by Smith, the Saints built there a huge temple large enough to hold 3,500 individuals.

No matter where the Mormons moved, controversy followed. In Nauvoo, the movement grew so large that the population nearly equaled that of Chicago, which made the Mormons even bigger targets for their enemies. In addition to the Book of Mormon, which continued to draw fire from other Christians, the Saints added several controversial doctrines, including baptism for the dead and "plural marriage," modeled on the polygamous practices in the Old Testament. Saints did not go public with plural marriage until the early 1850s, but Joseph Smith dictated a revelation endorsing it on July 12, 1842. Joseph Smith's wife, Emma Smith, was not happy with a revelation from God that gave permission for her husband to marry other women. Soon another revelation addressed this issue, commanding Emma Smith to "receive all those that have been given unto my servant Joseph, and who are virtuous and pure before me." Emma Smith was also commanded to remain faithful to Joseph as her only husband and threatened that "if she will not abide this commandment[,] she shall be destroyed, saith the Lord."[69]

Added to concerns about the Mormons' unusual beliefs and new scripture, many Americans worried that the Latter-day Saints were trying to build a "theocracy," which would enforce Mormon beliefs with civil power, perhaps even rivaling the United States. The situation escalated when the Saints called out a militia to defend themselves, which many saw as a hostile act. In 1844, Smith was charged with treason, and he and his brother Hyrum were jailed for attacking the office of the newspaper that had been critical of them. Before they could be released, a mob stormed into the jail and murdered them.[70]

Smith's death dealt a severe blow to the Saints, especially since he had left no clear instructions about who should succeed him. Most Saints accepted Brigham Young as their leader and moved farther west, finally settling in Utah. Yet several groups splintered off, and by 1860 one large group settled on Smith's son Joseph Smith III as their leader, calling themselves the Reorganized Church of Jesus Christ of Latter-day Saints. This group, which rejected some of Mormonism's more controversial ideas, such as plural marriage, never came close to the membership numbers of the main group under Young's leadership.

Although the Latter-day Saints were the largest and most enduring of the new religious movements that emerged during this period, others posed equally serious challenges to mainstream American society. Some were "communal movements," comprised of people who lived apart from the rest of society, in part to separate themselves from the temptations of "the world" and in part to show Americans how they should be organizing themselves. There were many such movements, and one of the earlier ones was the United Society of Believers in Christ's Second Appearing, often called the Shakers, who arrived in Albany, New York, in 1774.

Like the Quaker movement, to which they were related, the Shakers got their name from their ritualistic dancing. They were led by Ann Lee, whom they considered a prophet. They were also primitivists, like many Protestants, but taught that restoring the original Christian faith meant accepting that God had a dual nature, with both masculine and feminine perspectives, and that Ann Lee spoke for God. All sexual relations were sinful, Shakers taught, and men and women had equal status. Outsiders called them radicals who sought to undermine the traditional family. The Shaker village system worked, however, leading to commercial success in furniture manufacturing.[71]

Manufacturing was also a feature of the Oneida movement. Today when people think of "Oneida," they often think of flatware, but the history behind the expertly crafted spoons and forks is a utopian movement centered in upstate New York. Like so many religious folks in the period, including Finney and others we have discussed, the founders of the Oneida movement were seeking some form of the perfect life. The driving vision for Oneida came from John Humphrey Noyes (1811–86), a minister who graduated from Dartmouth and attended Yale and Andover. Like so many during these years, he was interested in Christ's second coming; but unlike most, he believed it had already occurred. So, Christians did not need to wait for Christ to return to achieve perfection; they could be perfect now. Preaching these ideas cost Noyes his ministerial credentials, but he rebounded by starting a society in Vermont composed of people who vowed to live by his principles that, if followed, would lead to a perfect society.[72]

Like others who formed new religious movements, including Joseph Smith and the Shakers, Noyes's ideas for a perfect society involved a new vision for sexual relationships. The Shakers demanded celibacy; Joseph Smith adopted plural marriage, allowing men to wed multiple women, but not allowing women to wed multiple men. In contrast, Noyes adopted "complex marriage," which allowed men and women in the community to have sexual relations with each other without the typical restrictions of monogamous marriage. Noyes was concerned with overpopulation, so he wanted procreation to be scientifically controlled through a method of birth control called "male continence," which he described in graphic detail in a book of the same title. Noyes recognized that abortion was commonly practiced, but he called it a "terrible deed."[73]

Noyes organized his group of "Bible Communists" in Vermont with two goals: first, "to develop the religion of the New Covenant and establish union with God"; and second, to establish "a new state of society by developing the true theory of sexual morality."[74] Not surprisingly, Noyes's community aroused opposition from its neighbors, so they had to leave Vermont and settled in Oneida, New York, in 1848. There the community expanded its experimentation with male continence as they expanded commercial ventures, especially production of flatware.[75]

The rapid changes in this new nation of promise led Americans to focus on the future, where they saw visions of success, both personally and nationally, but also warning signs of catastrophe and judgment if they went astray. They knew their Bible more than any other book, and they wrestled with some of its more confusing texts, including apocalyptic writings, especially the book of Revelation. With its bizarre symbols and visions of horrible beasts and bloody images of judgment, Revelation gave Americans a confusing and ominous anxiety about the end of the world and Christ's millennial rule.

Questions came from everywhere. Some, called "premillennialists," believed Christ's second advent, or second coming, would occur *before* the millennium (the 1,000-year reign of Christ that they saw predicted in Revelation 20 and elsewhere in Scripture). They expected world events to become worse as Satan gained more power over the world; finally Christ would come and take his people to glory. Others, "postmillenialists," believed things would improve as Christ gained more and more power over Satan, and Christ would not return until his millennial reign was over. Some pondered whether the United States was one of the signs of the millennium soon to begin or already in progress. These labels are helpful, but Americans' views of the end of the world were not always so tidy. Often confusion reigned, and people held a mixture of premillennial and postmillennial views.

If someone could predict exactly when Christ would return to earth, that would be valuable information. Some tried their hand at it, most famously William Miller (1782–1849), a Baptist farmer-preacher who lived in Low Hampton, New York. Using a calculation of various numbers from Scripture—which were as plentiful in apocalyptic texts as beasts with scary horns—Miller computed that Christ would return to earth on October 22, 1844. Miller's followers, known as "Millerites," responded by kicking aside anything that tied them to this world: houses, businesses, farms, and more. They put on "ascension robes" and waited for the greatest moment in history to arrive. October 22, 1844, did arrive as expected, but Jesus did not. Afterward, people referred to that day as "the Great Disappointment," but Miller's followers and others did not remain disappointed for long. They continued to calculate biblical figures and set future dates, thereby giving birth to Adventism, one of the most prominent themes in American religious history.

Arising from this movement were the Seventh-day Adventists, who admitted that while Jesus did not return physically on October 22, 1844, he did begin important work in heaven on that day, work that would lead to a later return to earth. While some Americans scoffed at Adventists after the Great Disappointment, others found in it renewed enthusiasm for prophetic visions, like those of Ellen G. White, who turned much of her attention to advice on health. She took her point of departure from Genesis 1:29: "God said, 'Behold, I have given you every herb bearing seed, which is upon the face of all the earth, and every tree, in the which is the fruit of a tree yielding seed; to you it shall be for meat.'" Her pronouncements about diet—advocating vegetarianism and forbidding alcohol, tobacco, tea, and coffee—had a substantial influence in American history. Inspired by the idea that one could not separate spiritual vitality from physical health, she helped found the Battle Creek Sanitarium in Battle Creek, Michigan, which became an example that similar institutions followed. White attracted the attention of John Harvey Kellogg, who moved to Battle Creek to learn more from her. Through her influence, the teenaged Kellogg became a leader in the church and editor of their magazine, *The Health Reformer*. The Adventist zeal for spirituality and nutrition inspired his research into breakfast cereals.[76]

The connection between health and religion was as old as religion itself. In the New Testament, Jesus healed the sick, fed the hungry (sometimes by miraculous means), and even raised the dead. The nineteenth century combined the rise of scientific knowledge, including medical research, with a strong Protestant culture; naturally, increasing numbers of Americans wanted to understand how medical science related to God's healing activity in the world. This connection would only grow in American history, giving birth to several new religious movements, as we will see in later chapters.

This chapter has described a dizzying array of religious movements that surged through the United States as the nation was coming to terms with its new identity on a vast continent. These years saw the expansion of evangelicalism, with Methodists and Baptists exploding in growth to the point that they almost dominated the American religious landscape—almost, but not quite. New religious movements appeared, so many that it was difficult for people at the time to keep track of them. Many such disappeared as quickly as they had appeared, but others staked a solid claim with a clear identity that attracted adherents for the long term. Like evangelicals, these new religious movements took advantage of the freedom the nation allowed to innovate with religion, even advancing new theories and radical new practices. Though many Americans despised this religious innovation, they often could do nothing about it. There was too much land and too many places for groups to move, allowing them to keep to themselves when that was needed.

During this time of religious experimentation and denominational rivalries, a key issue was authority. How could one prove authenticity? What evidence would convince others of the veracity of a church, a prophet, or a revelation? With no legally established churches declaring the final word on religious authority, the final word was often found in the Word, the Bible. It was the one book most read and most owned by Americans, many of whom owned few books. This confidence in Scripture never went uncontested, but it would encounter a fully blown crisis in coming years, with challenges from new historical methodologies for interpreting Scripture, new scientific theories of creation, and most tragically the crisis over slavery, which Americans failed to solve despite countless appeals to their most sacred text.

9. *Slavery and the Civil War*

The Civil War (1861–65) was the most catastrophic war in American history: over 700,000 Americans died. Through all the devastation, Americans looked to God and the Bible for support and consolation. For both the Union and the Confederacy, it was a sacred war, and slavery was at the center of it. Although various issues surrounded the war, including states' rights and loyalty to the Union, the main cause was the conflict over slavery. Nobody knew this better than Abraham Lincoln. In his Second Inaugural Address, delivered near the end of the war, he said it clearly: "Slaves constituted a peculiar and powerful interest. *All knew that this interest was somehow the cause of the war.*"[1]

Most Americans agreed that slavery was inseparable from religion. Some called it God's blessing, destined to enrich the South and to bring the gospel to "heathen" Africans; others called slavery the nation's curse, a diabolical institution that offended God and made a mockery of the nation's claim to be a land of liberty. Americans divided over slavery; they claimed God's endorsement for their views, transforming them into sacred convictions worth fighting (and dying) for by the hundreds of thousands. American views of religion, violence, and the nation's mission would never be the same.

Slavery and the Nation's Founding

As we have seen, the American Revolution tragically failed to abolish slavery. A new nation that claimed to be based on the principles of human equality and natural rights supported the enslavement of human beings. Recognizing this glaring contradiction, several prominent founders claimed that slavery was on the road to extinction. For much of the founding era, slavery was the elephant in the room—constantly thought about, sometimes complained about, but ignored whenever possible. The Constitution said nothing about freeing enslaved people, and it protected the slave trade until 1808. This was a relief for the founders, who wanted to put off the issue and let future leaders deal with it. Besides, many consoled themselves with the idea that slavery would die away on its own, so they did not want to argue about it. Best to wait until after 1808, when the nation would no longer participate in the international slave trade, and surely the end of slavery in the nation would follow.[2]

If the founders thought the issue was settled, they were wrong. This became clear on February 11, 1790, when Congress discussed two petitions to end the slave trade, presented by delegations of Quakers from Philadelphia and New York. These Quakers knew that the new Constitution had protected the slave trade until 1808, but that was not good enough for them: trading in enslaved people needed to end immediately. James Jackson, a congressman from Georgia, was immediately suspicious. This was not just about the slave trade, he said; it was a part of a menacing scheme to end slavery altogether. "Ridiculous," responded James Madison. If Jackson would just keep quiet about it, the petitions could be forwarded to a committee and dealt with quietly, never to be heard from again.[3]

Everything changed one day later, when the Congress received another petition, presented by the Pennsylvania Society for Promoting the Abolition of Slavery. As the name "abolition" indicated, this petition was not just about ending the slave trade; it called for "the abolition of slavery." This petition asserted that the "blessings of liberty" should "rightfully to be administered, without distinction of Colour, to all descriptions of People." The petitioners urged that the Congress and the Senate find a way to eliminate "this Inconsistency from the Character of the American People, that you will promote Mercy and Justice towards this distressed Race."[4]

This petition may have been dismissed as quickly as the other two but for one important reason: it came bearing the signature of the president of this abolition society, Benjamin Franklin, who was a legend in his own time, an American hero with irrefutable patriotic credentials. Congress had no choice but to give the petition due consideration.[5]

It was difficult to argue with a petition signed by "Dr. Franklin," but Southern representatives would attack abolitionist ideas with all their might, no matter who stood behind them. As the conversation grew heated, Representative Jackson of Georgia attempted to counter Franklin with God, turning to the Bible and religious arguments, claiming that God had endorsed slavery, and so should the nation. From there on the debate ensued, involving issues such as God's will, and economic necessity, the Constitution, legal restrictions, and practical necessities. They reached an impasse. In the following month, Congress deliberated on both the petition and a committee report on it, a discussion that featured one of the most extensive defenses of slavery and white supremacy ever made public, exhaustively presented by representatives from the Deep South, especially from Representative Jackson.[6]

Jackson's religious case for slavery made an impression, and it made the newspapers, but Benjamin Franklin was not done yet. Literally on his deathbed, Franklin published a parody of Jackson's speech, using the arguments Jackson made to enslave Africans as a model for similar arguments to enslave white Christians, published by a fictional Muslim from Algeria, Sidi

Mehemet Ibrahim. Northern newspapers widely reprinted Franklin's satire, and Southern newspapers ignored it. Franklin died three weeks later.[7]

Despite Franklin's endorsement, the petition failed in Congress. Even some of the founders who had negative things to say about slavery feared that legislation against slavery would throw the new nation into chaos. While Congress feared acting on emancipation because of its volatility, Benjamin Franklin feared putting off action against slavery, and he turned out to be correct. By failing to abolish slavery at the nation's formation, the founders put the United States on a path to civil war.[8]

The Expansion of Slavery

The founders made a tragic mistake by assuming that slavery would die a natural death. Far from it, as slavery was on the cusp of an expansion. This was another example of how technology helped to change history. As we see today with the Internet, smartphones, and social media, so too in early America new technology changed history as well, and never more dramatically than with the invention of the cotton engine (often called the "cotton gin") in 1793.

Developed by Eli Whitney (1765–1825), a Yale graduate who hailed from Massachusetts, the cotton gin expedited the painstaking task of removing seeds from cotton. The cotton gin made cotton production more efficient and more profitable. A little over a decade after Whitney's invention hit the market, production of cotton in Southern states skyrocketed, and the increase in cotton production increased the demand for enslaved people. While the North invested in transportation (including canals), industry, and banks, the South invested mostly in slavery.[9]

Religious Attacks on Slavery before the Civil War

The more that slavery expanded, the more Northerners commented on the contradiction represented in a nation of liberty that endorsed slaveholding. Opponents of slavery blasted this contradiction, and they often did so by claiming that slaveholding contradicted both the Declaration of Independence and the Bible.

One striking example came from David Walker, a free African American who published the *Appeal . . . to the Coloured Citizens of the World, but in Particular, and Very Expressly, to Those of the United States of America*.[10] This book struck like a lightning bolt from the press in 1829; it advocated violent attacks on slavery, a message that alarmed and enraged many Southern whites. "Have not the Americans the Bible in their hands?" Walker asserted. "Do they believe it? Surely they do not. See how they treat us in open violation of the Bible!!" It was obvious to Walker that slavery desecrated one of Scripture's central precepts, the Golden Rule: "All things whatsoever ye would that men should do unto you, do ye even so unto them" (Matthew 7:12). Despite this clear teaching, pro-slavery clergy ignored this teaching, and "an American minister, with the Bible in his hand, holds us and our children in the most abject slavery and wretchedness. Now I ask them, Would they like for us to hold them and their children in abject slavery and wretchedness?"[11]

Not only did Scripture oppose slavery; it also opposed racism, Walker argued. "How can the preachers and people of America believe the Bible? Does it teach them any distinction on account of a man's colour?" It did not, and this explained why slaveholders did not want enslaved people to learn how to read. "I cannot but think upon Christian Americans!!!—What Kind of people can they be?" As Walker wrote, "The whites have always been an unjust, jealous, unmerciful, avaricious and blood-thirsty set of beings, always seeking after power and authority."[12]

These were radical words, Walker knew, especially coming from a black American. But these were also words based on the nation's founding. As Walker wrote, "The Americans do their very best to keep my Brethren from receiving and reading my 'Appeal' for fear they will find in it an extract which I made from their Declaration of Independence, which says, 'We hold these truths to be self-evident, that all men are created equal.'"[13] Just as slavery violated the Declaration and contradicted the nation's supposed purpose as a nation of liberty, so did slavery violate Christianity and expose the hypocrisy of so-called ministers of the gospel who supported slavery.

DAVID WALKER: GOD'S JUDGEMENT ON SLAVERY

"What the American preachers can think of us, I aver this day before my God, I have never been able to define. They have newspapers and monthly periodicals, which they receive in continual succession, but on the pages of which, you will scarcely ever find a paragraph respecting slavery, which is ten thousand times more injurious to this country than all the other evils put together; and which will be the final overthrow of its government, unless something is very speedily done; for their cup is nearly full.—Perhaps they will laugh at or make light of this; but I tell you Americans! that unless you speedily alter your course, *you* and your *Country are gone!!!!!!* For God Almighty will tear up the very face of the earth!!!"*

*David Walker, *Walker's Appeal, in Four Articles* (Boston: David Walker, 1830), 44–45 (italics original).

Walker's uncompromising denunciation of slavery horrified and enraged many white Southerners, to the point that a price was put on his head.

Within a year after he published his *Appeal*, Walker was found dead. Reportedly there was no clear evidence of murder, but the timing was suspicious, to say the least.

A colleague of Walker's in Boston, Maria Stewart, became one of the first African American women to publish on political issues. She also worked with William Lloyd Garrison, one of the nation's most famous white abolitionists and publisher of *The Liberator*, the well-known abolitionist newspaper.

Like Walker, Stewart warned the nation about the consequences of slavery, insisting that both the nation's founding and Scripture opposed slavery. God "hath made all men free and equal," she said, paraphrasing the Declaration of Independence. As she wrote: "O, America, foul and indelible is thy stain! Dark and dismal is the cloud that hangs over thee for thy cruel wrongs . . . to the fallen sons of Africa. The blood of her murdered ones cries to heaven for vengeance against thee."[14]

David Walker, Maria Stewart, and many others employed religious language to warn America of the judgment and violence to come if the nation did not abandon slavery. Others, like Nat Turner, used such prophetic denunciations of slavery to make that judgment real, inciting violent attacks on slavery. When Turner planned a slave revolt (in Southampton County, Virginia) that would be the bloodiest and the most famous in American history, he claimed to be acting on a calling from God.[15]

All we know of Turner's thoughts comes from *The Confessions of Nat Turner*, written by Thomas R. Gray, a white lawyer who interrogated Turner while he was awaiting execution. Admittedly, this account may contain almost as many of Gray's thoughts as Turner's, but it is the best source historians have, and there is little doubt that it provides valuable insights into Turner's perspective.[16] Apparently Turner believed that God had commanded him to fight a war against slavery. Turner's descriptions of his visions echoed several biblical passages:

> I had a vision—and I saw white spirits and black spirits engaged in battle, and the sun was darkened—the thunder rolled in the Heavens, and blood flowed in streams—and I heard a voice saying, "Such is your luck, such you are called to see, and let it come rough or smooth, you must surely bare it." I now withdrew myself as much as my situation would permit, from the intercourse of my fellow servants, for the avowed purpose of serving the Spirit more fully—and it appeared to me, and reminded me of the things it had already shown me, and that it would then reveal to me the knowledge of the elements, the revolution of the planets, the operation of tides, and changes of the seasons. After this revelation in the year 1825, and the knowledge of the elements being made known to me, I sought more than ever to obtain true holiness before the great day of judgment should appear, and then I began to receive the true knowledge of faith. And from the first steps of righteousness until the last, was I made perfect; and the Holy Ghost

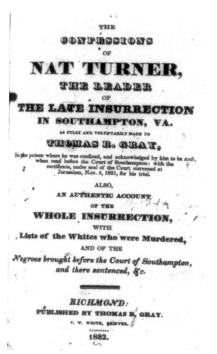

was with me, and said, "Behold me as I stand in the Heavens"—and I looked and saw the forms of men in different attitudes—and there were lights in the sky to which the children of darkness gave other names than what they really were—for they were the lights of the Saviour's hands, stretched forth from east to west, even as they were extended on the cross on Calvary for the redemption of sinners. And I wondered greatly at these miracles, and prayed to be informed of a certainty of the meaning thereof—and shortly afterwards, while laboring in the field, I discovered drops of blood on the corn as though it were dew from heaven—and I communicated it to many, both white and black, in the neighborhood—and I then found on the leaves in the woods hieroglyphic characters, and numbers, with the forms of men in different attitudes, portrayed in blood, and representing the figures I had seen before in the heavens. And now the Holy Ghost had revealed itself to me, and made plain the miracles it had shown me—For as the blood of Christ had been shed on this earth, and had ascended to heaven for the salvation of sinners, and was now returning to earth again in the form of dew—and as the leaves on the trees bore the impression of the figures I had seen in the heavens, it was plain to me that the Saviour was about to lay down the yoke he had borne for the sins of men, and the great day of judgment was at hand. . . . And on the 12th of May, 1828, I heard a loud noise in the heavens, and the Spirit instantly appeared to me and said the Serpent was loosened, and Christ had laid down the yoke he had borne for the sins of men, and that I should take it on and fight against the Serpent, for the time was fast approaching when the first should be last and the last should be first.[17]

For two days, Nat Turner and over sixty followers terrorized the countryside, killing fifty-seven people and beheading several of them. After Turner and his men were captured, white mobs retaliated by killing innocent blacks, many of whom they decapitated and mounted their heads on posts. Turner hid from authorities for over a month before his capture at the end of October 1831. Shortly before his execution, Thomas Gray asked Turner what he thought of his failed revolt. Turner replied, "Was not Christ crucified?"[18]

Divided Denominations and a Divided Bible

News of Nat Turner's revolt swept the nation. In the North, it helped to inspire abolitionists to work even harder to oppose slavery. In the South, the revolt enraged slaveholders and helped to motivate them to ramp up their defenses of slaveholding. A perfect storm was gathering. In times of trouble, Americans were used to looking to their ministers for divine wisdom, but now they looked on as their clergy disagreed over slavery just as fervently as had their politicians.

It was an ominous sign when the major Protestant denominations divided. Slavery was at the base of the Presbyterian divisions in 1837 and 1857, and slavery was the major cause when the Methodist Episcopal Church split along regional lines in 1844, and when the Baptists did the same in 1845. White Southerners in both denominations pulled away from Northern bodies: Methodists to establish the Methodist Episcopal Church, South; and Baptists to create the Southern Baptist Convention. Some Americans commented that this was a sign of a civil war to come.[19]

ONE BIBLE, BUT TWO WAYS TO READ IT

Not only did churches fail to heal the divisions between North and South; they also made the controversy worse. Both pro-slavery and anti-slavery ministers argued that God was on their side in the dispute, so both sides called theirs a holy cause, and they enlisted the Bible to support their positions. By the middle of the 1800s, the Bible was America's most read and most owned book, and Americans overall believed that it was the Word of God, the highest written authority on earth. Yet even this authority seemed divided over slavery.*

*See James P. Byrd, *A Holy Baptism of Fire and Blood: The Bible and the American Civil War* (New York: Oxford University Press, 2021) and Mark Noll, *The Civil War as a Theological Crisis* (Chapel Hill: University of North Carolina Press, 2006).

The same year that Baptists split into Northern and Southern factions (1845), two white Baptists published a debate over the Bible's word for America on slavery. No two men were more capable to hold up each end of the debate: Richard Fuller was a prominent minister in South Carolina, while Francis Wayland was president of Brown University. A look at this debate gives us a good overview of the main biblical issues at stake in countless arguments for and against slavery.

In his defense of slavery, Fuller pointed to the many references to slavery in the Bible. "The Old Testament did sanction slavery," Fuller wrote, and "in the Gospels and Epistles" of the New Testament "the institution" of slavery "is, to say the least, tolerated."[20]

In his response, Wayland dismissed any argument for slavery from the Old Testament, because these ancient Hebrew Scriptures endorsed many practices, including polygamy, that the New Testament prohibited. Turning to the New Testament, Wayland said that Jesus and his apostles opposed slavery "by promulgating such truths" that render "the slavery of a human being a manifest moral absurdity." Wayland cited Paul's statement from Acts: God "hath made of one blood all nations of men for to dwell on all the face of the earth" (17:26a). All people shared "the same nature, as we are all the children of one common parent." Regardless of physical differences, all shared a "*common nature.*" All had a right to hear the gospel, to receive the blessing of conversion, for all had immortal souls, crafted in God's image.[21]

Then Wayland quoted Jesus: "Thou shalt love thy neighbor as thyself" (Matthew 22:39). How could anyone obey this command and enslave another human? Also, did not slavery violate the Golden Rule? "Whatsoever ye would that men should do unto you, do ye even so unto them" (Matthew 7:12). According to the New Testament, therefore, slavery "is wrong, . . . a great moral evil. Can we conceive of any greater?"[22]

Fuller responded: If all this were true, why did neither Jesus nor his apostles *specifically* call out slavery as a sin? Why did they never demand that all enslaved people be set free? And why did the apostles discuss slavery and give advice to both enslaved people and slaveholders? These were sharp questions, and Fuller and other supporters of slavery posed them often.

Wayland had a response ready: It would not have worked for Jesus and his apostles to demand emancipation at that time because slavery was too embedded in Roman society. Direct attacks on slavery would have been dismissed out of hand, so preparatory work needed to be done before slavery could be successfully attacked. Jesus knew this, and he was well aware that slavery "could only be abolished by a change in the public mind, by inculcating those principles," including the Golden Rule, "which would show the whole community that [slavery] was wrong, and induce them, from a general conviction of its moral evil, to abandon it." By teaching these principles, Jesus and the apostles set the stage for slavery's demise.[23]

Fuller thought this was ridiculous. Neither Jesus nor his apostles would have neglected to condemn slavery because of "expediency," believing it was not the right time or place to speak against it. Since when did either Jesus or Paul neglect to call out sins for fear that people would reject their hard teachings? Both Jesus and the apostles condemned all other sins, large and small, and did so with a vengeance. And yet they breathed not "even a whisper against slavery, through fear of consequences!!"[24]

Fuller admitted that slavery could be a cruel institution, but he denied that slavery *had* to be cruel. Slavery, he wrote, was nothing more or less than requiring enslaved persons to work without their "consent" and without a "contract." All the cruelties that went along with slavery—including some that existed at the time of the apostles, such as torturing and starving enslaved people—were surely abhorrent to God, but these abuses were not necessary to slavery, Fuller claimed. Enslaved people were "property," Fuller noted, but he observed that there were many kinds of property, and property in a person was distinct from property in a chair or a horse, for example. Enslaved people were human beings, and "the slave has his rights, many of which are protected by our laws, and all by the Bible." Enslaved people should not be degraded "to the state of a chattel."[25]

Fuller's claims bore no resemblance to slavery in the real world, Wayland said. Slavery was *always* cruel. The definition that Fuller espoused, that slavery was *only* the demand for the enslaved person's labor without contract or consent, required brutality. If the master had a right to the enslaved person's labor without consent, then the master had "the right to use all the means necessary both to enforce and to render it permanent." So many of the evils of slavery existed to force enslaved people to work without their consent.[26]

Fuller and Wayland battled to a draw, neither Baptist convincing the other. Fuller's position fit with the literalistic way many Americans read the Bible. Fuller insisted that slavery was in both Testaments and that neither Jesus nor his apostles *specifically* condemned slavery. He cited chapter and verse, pointing to all the places where Scripture mentioned slavery. By contrast, Wayland could not cite specific texts that attacked slavery. Instead, he pointed to the Golden Rule and other texts that taught moral principles, such as "Love they neighbor," and drew the logical conclusion that these principles were inconsistent with slavery.[27]

The strength of Fuller's argument was its literalism: he could cite specific texts that supported slavery. The strength of Wayland's argument was its moral force: he challenged supporters of slavery to explain how one could enslave others and still be obedient to the Golden Rule and other moral commands of Scripture. The debates over the Bible and slavery introduced many Americans to doubts about the Bible's authority and its historical validity well before they had heard of higher criticism or the theory of evolution.[28]

"What to the Slave Is the Fourth of July?"

A year after Fuller and Wayland saw Baptists separate into Northern and Southern factions, the nation entered a controversial war with Mexico (1846–48). The United States won the war, but victory proved bitter. The nation acquired from Mexico vast territories: present-day Texas north of the Rio Grande, along with lands that later comprised much of California, New Mexico, Arizona, Utah, and Nevada. New territories meant new arguments. Would these new lands be open to slavery?[29]

After much wrangling on both sides, a deal was made: the "Compromise of 1850." This agreement included an updated Fugitive Slave Act, which passed into law on September 18, 1850, and made it the business of the federal government to capture any fugitive slaves and return them to slavery, even if they were in a free state. Now it was more dangerous than ever to be black in the United States. Slaveholders could falsely claim that free black people were escaped slaves. Once arrested, African Americans could not testify to defend themselves in court, nor could they show evidence they had been beaten or raped. Those who ran the Underground Railroad, helping fugitives to escape slavery, stood in more jeopardy than ever.[30]

The Fugitive Slave Act outraged many Northerners who wanted nothing to do with slavery. It also enraged abolitionists and inspired an upsurge of antislavery sentiment. Most influential was Harriet Beecher Stowe's *Uncle Tom's Cabin: or, Life among the Lowly*, the best-selling novel that, as James McPherson wrote, was "the most influential indictment of slavery of all time."[31] *Uncle Tom's Cabin* convinced thousands of Northern whites that slavery offended God's "higher law" of justice, no matter what the Constitution or other human laws said. As Frederick Douglass (1818–95) stated, "The touching, but too truthful tale of *Uncle Tom's Cabin*" aroused the emotions of many "who before cared nothing for the bleeding slave."[32]

Douglass was already famous when he wrote these words. Born in Maryland, Douglass escaped slavery and earned renown as a leading abolitionist, speaker, and best-selling author. Because of his publications, photographs, and speeches, Douglass was internationally famous.[33] In his religious views, Douglass distinguished between the corrupt, "slaveholding religion of this land" and "the Christianity of Christ," which opposed slavery and all injustice.[34]

FIGURE 9-2. Frederick Douglass, 1876, LC-DIG-ppmsca-56175 (Library of Congress)

FIGURE 9-3. Harriet Beecher Stowe, engraved by A. H. Ritchie, LC-DIG-ppmsca-49809 (Library of Congress)

SLAVERY AND PROPHETIC OUTRAGE

Frederick Douglass was never more prophetic than in a speech from 1852, titled "What to the Slave Is the Fourth of July?"* "What have I, or those I represent, to do with your national independence?" The nation's founding, especially its "principles of political freedom and of natural justice" had no relevance to blacks, Douglass proclaimed. "This Fourth of July is yours, not mine." So-called "Independence Day" was a farce. Douglass vented his outrage, "in the name of liberty which is fettered, in the name of the constitution and the Bible which are disregarded and trampled upon." Both the Bible and the nation's founding document thus contradicted slavery. "The existence of slavery in this country brands your republicanism as a sham, your humanity as a base pretense, and your Christianity as a lie."†

*D. H. Dilbeck, *Frederick Douglass: America's Prophet*, 1st ed. (Chapel Hill: University of North Carolina Press, 2018), Introduction. David W. Blight, *Frederick Douglass: Prophet of Freedom* (New York: Simon & Schuster, 2018), 229–31. †Frederick Douglass, *Great Speeches by Frederick Douglass*, ed. James Daley, Green ed., Dover Thrift Editions (Mineola, NY: Dover Publications, 2013), 32–34, 43–44.

**A War of
Providence
and Patriotism**

Abraham Lincoln's election to the presidency in 1860 divided the nation—literally. By the time of Lincoln's inauguration in 1861, already seven states had seceded from the United States (South Carolina, Mississippi, Florida, Alabama, Georgia, Louisiana, and Texas), and they had done so because Lincoln was the first President representing the Republican Party, which was widely known as the antislavery party. Although Lincoln was no radical abolitionist, it was no secret that he despised slavery. And a nation without slavery was a nation many white Southerners could not tolerate.[35]

As countless white Southerners saw it, they had no choice but to secede: they had had been forced into secession by a tyrannical and abolitionist government that was anti-God and anti-Bible. As the secessionist crisis expanded, white Southern ministers joined in the argument for slavery and secession based on white supremacy. Reverend James C. Furman, the first president of Furman University, published a racist letter with several colleagues, asserting, "The negro is not your equal, unless the Bible be untrue."[36] They also attacked the idea stated in the Declaration of Independence, "that every man is born free and equal." This idea "contradicts common sense, contradicts all history, contradicts the Bible."[37] Furman's was just one of many such racist claims.

When the Confederates started the war by firing on Fort Sumter in April 1861, Protestants dominated the American religious landscape. The nation had about 50,000 Protestant churches—an amazingly high figure when we consider that there were only about 77 Jewish synagogues or temples and only about 2,500 Catholic churches.[38] We have seen how important evangelicalism was to African Americans in the mid-nineteenth century. By the beginning of the war, there were about 450,000 enslaved Christians, the majority either Baptist or Methodist.[39]

Faith could comfort soldiers on the battlefield. It helped to think that they were under the care of God's providence, that their lives had purpose, and so did their deaths. This faith in Providence assured people that the world was not spinning out of control, that God was at the helm, supervising and directing everything that happened. God used wars to change the world—socially, politically, culturally, and more. Wars destroyed kingdoms and nations, and wars lifted them up. It was no wonder that people seemed more attentive to God's providence in wartime.[40]

When thinking about the war and Providence, Christians in the United States often called their nation special, chosen by God, seeing parallels with ancient Israel, God's chosen nation in the Hebrew Scriptures. Since the dramatic victory in the Revolutionary War, many Americans had believed their nation was providential, protected by God, chosen for a divine purpose.[41]

Emancipation

The American Civil War lasted for four devastating years, beginning in April 1861 and raging onward until April 1865. Many of the battles fought remain sealed in the nation's memory. Although here we cannot examine them all, we should not neglect the war's bloodiest *day*: September 17, 1862. The Battle of Antietam raged near Sharpsburg, Maryland, resulting in a staggering death toll: almost 6,000 dead, in addition to about 17,000 wounded.[42]

Less than a week after Antietam, Lincoln decided that it was time for his Preliminary Emancipation Proclamation, which he issued on September 22, 1862. In it he announced that on January 1, 1863, "All persons held as slaves within any State, or designated part of a State, the people whereof shall then be in rebellion against the United States shall be then, thenceforward, and forever free." The United States would "recognize and maintain the freedom of such persons" bound in slavery.[43]

Once Lincoln signed it the following January, the Emancipation Proclamation transformed the nature of the war. From that point onward, Union success in the war would threaten slavery in the South.[44] Lincoln was not naive; he knew that many Northern whites cared little about slavery and certainly did not want to sacrifice their lives in a war for emancipation. To them, Lincoln replied that emancipation was a military strategy for winning the war. Emancipation was, as Lincoln said privately, "a military necessity, absolutely essential to the preservation of the Union. We must free the slaves or be ourselves subdued. The slaves were undeniably an element of strength to those who had their service, and we must decide whether that element should be with us or against us."[45]

The Emancipation Proclamation was certainly not perfect, and many have critiqued it from the time Lincoln announced it to today. Yet it was a major step in the fight against slavery. Frederick Douglass called the Emancipation Proclamation "the greatest event in our nation's history, if not the greatest event of the century." With this proclamation, the Union war effort would be much stronger and the Confederate effort much weaker.[46] The proclamation made the Union army an army of liberation, and this army was greatly strengthened by thousands of African American soldiers who joined the fight. By the end of the war, "blacks comprised about 10 percent of the Union armies and nearly one-quarter of naval enlistments."[47] By fighting in the war, African American troops struck a devastating blow against slavery.

Battles were not only on the battlefield, however, and one of the heroic figures was Harriet Tubman (ca. 1822–1913). Before the war she was well-known as a leader in the Underground Railroad, a clandestine and dangerous system by which enslaved people from the South were assisted in escaping to the Northern states. Known as "Black Moses" because she led so many enslaved people to freedom, Tubman spied and scouted

FIGURE 9-4. Portrait of Harriet Tubman, taken between 1871 and 1876 by Harvey B. Lindsley, LC-DIG-ppmsca-54232 (Library of Congress)

for the Union army during the war, and her heroics are documented on the Central Intelligence Agency website: "Tubman's contribution to the Union cause was significant. When Tubman died in 1913, she was honored with a full military funeral as a mark of respect for her activities during the war."[48]

Gettysburg

Americans were never so convinced of the sacredness of courageous sacrifice than after the battle at Gettysburg, Pennsylvania, fought during the first three days of July 1863. It was the war's bloodiest battle: an estimated 40,000 died or were wounded, a sacrifice commemorated by Lincoln's famous Gettysburg Address, delivered at the dedication of the Soldiers' National Cemetery.[49]

This was one of the most famous speeches in American history, and it featured several religious references:

Fourscore and seven years ago our fathers brought forth on this continent a new nation, conceived in liberty and dedicated to the proposition that all men are created equal. Now we are engaged in a great civil war, testing whether that nation or any nation so conceived and so dedicated can long endure. We are met on a great battlefield of that war. We have come to dedicate a portion of that field as a final resting-place for those who here gave their lives that that nation might live. It is altogether fitting and proper that we should do this. But in a larger sense, we cannot dedicate, we cannot consecrate, we cannot hallow this ground. The brave men, living and dead who struggled here, have consecrated it far above our poor power to add or detract. The world will little note nor long remember what we say here, but it can never forget what they did here. It is for us the living rather to be dedicated here to the unfinished work which they who fought here have thus far so nobly advanced. It is rather for us to be here dedicated to the great task remaining before us—that from these honored dead we take increased devotion to that cause for which they gave the last full measure of devotion—that we here highly resolve that these dead shall not have died in vain, that this nation under God shall have a new birth of freedom, and that government of the people, by the people, for the people shall not perish from the earth.[50]

In this famous speech, Lincoln used language that sounded like the King James Bible (fourscore and seven), which accentuated the sacred importance of the address. He also spoke of the soldiers' deaths as sacred sacrifices for the nation. Lincoln used religious words like "consecrate" and "hallow" to declare that this battlefield was holy ground. He also cited these sacred

FIGURE 9-5. Matthew B. Brady. *Print of a Brady Photograph of Lincoln.* United States Washington D.C. Washington, 1891. M. B. Rice, Washington D.C. Photograph. www.loc.gov/item/scsm000986/ (Library of Congress)

sacrifices to inspire those who were still fighting the war: "We here highly resolve that these dead shall not have died in vain; that this nation, under God, shall have a new birth of freedom; and that government of the people, by the people, for the people, shall not perish from the earth."[51]

"Both Read the Same Bible"	The Gettysburg Address was a great speech when a great speech was called for, and that was typical of Lincoln. Lincoln's Second Inaugural Address, delivered near the end of the war, was one of those great presidential speeches, just as it was one of the most insightful assessments of the war's meaning, more insightful in fact than that of most esteemed ministers and theologians of the day. As Frederick Douglass said, the Second Inaugural Address "sounded more like a sermon than a state paper."[52]

In one of his most profound statements, Lincoln noted that "both [North and South] read the same Bible and pray to the same God, and each invokes His aid against the other." Both sides fought for God, yet they fought and killed each other in God's name. Even though it appeared that the Union would win the war, Lincoln had no patience for celebration. This was a time to process the tragedy of the war, not a time for self-congratulation. Those in the North who hated slavery may have been horrified that white Southerners dared to "ask a just God" to endorse slavery. Yet Lincoln warned, "Let us judge not that we be not judged," quoting Jesus (Matthew 7:1). The North had no cause to be self-righteous because many white Northerners were complicit in slavery as well as white Southerners. Slavery was the nation's sin, not just the South's.[53]

Despite the attempts of both the Union and the Confederacy to claim that God was on their side, "the Almighty has His own purposes," Lincoln said, and perhaps God had used the war to punish both sides for slavery. The punishment would continue until God was satisfied: "If God wills that [the war] continue until all the wealth piled by the bondsman's two hundred and fifty years of unrequited toil shall be sunk, and until every drop of blood drawn with the lash shall be paid by another drawn with the sword, as was said three thousand years ago, so still it must be said[,] 'The judgments of the Lord are true and righteous altogether.'"[54]

Lincoln ended with words of reconciliation: "With malice toward none, with charity for all, with firmness in the right as God gives us to see the right, let us strive on to finish the work we are in, to bind up the nation's wounds, to care for him who shall have borne the battle and for his widow and his orphan, to do all which may achieve and cherish a just and lasting peace among ourselves and with all nations."[55]

This Second Inaugural Address has been one of the most famous and most scrutinized speeches in American history; historians have never tired

FIGURE 9-6. Abraham Lincoln delivering his Second Inaugural Address as President of the United States, Washington, D.C., March 1865, LC-DIG-ppmsca-23718 (Library of Congress)

of examining it. According to Mark Noll, the Second Inaugural Address was "a theological statement of rare insight." Specifically, "the contrast between the learned religious thinkers and Lincoln in how they interpreted the war poses the great theological puzzle of the Civil War." Lincoln had "propounded a thick, complex view of God's rule over the world and a morally nuanced picture of America's destiny" that put the sermons of most ministers to shame. For all their theological training, many of them could not see beyond their own agendas, which led them to proclaim that God was exclusively on their side.[56]

Jill Lepore had some great advice for newly elected presidents: "A good idea, before writing your presidential inaugural address, is to read everyone else's. Or, you could skip the rest, and just read Lincoln's."[57] The Second Inaugural proved her point. Yet, at the time, Lincoln's speech suffered from mixed reviews. The speech was "not immediately popular," as Lincoln put it, mostly because "men are not flattered by being shown that there has been a difference of purpose between the Almighty and them. To deny it, however, in this case, is to deny that there is a God governing the world. It is a truth which I thought needed to be told."[58]

The ultimate sacrifice at the end of this war of unprecedented death was the Lincoln assassination. Only five days after Confederate General Robert E. Lee surrendered at Appomattox, Virginia, John Wilkes Booth shot President Lincoln at Ford's Theatre in the nation's capital. For Christians, it was Holy Week, and Booth assassinated Lincoln on Good Friday. Northerners had been looking forward to an Easter Sunday celebration of the war's end. When the news of Lincoln's death came (most heard about it on Saturday afternoon), Northern ministers quickly scrapped the Easter sermons they had planned on preaching and turned their thoughts from celebration to mourning.

On that Easter Sunday as preachers honored Lincoln's legacy, they had to ask *why*. Why would God take Lincoln away, just as the war was won? Of all the war's sacrifices, this one seemed to hurt the most for many Americans. But, as the sacrifices of thousands of soldiers made the nation sacred, so did the assassination confirm Lincoln's status as a sacred leader. Preachers could find no better evidence than the fact that God allowed Booth to assassinate him on Good Friday. There could be no clearer comparison between Abraham Lincoln and Christ. God had aligned it providentially, many believed, and this image of Lincoln as a martyr president survived. Historians have never tired of studying Lincoln, examining his virtues and flaws, including his racism. In recent years both Democrats and Republicans have frequently tried to claim Lincoln's support for their positions on issues. He remains one of the most admired and most criticized presidents in American history.[59]

Civil War and Civil Religion

Lincoln's assassination, along with the unprecedented death of American soldiers on both sides in the war, convinced many Americans that there had to be some meaning in all this loss. "The Civil War was indeed the crimson baptism of our nationalism," Harry S. Stout argues. The war's "final great legacy" was "the incarnation of a national American civil religion."[60] The Civil War strengthened this belief for Americans on both sides of the fighting. Northerners gained confidence that God was on their side as they fought for the Union; meanwhile many white Southerners believed that they were God's people and that God stood with them even in defeat. The white, Southern brand of civil religion emerged in full strength after the war, as white Southerners struggled to cope with defeat. Despite their deep sense of loss, white Southerners often reaffirmed their belief that God had been on their side.[61] White Southerners celebrated their Confederate heroes and the Confederacy's sacred honor and white Southern culture as a "Lost Cause." Artifacts of white Southern civil religion exist in Confederate monuments, most of which were erected in the early twentieth century by the United Daughters of the Confederacy.

These remnants of the Civil War and their meaning for the nation provoked sharp debates into the twenty-first century. To many, the Confederate monuments and flag represented the violence of white supremacy in America, part of an effort to oppress any expansion of civil rights for African Americans. Debates on the issue included conflicting interpretations of the Civil War. Although the war has been over for more than 150 years, the war over the Civil War continues, and at its center are issues of justice, morality, and civil religion.

10. The Second American Revolution

Emancipation, Immigration, and Reckoning with Life and Death

Americans emerged from the Civil War as transformed as was the revolutionary generation. For the formerly enslaved freedmen, early hopes in Reconstruction were soon dashed, but the era was one of enormous religious importance for the growth of new black churches, schools, and colleges in the South. Elsewhere, Eastern cities and Western states were flooded with immigrants bringing new religious expressions to the American mix. Families who had lost members in America's bloodiest war turned from sentimental views of the good death and increasingly to spiritualist and related ideas for comfort.

On the night of December 31, 1862, the ministers and members of black churches throughout the Northern states gathered in anticipation for a "Watch Night" service. Since the Moravians had brought the practice of gathering in church from seven in the evening to midnight as an act of piety meant to renew one's covenant with God and John Wesley's Methodists had adopted and spread the practice, Americans had gathered for these nighttime services of worship and prayer. For black Christians, New Year's Eve 1862 took on a new significance. They were waiting in hope to see if President Abraham Lincoln's Emancipation Proclamation issued in September 1862 would actually go into effect, or whether some last-minute change would lead to disappointment. The Proclamation read, in part:

> That on the first day of January, in the year of our Lord one thousand eight hundred and sixty-three, all persons held as slaves within any State or designated part of a State, the people whereof shall then be in rebellion against the United States, shall be then, thenceforward, and forever free; and the Executive Government of the United States, including the military and naval authority thereof, will recognize and maintain the freedom of such persons, and will do no act or acts to repress such persons, or any of them, in any efforts they may make for their actual freedom.[1]

The apprehension that made this Watch Night unique was justified. On September 22, 1862, when Lincoln originally announced what was coming, he issued a preliminary warning that he would order the emancipation of all slaves in any state that did not end its rebellion against the Union by January 1, 1863. The Proclamation provided that all enslaved persons making it to Union lines in the South were free and that the men among them could enlist in the Army in the cause of their own freedom. Even though slavery in border states was unaffected by Lincoln's war order, the die was cast for freedom and against the option of return to the previous status quo, with some states free and others not free. To this day, Watch Night on New Year's Eve continues to be a major date of observance in black churches, and an early commemorative card is shown in figure 10-1.

As the Civil War came to a close, the war's cause—the "peculiar institution" of slavery—was coming to an end as well. In a short matter of months, some two and a half centuries of slavery on American soil was forever ended, and four million African Americans began to experience freedom under the law, most of them for the first time in their lives. From the vantage point of another 150 years later, we can see how momentous emancipation figured as a moral moment in the life of the nation. Consequences were substantial for the religious life of the newly freed people (called freedmen), together with already free persons of color, as we shall see. Addressing the immediate plight of the formerly enslaved could have, and doubtlessly should have, occupied the entire nation's energies after the war. Reconstruction was the effort to remake the South on a fundamentally different basis than the antebellum plantocracy. It was designed to help meet the economic, educational, political, and safety needs of the freed men, women, and children. Yet this

FIGURE 10-1. Watch Night Commemoration Card, Dec. 31, 1862--Waiting for the hour / Heard & Moseley, Cartes de Visite, 10 Tremont Row, Boston. (Library of Congress https://lccn.loc.gov/98501210)

federal program was short-lived and met with violent resistance. Reconstruction also competed for Americans' attention to the grief of war widows and orphans, the injuries of veterans, massive immigration, and westward expansion during these critical years. All these dimensions of the American experience fundamentally shaped America's religious life.

Reconstruction

The earliest efforts at education of a large group of newly liberated persons began in 1862 in the South Carolina Sea Islands, in what became known as the Port Royal Experiment, for Port Royal was the U.S. government's name for the sea islands of the Beaufort District.

Teachers and missionaries from the American Home Mission Society in Boston, known as Gideon's Band (for their few numbers against long odds), went to the Sea Islands to work with the ten thousand freed people who had been left behind by deserting plantation owners and then liberated early in the war by Union Navy and Army troops. To deal with this humanitarian crisis, the military called upon religious charities to help. The missionaries who answered the call included Charlotte Forten (black) and Laura Towne (white), both abolitionists who went on to fame, Forten for her writing, and Towne for her educational innovations and tenacity at Penn's School, St. Helena Island, South Carolina. The women taught formerly enslaved adults and children to read, write, do arithmetic, and learn the history of the nation in which they hoped to become recognized citizens. They also distributed farming manuals and clothing sent to them by Northern freedmen's aid associations. It was in the Beaufort district that the first independent black congregations in the South were formed and their church buildings built, a mix of Baptist and African Methodist Episcopal churches. These churches were the first institutions in the South to be entirely controlled by black persons. On January 1, 1863, Charlotte Forten wrote in the *Atlantic Magazine*, "We enjoyed perfectly the exciting scene on board the *Flora*. There was an eager, wondering crowd of freed people in their holiday attire with the gayest of head-handkerchiefs, the whitest of aprons, and the happiest of faces. The band was playing, the flags streaming, everybody talking merrily." They were on their way to the former Smith plantation, now become a U.S. Army camp where thousands would gather to hear the Emancipation Proclamation read aloud and celebrate their freedom. Some men in the gathering also celebrated the fact that the proclamation allowed African Americans to enlist in their own defense. Soon they would be fighting Confederate soldiers along the Edisto River in this same area and participating in the assault on Charleston.

A presidential wartime order has limited application. To finish the work of emancipation, a constitutional amendment, which when ratified became the 13th Amendment, was passed by Congress (Lincoln was so enthusiastic that he signed it himself, even though presidents have no role in amending the Constitution). All Northern states ratified the Amendment quickly, and ratification of the Amendment was a condition of rejoining the Union for states of the former Confederacy. The text of the Amendment was short and to the point:

"Section 1. Neither slavery nor involuntary servitude, except as a punishment for crime whereof the party shall have been duly convicted, shall exist within the United States, or any place subject to their jurisdiction.

"Section 2. Congress shall have power to enforce this article by appropriate legislation."

To give thanks for passing the Amendment in the House and in honor of Abraham Lincoln's 56th birthday on February 12, 1865, a Sunday service of worship was held in the U.S. House of Representatives chamber. The preacher for the occasion was the Reverend Henry Highland Garnet, pastor of the District's Fifteenth Avenue Presbyterian Church, himself a former slave and a noted abolitionist. More remarkably, he was the first black man to be permitted on the House floor since 1820, a sign of things to come. He used his spellbinding sermon to praise and encourage advocates of the 13th Amendment, and he spoke of his great hope for what might come for all members of his race.

FIGURE 10-2. Rev. Henry Highland Garnet, 1815–82 (National Portrait Gallery, Smithsonian Institution NPG.89.189)

HENRY HIGHLAND GARNET:
"LET THE GIGANTIC MONSTER PERISH"

"We ask, and only ask, that when our poor, frail barks are launched on life's ocean—

> Bound on a voyage of awful length
> And dangers little known, [William Cooper]—

that, in common with others, we may be furnished with rudder, helm and sails and charts and compass. Give us good pilots to conduct us to the open seas; lift no false lights along the dangerous coasts, and if it shall please God to send us propitious winds or fearful gales, we shall survive or perish as our energies or neglect shall determine. We ask no special favors, but we plead for justice. While we scorn unmanly dependence; in the name of God, the universal Father, we demand the right to live and labor and enjoy the fruits of our toil. The good work which God has assigned for the ages to come will be finished when our national literature shall be so purified as to reflect a faithful and a just light upon the character and social habits of our race, and the brush and pencil and chisel and lyre of art shall refuse to lend their aid to scoff at the afflictions of the poor or to caricature or ridicule a long-suffering people. When caste and prejudice in Christian churches shall be utterly destroyed and shall be regarded as totally unworthy of Christians, and at variance with the principles of the Gospel. When the blessings of the Christian religion and of sound religious education shall be freely offered to all, then, and not till then, shall the effectual labors of God's people and God's instruments cease.

"If slavery has been destroyed merely from necessity, let every class be enfranchised at the dictation of justice. Then we shall have a Constitution that shall be reverenced by all, rulers who shall be honored and revered, and a Union that shall be sincerely loved by a brave and patriotic people, and which can never be severed."*

*Henry Highland Garnet, "Let The Monster Perish" (1865), www.blackpast.org/african -american-history/1865-henry-highland-garnet-let-monster-perish/.

After the hostilities ended with the South's surrender at Appomattox Court House on April 9, 1865, the period of Reconstruction began with U.S. Army troops occupying the Southern states until they were first readmitted by accepting the 13th, 14th, and 15th Amendments providing for black freedom, citizenship, equal protection, and male suffrage. Several of the states agreed with what can only be called duplicitous intent to get out from under federal military occupation, while scheming how to enact vagrancy and other laws to effectively re-enslave persons under the cover of law. Still, during the presidential administrations of Andrew Johnson and Ulysses S. Grant, active attempts were made by a combination of government and nongovernmental groups to help the freedmen establish themselves educationally, spiritually, economically, and politically. During these years numerous colleges and schools were established by northern philanthropists and mission agencies, including by black church denominations. Clark Atlanta, Fisk, Howard, Dillard, Tuskegee, Hampton, Virginia Union, and Claflin universities; and Morehouse, Benedict, Rust, Barber-Scotia, and Stillman colleges—these are just a few of the thirty-five Historically Black Colleges and Universities (HBCUs) founded during Reconstruction. Education was vital to mobility within a society based upon free labor and to exercising the political rights provided by freedom, yet scholars estimate that only 10 to 15 percent of the Southern black population were literate in 1865; many of these were the free persons of color who formed the real backbone of the schools for African American children and adults. The results of freed adults and children attending school side by side were so dramatic that black adult illiteracy was effectively cut from 80 percent in 1870 to 30 percent in 1910.[2]

Educated black leaders, many of them ordained ministers, rose to political prominence during Reconstruction, serving as elected leaders in their state assemblies and even the U.S. House and Senate. All of this political participation came to a halt beginning with the presidential election of 1876, when Democrat Samuel J. Tilden got more popular votes than Republican Rutherford B. Hayes but lacked the electoral votes to declare victory. Both candidates claimed the remaining twenty unresolved votes. To settle the ill will between parties, it was agreed in the Compromise of 1877 that Hayes would become President and, in return, federal troops and oversight would be removed from former Confederate states, giving white Democrats a chance to retake power. In 1877 what Southern whites termed "Redemption" (borrowing the language of religious salvation) began. What ensued was a reassertion of white supremacy in society, commerce, and especially government. A regime of Jim Crow laws was imposed to force the legal separation of black from white persons in transportation, accommodations, education, and even public facilities like water fountains.

With the rapid descent into legalized white-over-black racial discrimination, did Reconstruction produce nothing of value? On the contrary; though the end of the era stripped away many gains, two key institutions of black freedom, dignity, and progress had been built: the church and the school. Attending church under conditions of slavery most often entailed sharing the master's religious space or worshiping surreptitiously in "hush harbors" on the edge of plantations. The opportunity to erect a church of one's own and worship without oversight or restriction was central to the emancipated person's conception of freedom. Though the African Methodist Episcopal (AME) Church, based largely in the North, was well organized and made significant successful efforts to establish new congregations in postbellum Southern states, Baptists had the most growth. Each black Baptist congregation was locally formed and supported. It chose its own deacons and minister and took no oversight from elsewhere. The Baptists were the epitome of Christian liberty and actual freedom exercised locally. Although there were some independent black Baptist churches before emancipation, the majority of African Americans attending Baptist churches in the South before 1865, be they free or enslaved, were in white-controlled congregations. After the war, numerous freemen discovered that emancipation did not extend to white Christians' religious attitudes, as in the case of South Carolina Baptists who still expected blacks to obey the old "slavish custom" and worship separately from the balcony or by listening while standing outside the church building. From a black Christian perspective, this was intolerable; due regard for Christians of the other race as brothers and sisters was only achievable in separate congregations.[3] By 1906 churches associated with the National Baptist Convention founded in 1866 would count more than two million members and have 61 percent of the overwhelmingly still southern black American population.[4]

The federal government's Freedmen's Bureau mostly coordinated and funded the activities of charitable organizations, and most of these were religious in character, like the American Home Mission Society. African Methodist Episcopal (AME) missionaries and educators were some of the most active and had a long-lasting impact. They came beginning in 1863 with the Port Royal Experiment in the South Carolina Sea Islands. James Lynch and J. D. S. Hall established a half dozen churches within their first year, and with them they started schools. When federal troops went into Charleston and then Savannah, Lynch followed them. AME Bishop Daniel Payne himself returned to his native Charleston to resume his lifelong work of promoting religion and education. In all, it is estimated that at least 70 AME missionaries worked in the South during the years 1863 to 1870 alone.[5] This well-organized church alone gathered in an estimated 137,000 new members in the South, tripling its overall national membership from 1866 to 1876. By 1880 the denomination was operating 2,000 schools in the South out of its churches, with 155,000 students.[6]

The extraordinary success of the AME and the smaller AME Zion was due in part to whites' abandonment of ministry to the formerly enslaved. A third Methodist Church, the Colored Methodist Episcopal (CME) Church, was founded for the congregations and black ministers of the Methodist Episcopal Church South that were separated out from their white brethren into a new denomination. This action of forced separation, however, was matched by a separatist impulse, wherein black Christians throughout the South founded their own churches, benevolent societies, fraternal orders, and mutual aid organizations. Freedom meant the right to assembly without white supervision. Alexander Wayman, the minister opening the first AME church in Virginia, chose as his sermon text Genesis 37:16: "I seek my brethren." The brethren Wayman had in mind were the Christians of African descent who had borne the same sufferings in the years of slavery. As churches were founded from Maryland to Florida and over to Texas, the sentiment was the same, and that scriptural text became a standard for such events.[7]

In May or early June of 1866 in Pulaski, Tennessee, six Confederate veterans gathered in a law office to form a fraternal order, the Ku Klux Klan, replete with much of the pseudo mysticism common to college fraternities and lodges of the day. It remained dormant until Tennessee enfranchised its freedmen in 1867, and then for the next two years grew into the leading white terrorist movement in the South under the leadership of Nathan Bedford Forrest, its Grand Wizard. As black voters flocked to the Republican Party of Lincoln, conservative Democrats employed a strategy of intimidation and violence until the Klan's disbanding under state pressure in 1869. Nevertheless, much is known about the early days of the Klan and its legitimacy even among white Christians because its history was preserved by some of the Pulaski founders' Presbyterian minister, D. L. Wilson, more than a decade later.[8] What is chilling for modern readers to encounter in Wilson's words is the repeated assumption of the right to use violence and intimidation to put black citizens back in their presumed places. That 3.6 million black Christians could find their way into the membership of a handful of black Methodist and Baptist denominations in the forty years after emancipation is a testimony to the strength of the refuge they found together in the face of organized and abiding oppression from without. During these years the early promises of freedom—voting, fair access to property, service on juries, equal rights under the law—would nearly completely disappear. Yet the churches and the schools, together with the family, were the cornerstones of black society and the foundation from which freedom would be reclaimed in the twentieth century.

Immigration

At the same time that Reconstruction was remaking the lives, religious experiences, and possibilities of black Americans in the South, immigration was bringing a larger number of people to the United States from overseas, particularly in the North, the Midwest, and the Western states and territories. These immigrant groups brought their religious institutions with them and settled in clusters in particular areas. In retrospect, as they set up their Irish, German, Swedish, or even Canadian enclaves, they often seem remarkably oblivious to the fact that a Civil War had been fought, let alone its causes. Sometimes, however, the new immigrants learned American prejudices all too fast; such was the case in the New York City Draft Riots of July 1863.

The critical shortage of volunteer federal troops in the winter of 1863 led the Lincoln administration to devise a draft in which all male citizens between 20 and 35 and all unmarried men between 35 and 45 were subject to military duty, to be chosen by lottery. Black men were excluded because in most places they were not considered to be citizens. Wealthier men, meanwhile, could pay the government $300 (the rough equivalent of $5,000 today and equal then to a workingman's total annual wage) to be released from obligatory service and to fund a replacement. The draft led to riots in Detroit and Boston, but nowhere was it so unpopular or as violently met as in New York City, where the issue had been weaponized by the wealthy, the political leaders of at-risk immigrants, and white workingmen who hated working alongside black men.

The city's Wall Street financiers had resisted the war with the South from the beginning because their economic interests were closely tied to the international cotton trade. The Democratic Party machine of Tammany Hall and its allied newspapers framed the issue of the impending draft as a burden falling disproportionately on their Irish and German immigrant constituents, all for the sake of Republican abolitionists and blacks. Men fresh off the boat from Ireland and Germany found themselves quickly registered as citizens so they could add to Tammany's voting bloc; now they found themselves facing a military draft into a cause they did not understand and which their new leaders told them to resist. Many immigrant longshoremen and dockside workers already resented working beside free men of color.

When July 11, 1863, arrived and with it the scheduled week for the draft, all was quiet for 24 hours; then on Monday, July 13, violence broke out, lasting for four days and producing the worst death toll in America's history of civil unrest events to this day, with 119 or 120 killed and 2,000 injured.[9] After an initial focus on government buildings, the attacks shifted to the homes of abolitionists and black residents, and upon the persons of black men and women. The city's African American orphanage was burned to the ground in a matter of minutes, displacing 233 children. At least 11 black men were lynched, and by the end of the fourth day 3,000 black New Yorkers were left homeless. These black citizens largely departed for Brooklyn, then a separate city. Irish laborers did most of the destruction and committed most of the violence, which only ended when 4,000 federal troops, members of the New York volunteers and militia, were diverted home from the Battle of Gettysburg to quell the riots on their third day.

As important as the draft riots are in American history, their place in the history of American religion is demonstrated by just how separate Irish Catholics felt themselves to be from the causes of war that enveloped their fellow Americans. This became clear in the life and work of New York's Archbishop John Hughes, who tried unsuccessfully to quell the riots as they happened and then spoke eloquently to what had gone wrong in the aftermath. He had issued a flyer calling for restraint by Irish Catholics during the riots, and on Friday the ailing Hughes spoke to an estimated crowd of five thousand from the steps of his residence:

FIGURE 10-3. Archbishop John Hughes, 1797–1864 (Library of Congress loc.gov /item/97508251/)

Every man has a right to defend his home or his shanty at the risk of life. The cause, however, must be just. It must not be aggressive or offensive. Do you want my advice? Well, I have been hurt by the report that you were rioters. You cannot imagine that I could hear these things without being grievously pained. Is there not some way by which you can stop these proceedings and support the laws, none of which have been enacted against you as Irishmen and Catholics? You have suffered already. No government can save itself unless it protects its citizens. Military force will be let loose upon you. The innocent will be shot down and the guilty will be likely to escape.[10]

In many ways the powerful Hughes was a man of many parts representing both his own gifts and contradictions and the aspirations of the Irish and Catholics he represented. The anger he encountered in young Irish immigrants was something he recognized from his own life. Born in Tyre County, Ireland, he remembered the humiliation of his sister being denied a Catholic burial because the ruling English had forbidden Catholic priests from setting a foot inside a cemetery. Instead, he was given a handful of consecrated dirt by the priest to throw on his sister's grave and vowed to cast off the impotency of the priesthood he knew in Ireland. Immigrating to Maryland in 1817 at the age of twenty, he presented himself at Mount Saint Mary's Seminary in Emmitsburg, hoping to study for the priesthood. There the seminary's rector, an elite clerical refugee from the French Revolution named John Dubois, declared him fit only to be a gardener. Luckily for this young gardener, three years later he came under the sponsorship of a rich widow and Catholic convert, Elizabeth Ann Bayley Seton, who interceded on his behalf and got him admitted after all.[11]

Ordained to the priesthood, Hughes was called to service in Philadelphia and became a hero for his ministry to his flock and beyond during the 1834 cholera epidemic, when Protestant clergy notably fled the swampy city. He gained further distinction by debating the aristocratic Presbyterian clergyman John Breckenridge. Then in 1837, John Dubois, the Bishop of New York, became so ill that the diocese required a coadjutor bishop (a designated successor) to be appointed to actually carry out his episcopal duties. John Hughes then received the delicious honor of replacing the haughty cleric who would not have him as a seminarian so many years earlier.

What Hughes found on coming to New York was shocking. There were legal disputes with lay trustees over who controlled the parishes and their buildings, even the appointments of priests. Many Catholics were impoverished, with hungry children running in the streets. Perhaps worst of all, there were as many as fifty thousand Irish Catholic girls and women working as prostitutes in New York for lack of other meaningful work, while the Protestant hierarchy of the city regarded the Irish as a plague and another race entirely. Priests and the members of religious orders seemed to accept these facts as unalterable. Bishop Hughes addressed the problem at hand by preaching a tireless doctrine of sexual purity and insisting that his priests and religious teach the same. Hughes made clear the value of Irish womanhood in the eyes of the church, no small task in a city where women outnumbered men and families had disintegrated. In the words of William J. Stern:

> [Hughes] did this by putting Catholicism's Marian Doctrine right at the center of his message. Irish women would hear from the priests and nuns that Mary was Queen of Peace, Queen of Prophets, and Queen of Heaven, and that women were important. The "ladies of New York," Hughes told them, were "the children, the daughters of Mary." The Marian teaching encouraged women to take responsibility for their own lives, to inspire their men and their children to good conduct, to keep their families together, and to become forces for upright behavior in their neighborhoods. The nuns, especially, encouraged women to become community leaders and play major roles in church fund-raising activities—radical notions for a male-dominated society where women did not yet have the right to vote. In addition, Irish men and women saw nuns in major executive positions, managing hospitals, schools, orphanages, and church societies—sending another highly unusual message for the day. Irish women became important allies in Hughes's war for values; by the 1850s they began to be major forces for moral rectitude, stability, and progress in the Irish neighborhoods of the city.[12]

Hughes also took on the Protestant public schools where Catholic children were forced to read from the King James Version of the Bible and told by teachers that their religion was false, in league with the "Whore of Babylon" and worse. Because of this pervasive nativism and religious bigotry, Hughes wanted state money for separate Catholic schools and, barring that, the freedom for Catholics to start their own schools. He became the leading voice in New York and nationally for the development of a parochial school system. Plenary meetings of the American Catholic hierarchy in 1852, 1866, and 1884 would intensify this emphasis long after Hughes's own death. In New York, Hughes built 65 parishes and 100 schools, and founded Fordham University and also Manhattan, Manhattanville, and Mount St. Vincent colleges.

Politically, Archbishop Hughes also allied himself with the nascent Republican Party so as to have leverage on the schools issue and took on international diplomacy for Abraham Lincoln on behalf of the Union cause early in the Civil War; but he, like many of his brethren, was opposed to abolitionism. Hughes believed in human freedom but thought that the mostly Protestant abolitionists were so radical in their aims that no good could come to Catholics from associating with them. When on his deathbed he sought one last time to control the Irish for the sake of their souls and to prevent the destruction of black lives and property, he proved an imperfect messenger. Still, Hughes was the model for most of the American Catholic hierarchy during the next fifty years: the Irish were committed to a separate development in church, school, and culture. Their names stand out as the leaders who built parishes, schools, colleges, and seminaries for their flocks as they grew dramatically over the same time.[13]

NUMBER OF AMERICAN ROMAN CATHOLICS BY YEAR

1850   1.6 million (1 in every 15 Americans)
1860   3 million (1 in every 10 Americans)
1870   4 million (1 in every 10 Americans
1880   6 million (1 in every 8.5 Americans)
1890   9 million (1 in every 7 Americans)
1900   12 million (1 in every 6.4 Americans)
1920   17.6 million (1 in every 6 Americans)*

*Michael Glazier and Thomas J. Shelley, eds., *The Encyclopedia of American Catholic History* (Collegeville, MN: Liturgical Press, 1997), 288.

Bishops with names like Conroy, McCloskey, Kane, Keane, McQuaid, Purcell, Ryan, Corrigan, Gibbons, and O'Hara constituted the overwhelmingly Irish and traditionalist church that would meet immigrant Catholics for decades to come, even though after 1890 the majority of those Catholics would be from Poland and Italy. They would be taught the Baltimore Catechism and infused with a strong Marian piety in close step with Rome on matters spiritual and temporal. Over time, not just New York City's Irish Catholics went from being impoverished new immigrants associated with social problems but all Irish Catholics grew into a subculture of model American citizens, supplying much of the police, firefighters, and political leadership of American cities and exhibiting the strongest of family values.

When it came to how closely Catholics should align themselves with broader American values, an alternative view to the traditionalists was associated with Minnesota's John Ireland, Archbishop of Saint Paul, who believed that the American arrangement of separation of church and state provided the conditions for Catholicism to thrive. A friend to African Americans, Ireland had been a chaplain during the war and a popular figure in the Grand Army of the Republic afterward. He became a friend to Presidents McKinley and Theodore Roosevelt and took an active hand in recruiting Catholics from crowded Eastern Seaboard cities to "colonize" the rural parts of his state. His enthusiasm for America caused him to require immigrant children and parishioners to learn English and to sell parochial schools to local school boards. These schools continued to be staffed by nuns, but no religious teaching occurred. For this innovation Ireland was called to Vatican City to explain himself, which he did. Ideas like these, however, were condemned by Rome as "Americanism" and a heresy by Pope Leo XIII, first in an encyclical, *Longinqua oceani* (1895; "Wide Expanse of the Ocean"). Though Leo had many positive things to commend in the American church, he observed that the church "would bring forth more abundant fruits if, in addition to liberty, she enjoyed the favor of the laws and the patronage of the public authority." In sum, separation of church and state was not to be endorsed as a system by Catholics. Four years later, Leo followed up on his concerns in a letter *Testem benevolentiae nostrae* (January 22, 1899; "Witness to Our Benevolence") to James Cardinal Gibbons of Baltimore and, through him, all American prelates. The pope expressed his concerns that American Catholics might be subject to the liberal tendency to choose which of the church's magisterial teachings they wished for themselves to believe and practice. The pope made it clear that Catholicism was an all-encompassing deposit of faith. The result of the Americanist crisis was that American prelates both redoubled their efforts for another sixty years to toe the traditionalist line and also made certain they had their own connections in Rome to help with future power struggles.[14]

American immigration patterns up through 1860 were remarkably stable. Ireland contributed the largest number of foreign-born residents, 1.6 million; Germany was just behind, with 1.3 million; and people from all over the United Kingdom (including Scotland) amounted to 800,000 persons. Canada and France rounded out the last two main contributors of foreign-born residents to America with 200,000 and 100,000 persons, respectively. The general pattern was that Irish Catholics predominated in every Eastern and Southern state from New Hampshire down to Mississippi; Germans (divided between Catholics, Lutherans, and some Reformed) dominated the Midwest from Minnesota to Ohio and down to Louisiana and Texas. Altogether 4.1 million, or 13.2 percent, of the 31.4 million Americans enumerated in the 1860 census were foreign-born. Those numbers grew to 14.4 percent of the population by 1870, with the Irish and Germans still supplying the greatest numbers; during this decade 1.5 million additional foreign-born people immigrated to America despite the Civil War underway for half the decade.

During the 1860–70 decade the transcontinental railroad was completed, several territories were made states, and the West dramatically opened for settlement. Canadians began to dominate the influx in upper New England, Mexicans in Texas and in what would become New Mexico and Arizona. Over the next ten years, from 1870 to 1880, China became the largest supplier of foreign-born population in the five westernmost states; Sweden and Norway began to displace France in significance, especially for the upper Midwest.

What then was happening religiously as a result of these movements? The Roman Catholic Church was becoming the single largest religious body in the nation, displacing the Methodist Episcopal Church for that honor. Yet the flavor of Catholicism that was practiced differed greatly depending on whether one lived in Louisiana; New York City; or St. Paul, Minnesota. Even so, Irish bishops were coming to dominate church hierarchy, which early in the century had been filled by prelates of English and French stock.

The influx of Lutherans from Sweden, Norway, Germany, Finland, and Denmark did not simply provide different local flavors of Lutheranism, but actual different denominations since European Lutheranism was divided into different bodies along national, linguistic, and theological lines. By 1900, as some of these churches began to also evolve English-speaking American variants, there would come to be no fewer than four hundred distinct Lutheran bodies in America.

Smaller groups of religious believers also immigrated from Western Europe, seeking to take advantage of religious freedom and good farming land: German Seventh Day Baptists, Moravian Brethren, Swiss-German-speaking Mennonites and Amish from Switzerland and Alsace-Lorraine. Many of these went to Ohio, Indiana, Illinois, and Missouri. Others, like the Welsh Calvinistic Methodists, came to Pennsylvania to mine coal and made the environs of Scranton, Pennsylvania, the largest concentration of Welsh outside Wales from the Civil War through 1918.[15]

Just how isolated immigrants could be ethnically, geographically, and religiously is clear from the account of Thomas P. Christensen, who relates the tale of Rev. Lars Jorgensen Hauge, who managed to attract such a large number of Danish Baptists to the area in and around Freeborn County, Minnesota, in the 1860s and 1870s that it was a virtual Danish Baptist colony within a U.S. state:

In 1858 he emigrated to Wisconsin, where there was already a small congregation of Danish Baptists. Soon Hauge was one of their most active preachers and evangelists, working intensely and traveling widely in the interest of his church. He married in 1863, and with his young bride and other Danes he set out by ox team in the same year from Raymond, Racine County, Wisconsin, for western Minnesota. On the way these immigrants were warned against settling so near the region where Sioux tomahawks had recently been at work. To all such warnings the young zealot, anxious to scatter the pure seed of the Baptist faith as well as to find suitable lands for settlement, turned "the deaf ear." The immigrants pushed across the Mississippi but did not go far to the west. Instead, they located near Lake Geneva in Freeborn County, where they met a few other Danish families, who had come the same year from Waushara County, Wisconsin. Hauge made trips to Raymond both in 1863 and 1864, each time bringing back more settlers, and he wrote a small pamphlet about the Danes in the United States which was published in Copenhagen.[16]

But like many errands in the American wilderness, Hauge's was not without difficulties, for having studied the Scriptures diligently, he "soon came to the conclusion that evangelical Christians should observe the Sabbath on Saturday rather than Sunday. In this he met opposition from his congregation and a fight, not figuratively speaking, was at one time imminent in the little log church." Hauge's parishioners accused him of heresy, and Hauge himself turned to his other great enthusiasm: dairying. But all his religious interests were not spent, for as Christiansen relates, "he spent the greater part of the remainder of his long life as a free-lance missionary among the Sioux Indians," another in a long line of immigrants bringing their faith to native people whose lands they had displaced.

The Spiritual Work of Mourning

Wars inevitably change relations between women and men as men leave home for military duty and return mentally changed and wounded, or never return at all. Meanwhile, women are less confined to traditional gender roles during wars and manage families, households, finances, and farms for the duration of hostilities and sometimes for decades afterward. This fact of life under conditions of war was particularly true in the case of the American Civil War and its aftermath.

The total rate of death alone is hard to imagine when the raw figure of 750,000 Civil War deaths is used. On a percentage basis, it would compare to contemporary America losing 7.5 million of its young male population over a four-year period to war. And for the South, the losses were even more catastrophic. The historian J. David Hacker estimates, "More than 20 percent of the men ages 20–24 in 1860 who were born in the South died as a result of the war. A huge proportion of Southern women remained widowed in 1880." The loss of men in their prime affects more than marriage. We know that the Southern economy struggled for a long time.[17] Put another way, in the South, 13.1 percent of all white men of military age in 1860 died as a result of the war, and 200,000 white women were widowed, and hundreds of thousands of children were orphaned. We also know that at least 36,000 of the 179,000 black soldiers who fought for the Union died (1 in 5), leaving unnumbered widows and orphans.[18] Of those who returned home, an extraordinary number of the recorded 475,881 wounded did so with amputated extremities.[19]

The disruption of war meant deep disruptions in religious assumptions, patterns of piety, and spiritual innovations as well. Spiritualism was a new religious movement that was determined to provide evidence of the immortality of the soul. While other new religious movements of the time were tightly organized around (usually) male figures teaching a new revelation or doctrine, spiritualism was more diffuse and featured many women advocates and mediums. Though the movement quickly developed detractors, the idea of contacting the dead proved irresistible to those who lost loved ones abruptly or to untimely deaths. In an age that taught Anglo-Americans to revere the good death, casting off one's mortal body, surrounded by loved ones, and seeing heaven unfolding before them like a door to the night being open—anything less was a desperate disappointment. Families were accustomed to displaying their deceased loved one's body at home in the parlor or in the dining room, for as long as the ice held out. Grief work, praying the dead on their way to the next life, was important. The war made things much, much worse. Disordered, messy bodies; sons and husbands gone forever: these drove many innovations in the American way of death. A Pennsylvania undertaker, Dr. Thomas Holmes, offered to go and recover officers' bodies for a fee and preserve them by using an arsenic compound, the first modern use of embalming. The practice of recovering mortal remains of the war dead led Union women to press the government's U.S. Sanitary Commission to keep working until every last boy or man in blue had been decently buried in the North. As for the proportionately greater Confederate losses, these bodies were outside of the Commission's work. And so, Southern mothers and wives and daughters added the work of cemeteries and memorialization to their many other labors, and no women excelled the way Southern ladies' memorial associations did in creating cemeteries that glorified the defeated lions of Southern white manhood.[20] Staying in touch with the dead took a decidedly different form especially in the North, where spiritualism became an incredibly vital movement for a brief time.

In their *History of Woman Suffrage*, editors Elizabeth Cady Stanton and Susan B. Anthony called spiritualism "the only religious sect in the world . . . that has recognized the equality of women." The movement's leaders included many women and perhaps, most importantly, internally resisted the ideas of a gender hierarchy and indeed any individual's spiritual superiority over any other. To a public confused by biblical debates and theological "evidences" for God's existence and eternal life, spiritualism offered a more direct, experiential approach to the same end: confirmation of life after death, spirit communication. Like every other claim to direct revelation available to individual persons without a church or priesthood, spiritualism was radical in its social implications.

Spiritualism's beginnings came in the same upstate New York region that had given birth to so many other religious innovations, including Charles G. Finney's New Measures (1826), Mormonism (1827), and the Millerites (1840). In this instance two young sisters named Kate and Margaret Fox, ages 14 and 12, who had previously reported the strong "rappings" of a purportedly murdered peddler in their home in Hydesville, New York, came to live near Rochester, New York. There they made contact with Congregational Quakers who had left even the Hicksite Quakers (who preferred the inner light to the Bible as a source of authority) so as to pay greater attention to the inner light, as the spirit moving from within an individual was known, without the increasing constraints of Quaker social conformity. Already attuned to the inner light, these Quakers began to inquire as to the Fox sisters' good faith and integrity and could find no fault with them. So it was that they began asking of the spirits with whom they communicated direct questions that could be answered yes or no with knocks, or raps, as in this interchange between the girls and a Dr. Chase, recorded by Isaac Post in November 1848:

INQUIRING OF THE SPIRITS OF THOSE DEPARTED

"Dr. Chase who had recently lost his mother, asked if his Mother's Spirit was present. The answer was, she was. Whether she was happy she was, whether her knowledge had increased since she passed away it had. Whether she continually watched over him/she did. Then he asked about . . . a sister, whether his suspicions in regard to her death were correct. The answer, they were not. Would she have lived if other means had been used? The reply, she would not. Then he asked if [he] could be convinced that there could be spiritual manifestations[;] then he could get no more answers."*

*As quoted in Ann Braude, *Radical Spirits: Spiritualism and Women's Rights in Nineteenth-Century America* (Boston: Beacon Press, 1989), 12.

Soon, the Fox sisters' fame spread among East Coast literati who experienced similar communication with the dead in their presence. These included James Fenimore Cooper, Horace Greeley, George Bancroft, and William Cullen Bryant. These séances, as the experiences were known, grew in popularity in the 1850s; but just as importantly, they were no longer associated only with the Fox sisters. More and more, people were testing the spirits themselves through mostly female mediums. As historian Ann Braude has noted, "by identifying mediumship with characteristics believed to be inherent in women, Spiritualists echoed the language of the larger culture, which identified the qualities of piety with the qualities of femininity."[21] And as in Victorian America the woman's place was in the home, so too spiritualism's religiosity was quintessentially practiced in the home.

Spiritualism outside the home took on several manifestations that became especially strong in the years immediately after the Civil War. The first was the lecture from a spiritualist adept in presenting the practices' promise and results. These lectures, confined to Eastern Seaboard northern cities prior to 1865, more than doubled in number after the war as women in the Midwest and interior East clamored for ways to speak with loved ones beyond the grave. Three-quarters of the spiritualists' public meetings—as revealed by their two principal newspapers, the *Telegraph* and the *Banner of Light* after the war—occurred in just seven states; listed from most to least active: Massachusetts, New York, Ohio, Maine, Illinois, Connecticut, and Michigan.[22]

FIGURE 10-4. Mrs. Fanny Conant with the ghost of her brother, Charles H. Crowell (1868) by William H. Mumler, Boston. Albumen print carte de visite (Getty Open Content Program www.getty.edu/art/collection /objects/95766/william-h-mumler -mrs-conant-american-1862-1875/)

The other manifestation of spiritualism beyond the home was increasing interest in capturing evidence of spirit visitation in séances through the new medium of wet-plate photography. This new "evidence of things not seen" (cf. Hebrews 11:1) had to be obtained mostly in photographic studios or under otherwise controlled circumstances. Positively, the wonderful photographs, with their ghostly images of loved ones in the background, seemed to provide concrete evidence to skeptics. Negatively, given the profit motive in exploiting the grief of others, photographers learned to fake the images with double exposures. The exposure of fakes soon caused people to doubt the "evidence" of their eyes. An example of these "spirit photographs" is the visiting card created for Fanny Conant in Boston by William H. Mumler, a spirit-medium photographer who ran into legal challenges to his work.

Though an interest in contracting spirits of the deceased continued, spiritualism declined rapidly in the 1870s as the movement faced concerns over fraud. It was also self-limiting in the sense that either people obtained the contact they desired, or they did not. For those seeking alternatives to the prevailing evangelical Protestantism of the day, spiritualism was displaced by two related religious movements: Christian Science and Theosophy. Mary Baker Eddy's *Science and Health, with Key to the Scriptures*, first published in 1875, was particularly hard on spiritualism for being insufficiently based in the Scriptures. Her central argument was that ailments and disappointments of living were the result of errors in perception, for which Christ, the Scientist, had left a suitable set of prescriptions. Eddy (1821–1910) linked her teachings about health to the teachings of Jesus in the Gospels, but it is health and right thinking that predominate in her teachings: "This is the doctrine of Christian Science: that divine Love cannot be deprived of its manifestation, or object; that joy cannot be turned into sorrow, for sorrow is not the master of joy; that good can never produce evil; that matter can never produce mind nor life result in death. The perfect man—governed by God, his perfect Principle—is sinless and eternal."[23] It is hard now to imagine how popular, in an age filled with quack medicines and dubious remedies aimed especially at the complaints of women, Eddy's alternative approach to healthy living through healthy thinking and homeopathy became. Eddy went on with her students and followers to establish the Christian Scientists in 1879 as a Christian denomination dedicated to spiritual healing.

Theosophy as a movement dates to the meeting of Madame Helena Petrovna Blavatsky (1831–91), who immigrated to the United States in 1872, and Colonel Henry S. Olcott (1832–1907), a lawyer interested in the relation of religion to science. Blavatsky was known as a medium, had dabbled in mesmerism, and was said to be channeling the souls of what she called "mahatmas" (the Hindu term for "great souls"). Together they formed the Theosophical Society in 1875; through the doctrines channeled through Blavatsky, in such books as *Isis Unveiled: A Master-Key to the Mysteries of Ancient and Modern Science and Theology* (1877) and *The Secret Doctrine*

(1888), they taught that all religious wisdom was perennial, emanating from a single source, and that life emanated from a divine spark. They introduced Americans to Eastern religions, minimized the uniqueness of the teachings of Jesus, and also sought to correlate Darwinian science with older forms of thought, including reincarnation. Though never any larger than ten thousand members, Theosophy begot a nearly endless series of other esoteric religious interests in America under many labels, eventually undergirding interests in learning more about Buddhism and Hinduism and New Age experiments in the later twentieth century.

11. The New Science and the Old-Time Religion

The fifty years from 1835 to 1885 saw more technological developments in the span of a single lifetime than ever before. Americans went from traveling no faster than a horse could move to riding in railcars traveling over 60 miles an hour and communicating at the speed of light. It is appropriate, then, that the message Samuel F. B Morse used on May 24, 1844, to officially open the Baltimore–Washington telegraph line was a phrase from the book of Numbers (23:23), "What hath God wrought!" Cyrus McCormick's mechanical reaper was an international success by 1851. The Otis safety elevator was invented in 1852, allowing buildings to rise beyond the number of floors a person could climb. The telegraph tied the nation together with election results and news. So did the First Transcontinental Railroad, a 1,912-mile continuous railroad line constructed between 1863 and 1869 that connected the existing eastern U.S. rail network at Omaha, Nebraska, with the Pacific coast at San Francisco, California.

It was the golden age of inventors. A young George Westinghouse invented railroad safety air brakes in 1869 and later pioneered mass electrical power distribution in the 1880s. In March 1876 Alexander Graham Bell used the telephone for the first time to speak to his assistant, saying, "Mr. Watson, come here. I want to see you." Thomas Edison would follow with the first practical light bulb in 1879, the phonograph, and more. These inventions were making their creators wealthy and transforming America from a mostly rural, agrarian nation to an increasingly urban and industrial one. The age was one of scientific and technical progress, but also of extremes in wealth and poverty as American laborers found themselves working in factories for men like Andrew Carnegie and Henry Clay Frick, who could respond to demands for wage increases by first locking them out and then cutting their prior wages in half. Progress brought with it social pains that religious leaders would address in a variety of ways. Some scientific ideas also seemed to directly challenge religion itself.

Americans were inclined to see the technical developments around them as a case of human mastery of the physical world through engineering and the use of the laws of nature. When it came to natural science, however, Charles Darwin's writings provoked a sustained religious self-examination and a defense of the Bible as a source of knowledge, especially about human

FIGURE 11-1. Charles Darwin, 1809–82 (Library of Congress loc.gov/item/2004674431/)

origins and destiny. Darwin, an English naturalist (the term then in use for biologists), undertook the research upon which his reputation would be made in the 1830s on a five-year voyage on the HMS *Beagle*. On the ship he traveled to Africa, Australia, South America, multiple isolated islands in the Pacific and Atlantic, and perhaps most significantly the Galápagos Islands off Ecuador. As naturalists had before him, Darwin catalogued the different species he found. Something else he found along his travels were subtle differences in varieties of the same fauna that could only be explained by adaptation to the environment. While he published the basic account of his travels and findings in the *Voyage of the Beagle* in 1839, Darwin sat on the publication of his evolutionary theory for twenty years because he knew how challenging it would be to the contemporary worldview held by Christians, including his own family members. Only as competing theories of evolutionary change—wrong ones, in his view—began to be published and discussed did Darwin publish *On the Origin of Species by Means of Natural Selection, or, the Preservation of Favoured Races in the Struggle for Life* in 1859. By the next year, the English scientific community was taking Darwin's conclusions seriously. By 1871, with his publication of *The Descent of Man: and, Selection in Relation to Sex* (2 vols.), there were few learned

FIGURE 11-2. Caricature of Samuel Wilberforce, 1805–73. *Vanity Fair*, 24 July 1869 (commons.wikimedia.org/wiki /File:Carlo_Pelligrini-Samuel_Wilberforce _Not_A_Brawler.jpg)

FIGURE 11-3. Caricature of Thomas Henry Huxley, 1825–95. *Vanity Fair*, 28 January 1871 (https://commons.wikimedia.org /wiki/File:Thomas_Henry_Huxley01.jpg)

people in America, Britain, or Europe who had not formed an opinion as to whether humanity descended from lesser forms of life or directly from Adam and Eve.

The particular forms the debate in America would often take were prefigured by the so-called 1860 Oxford evolution debate between Bishop Samuel Wilberforce and the noted biologist Thomas Huxley at the conclusion of the meeting of the British Science Academy in June 1860. Although other figures had actually discussed *Origin* in positive terms, the memorable fireworks came when Wilberforce is said to have responded to Huxley's claim that it did not bother him to have descended from a gorilla or not, "whether he had a preference for the descent being on the father's side or the mother's side?" Huxley then retorted that he would sooner "claim kindred with an Ape than with a man like the Bp., who made so ill a use of his wonderful speaking powers to try and [suffocate], by a display of authority, a free discussion on what was, or was not, a matter of truth." Huxley's point was that on "questions of physical science, [churchly] 'authority' had always been bowled out by investigation" and used as his examples astronomy and geology.[1]

Huxley's appeal to geology and astronomy was apt, for by 1860 it was widely accepted that contemporary geological discoveries indicated a very

FIGURE 11-4. An illustration of racist theories of polygenesis. (In *Indigenous Races of the Earth* [Philadelphia: J. B. Lippincott, 1857], by Josiah Clark Nott and George Robins Gliddon)

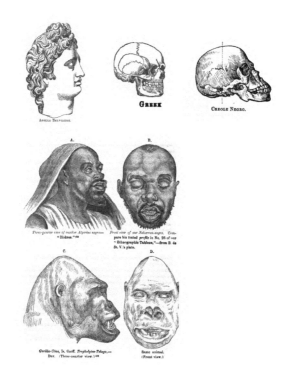

old earth, featuring a sequence of different populations in the fossil record. Therefore, among most educated clergy it was recognized that the Genesis creation story was figuratively true, not literally true. It was common to say that, with God, an aeon is like a day. To explain the fossils, there were also several theories of "transmutation" or "development" to explain how great and small creatures of the past came and went. So what was different and more upsetting about Darwinism? The assertion of the randomness of natural selection was at odds with prevailing religious understandings of a divinely created and controlled universe. If nature changes by random chance and sexual selection for surviving traits, how could it continue to be said that human beings really hold a special place in God's world? Perhaps just as disturbingly, Darwin's natural science could be read to mean that the only measure of good and evil was survival, thus making the ethical and moral teachings of Bible appear pointless.

The problems for religion and society did not end with Darwin's teachings properly understood. They were often truncated into a simple "survival of the fittest," which as interpreted by Herbert Spencer and others came to be seen as "Social Darwinism." This idea held that some individuals were more adapted to survival in the modern age; other poorer and less developed types should be allowed to wither and die. False views of evolution also propped up the "scientific" racism of polygenesis, wherein the different human races were believed to be separately created, and some humans were therefore, according to race, inferior to others. The effect of such approaches to evolution was to buttress notions of white supremacy. These theories were propagated on both sides of the Atlantic by anthropologists like Josiah Clark Nott (1804–73) and George Robins Gliddon (1809–57), and by Harvard's American Swiss biologist Louis Agassiz (1807–73). Whether well understood, or not, Henry Adams commented upon evolution's appeal among the intelligent classes: "Unbroken Evolution under uniform conditions pleased every one—except curates and bishops; it was the very best substitute for religion; a safe, conservative practical, thoroughly Common-Law deity."[2]

Reception of Darwin: American Responses

One of the religious leaders who thought he understood Darwin and did not like the implications for an understanding of God's role in the world was Princeton Theological Seminary theologian Charles Hodge (1797–1878). In 1874, northern Presbyterianism's most distinguished theologian published *What Is Darwinism?* In it he wrote: "Darwinism includes three distinct elements. First, evolution or the assumption that all organic forms, vegetable and animal, have been evolved or developed from one, or a few primordial

FIGURE 11-5. Charles Hodge, 1797–1878 (Library of Congress LC-DIG-cwpbh-02865)

living germs; second, that this evolution has been effected by natural selection, or the survival of the fittest; and third, and by far the most important and only distinctive element of his theory, that this natural selection is without design being conducted by unintelligent physical causes."[3] It was the last of these three qualities that most upset Hodge. The mere idea that the marvel of the human eye was the result of unintelligent, random causes was an insult to God as the great designer and upholder of all things.

Meanwhile just across town, in 1868 the College of New Jersey (now Princeton University) had inaugurated a new president, James McCosh (1811–94); in his first week on campus, he told upper-class students that he believed in evolution. Over the next two decades he supported scientific research at the college and lectured extensively on his views about evolution. In the end, his position was not diametrically opposed to Hodge's concerns about design in creation. In McCosh's *Christianity and Positivism* (1871) he made clear that just because evolution occurred in nature did not mean one had to adopt the atheist determinism of Spencer and Huxley (or Darwin, for that matter). In *Religious Aspects of Evolution* (1888), McCosh insisted on the principle of design in nature, interpreting the Darwinian discoveries as more evidence of the prearrangement, skill, and purpose in the universe. In other words, God was so marvelous as to have worked through evolution. Critically, however, McCosh also drew the line on evolution happening to human beings. This religious embrace of redefined evolution became the brand most other brave clerical harmonizers of evolution with Christianity embraced.[4]

As moderate as McCosh's position seems a century and half later, a similar position got the uncle of future President Woodrow Wilson convicted

FIGURE 11-6. James Woodrow, 1828–1907 (wilsonboyhoodhome .org/learn/about-woodrow-wilson /correspondence/)

of heresy. James Woodrow (1828–1907), the only academic appointed to a science chair in an American theological school, interpreted evolution both as the Harvard- and Heidelberg-trained biologist he was and as an ordained minister in the Presbyterian Church in the United States. His professorial chair at Columbia Theological Seminary, "the Perkins Professorship of Natural Science in connexion with Revelation," was designed "to evince the harmony of science with the records of our faith, and to refute the objections of infidel naturalists." In his inaugural address in the fall of 1861, after leaving Oglethorpe University to take up his new post, Woodrow outlined his understanding of the possible purposes of the Perkins professorship. He noted three options. First, he could "pursue classical natural theology, seeking evidence of God's existence from nature." Second, he could make analogies between nature and Scripture, seeking to "show that they were works of the same Author." Instead, Woodrow announced his intention "to scrutinize the nature and the force of current and popular objections to the Scriptures, to meet them, and to set them aside, by proving that they spring either from science falsely so called, or from incorrect interpretations of the words of the Holy Bible." This he continued until it cost him his position, for though he initially doubted the validity of evolution, over the next two decades he became more and more convinced of its truth.[5]

Among his southern Presbyterian brethren, James Woodrow stood at the opposite end of the religion and science spectrum from Robert Lewis Dabney (1820–98), a professor at Virginia's Union Theological Seminary. Dabney went so far himself as to write a refutation of the findings of geologists, titled "Geology and the Bible," because they found the earth to be older than depicted in Scripture. Woodrow fired back a published essay, "Geology and Its Assailants." The continued squabbling within the pages of denominational journals led the Columbia Seminary Board in 1884 to require that Woodrow "give fully his views . . . upon Evolution, as it regards the World, the lower Animals and Man." Later that year he addressed members of the Columbia Theological Seminary alumni association on the topic "Evolution." At a key point in his lengthy address, he argued that to answer the question what to think of evolution, he needed to ask first what one meant by evolution:

> When thinking of the origin of anything, we may inquire, Did it come into existence just as it is? or did it pass through a series of changes from a previous state in order to reach its present condition? For example, if we think of a tree, we can conceive of it as having come immediately into existence just as we see it; or, we may conceive of it as having begun its existence as a minute cell in connexion with a similar tree, and as having reached its present condition by passing through a series of changes, continually approaching and at length reaching the form before us. Or thinking of the earth, we can conceive of it as having come into existence with its present complex character; or we may

conceive of it as having begun to exist in the simplest possible state, and as having reached its present condition by passing through a long series of stages, each derived from its predecessor. To the second of these modes, we apply the term "Evolution." It is evidently equivalent to "derivation"; or, in the case of organic beings, to "descent."[6]

This definition or description of evolution, Woodrow noted, did not include any reference to source behind origination, but rather to the mode of change alone. Immediate existence might be attributed to God or to chance. Evolution did not settle whether natural laws or an "almighty personal Creator, acting according to laws of his own framing," accounted for the origin of matter and species. Creation and evolution were therefore not mutually exclusive. By the same token, evolution could no more be termed atheistic or theistic, than to call it "square or round," Woodrow said. Instead evolution was like any other hypothesis in science; it stood to be proved true or false. About God, Woodrow asked,

> How can our belief in this doctrine tend to weaken or destroy our belief that he is infinite, that he is eternal, that he is unchangeable, in his being, or his wisdom, or his power, or his holiness, or his justice, or his goodness, or his truth? Or how can our rejection of the doctrine either strengthen or weaken our belief in him? Or how can either our acceptance or rejection of Evolution affect our love to God, or our recognition of our obligation to obey and serve him—carefully to keep all his commandments and ordinances?[7]

A few minutes later Woodrow was quoting no less an authority than John Calvin himself, to the effect that the Bible was not intended as a science book: "So much at least seems clear—that whatever the Bible may say touching the mode of creation, is merely incidental to its main design, and must be interpreted accordingly. Well may we repeat with Calvin, 'He who would learn astronomy and other recondite arts, let him go elsewhere.'"[8]

Tried for heresy, Woodrow was first acquitted yet then convicted. He left the seminary to become president of the University of South Carolina. Yet the conflict continued to roil the church, whose General Assemblies in 1886, 1888, 1889, and as late as 1924 were moved to affirm the historicity of the creation of Adam, such as affirming "that Adam and Eve were created, body and soul, by immediate acts of Almighty power, thereby preserving . . . perfectly race unity; that Adam's body was directly fashioned by Almighty God without any natural animal parentage of any kind, out of matter previously created from nothing; and that any doctrine at variance therewith is a dangerous error."[9] Of course, the need to affirm this specific view of creation says just as much about prevailing understandings of the Bible and its interpretation as it does about Darwinian evolution.

Reception of Evolution: Progressive Responses

Not everyone who endorsed evolution did so with as great a technical understanding as had Woodrow, or a fear for what its acceptance might portend as had his opponents. Two cases in point were the extremely popular Congregationalist ministers Henry Ward Beecher (1813–87) and Lyman Abbott (1835–1922), who served the influential Plymouth Congregational Church of Brooklyn, New York, one after the other for most of the last half of the nineteenth century and together edited the *Christian Union* (later the *Outlook*). Beecher, declaring his stand for evolution about 1880, was probably the first prominent American preacher to accommodate himself to the newer view. In a book based on his sermons, *Evolution and Religion* (1885), he concluded that science was simply "the deciphering of God's thought as revealed in the structure of the world."[10] Reading Beecher, one sees that he was mainly interested in human evolution as the development of moral beings and in Christianity as a great help in improving religion. He was less interested in sticky questions concerning random accidents of biology. As with McCosh, then, there was still a Great Designer behind the process of evolution.

In 1882 Beecher's and Abbott's *Christian Union* confidently announced (prematurely, as we shall see) that "the time when ministers scoffed and derided Darwin and his disciples has forever passed."[11] Lyman Abbott, for his own part, deflected the biblical literalists' worries with humor, saying, "I would as soon have a monkey as a mud man for an ancestor."[12] Thus,

FIGURE 11-7. Henry Ward Beecher, 1813–87 (Library of Congress loc.gov /item/2017895649/)

having repudiated the traditional view of creation by God taking up clay, Abbott adopted a position of creation by evolution, what he termed "God's way of doing things," again converting evolution into a religious metaphor:

> And the consummation of evolution, the consummation of redemption,—the one term is scientific, the other theological, but the process is the same,—the consummation of this long process of divine manifestation, which began in the day when the morning stars sang together, will not be until the whole human race becomes what Christ was, until the incarnation so spreads out from the one man of Nazareth that it fills the whole human race, and all humanity becomes an incarnation of the divine, the infinite, and the all-loving Spirit. What Jesus was, humanity is becoming.

Abbott also rejected the old explanation of sin. He labeled Genesis's account of the fall of humanity "a beautiful fable." Sin, therefore, was a lapse into the animal nature from which man subsequently "ascended." Evolution was not, therefore, a struggle for the survival of the fittest, but rather "the doctrine of growth applied to life."[13]

The kind of updating of the Bible's meaning that Beecher and Abbott promoted was paralleled in the American Jewish community's Reform movement, whose greatest light was Rabbi Isaac Mayer Wise (1819–1900). This movement of mostly assimilated German Jews, who had arrived in the United States earlier in the nineteenth century, found the relative freedoms (political, religious, and economic) conducive to self-expression and to some revision of received doctrines. In the second article of the Pittsburgh Platform, the founding document of Reform Judaism that Wise had a strong hand in writing, American Jews held that they had nothing to fear from science and would not be overly bound by biblical worldviews when they conflicted with science:

SCIENCE AND RELIGION:
THE PITTSBURGH PLATFORM OF REFORM JUDAISM

"We recognize in the Bible the record of the consecration of the Jewish people to its mission as the priest of the one God, and value it as the most potent instrument of religious and moral instruction. We hold that the modern discoveries of scientific researches in the domain of nature and history are not antagonistic to the doctrines of Judaism, the Bible reflecting the primitive ideas of its own age, and at times clothing its conception of divine Providence and Justice dealing with men in miraculous narratives."*

*Reform Judaism, *The Pittsburgh Platform*, November 1885, www.jewishvirtuallibrary.org/the-pittsburgh-platform.

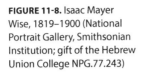
FIGURE 11-8. Isaac Mayer Wise, 1819–1900 (National Portrait Gallery, Smithsonian Institution; gift of the Hebrew Union College NPG.77.243)

Biblical Criticism Comes to America

Prior to the Enlightenment the Bible belonged to the church. Even as Protestants split from Catholicism in the Reformation and from one another after that, the terms of their disagreements were overwhelmingly about the church and its leaders' readings of the Bible and what proposed alternative interpretations might mean for the communal life of the faithful. The Enlightenment provided the opportunity for scholars not affiliated with a church to examine Scriptures and offer, without threat to their own lives, opinions as to their origin and validity. Baruch Spinoza (1632–77), David Hume (1711–76), John Locke (1632–1704), and Thomas Paine (1737–1809) each called into question revealed religion without lightning striking them dead, but only in the nineteenth century did biblical criticism become a thing happening inside the church-related universities and theological schools of Europe, the United Kingdom, and then the United States. The "scientific" examination of the Bible—its origins, parts, inconsistencies, and parallels with other ancient Near Eastern and Hellenistic-Roman religions—made its way into American churches and culture through seminary education and popular journals as Enlightenment attacks had not. Some people believed knowing about the Bible in this way increased their faith: trips to the "Holy Land" were never so popular as in the late nineteenth century, even though Mark Twain commented humorously that on his visit to places like the tomb of Adam, the evidence amounted to there being no "question that he is actually buried in the grave which is pointed out as his—there can be none—because it has never yet been proven that that grave is not the grave in which he is buried." Nevertheless, even as he mocked the emotionality of the experience,

Twain simultaneously provided a sense of what Western travelers found to confirm their faith in Palestine:

> The tomb of Adam! How touching it was, here in a land of strangers, far away from home, and friends, and all who cared for me, thus to discover the grave of a blood relation. True, a distant one, but still a relation. The unerring instinct of nature thrilled its recognition. The fountain of my filial affection was stirred to its profoundest depths, and I gave way to tumultuous emotion. I leaned upon a pillar and burst into tears. I deem it no shame to have wept over the grave of my poor dead relative. Let him who would sneer at my emotion close this volume here, for he will find little to his taste in my journeyings through Holy Land. Noble old man—he did not live to see me—he did not live to see his child. And I—I—alas, I did not live to see *him*. Weighed down by sorrow and disappointment, he died before I was born—six thousand brief summers before I was born. But let us try to bear it with fortitude. Let us trust that he is better off where he is. Let us take comfort in the thought that his loss is our eternal gain.[14]

Yet trips to the Holy Land, along with maps and books about the time of Christ, only confirmed others' worries that the old-time religion was under an attack from within by a far greater threat even than evolution: biblical criticism.

Biblical criticism took several forms during the nineteenth century. So-called lower criticism focused on translation from original languages and textual variations of ancient manuscripts. Although most laity were unaware that there were hundreds of ancient copies of parts of the Bible, but none going back to even the early second century CE, this form of criticism was uncontroversial. The so-called higher criticism of the Bible, also known as the historical-critical method, was much more controversial. It sought to reveal the world behind the text and was interested in the meaning and intent of texts in their original context. Historical criticism focused on issues of authorship, audience, agenda, historical setting, genre, cultural assumptions and influences. By giving the Bible and its parts a human history, it threatened its status as given by God at a particular point and threatened the prevailing Protestant assumption that its meaning could be understood by ordinary believers using their "common sense."

Even lower criticism could spark theological changes. Earlier in the century Edward Robinson (1794–1863) and Moses B. Stuart (1780–1852), both great philologists who taught at Andover Seminary in Massachusetts, had begun to improve the historical understanding of the Bible, with Stuart arguing persuasively that the book of Revelation was about Christians under the Roman emperor Nero and not a prediction of the future. Likewise, William Ellery Channing (1780–1842) and Andrews Norton (1786–1853) had been key early Unitarian theologians of an alternative to Trinitarian evangelicalism precisely on biblical grounds.

Meanwhile in Germany, David Friedrich Strauss (1808–74) published a controversial work in 1835, *Das Leben Jesu, kritisch bearbeitet*, later published in English by the novelist George Eliot (Marian Evans, 1819–80) under the title *The Life of Jesus, Critically Examined*. Strauss's book provided an intriguing source-critical analysis of the Synoptic Gospels, John, Acts, and the Pauline Epistles, demonstrating which document's authors or editors had access to which other materials. The scandal of Strauss's work was that he interpreted the miracles of Jesus as myths created by the early Christian community to prop up their claim that Jesus of Nazareth was the Jewish Messiah. Despite the scandal, Strauss helped make Germany (along with England and Scotland) a place for Americans to undertake graduate work in biblical studies. In most years during the 1890s, over four hundred American students were enrolled in German theological schools.

Some of the American interest in German higher criticism was fostered by influential English theologians and academics. The revered Anglican classicist Benjamin Jowett (1817–93) had carried on his own German correspondence when in 1860 he published his *Essays and Reviews*. Appearing just four months after Darwin's *Origin of Species*, Jowett's collection included a stirring essay, "On the Interpretation of Scripture." In it, he urged Christian academics to err on the side of being fully rational, saying, "Doubt comes in at the window, when Inquiry is denied at the door." Throughout he maintained that the job of the interpreter "is to read Scripture like any other book."

One German interpreter who followed Jowett's advice to stunning effect was Julius Wellhausen (1844–1918). In 1878 Wellhausen published *Geschichte Israels* (English translation, *History of Israel*, 1885), elaborating a "documentary hypothesis" arguing that the first six books of the Bible (Genesis–Joshua) were composed by different authors/editors at different times. The sources Wellhausen posited were as follows:

J   (Yahwist), composed about 950 BCE, in Judah. This source referred to the God of Israel as "Yahweh" (the German *J* is the equivalent of the English *Y*).

E   (Elohist), composed about 850 BCE, in Israel. This source referred to another Hebrew word for God, "Elohim," that was also used in sections of Genesis, from another era of history.

D   (Deuteronomist), composed about 600 BCE, in Jerusalem. The Deuteronomist was posited as the source of the book of Deuteronomy and the historical sources of the books of Joshua, Judges, Samuel, and Kings, all composed separately.

P   (Priestly source), composed about 500 BCE, in exile in Babylon and back in Jerusalem. Priestly portions of the text represented an interest in reinforming ritual observance in the post-exilic situation.

Wellhausen used his hypothesis to explain some things faithful readers had probably always wondered, such as why the Bible begins with two different creation stories (answer: different sources with different agendas). Yet the implications for the history of Israel's religion were far-reaching. He depicted the early faith of Israel as polytheistic and family-based (JE), only promoting ethical monotheism with prophetic, priesthood, and royal support (D) during a later period of centralization in Jerusalem. This Wellhausen also depicted as supplanted after the exile, when priests (P) took over the authority once accorded the monarchy.

As exciting as this and other theories were to scholars, biblical criticism challenged traditional ideas of authorship by inspired prophets and apostles. Christians had long thought that Moses, Matthew, Peter, and others wrote the books associated with their names and did not take alternate histories well. At base the new criticism challenged the reliability of biblical history and prehistory, just as evolutionary theory did. Any possible human activity and creativity in the formation of the Bible called into question the Bible's inspiration. So what kind of book was the Bible, and how authoritative could the Bible be?

Many American religious leaders felt a need to defend older understandings of the Bible's inspiration as truth, terming the Bible "inerrant," thus containing no errors in presenting the intent and voice of God. The theologian Charles Hodge offered a defense of qualified biblical inerrancy. The Bible, he argued, was wholly accurate if one disregarded trivial discrepancies in numbers and dates; allowed for minor errors in copying and translation; distinguished between what biblical authors personally believed and formally taught; used commonsense standards of what constitutes accuracy—such that "the sun rising" was understood as language of everyday life, not as a theological pronouncement of how the sun relates to the earth. One of Hodge's successors, Benjamin B. Warfield (1851–1921), went further in defending the Bible's "inerrancy," writing in 1881, "The scriptures not only contain, but ARE THE WORD OF GOD, and hence . . . all their elements and all their affirmations are absolutely errorless, and behind the faith and obedience of men."[15]

Reception of Biblical Criticism: A Progressive Response

Fifty miles away in Manhattan, an Old Testament scholar named Charles A. Briggs (1841–1913) at Union Theological Seminary was earning Warfield's wrath by accepting most of higher criticism's historical findings. But Briggs also defended the supernatural elements of the Bible that Christians most cared about. For all this, his fellow Presbyterians tried him for heresy in 1892, and he ended up being ordained a priest in the Episcopal Church in 1893. Briggs's seminary left the Presbyterian Church along

FIGURE 11-9. Charles Augustus Briggs, 1841–1913 (commons.wikimedia .org/wiki/File:CharlesAugustusBriggs.jpg)

with him, becoming the first nondenominational theological school in the country.

A decade after his heresy trial, Briggs offered a mature defense of what history could do for living faith in an essay titled "The Higher Study of Theology." In it he hoped for theology to reclaim its rightful place as "Queen of knowledge, . . . by divine right grounded in the very nature of things." Ever the Old Testament professor, he quoted Wisdom speaking in Proverbs 8:22–35, which ends:

> For whoso findeth me findeth life,
> And shall obtain favour of the LORD.

The problem, Briggs thought, was not a half-century battle between science and religion, but science and true religion against ecclesiastical domination. Theology was in danger of being domesticated to what denominations held dear. As for half a century of uncovering the cultural origins of the Christian faith, this activity made Briggs more rather than less of a believer in Jesus and his message:

> There are some who think that the whole fabric of Christianity is imperiled by these historical facts. They have been accustomed to think that the whole of Christianity had a unique divine source. When such a one learns that the greater part of the structure is human in origin, and can be explained by Greek philosophy and Roman law, without thinking at all of the Scriptures of the Old and New Testaments, Christianity seems shaken to its foundations. But, in fact, there is no real cause

for alarm, but rather for thankfulness; for we are now able to make distinctions which are indispensable for the progress of theology and of Christianity. It is certainly true that the great fundamental doctrines of the person of Christ and of the holy Trinity were stereotyped in the forms of Greek philosophy. It is as certainly true that Christian institutions were stereotyped in Roman forms. No one can fully understand them unless he studies them in these forms. It is necessary, if they are to be translated and explained to the modern mind, that we should be able to discriminate the forms from the substance; we must ascertain all that is really Greek, all that is really Roman, all that is really Hebrew, and all that really came as a new formative and divine teaching from Jesus Christ himself.[16]

Church history, Briggs believed, could help sort out all these problems. But even after the fullest examination, Christians would be left with the question "What shall we say?" He asked, "Is Christian only that which can be traced to Jesus Christ himself? Is there no other Christianity save the essence of Christianity?" Instead, Briggs thought, "Jesus promised his disciples the divine Spirit to guide them unto all truth. He gave them a few simple, original, formative, divine principles, and commanded them to teach all nations and make the whole creation Christian."[17]

Briggs expressed his desire that the universal message of the faith be separated from its Western cultural influences and denominational trappings now just so that it could be shared in East Asia and Central Africa, saying, "We have learned something from the past. We ought not to think of making these nations sectarian Christians or American Christians. We should be content to have them become *real* Christians, leaving them to organize their Christianity in accordance with the genius of their own races."[18]

Popular Understandings of the Bible in the Later Nineteenth Century

Throughout the late nineteenth century, academics and clergy battled one another for right understandings about the relation of religion to science, and about the history of the Bible in relation to its meaning and truth. The unresolved strife would have huge implications for religion in the twentieth century as the broad evangelical Protestant majority would be rent asunder over these and other issues. At the same time other influential voices among Christian lay leaders were also shaping the public's view of the Bible. Among conservatives, Phoebe Palmer and Dwight L. Moody stand out as perhaps far more influential in their own time than any member of the clergy.

Dwight L. Moody (1837–99) modeled one of the predominant stories of his time when he left his boyhood farm at the age of 18 to seek his future in the big city. In his case the city was Boston; success was found by selling shoes in his uncle's store. Moody went to church with the same uncle, discovering the Bible and experiencing a calm conversion, accepting Christ, and becoming a church member, all within two years. Then he moved to Chicago. There he not only became renowned for his salesman's gifts; he also joined the Plymouth Congregational Church and rented pews for collecting people from wherever to fill them each Sunday. Moody was becoming an evangelist. Soon he was also in charge of a mission Sunday school in the Sands district north of the Chicago River, had gathered 1,500 poor and homeless people into a church, and caught the attention of some of Chicago's wealthiest men.

By 1861 Moody had left business forever to do Christian work as a missionary, an agent for the Christian Commission during the Civil War, and then as president of the Chicago YMCA. Everywhere Moody went, he was determined to sell people on Christ, learning along the way the love of God for sinners. In 1870 he persuaded Ira Sankey (1840–1908) to be his song leader; the two spent the rest of their careers leading revivals. Moody and Sankey first experienced tremendous approval for their efforts in Great Britain: on an extended tour in 1873–75 they reached as many as four million souls. When Moody came back to the States as a transatlantic celebrity, he led gigantic weeks-long revivals in Brooklyn, Philadelphia, and from the Atlantic to the Pacific.

FIGURE 11-10. "The Great Revival—Mr. Moody Preaching at the Hippodrome," *Harper's Weekly,* March 11, 1876

Moody preached the salvation of souls. Holding a Bible aloft, he would speak of eternal life, "Come forward and t-a-k-e, TAKE!" Then he told his new converts to join a church—any church, it did not matter which. This disdain for denominational distinctives was a layman's answer to what was important and what was not. Besides excellent advance planning for every revival, Moody's genius lay in a reasoned, businesslike approach to his topic. He was not overly dramatic, always looking and acting like the businessman he was. His sermons were homey, even sentimental, stressing the love of God over wrath. He also repeated his core message at every opportunity. Moody preached of the "3 Rs":

Ruin by Sin
Redemption by Christ
Regeneration by the Spirit

Moody's posture as a layman was decidedly anti-intellectual, and he worked to make religion as simple as possible. Still, his messages contained swipes at the controversies of the day, showing that he knew what was in the air. At times he made it clear that he eschewed higher criticism of Scripture, telling ministers, "I don't see why you men are talking about two Isaiahs [discussing the theory that the biblical book of Isaiah was written by more than one author]; half the people in the country do not know that there is one Isaiah yet; let's make them know about one before we begin to tell them about two." Nevertheless, when it was time to plan or publicize a revival, Moody worked with liberals, too. When asked about his theology, he famously answered, "My theology! I didn't know I had any!" In fact, his theology was premillennialist, expecting things to get worse and worse in a fallen world until the coming of Christ. As usual, however, Moody put it more simply, "I look upon this world as a wrecked vessel. God has given me a lifeboat and said, 'Moody, save all you can.'" When told that some ministers complained, finding it "undignified" to advertise religious services, Moody shot back that it would be more "undignified" to preach to empty pews.[19]

As influential as Moody's revivals were in promoting a simple gospel message in the face of higher criticism, so too was the teaching of Phoebe Worrall Palmer (1807–84), a New York City Methodist who in the 1830s began offering a Tuesday Meeting where she taught people how to pray, read the Scriptures for themselves, and seek holiness as a step beyond conversion. In 1865 she said what she really thought about all the fuss clergy and academics made over Scripture: "The Bible is a wonderfully simple book; and, if you had taken the naked Word of God as . . . your counsel, instead of taking the opinions of men in regard to that Word, you might have been a more enlightened, simple, happy, and useful Christian."[20] Palmer's public speaking—not preaching (for women were banned from preaching in almost every tradition at the time), but instead speaking as a Christian laywoman—made her an advocate for Bible reading and testifying to spiritual experiences. The Tuesday Meetings movement spread so that by 1886, two years after Palmer's death, there were two hundred separate meetings happening simultaneously, with laity and clergy encouraging one another to practice the ways of holiness, consecrating all to God with faith in God's promises to deliver. A taste of the faith inspired by this movement can be grasped in words from the popular hymn "Blessed Assurance," written by Palmer's daughter Phoebe Palmer Knapp and Fanny Crosby in 1873:

> Blessed assurance, Jesus is mine!
> O what a foretaste of glory divine!
> Heir of salvation, purchase of God,
> Born of His Spirit, washed in His blood.

The refrain followed each verse:

> This is my story, this is my song,
> praising my Savior all the day long;
> this is my story, this is my song,
> praising my Savior all the day long.

The last two verses speak of "perfect submission" and becoming "lost in His love." The hymn first appeared in the July 1873 issue of *Palmer's Guide to Holiness and Revival Miscellany*, a magazine printed by Phoebe Palmer and her husband.

FIGURE 11-11. Phoebe Worrall Palmer, 1807–84 (smu.edu/Bridwell /SpecialCollectionsandArchives /Exhibitions/FiftyWomen /19thCenturyAmericans/Palmer)

Among progressives, the *Woman's Bible* caused a stir of major proportions by asking explicitly how good the Bible was for women. Published in two volumes in 1895 and 1898, it was the work of noted suffragist Elizabeth Cady Stanton and a committee of twenty-six women. The book challenged the traditional position of religious orthodoxy that women should be subservient to men. The authors' comments pointed out the few places where women are mentioned in the Bible. Though it was really not so much a Bible as a women's commentary on these issues, Stanton still could not get well-positioned and trained scholars to sign on to the project. Her experience demonstrates that while Darwinism and higher criticism were safe topics for religious scholars of the 1890s, sex, gender, and the Bible were not. The project itself shows learned amateur acquaintance with contemporary biblical scholarship. Yet these first-wave feminists pull no punches in what they think. A typical entry signed by Stanton herself is this paragraph from Genesis 2:

THE WOMAN'S BIBLE

"All the commentators and publicists writing on woman's position go through an immense amount of fine-spun metaphysical speculations, to prove her subordination in harmony with the Creator's original design.

"It is evident that some wily writer, seeing the perfect equality of man and woman in the first chapter, felt it important for the dignity and dominion of man to effect woman's subordination in some way. To do this a spirit of evil must be introduced, which at once proved itself stronger than the spirit of good, and man's supremacy was based on the downfall of all that had just been pronounced very good. This spirit of evil evidently existed before the supposed fall of man; hence woman was not the origin of sin as so often asserted. E. C. S."*

*Elizabeth Cady Stanton, *The Woman's Bible: A Classic Feminist Perspective* (Mineola, NY: Dover Publications, 2002), 20–21.

Although Susan B. Anthony tried to dissuade her colleague Stanton from even undertaking the project as a distraction to the goal of women's rights, she could not prevent younger feminists from pushing the National American Woman Suffrage Association to dissociate itself from the project. Stanton knew she had touched several nerves; she wrote her friend Reverend Antoinette Brown Blackwell in April 1896, observing: "Our politicians are calm and complacent under our fire, but the clergy jump round the moment you aim a pop gun at them 'like parched peas on a hot skillet.'" This matter of Bible interpretation could be quite contentious.

By the end of the nineteenth century, the fault lines of future conflicts were set. Conservative Protestants were skeptical of both science and higher criticism and proposing new forceful doctrines of biblical inerrancy or infallibility. A liberal Protestant wing professed its confidence in science, seeing the Bible as *witness* to revelation, not so much *revelation* per se. Eventually neo-orthodox and neo-evangelical positions would try to bridge the looming gap, but not before active hostilities broke out in the churches. And most Protestant Christians of the late 1800s probably just wanted to follow the example of Palmer and Moody and sing Anna B. Warner's 1860 hymn that became popular just as Darwin's *Origin of Species* was being read for the first time:

> Jesus loves me! This I know,
> For the Bible tells me so;
> Little ones to Him belong;
> They are weak, but He is strong.
>
> Yes, Jesus loves me!
> Yes, Jesus loves me!
> Yes, Jesus loves me!
> The Bible tells me so.

12. Mass Immigration and the Closing Western Frontier

The closing years of the 1800s brought intense conflict over land, the influx of new kinds of people, and the attempts to stop these changes from occurring. Most of the era's conflicts had religious dimensions, and some were intensely religious in nature. So-called "Christian friends of the Indians" interrupted tribal and family life. German Jews found their beliefs and practices challenged by the influx of the huge number of Jews from Eastern Europe and Russia. Irish Catholics found themselves at odds with German and Italian Catholics, who believed in worshiping differently, and also with immigrant Orthodox Christians from eastern and central Europe, who did not recognize the pope in Rome. Anglo-Saxon Protestants, convinced of their own superiority, viewed all demographic change with alarm and issued calls to shore up their dominance, excluding Chinese immigrants, deriding Jews and Catholics, and preventing Utah Mormons from achieving statehood until they gave up polygamy. By 1900, however, all the elements of twentieth-century multifaith and multicultural America were set in place, even if not yet celebrated as constituting America's greatness. America became even more diverse, down to our time in the twenty-first century, and the conversation about the meaning of religious and ethnic diversity in America continues.

In 1909 the Census Bureau published a book titled *A Century of Population Growth from the First Census of the United States to the Twelfth, 1790–1900*. In the volume the bureau celebrated the enormous growth of the United States over 110 years as measured by the constitutionally mandated decennial census. One chapter sticks out, however, with its attention to what the writers describe as the "foreign element" in America and its growth in the most recent decades.

The census data presented this way shows that by 1900 more than half of the population in New England and the middle states of the Eastern Seaboard, then the most populous part of the country, were born abroad or born of foreign-born parents. The South was growing very little in these years since it was still in a prolonged economic slump and agrarian in nature. In the "Added area" consisting of states and territories added since 1790, nearly 40 percent had been born abroad or were native (USA) born of parents who had immigrated. What this underscored was that America was

FIGURE 12-1. Census data, 1790–1900, in *A Century of Population Growth from the First Census of the United States to the Twelfth, 1790–1900* (Washington: Government Printing Office, 1909, 128)

Upon combining the number of foreign born and their native children, who comprise what may be termed the distinctly foreign element, the following proportion in each 1,000 of white population appears:

TABLE **57.**—*Number of persons of foreign birth and of native birth and foreign parentage, in each 1,000 of the white population: 1870, 1890, and 1900.*

YEAR.	ORIGINAL AREA.				Added area.
	Total.	New England.	Middle states.	Southern states.	
1870	306	331	427	94	340
1890	352	477	479	85	393
1900	378	546	507	79	394

visibly changing, nowhere so fast as in its cities, and the perception from self-designated "Old Stock" groups was that these changes were not for the better. They assessed their new neighbors through the lenses of religion and ethnicity, and often they did not like what they saw.

Perhaps no writer so captured the new nativism of the late nineteenth century as did the Reverend Josiah Strong (1847–1916). He was asked to write a book for a limited purpose: to encourage Protestant churches to engage in foreign and domestic missions. Instead, he managed to deliver an 1885 viral sensation promoting the idea of Anglo-Saxon supremacy, titled *Our Country: Its Possible Future and Its Present Crisis.* Even a brief excerpt demonstrates how the Congregational clergyman whipped up bigotry as he strived to encourage his fellow religionists:

> It seems to me that God, with infinite wisdom and skill, is training the Anglo-Saxon race for an hour sure to come in the world's future. Heretofore there has always been in the history of the world a comparatively unoccupied land westward, into which the crowded countries of the East have poured their surplus populations. But the widening waves of migration, which millenniums ago rolled east and west from the valley of the Euphrates, meet to-day on our Pacific coast. There are no more new worlds. The unoccupied arable lands of the earth are limited, and will soon be taken. The time is coming when the pressure of population on the means of subsistence will be felt here as it is now felt in Europe and Asia. Then will the world enter upon a new stage of its history—*the final competition of races, for which the Anglo-Saxon is being schooled.* Long before the thousand millions are here, the mighty

centrifugal tendency, inherent in this stock and strengthened in the United States, will assert itself. Then this race of unequaled energy, with all the majesty of numbers and the might of wealth behind it—the representative, let us hope, of the largest liberty, the purest Christianity, the highest civilization—having developed peculiarly aggressive traits calculated to impress its institutions upon mankind, will spread itself over the earth. If I read not amiss, this powerful race will move down upon Mexico, down upon Central and South America, out upon the islands of the sea, over upon Africa and beyond. And can any one doubt that the result of this competition of races will be the "survival of the fittest"?[1]

Thus Strong combined manifest destiny and social Darwinism and baptized them together. Yet what he said about the America of his time was even more memorable. Strong outlined seven perils confronting the country—immigration, Romanism (Roman Catholicism), Mormonism, intemperance, socialism, wealth, and cities—decrying each as evil; he called for reform led by Anglo-Saxons, representatives of civil liberty, and "pure, spiritual Christianity." Perhaps his most concentrated blow was reserved for the modern city, because in his view "the city has become a serious menace to our civilization, because in it . . . each of the dangers we have discussed [here he meant Roman Catholicism, socialism, wealth, intemperance, immigration—every danger except Mormonism] is enhanced, and all are focalized; . . . the rich are richer and the poor are poorer, in the city than elsewhere." The United States had a "divine mission" in realizing the kingdom of God as God's own chosen instrument, but first it had to reform itself. Strong went on to serve as general secretary of the Evangelical Alliance from 1886 to 1898. The Alliance was an early attempt to bring about Protestant cooperation, designed to show the superiority of a democratic society and spiritual unity, but Strong the liberal Protestant and his organization combined remarkable ethocentricism and pride in their approach to others.

Strong's version of a better America had already been put into practice in the Page Act of 1875, America's first restrictive federal immigration law. It prohibited the entry of Chinese women, alleging that they were in the United States only for immoral purposes like prostitution. This marked the end of an open-borders policy, where anyone could come. The first frontier to close was not the American West so much as the American mind about who could and should immigrate to America. In 1882, the Chinese Exclusion Act extended the immigration ban to Chinese men as well. Though that act was planned to last for ten years, it was renewed and made permanent in 1902. Only in 1943, when China was an ally in World War II, did the passage of the Magnuson Act allow Chinese again to immigrate to the U.S. Even then their numbers were limited to 105 persons per year. Direct racial barriers were removed in the 1952 Immigration and Nationality Act. Yet only the Hart-Celler Immigration and Nationality Act of 1965 finally abolished the

National Origins Formula. For almost a century, therefore, the United States was effectively closed to immigration from most Asian countries, a factor that shaped the religious development of the nation.

New Jewish Immigrants from Eastern Europe

While Congress was restricting Chinese immigration on the West Coast, the East Coast port cities were receiving large numbers of immigrants from places where few persons had come earlier. These new immigrants posed strong challenges inside the Jewish and Catholic religious communities already established in nineteenth-century America. For Jews, the small colonial communities of *Sephardic* Jews (*Sephard* is the Hebrew word for Spain; *Sephardic* identifies Jews of Iberian descent) on the Eastern Seaboard were supplemented throughout the first two-thirds of the 1800s with so-called German Jews, highly assimilated Ashkenazic Jews from German-speaking lands and Western Europe. These mid-nineteenth-century Jewish immigrants included a large number of Polish Jews, so the modifier "German" can be misleading. They settled in eastern cities, the new cities of the industrial heartland (Pittsburgh, Cincinnati, Chicago), and the commercial South (Atlanta, Natchez, New Orleans). The Judaism they founded in the United States was progressive, educated, and intelligible to non-Hebrew speakers. It could be found in Cincinnati at Hebrew Union College (1875) for training rabbis, in the Reform movement that gathered the leading rabbis, and in lay leaders of the nearly one-quarter million American Jews living in America in the 1870s. The Reform movement formulated and announced its principles in the Pittsburgh Platform, so-called because of its adoption at a conference held in 1885 under the leadership of Kaufmann Kohler and, especially, Isaac M. Wise. As you read the eight points of the Pittsburgh Platform, ponder how modern these ideas might sound then, or even now, to more traditional believers:

> 1. We recognize in every religion an attempt to grasp the Infinite, and in every mode, source or book of revelation held sacred in any religious system the consciousness of the indwelling of God in man. We hold that Judaism presents the highest conception of the Godidea as taught in our Holy Scriptures and developed and spiritualized by the Jewish teachers, in accordance with the moral and philosophical progress of their respective ages. We maintain that Judaism preserved and defended midst continual struggles and trials and under enforced isolation, this Godidea as the central religious truth for the human race.
>
> 2. We recognize in the Bible the record of the consecration of the Jewish people to its mission as the priest of the one God, and value it as the most potent instrument of religious and moral instruction. We hold that the modern discoveries of scientific researches in the domain

of nature and history are not antagonistic to the doctrines of Judaism, the Bible reflecting the primitive ideas of its own age, and at times clothing its conception of divine Providence and Justice dealing with men in miraculous narratives.

3. We recognize in the Mosaic legislation a system of training the Jewish people for its mission during its national life in Palestine, and today we accept as binding only its moral laws, and maintain only such ceremonies as elevate and sanctify our lives, but reject all such as are not adapted to the views and habits of modern civilization.

4. We hold that all such Mosaic and rabbinical laws as regulate diet, priestly purity, and dress originated in ages and under the influence of ideas entirely foreign to our present mental and spiritual state. They fail to impress the modern Jew with a spirit of priestly holiness; their observance in our days is apt rather to obstruct than to further modern spiritual elevation.

5. We recognize, in the modern era of universal culture of heart and intellect, the approaching of the realization of Israel's great Messianic hope for the establishment of the kingdom of truth, justice, and peace among all men. We consider ourselves no longer a nation, but a religious community, and therefore expect neither a return to Palestine, nor a sacrificial worship under the sons of Aaron, nor the restoration of any of the laws concerning the Jewish state.

6. We recognize in Judaism a progressive religion, ever striving to be in accord with the postulates of reason. We are convinced of the utmost necessity of preserving the historical identity with our great past. Christianity and Islam, being daughter religions of Judaism, we appreciate their providential mission, to aid in the spreading of monotheistic and moral truth. We acknowledge that the spirit of broad humanity of our age is our ally in the fulfillment of our mission, and therefore we extend the hand of fellowship to all who cooperate with us in the establishment of the reign of truth and righteousness among men.

7. We reassert the doctrine of Judaism that the soul is immortal, grounding the belief on the divine nature of human spirit, which forever finds bliss in righteousness and misery in wickedness. We reject as ideas not rooted in Judaism, the beliefs both in bodily resurrection and in Gehenna and Eden (Hell and Paradise) as abodes for everlasting punishment and reward.

8. In full accordance with the spirit of the Mosaic legislation, which strives to regulate the relations between rich and poor, we deem it our duty to participate in the great task of modern times, to solve, on the basis of justice and righteousness, the problems presented by the contrasts and evils of the present organization of society.[2]

Isaac Mayer Wise (1819–1900, seen above in figure 11-8) was a rabbi born in Austrian Moravia who had come to America in 1846. First in his ministry in Albany, New York, and then in Cincinnati, Ohio, Wise introduced many firsts that foreshadowed the affirmations of the Pittsburgh Platform. His Albany synagogue was the first to seat men and women together, the first to count women to make up a minyan (the ten adult Jews required to conduct public worship), to have a mixed-gender choir, and to eliminate the bar mitzvah in favor of a confirmation at a later age. Rationality in religious life was of supreme importance to Wise. It was ever his dream to organize unions of all the rabbis and all the congregations of Jews in America. In the end, he was successful in organizing those who agreed with him, yet also stimulating organization of Jews who thought the Reform movement had rejected too much that was key to their observance of Judaism. The critical moment of division between the two came as the result of what was to have been a high point in the movement.

On July 11, 1883, at Hebrew Union College more than two hundred dignitaries gathered for a banquet in celebration of the first graduating class of new rabbis. Guests came locally from Cincinnati and from as far away as New York. The menu was lavish. It also combined prohibited foods (clams, crabs, shrimp, frogs' legs) with foods that should not be mixed (meat and dairy). Though wealthy Jewish families from Cincinnati paid for the meal and made certain not to serve pork, rabbis from the East rose out of their seats and left when shrimp appeared on their plates. Wise refused to apologize, calling the rabbis' halakic scruples "kitchen Judaism." (*Halakah* [literally, "the way" in Hebrew] denotes the body of Jewish religious law, including laws about forbidden foods.)

The "Trefa banquet" (*Trefa*: food not meeting the requirements of Jewish law), as the incident was called, became a key basis for the formation of Conservative Judaism, with its own rabbinical and congregational unions and its own seminary, the Jewish Theological Seminary based in New York City. Its commitment to conserving tradition was based not on divine command, but on the tradition's importance in Jewish life. These ritual practices could be subject to development or change, but not to the outright dismissal demonstrated by Wise and others. This Conservative tradition initially occupied a position between assimilated Reform Judaism and the Orthodox Judaism practiced by others. During the twentieth century, however, Conservative Judaism would grow in influence and in numbers of adherents, in part because of what was happening at the very moment it began: the influx of Eastern Jews, from Russia or its adjacent areas.

Jews in Russia from the time of Catherine II in the late eighteenth century and onward were confined to an area called the "Pale of Settlement," which stretched over what is now Belarus, Lithuania, eastern Poland, and Ukraine. There they were treated more as a race to which a person always belonged than as a religion one could leave if one so chose. They were also subjected to certain disabilities, like paying twice the taxes paid by Christians. Under Czar Alexander II in the 1880s, anti-Jewish policies and attacks known as pogroms were stepped up. This led directly to the mass exodus of more than

FIGURE 12-2. Thomas Nast, Exiles from Russia—their first day in New York. From a sketch by S. F. Yeager, 1882 (loc.gov/item/92513488/)

two million Russian Jews between 1880 and 1920. The great preponderance of these people fled to the United States and to British-controlled Palestine, which eventually became the State of Israel (in 1948).[3]

Because Russian Jews had lived off by themselves in villages and shtetlach, or ghettos, they had not assimilated as much to prevailing European ways as the German Jews who came to the U.S. earlier. They seemed exotic to American gentiles and Jews alike, as the illustration from *Harper's Weekly* demonstrates. They also were accustomed to a highly Orthodox form of religious observance that guided every aspect of life in the old country. We find a helpful description from Mary Antin, a young immigrant:

> As I look back to-day I see, within the wall raised around my birthplace by the vigilance of the police, another wall, higher, thicker, more impenetrable. This is the wall which the Czar with all his minions could not shake, the priests with their instruments of torture could not pierce, the mob with their firebrands could not destroy. This wall within the wall is the religious integrity of the Jews, a fortress erected by the prisoners of the Pale, in defiance of their jailers; a stronghold built of the ruins of their pillaged homes, cemented with the blood of their murdered children.
>
> Not on festivals alone, but also on the common days of the week, we lived by the Law that had been given us through our teacher Moses. How to eat, how to bathe, how to work—everything had been written down for us, and we strove to fulfil the Law. The study of the Torah was the most honored of all occupations, and they who engaged in it the most revered of all men.[4]

Mary Antin wrote eloquently of the old country, where her father provided a comfortable living for his family, but where he was oppressed at every turn by gentiles. She wrote of the immense honor given to study and the role of the scholar, but as a girl she never attended a day of school until the family joined her father in Boston. There she quickly learned English and by February of her first year in school was writing poems about the father of her country, George Washington. Her autobiography, *The Promised Land*, carries in its very title a double meaning. For many Russian Jews, the promised land was not across the river Jordan, but across the Atlantic Ocean. Nearly two million Russian Orthodox Jews came to the United States, with many (like Mary Antin) enjoying the opportunity to explore secular freedoms and even taste forbidden foods. Her father allowed her mother to continue to keep a kosher kitchen, but he wanted his children to have the freedom to accept invitations with gentiles. Mary's father even avowed atheism. His daughter later shocked the schoolyard by denying the existence of God. Antin's schoolteacher was Miss Dillingham, a gentile Christian who later invited Mary to tea and put her to an unwitting test, as Antin relates:

> All went well, until a platter was passed with a kind of meat that was strange to me. Some mischievous instinct told me that it was ham—forbidden food; and I, the liberal, the free, was afraid to touch it! I had a terrible moment of surprise, mortification, self-contempt; but I helped myself to a slice of ham, nevertheless, and hung my head over my plate to hide my confusion. I was furious with myself for my weakness. I to be afraid of a pink piece of pig's flesh, who had defied at least two religions in defense of free thought! And I began to reduce my ham to indivisible atoms, determined to eat more of it than anybody at the table.[5]

Still, the event proved decisive to Antin's determination to hide her Jewishness. "That Spartan boy who allowed the stolen fox hidden in his bosom to consume his vitals rather than be detected in the theft," wrote Antin, "showed no such miracle of self-control as did I, sitting there at my friend's tea-table, eating unjewish meat."[6]

Mary Antin—or Maske, as she was known before she enthusiastically Americanized herself—represents one form of Eastern European Jews' religious adaptation to their new home. The historian Jonathan Sarna has written, with only slight exaggeration, that there were as many forms of Judaism as Jews in this period. Some Orthodox Jews renewed the faith of the old country, based in home and *shul* (Yiddish for *synagogue*). Others sent sons to attend Jewish Theological Seminary and helped the Conservative movement grow. Still others created their own theological seminaries that bridged the American college model and the yeshiva. And many of the two million who came from 1880 to 1924, when immigration stopped, were minimally religious and never belonged to a synagogue in the United States. Yet Sarna writes that, having left parents behind in Europe, American Jews were particularly apt to honor their mothers and fathers in death, saying the Kaddish, the mourner's prayer in which God is magnified and praised. Even, and especially, in the face of the loss of a loved one, the God who created life is praised. Sometimes these mourners had made religious and life choices that their parents would not have approved of, but as one observer noted, "Death sustains the life of American Judaism." It was a time that bound together the most religiously observant with their nonreligious contemporaries.[7]

Even among the religious Orthodox, there was a great movement in building new, decorous, and refined synagogues to copy the middle-class respectability formerly associated with the Reform movement.[8] It was also in cities like New York that Orthodox Jews from all parts of Eastern Europe—Galicia, Hungary, Lithuania, Poland, Romania, Russia—began to gather in single-neighborhood synagogues and leave aside the marks of distinction that had divided their previous practice in the old countries. In this way they too were Americanized. And for philanthropists like Jacob Schiff (1847–1920), these signs of assimilation were welcome. Having come from Germany in his teens, he used the immense wealth he made on Wall Street to raise up the Jewish people. He helped fund both Jewish Theological Seminary and the Hebrew Union College, and both fledgling Orthodox seminaries in New York, one of which would become Yeshiva University. Additionally, Schiff made large contributions to the relief programs for the Jewish victims of the Russian Czar's anti-Semitic pograms, even as he worried about signs of American anti-Semitism and general xenophobia expressed toward the new immigrants arriving at Ellis Island in New York Harbor. For that, he and other successful and assimilated Jews supported the Henry Street Settlement House, modeled on similar Protestant efforts, which took poor immigrants under its wings and provided the training, social capital, and skills necessary to achieve the first steps on the American ladder of success.[9] So too did the Young Women's Hebrew Association (YWHA) founded in New York in 1988 especially for the purpose of immigrant education. At Henry Street, the YWHA, and in organizations like the National Council of Jewish Women (1893), Jewish women found a place in religious and community life they had never experienced before.

Did Jacob Schiff, the YWHA, and leaders of the Jewish community need to worry about what other Americans thought? We can gauge part of the sentiment of the Protestant majority by viewing Frank Beard's cartoon, "The Stranger at Our Gate," in figure 12-3. It is clear that the image has anti-Semitic elements, along with other signifiers particularly aimed at Catholics coming from eastern and southern Europe where "superstition," "anarchy," "disease," "Sabbath desecration" (from drinking and dancing on Sundays), and "intemperance" were especially thought to have emanated.

The editors of *The Ram's Horn* indicated what they thought should happen to additions to the "melting pot" in a text that ran with the color cartoon: "When that stream is polluted with the moral sewage of the old world, including its poverty, drunkenness, infidelity and disease, it is well to put up the bars and save America, at least until she can purify the atmosphere of

FIGURE 12-3. "The Stranger at Our Gate" (Cartoon by Frank Beard, in *The Ram's Horn* magazine, Chicago [April 25, 1896])

THE STRANGER AT OUR GATE.

EMIGRANT. Can I come in? UNCLE SAM. I 'spose you can; there's no law to keep you out.

contagion which foreign invasion has already brought." And then without pausing to think about the source of their biblical warrant, the editors closed by invoking Jeremiah 7:2–3:

> Stand in the gate of the LORD's house,
> and proclaim there this word: . . .
> Thus saith the LORD of hosts,
> the God of Israel,
> Amend your ways and your doings,
> and I will cause you to dwell in this place.[10]

Other World Religions Appearing

Some immigrants coming in small numbers—Muslims as laborers from Syria, Turkey, and Lebanon—blended in with darker-skinned Europeans in American cities in the late nineteenth century. But Sikh, Chinese, and Japanese immigrants were not so lucky. In the Pacific Northwest, Sikh men from the Punjab of India were noticeably different because of the turbans they wore. Even Hindus who also came from India treated them poorly because of their religious beliefs, which were monotheistic as in Islam and incorporated reincarnation as the consequence of an insufficiently virtuous life, as in Hindu belief.

On the West Coast and intermountain West, Chinese men were brought over to work on railroad building in the middle of the nineteenth century, yet with relatively few women; they worked in mining camps in towns afterward. There they were perceived as a threat to native labor. In a nation that had since 1790 restricted citizenship by law to whites only, Asians had no long-term security. This point was made clear by the Chinese exclusion acts of 1888, 1892, and 1902, plus other measures. Japanese-Americans who largely made their way in the new land as couples and families in the San Francisco Bay area fared slightly better, going so far as to start Young Men's (and) Women's Buddhist Associations in West Coast cities by the end of the century and hosting a Buddhist Mission to the United States. These Isei and Nisei (first- and second-generation) Japanese Americans were choosing the assimilation route, even converting these YMBAs into American Buddhist Church congregations shortly after the turn of the twentieth century. Still, no matter how far Japanese Americans ascended professionally, and how much Buddhism was made like Protestant congregational life, race limited their full acceptance, a reality made glaringly evident when the United States Supreme Court denied citizenship to Takao Ozawa in 1922 after twenty years in the country because he was not white.[11] America was wrong to be racially exclusionary, yet religiously something new had happened: immigrants brought Islam, Buddhism, and Confucianism to American shores for the first time, unnoticed by the average American.

The World Parliament of Religions

The end of the nineteenth century saw an increased awareness that other non-Western religions were also being practiced in America. The West Coast hosted the greatest number of Chinese and Japanese immigrants and therefore the most significant number of practitioners of Buddhism and also of Chinese folk religion derived from Taoism, Confucianism, and Pure Land Buddhism. From 1875 onward, there was always a physical house of worship in San Francisco for Chinese religion. Sometimes there were many.

Many Americans first encountered other world religions besides Christianity and Judaism at the Columbian Exposition of 1893 in Chicago. This world's fair, of sorts, was held in commemoration of Columbus coming to America four centuries earlier. Many nations occupied pavilions alongside halls dedicated to industry and agriculture. A Unitarian, Jenkin Lloyd Jones, conceived of the Parliament. He, together with mostly liberal Protestants with some participation by Catholics and Jews, planned to hold a World Parliament of Religions at the Exposition and invited religious leaders from around the world to gather in the Auxiliary Building, later the home of the Art Institute of Chicago. Those who responded and attended were predominantly Christians from other nations, but the attention of the public was drawn to the learned and eloquent representatives of Asian religious traditions such as the Hindu Swami Vivekananda (1863–1902) and the Japanese

Buddhist priest Shaku Soyen (1860–1919). Buddhist monks in colorful robes drew so much attention that they were given their own room. Muslim and Baha'i leaders also attended.[12]

The Parliament's purpose was educational: to promote understanding of the world's major (and some minor) religious traditions. Jain preacher Virchand Gandhi spoke of that tradition's cosmology and code of conduct. Buddhism's first global missionary, Anagarika Dharmapala (1864–1933), represented Sinhalese, nonviolent Theravada practices. Swami Vivekananda went the goal of understanding one better by leaving behind Vedanta Societies, which brought the knowledge of and respect for Hindu religious ideas and practices to Victorian-era Americans. Since very few ethnic Hindus were in America, most of the Vedanta Society's early members were well-educated Americans who were looking for an older, more esoteric wisdom than that contained in the predominant evangelical Christianity of the day. Many of these also explored Theosophy and New Thought. This constituted the first instance of a kind of export Hinduism, which in the twentieth century would come to include Swami Paranahansa Yoganda's (1893–1952) Self Realization Fellowship (1925), Transcendental Meditation (TM) introduced to this country in 1959 by the Maharishi Mahesh Yogi (1911–2008), and the International Society for Krishna Consciousness (ISKCON), brought by A. C. Bhaktivedanta Swami Prabhupada (1896–1977) in 1965. Each of these groups introduced meditation and yoga to America in the decades before and alongside later large-scale ethnic Hindu immigration following the 1965 immigration act. Therefore, though the elite liberal Protestants and Jenkin Jones himself had hoped to promote the superiority of liberal Protestantism, the seventeen-day event's breakout hits were charismatic religious leaders

FIGURE 12-4. Parliament of Religions, September 1893. On the platform, left to right, Virchand Gandhi, unknown, Anagarika Dharmapala, Swami Vivekananda, G. Bonet Maury, unknown, and Nikola Tesla. (commons .wikimedia.org/wiki/File :Swami_Vivekananda _at_Parliament_of _Religions.jpg)

from elsewhere in the world, especially those from the British Empire who expressed their learned ideas in polished English.

Shaku Soyen, a Japanese Zen priest, was also a central figure from abroad. His version of Buddhism was communicated even more effectively by his students who stayed behind in America and by a lay follower: D. T. Suzuki (1870–1966), who became the teacher most associated with Buddhism for Americans in the middle of the twentieth century (see chap. 15). In these various ways the World Parliament of Religions succeeded not so much in promoting a relaxed Protestantism as fostering the beginning of pluralism in American thought: the idea that other religions have an equal claim to the ultimate truths of meaning in existence.

Shifting Catholicism and Eastern Orthodoxy

In the late nineteenth century the pattern established in American Catholic life at midcentury was stretched. First, after the unification of Germany in 1871 under Chancellor Otto von Bismarck, the pattern of German-speaking immigrants shifted from northern Protestants to mostly southern Catholics. This led to a great expansion of Catholic presence in cities like St. Louis, Milwaukee, and St. Paul. But since the church hierarchy in those places was already of Irish descent, it took some time to work out linguistic issues, parish boundaries, and other matters. Fortunately, the Germans were relatively prosperous and began to support their church quickly. Then there was another potato famine, which led to another influx of Irish immigrants. Next came the Italians, followed by other Southern Europeans.

In 1870, there were only about 25,000 Italian immigrants living in America, and many of these were from northern Italy. Not a few of these had left during the wars for Italian independence and unification, called the Risorgimento (rising again), that came in many parts from 1815 until 1871, when Rome was at last declared capital of a unified Italy. Between 1880 and the effective halt of immigration in 1924, more than four million Italians immigrated to the United States, half of these from 1900–1910 alone.

What led the millions to leave Italy? The intense poverty in southern Italy, including the islands of Sardinia and Sicily, drove agrarian people from their homes to seek out the promise of new ways of life. It was said that many did not know they were Italian, the level of education was so low and the commitment to one's village of origin was so high. For the American Catholic Church, this massive influx in places like New York, Boston, Providence, Newark, Philadelphia, and Chicago posed special problems. One contemporary observer, Julian Miranda, spoke to this perception and to Catholic Italians' own sense of piety in an Irish-dominated church:

> On the topic of the church, it must be remembered that Southern Italian men were not so church scrupulous as the women although they

were Catholic. I think no one should mistake their non-church attendance for a lack of belief in the Roman Catholic faith. The seeming lack
of scrupulosity in Italians should not delude anybody about their lack
of commitment to Christianity and its central ideas. I think there is a
great paradox and a great ambivalence there. Basically they dislike the
clergy, and if they dislike the Italian clergy, they despise the American
clergy. They were very cruelly treated by this group.

I remember when I was a child going for my First Communion,
and I was asked by one of the nuns to recite the Our Father. I had only
known it in either Sicilian or Latin [dog Latin]. I knew what was going
to happen, but I got up and recited it, and of course the class guffawed
and the nun made fun of me. In a rage, I left the class. It was a Sunday
and my grandfather was coming to the house, saw my face, and said,
"*Die succedio* [What happened]?" At first, I did not want to tell him
because of the *omerta* [You did not whine], but I finally told him that
I said my prayer in Sicilian, and they laughed at me. Inside of thirty
seconds he had me by the arm and had propelled me up to the church.
There, he got hold of Fr. Fitzsimmons and the nun and verbally laid
them out. Nevertheless, this affected my church attendance.

The lack of concern by the church for the immigrants and the cultural difference between the Italian and Irish Catholicism were responsible for a lot of the movement of Italians out of the Church toward
Protestantism. This was also, however, a way to upward mobility. Had
there been Italian clergy, there is no question but that it would have
made a difference. First of all, the mere fact of being able to converse
with the priest in your own language is important, but the role of the
priest has been limited until very recently. The priest was not really a
social agent by and large. I do not think priests gave social assistance
beyond the performance of their strictly religious functions.[13]

If the Italians had a difficult time being accepted in the Catholic Church
of the late nineteenth century, more so did the Poles, who began to arrive
in large numbers during the same period. The U.S. church had no Polish
bishops and few Polish priests and did not allow Polish to be taught in parish
schools. Meanwhile, the church in Poland had split apart over Vatican I and
other divisions. The First Vatican Council (1869–70), a plenary council of
the Roman Catholic Church, had promulgated the doctrine of Papal Infallibility: that when teaching on matters of faith, the pope, as the representative
of Jesus Christ, cannot err. Some Catholics did not accept the new teaching
and started declaring their churches faithful to older doctrine. Old Catholics, the products of such a split, were not welcome in the Roman Catholic
dioceses in which they set up parishes affiliated with the Polish National
Catholic Church on their own initiative. Neither were Uniate Catholics
made welcome. Uniate Catholics acknowledge papal supremacy but retain
their own liturgy based in Eastern Orthodox Christianity. A turning point
for Uniate Christians, and for Orthodox Christians more generally, came in

December 1889, when Alex Toth, an Eastern-rite Catholic priest, went to the local Roman Catholic archbishop, John Ireland, to seek permission to serve a new parish of Carpatho-Russians in Minneapolis. Toth later wrote an account of what happened:

> The place of my appointment was Minneapolis, Minnesota, in the dio-cese of Archbishop John Ireland. As an obedient Uniate, I complied with the orders of my bishop [the bishop of Prešov], who at that time was John Valiy, and appeared before Bishop Ireland on December 19, 1889. I kissed his hand, as I should have, according to custom (fail-ing, however, to kneel before him, which as I learned later was my chief mistake), and presented my credentials. I remember well that no sooner did he read that I was a "Greek Catholic" than his hands began to shake! It took him almost 15 minutes to read to the end, after which he asked me abruptly (the conversation was in the Latin language):
> "Do you have a wife?"
> "No."
> "But you had one?"
> "Yes. I am a widower."
> Hearing this, he threw the paper on the table and loudly shouted: "I have already written to Rome protesting against this kind of priest being sent to me."
> "What kind of priest do you mean?"
> "Your kind."
> "But I am a Catholic priest of the Greek rite. I am a Uniate, and I was ordained by a lawful Catholic bishop."
> "I do not consider that either you or that bishop are Catholic. Besides, I do not need any Greek Catholic priests here. A Polish priest in Minneapolis is more than enough. He can also be the priest for the Greeks."
> "But he belongs to the Latin Rite. Besides, our people will not understand him and so they will hardly go to him. That was the reason that they built a church of their own."
> "I did not give them permission to do that, and I do not grant you jurisdiction to serve here."
> I was deeply hurt by this kind of fanaticism of this representative of papal Rome and sharply replied to him: "In that case I neither ask from you a jurisdiction nor your permission. I know the rights of my church. I know the basis on which the Unia was established, and I will act according to them."
> The archbishop lost his temper. I lost mine just as much. One word led to another. The thing went so far that it is not worthwhile to recon-struct our entire conversation further.[14]

Rome ordered Toth and seven other Greek Catholic priests to return to Europe. Toth's congregation had other ideas and suggested receiving per-mission from the Russian Orthodox Archbishop Vladimir, whose see had been relocated from Alaska to San Francisco. Soon Toth was received and shortly after that the whole congregation of 361 was received by the arch-bishop personally into the Orthodox Church. This in turn led, thanks to Toth's efforts, to 65 Greek Catholic communities with 20,000 people becoming Orthodox (predominantly in the Northeast). Added to this were Serbian, Greek, Albanian, Romanian, Bulgarian, Ukrainian, Syrian, and Russian and other Orthodox Christians coming to the United States, all between 1870 and 1924. What most had in common was the remarkable practice of gathering together a parish of like-minded believers and then asking a bishop from the old country to send them a priest. By the 1926 U. S. Religious Census, the total number of Orthodox had grown from a mere handful in 1875 to 259,394.[15]

Native American Religious Life

Native American religious life changed dramatically from the 1830s to the 1890s under pressure from land-hungry settlers, American politicians, and a U.S. military engaged in a nearly continuous process of confining indigenous peoples and their tribes to reservations. The reservation system was based upon the idea of Native people having sovereign rights as separate and defined nations. For their part, the Native tribes, who signed treaties with the federal government (effectively at gunpoint) agreed to remain on a defined reservation in return for specific guaranteed annual amounts of food and trade items to be administered by agents of the government. These agents were nearly all white and notoriously corrupt in practice. Congress itself, every Indian nation's treaty partner, also frequently reduced the terms of its annuity payments.

The annals of the Bureau of Indian Affairs (BIA) are full of complaints that the government was not fulfilling its side of treaty obligations. Worse still, the reservations were often unilaterally made smaller or moved when settlers or miners found something on Native-held land that they wanted (like gold in California and the Black Hills). Sometimes the people who signed the treaties on behalf of Native Americans did not have the authority to do so, and tribes resisted leaving their ancestral lands for inferior reservations to which they had not agreed to move. This was true in the case of the Wal-lam-wat-kia band of the Nez Perce nation led by Chief Joseph (In-mut-too-yah-lat-lat), who took his people's case all the way to Washington, D.C., in 1879. Two years earlier his band had been forcibly removed from the land they were promised in their native Oregon and relocated in Idaho. The case involving white deceit and government recklessness received national newspaper coverage. Chief Joseph's speech, made in a public auditorium in Washington, was published in its entirety in the then popular *North American Review*. Chief Joseph made an impassioned moral and religious argument to federal government leaders, as we can see in his words taken from that speech.

CHIEF JOSEPH'S (IN-MUT-TOO-YAH-LAT-LAT)
SPEECH IN WASHINGTON, D.C.

"My friends, I have been asked to show you my heart. I am glad to have a chance to do so. I want the white people to understand my people. Some of you think an Indian is like a wild animal. This is a great mistake. I will tell you all about our people, and then you can judge whether an Indian is a man or not. I believe much trouble and blood would be saved if we opened our hearts more. I will tell you in my way how the Indian sees things. The white man has more words to tell you how they look to him, but it does not require many words to speak the truth. What I have to say will come from my heart, and I will speak with a straight tongue. Ah-cum-kin-i-ma-me-hut (the Great Spirit) is looking at me, and will hear me.

"Our fathers gave us many laws, which they had learned from their fathers. These laws were good. They told us to treat all men as they treated us; that we should never be the first to break a bargain; that it was a disgrace to tell a lie; that we should speak only the truth; that it was a shame for one man to take from another his wife, or his property without paying for it. We were taught to believe that the Great Spirit sees and hears everything, and that he never forgets; that hereafter he will give every man a spirit-home according to his deserts: if he has been a good man, he will have a good home; if he has been a bad man, he will have a bad home. This I believe, and all my people believe the same."*

*In-mut-too-yah-lat-lat, "Speech at Lincoln Hall" in Washington, D.C., 1879; in *North American Review* 128, no. 269 (April 1879): 412–34, www.jstor.org/stable/i25100738.

FIGURE 12-5. Chief Joseph (National Portrait Gallery, Smithsonian Institution NPG.78.68)

Chief Joseph went on to explain that while his band of Nez Perce had refused to sell their land, so-called Indian agents and other Nez Perce had sold what was not theirs to sell. Chief Joseph compared this to a man selling someone else's horse, saying, "Suppose a white man should come to me and say, 'Joseph, I like your horses, and I want to buy them.' I say to him, 'No, my horses suit me, I will not sell them.' Then he goes to my neighbor, and says to him: 'Joseph has some good horses. I want to buy them, but he refuses to sell.' My neighbor answers, 'Pay me the money, and I will sell you Joseph's horses.'"

The indigenous people's land had been thus stolen. Then Joseph said, "I only ask of the Government to be treated as all other men are treated. If I can not go to my own home, let me have a home in some country where my people will not die so fast." The chief reported that three of his people had died since he left for Washington. Meanwhile his heart was made heavy by people of his race being treated like animals and herded from country to country. Instead of this continued mistreatment, he asked only for "an even chance to live as other men live. We ask to be recognized as men. We ask that the same law shall work alike on all men. If the Indian breaks the law, punish him by the law. If the white man breaks the law, punish him also." Chief Joseph concluded memorably:

> Let me be a free man—free to travel, free to stop, free to work, free to trade where I choose, free to choose my own teachers, free to follow the religion of my fathers, free to think and talk and act for myself— and I will obey every law, or submit to the penalty.
> In-mut-too-yah-lat-lat has spoken for his people.[16]

From even this description of Chief Joseph's plea, we can see how well he understood American cultural values of the time and was able to appeal to them to make his case. Chief Joseph's arguments did not fall on completely deaf ears. His speech generated substantial support and goodwill for the Nez Perce; yet many of the more than five hundred other tribal groups were undergoing similar hardships of dislocation and even genocidal attacks by the Army. The Wal-lam-wat-kain band of the Nez Perce did not get to stay in Oregon, but they did end up in the state of Washington, on the Colville reservation. Meanwhile, the reservation system had developed to be such a scandal that some American citizens (and note that Native Americans were not permitted to be citizens until 1924) declared themselves the "Christian Friends of Indians." These citizens began to advocate for measures that would break up the reservation system. One of their number, Richard Henry Pratt, described his mission this way:

> A great general has said that the only good Indian is a dead one, and that high sanction of his destruction has been an enormous factor in promoting Indian massacres. In a sense, I agree with this sentiment,

but only in this: that all the Indian there is in the race should be dead. Kill the Indian in him, and save the man. . . . Theorizing citizenship into people is a slow operation. What a farce it would be to attempt teaching American citizenship to Negroes in Africa. . . . Neither can the Indian understand or use American citizenship theoretically taught to them on Indian reservations. They must get into the swim of American citizenship. . . . They must feel the touch of it day after day, until they become saturated with the spirit of it, and thus become equal to it.[17]

The plans of do-gooder activists like Pratt included privatization of native properties upon a formula entirely devised from above, with male heads of household receiving a half section (320 acres), and with women and other dependents receiving various lesser amounts of land. Of course, these lands were almost by definition unsuitable for private cultivation. As for Native children, the plan to "kill the Indian inside the man" led to the establishment of thousands of Indian schools, of which the one founded at an old Army base at Carlisle, Pennsylvania, by Pratt was just the most famous. Children as young as five were sent across the country to the school and forbidden to speak their native languages upon punishment of having their mouths washed out with lye soap. Children also exchanged their familiar native clothes for the starched and "uncomfortable" clothing of Victorian America. Because the schools did not pay for travel, Native American schoolchildren might go for years without ever returning to their homes and families. Some never made it home: there are more than 180 graves of children who died and were buried at Carlisle Indian Industrial School alone. Though Carlisle was the biggest from 1879 until its closure in 1918, Catholics, Episcopalians, Presbyterians, Baptists, and Methodists founded other such boarding schools across the West, some of which continue to operate.

While Washington was pursuing a policy of dismantling reservations under the legal auspices of the Dawes Act (1887) and its private allotment system, other things were happening to indigenous peoples. In California, the small size of typical groupings (roughly 250 and below per band) led to their near annihilation by incoming settlers and miners and the diseases they carried with them. The Navajo (Diné) were fighting not to be relocated to unfamiliar Oklahoma; eventually they returned to their four corners homeland of Arizona, Utah, Colorado, and New Mexico. The Western Sioux, or Lakota, were pacified by extreme force after killing George Armstrong Custer and his troops at Little Bighorn (1876) and then were not so lucky. They faced repeated retribution, and yet the vessel for their great misfortune at the massacre at Wounded Knee (1890) was occasioned, in part, through a pan-tribal religious movement begun nearly 1,200 miles away by a member of the Northern Paiute, one named Wovoka, who also went by the name Jack Wilson.

Ghost Dance Religion

The Northern Ute made their home in the fragile Great Basin area of the American West; their people lived on nuts, fish, and birds. The coming of farmers and ranchers to Nevada led to water diversions and massive trout deaths, ending their way of life along the Walker and Truckee Rivers. So Northern Paiutes adapted, scrounging for wood, food, and working for white men. Jack Wilson, as he was called by the Wilson rancher family, with whom he had worked for years, had a vision and began to tell others about it. Wovoka, as he was among his own people, fell into a trance lasting a reported twelve to fourteen hours. Upon rising he prophesied that Native Americans would soon repossess the country and the whites would disappear. John Mayhugh, a special census agent who reported on these events from Nevada, indicated that these prophecies were not seen as a threat to whites. Some of them even joined the dances that Wovoka instructed his listeners to do to bring about the restoration. Why? Historian Louis Warren believes that for indigenous people and whites alike, the Great Basin was experiencing a kind of apocalypse, where the dreams of American progress had exhausted the land and made everyone desperate.[18]

FIGURE 12-6. Ghost Dance of the Sioux Indians in North America, *Illustrated London News*, January 3, 1891 (Library of Congress loc.gov/item/2006681363/)

Beginning with a solar eclipse on January 1, 1889, Wovoka began preaching that God (and sometimes Christ) told him to do the Ghost Dance—a circular ritual dance that would bring about the return of the bison to all Western native tribes, the departure of all whites, and the resurrection of their dead. Wovoka knew these things because he had himself died and been raised and talked, he said, with Christ. As millenarian and utopian as this message was, predicting the restoration of all lost things, Wovoka's teaching about how change was to happen was as down-to-earth as the Presbyterian and Mormon teachings he had been exposed to among the Wilsons. Wovoka taught that Indians should farm their land, work jobs for wages, and refrain from waging war, even on the white man. Wovoka, in other words, offered a full-blown religion with hope for the here and now and also for a time when all things would be restored.[19]

Word spread about the Paiute who had died and risen and talked to Christ *and* who could control the weather. Native Americans from all over the West hopped rides on trains and wagons to meet Wovoka during 1889 and 1890. Perhaps no religion, ancient or modern, spread so quickly and far. This brings us back to the Western Lakota, who liked what they heard about the Ghost Dance religion. The restoration of the sacred bison was one feature. Another was the belief that ghost dancers wearing specially embroidered shirts would be impervious to bullets. Unfortunately, the units of the U.S. Army under General Nelson Miles were keeping their ears and eyes on the Lakota as talk circulated of warriors who could not be killed by Winchester bullets. Rumors swirled for months in 1890 that the Ghost Dance was a prelude for an organized uprising, and General Miles ordered the dancing (depicted just months later in a London news magazine) stopped. Meanwhile, the dancing went on, and Army Lieutenant Colonel Guy Carlton tried to explain matters to his superiors back in Washington: "They believe that the 'Messiah' dance is a prayer to the 'Messiah' to come and bless them, and they want to know why the whites object to their dance (prayer) and will naturally soon think that they (the whites) are afraid of his coming and are trying to prevent it by preventing the Indians' dancing, i.e., praying for him to come."[20]

When Spotted Elk was ordered to take his group of 350 and report to the Pine Ridge Reservation in late December 1890, they moved slowly in the winter weather. They were overtaken some miles from the reservation by a detachment from the Seventh Cavalry and ordered to make camp at Wounded Knee Creek (in southwestern South Dakota). The next morning, they were surrounded by a larger contingent of cavalry armed with Hotchkiss guns, an early machine gun. Amid miscommunication, Ghost Dancing, and resistance, gunfire began, and then the Hotchkiss guns were deployed. Within an hour at least 150 Lakota men, women, and children were dead, and the Army had killed 25 of their own men with their guns in crossfire. Many more were wounded on both sides, and the dead lay frozen on the ground amid a blizzard.

In 1893 at the World's Columbian Exposition in Chicago, just three years after the worst massacre of indigenous people on their own land in American history, Frederick Jackson Turner stood before the gathering of the American Historical Association and offered an interpretation based upon the 1890 Census's finding that the frontier had closed. American democracy, Jackson said, and all that went with it was not imported from Europe, but instead forged in the forest and on the plains by successive generations of settlers discarding the aristocracies, customs, and churches of the old world and making their own institutions as they went. In the years that followed, many historians embraced Turner's thesis; other Americans, like Josiah Strong, worried about what would happen once the basically free land was gone. Little noticed was Turner's contention that violence had accompanied westward movement at every step of the journey. Native peoples, the formerly enslaved, and America's newest immigrants, however, knew this only too well. The high price for multicultural and multifaith America was paid mostly by them and their children.[21]

13. A Social Gospel and Black Religious Life in the Nadir

The closing decades of the nineteenth century are often called the Gilded Age. From 1865 till well into the 1920s, American industrialists became rich beyond the belief of their contemporaries and used new legal mechanisms like joint-stock ownership corporations and anti-competitive trusts to ensure still greater profits and secure these gains for their families beyond the grave. Meanwhile, the robber barons who owned steel mills, railroads, textile mills, mines, and oil companies employed more and more of the American population at barely livable wages—sometimes even owning the very housing where their workers and workers' families lived and appointing onsite religious leaders to align with company values. At the same time, black Americans were slipping backward under a Jim Crow racial regime in which the freedoms granted to them under the Constitution were erased under the color of law and custom. The American nation was divided, and religious people sought to respond to these challenges of economic and racial injustice.

In chapter 11, we already encountered one conservative line of response in Dwight L. Moody's metaphor of the dying world and the lifeboat. Moody and his fellow premillennial dispensationalists expected the world to get worse until the second coming of Christ. Two other groups of late nineteenth- and early twentieth-century Americans were determined to do all they could to reform America and even the world to bring it into conformity with what they identified as the kingdom of God. This chapter features an extraordinary cast of characters including Washington Gladden, Walter Rauschenbusch, Francis Grimké, W. E. B. Du Bois, Booker T. Washington, and Ida B. Wells. Their joint story is one of hope and progress tempered by outside hostility.

It is helpful to get a sense of the religious landscape of the late nineteenth century before surveying the social and economic scene and seeing how religious groups and their leaders interacted with the events of the day. The first and by far the largest group were the *evangelicals*, consisting of the Methodists, Baptists, Presbyterians, Congregationalists, the Dutch and German Reformed churches, the Disciples of Christ, Churches of Christ, Nazarenes, some Episcopalians, and some Lutherans. They were evangelical Protestants in the sense that preaching and sharing the faith with society (and the world) in word and good deeds united them, even as denominational "distinctives," or theological and ethnic origins, differentiated them from one another. Nevertheless, this was a broad group, combining conservatives like Dwight L. Moody, Holiness advocates like Phoebe Palmer, and liberals like Henry Ward Beecher—all in one broad movement. Splits over Pentecostalism, fundamentalism, and modernism were all in the future. These mostly white churches also had some African American members and ministers, but most black evangelicals belonged to the African Methodist Episcopal, African Methodist Episcopal Zion, Christian Methodist Episcopal, and National Baptist churches, which we can now designate as the *black church.*

Also large in number were those we may designate *liturgicals:* Christians whose worship life was centered on the celebration of the Eucharist, more than on the preached word by itself. The liturgicals included most Lutherans, Episcopalians, Roman Catholics, and the various Orthodox churches. The fact that they were "high church" and centered on liturgical rituals like a weekly Eucharist set them apart from their white and black evangelical church counterparts. For a time, it also meant that these churches were less likely to engage in either missionary activity or the political issues of the day.

Finally, our conceptual map needs a space around its borders for the forms of religious practice present at the turn of the twentieth century in America that do not fit the evangelicals, black church, and liturgical categories. Here we find groups that are comfortable in their own identities and locations, such as Boston's Unitarians and Utah's Mormons, who are related to but different from the evangelicals for belief reasons. We also find an increasing number of new religious movements: the Seventh-day Adventists, Jehovah's Witnesses, followers of New Thought, Christian Science, and the small numbers of Chinese and Japanese Buddhists, alongside Muslims and Baha'is. Add to these the two and a half million American Jews, representing a variety of sects, practices, and length of time in the U.S. Most of these movements did not yet have wide representation in America's towns and villages, but all of them were on a more or less equal footing at the 1893 World's Parliament of Religions held at Chicago's Columbian Exposition.

America was slowly becoming more religiously diverse. In this chapter, however, it is those from the evangelical and black church traditions that will speak the loudest to the crises of class and race out of their respective senses of stewardship for souls and bodies beyond the temple precincts alone.

The Gilded Age

Humorist Mark Twain and his co-author Charles Dudley Warner effectively lent the title of their 1873 novel, *The Gilded Age*, to the period that stretched from 1870 until the 1910s. Gilding is the process of placing a superficial layer of gold over a common object. Their obvious comparison is to any other "golden age," for as it becomes clear in the novel, their subject is money-mad

America, with the few filthy rich on top, the many poor below, and a culture of corruption that maintains the distance between the two. Two years earlier, Twain had parodied the Westminster Shorter Catechism's famous first question by rephrasing it: "What is the chief end of man? —to get rich. In what way? —dishonestly if we can; honestly if we must." Mark Twain was no fan of the Gilded Age, or its conspicuous wealth. In just one memorable event, New York's Mrs. Stuyvesant Fish threw a dinner to honor her dog, which arrived in a diamond collar worth $15,000 or roughly $400,000 in today's money. Meanwhile, it was estimated that 11 million of the 12 million American families in 1890 brought home less than $1,200 per year.[1]

The economic shifts of the era were dramatic, supplanting an economy dominated by agriculture with a more diverse one that now included an industrial sector emphasizing manufacturing, and employing ever-increasing numbers of Americans in factory labor—except when businesses and banks failed, leading to mass unemployment. Congress further emphasized the shift away from farming and toward manufacturing by adopting a protectionist tariff making it prohibitively expensive to buy imported goods. This was favorable for manufacturers and hard on farmers and owners of small businesses. Mechanization also made farmers more productive. But with resulting low prices, high railroad fees, and no external market, farmers became less prosperous for all their productivity. Finally, stock speculation in railroads, shipping ventures, factories, and new inventions like electric light distribution, made and broke millionaires overnight. Often these investment failures led directly to bank failures; since there was no Federal Reserve Bank (1913) to restore liquidity nor a Federal Deposit Insurance Corporation (1933) to insure depositors, when banks failed, large and small depositors lost everything. Between 1865 and 1914, the U.S. suffered thirteen panics, recessions, and depressions, each event lasting from eight months right up to five years and ten months in the case of the Panic of 1873.

Even when a worker had a job, there was no guarantee that weekly wages kept up with the cost of living. There were occasions when their employers, like the Union Pacific Railroad and the McCormick Harvesting Machine Company, unilaterally cut wages, sometimes by half. Forming a union to bargain collectively or strike did not always counter these strategies of the so-called robber barons. In 1889 a strike against Carnegie Steel Company resulted in higher wages, but three years later Andrew Carnegie was determined to break the union. Henry Clay Frick, the company's plant manager at Homestead, Pennsylvania, carried out anti-labor plans by first stepping up the production quotas and then, when the union balked, by locking the workers out. Though only about 20 percent of workers, those most skilled, ever belonged to the steel workers' union, when faced with oppression from above, the rest of the plant's workers voted to strike, too. The result was violent clashes between strikers and Pinkerton detectives, and later a state militia numbering in the thousands. In the end Frick reopened the plant

HISTORY REPEATS ITSELF.——THE ROBBER BARONS OF THE MIDDLE AGES, AND THE ROBBER BARONS OF TO-DAY.

FIGURE 13-1. Cartoon from *Puck*, New York, November 6, 1889, pp.170–71

and instituted longer hours and lower wages.[2] Another notable case of wage disputes leading to violence was Chicago's Haymarket Square riots in May 1886. There three years of labor disputes with McCormick had led nowhere. A rally planned for May 4 went awry when a bomb exploded, and assembled police fired into the crowd. Seven police and four civilians eventually died, while an estimated fifty were injured; anarchists were blamed, and some were jailed and executed.[3]

There was clearly something deeply wrong in industrial America, where some became fabulously wealthy on the backs of the many leading lives of misery. At this moment religious leaders began stepping forward. An Episcopal priest and labor activist, James Otis Sargent Huntington (1854–1935), responded to the Haymarket riot by starting the Church Association for the Advancement of the Interests of Labor (CAIL). Christians like Huntington were moving to add social structural change to their standard response of charity for the poor. Rev. Henry Codman Potter (1834–1908), of Grace Episcopal Church in New York, had responded with concern to the Panic of 1873 around him; in his annual report of parish work, he stated that on the one hand, there were "professional paupers . . . not entitled to the indiscriminate benefactions," which would increase the number of such paupers. For these, Potter believed, a "truer and more Christian charity" would be to help them find work. On the other hand, Potter observed, those with "the clearest claim upon our sympathy and help [were] the sick, the crippled, the blind or imbecile, or otherwise incapacitated; poor women and untaught childhood; children and young girls left orphaned or alone in this great city; persons of gentle nurture and antecedents who have met with reverses; all these at our doors, and then the family of the stranger and the missionary beyond them, alike have a claim." These were those most deserving of Potter's well-to-do church's charity. He ended by cautioning that "the cynicism and indifference which sneers at all charity alike [was worse than] the sentimentalism of indiscriminate and thoughtless charity."[4] By the time Huntington had founded CAIL, Bishop Potter (he had been elected Bishop of New York in 1883) was firmly in the justice-for-laborers camp. Potter issued a pastoral letter to his clergy in 1886 instructing them, "What the laborer wants from his employer is fair and fraternal dealing, not alms-giving; and a recognition of his manhood rather than a condescension to his inferiority." Personally, he went further, working to mediate the steel strike of 1901 and the coal strike of 1902 among other activities. When he was challenged by a coal-interest president: "Cannot I do what I will with my own?" Potter shot back his own question: "Ah, well, but what is my own?"[5]

In places like Chicago, the efforts of middle- and upper-class clergy to sympathize with and address the problems of labor did not stand alone. Instead, as historian Heath Carter has pointed out, laborers and their advocates pushed the clergy from below to do more. Andrew Cameron, publisher of the *Workingman's Advocate* and a believer in free republican labor (as opposed to state or socialist labor movements), was one such voice who helped wean Protestant clergy away from belief that laissez-faire economics would suffice. Cameron hit early and hard those ministers who stood in the way of labor reform:

> While we cheerfully concede that a number of our so-called ministers of the gospel are little else than political clackers, we fail to see the argument presented thereby against an undefiled Christianity. The fact that a counterfeit note has been presented at any of our banking institutions does not prove that a genuine bill is worthless. On the contrary, it may be accepted as prima facie evidence of the ability and readiness of the institution upon which the forgery has been committed, to redeem its obligations. On the same principle we claim that the fact that political charlatans are found in our pulpits and theological seminaries does not prove that religion, pure and undefiled, is a fraud, but rather that these impostors are frauds on religion.... While we believe in a liberal, catholic Christianity, a Christianity which concedes to all classes the privilege of worshiping God beneath their own vine and fig tree according to the dictates of their own conscience, we do not believe in a Liberalism without a Christianity.[6]

Cameron, in short, advocated for a Christianity less captive to the class interests of classical economic liberalism and more associated with needs of the poor. This interest would grow, as many clergy found attractive the economic ideas of Henry George (1839–97), a popular political economist and journalist, who wrote in his wildly successful book *Social Problems*, "The rapid changes now going on are bringing up problems that demand the most earnest attention. . . . Symptoms of danger, premonitions of violence, are appearing all over the civilized world. Creeds are dying, beliefs are changing, the old forces of conservatism are melting away. Political institutions are failing, as clearly in democratic America as in monarchical Europe. There is a growing unrest and bitterness among the masses, whatever be the form of government, a blind groping for escape from conditions becoming intolerable."[7] George's own favorite remedy was a single tax on land, but he was just one individual getting people to think of the economy as humanly manageable to moral ends, rather than being moved by Adam Smith's "invisible hand" or collective "enlightened self-interest." The most important figure bridging political economy, and particularly labor and the church, however, was economist Richard T. Ely (1854–1943).

Best remembered today as the founder of the American Economic Association, Ely was one of the first Americans to obtain a PhD at Heidelberg in Germany. His accounts of labor, taxation, and monopolistic trusts changed the field of economics rapidly, but he also brought his penetrating mind to bear on what he called the "Social Aspects of Christianity" in a book by the same name, which began as lay sermons and articles for Presbyterians, Congregationalists, and Baptists. In many of these talks and articles he found himself speaking for the simple ethics of Jesus to businessmen who wanted to do well without losing their souls. Ely wrote in his book *Social Aspects of Christianity* what he had repeatedly told church groups, beginning with a lay sermon in his hometown of Fredonia, New York:

> Nothing is more difficult, nothing requires more divine grace, than the constant manifestation of love to our fellows in all our daily acts, in our buying, selling, getting gain. People still want to substitute all sorts of beliefs and observances in the place of this, for it implies a totally different purpose from that which animates this world. It is when men attempt to regulate their lives seven days in the week by the Golden Rule that they begin to perceive that they cannot serve God and mammon; for the ruling motive of the one service—egotism, selfishness—is the opposite of the ruling motive of the other—altruism, devotion to others, consecration of heart, soul, and intellect to the service of others. Men are still quite willing to make long prayers on Sunday, if on week days they may devour widows' houses; or, as Reverend Mark Guy Pearse said two summers since at Chautauqua, they are ready to offer their prayers and their praise on Sunday, if on Monday they may go into the market place and skin their fellows and sell their hides.[8]

Through his writings and speeches Ely became one of the leading figures associated with the social gospel—a movement that at its simplest meant that the gospel stood for the "Fatherhood of God and the brotherhood of man." This phrase (meant inclusively in its own time) aimed at bringing all human beings and their institutions—religious, economic, and political—under the reign of God. Social gospel advocates also intended to sweep away the lines of class, ethnicity, and race that characterized the social relations between persons as not in keeping with the teachings of Jesus. This kind of zeal figured prominently in social gospel thought. In this, the American social gospel paralleled a movement in Great Britain called social Christianity that likewise sought to apply the teachings of Jesus to industrial society. One of the English movement's writers, William T. Stead (1849–1912), wrote a particularly scathing attack on American labor conditions and social relations, titled *If Christ Came to Chicago!*[9] Alongside the heartrending New York photography of Danish immigrant Jacob Riis in *How the Other Half Lives* (see figure 13-2), presented first to church and other groups in 1888 and in 1890 as a book, Stead's "plea for the union of all who love in the service of all who suffer" attracted middle-class sympathies to what working people already knew about daily life in the city. Being poor in a Gilded Age city was hard, and it could end all too quickly, leaving your loved ones absolutely destitute.[10]

William Stead's work lived on in a social gospel novel by a Topeka, Kansas, minister who posed the contemporary dilemma as a question, "What

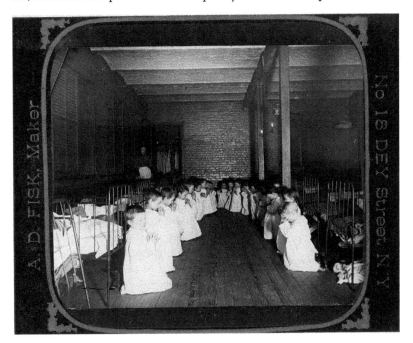

FIGURE 13-2. Prayer time in Nursery of the Five Points Mission and Five Points House of Industry by Jacob A. (Jacob August) Riis, 1849–1914. Museum of the City of New York, 90.13.2.70.

Would Jesus Do?" and proceeded to answer it. Charles M. Sheldon's (1846–1957) spiritual classic *In His Steps* (1896) featured a bourgeois congregation as equally proud of its beautiful church as its pastor, Rev. Henry Maxwell, is of his erudite sermons. While he is preparing one of these sermons, Maxwell turns away an unemployed man, described through his eyes as a "tramp," who later interrupts the Sunday service, tells his tale of a job lost due to automation, and his anxious search for someone who will help him and his little girl: "Somehow I get puzzled when I see so many Christians living in luxury and singing 'Jesus, I my cross have taken, all to leave and follow Thee,' and remember how my wife died in a tenement in New York City, gasping for air and asking God to take the little girl too. Of course I don't expect you people can prevent every one from dying of starvation, lack of proper nourishment and tenement air, but what does following Jesus mean?"

The unwanted visitor collapses in church and dies the next day. By the next Sunday the congregation is uncomfortable, none more so than Rev. Maxwell, who challenges his congregation to live what they say they believe, saying, "Our motto will be, 'What would Jesus do?' Our aim will be to act just as He would if He was in our places, regardless of immediate results. In other words, we propose to follow Jesus' steps as closely and as literally as we believe He taught His disciples to do. And those who volunteer to do this will pledge themselves for an entire year, beginning with today, so to act." What follows are the hard choices faced by several members who take Maxwell up on his guidance to live as Jesus would live if he were there now and confronted by modern dilemmas. These WWJD Christians include Rev. Maxwell himself; when the novel ends, he is no longer as popular a preacher as before.[11]

Another Congregationalist, Washington Gladden (1836–1918), was also an enduring social-gospel figure. The pastor of First Congregationalist Church in Columbus, Ohio, Gladden was a prolific author of hundreds of poems, articles, and hymns and more than thirty books. Ely, Potter, and Sheldon offered many social critiques and encouragements; alongside all that, Gladden took an interest in how congregations and denominations could and should structure their affairs to meet the needs of the age. Gladden advocated the "institutional church," an urban church edifice with a program capacious enough so that it could teach English, train recent immigrants in useful skills such as how to use sewing machines, feed the hungry, and do job retraining and literacy work on weekdays. He favored all kinds of groups meeting under church auspices for the purpose of Christianizing civilization one congregation at a time. In Gladden's view, the church was always instrumental to the kingdom of God, an idea taught by Jesus and comprehending the entire organism of society. Indeed, the church in former ages had sponsored hospitals, education, work for the poor, and relief for widows and orphans and others unable to work. But Gladden told the graduating class at the Oberlin Graduate School of Theology:

WASHINGTON GLADDEN: OBSTACLES OF THE KINGDOM

"What may be truthfully said is this: that there are local churches—a considerable number of them—whose administration is such that they hinder more than help the progress of the kingdom. And it may also be that there is a pretty strong tendency, in many churches, to forget the instrumental character of the church; to forget that it is a part and not the whole, a means and not the end; and to be content with building up the church, or the denomination, instead of studying to make the church serviceable in building up the kingdom."*

*Robert T. Handy, *The Social Gospel in America, 1870–1920* (New York: Oxford University Press, 1966), 111.

Churches that sought only to build themselves were an obstacle to the kingdom of God, Gladden said. Christians and the church itself had social obligations to the kingdom of God in government structures and beyond. The church needed to live out its social principles, but Gladden was realistic: "When any attempt is made to call the attention of people of the churches to their continuing responsibility for the care of those interests" certain people could be counted on to protest, "'We don't want politics,' they cry, 'we don't want sociology; give us spiritual sermons; preach the gospel.'"[12]

Gladden also took an interest in "race uplift," improving the lives and prospects of black Americans through education and training; yet, as we shall see, he had to learn along the way about how best to help. Finally, as the nation's most prominent Congregationalist minister of the time, Gladden memorably opposed his own denominational mission board's acceptance of a $100,000 ($2.6 million today) gift in 1905 from John D. Rockefeller. It was "tainted money," Gladden insisted, because Rockefeller had become the world's richest man through predatory practices with workers and competitors alike, values that Gladden thought the church must oppose. Instead, he thought Rockefeller's morals came along with his money in ways it was hard to protest: "It is idle to say that we can take this man's money and then turn and fight him. It is not an honorable thing to do. It is not dealing fairly with Mr. Rockefeller; he would not have given it if he had expected us to set ourselves in array against him."[13] The Christian Socialist Vida Scudder, a female Wellesley professor, was one of the few figures to support Gladden's case in public with crisp prose of her own. However convincing Gladden's argument might have been morally, the American Board of Commissioners for Foreign Missions still overwhelmingly found a way to accept Rockefeller's funds. Tainted money, it seemed, could be made pure if one gave to the right cause.

Rockefeller himself and Andrew Carnegie spent the second half of their lives trying to give away their wealth to good causes. They founded the University of Chicago and Spelman College (Atlanta), funded public libraries for small towns and Carnegie University (Pittsburgh), and established foundations that would keep giving. Carnegie even wrote an essay titled "The Gospel of Wealth," which claimed, "The man who dies rich, dies disgraced." Wealth, however gotten, was being redeemed in some eyes by the use to which it was put.

Some ministers went even further to make friends with money in the Gilded Age. Russell H. Conwell (1843–1925), a Yale-educated Baptist minister and founder of Temple University in Philadelphia, became famous for the inspirational lecture "Acres of Diamonds," which he delivered more than 6,000 times in his life. In it, he argued that wealth was everywhere for those who had eyes to see the possibilities: "I say that you ought to get rich, and it is our duty to get rich. How many of my pious brethren say to me, 'Do you, a Christian minister, spend your time going up and down the country advising young people to get rich, to get money?' 'Yes, of course I do.' They say, 'Isn't that awful! Why don't you preach the gospel instead of preaching about man's making money?' 'Because to make money honestly is to preach the gospel.'"[14] Evangelical Protestantism itself was being divided on the question of wealth.

The greatest and last of all social gospel leaders was Walter Rauschenbusch (1861–1918), a German American Baptist pastor and theologian who was influenced by Washington Gladden and would in turn influence Martin Luther King Jr. In 1948 King entered Crozer Theological Seminary. He describes reading Rauschenbusch's *Christianity and the Social Crisis* (1907)

FIGURE 13-3. Walter Rauschenbusch, 1861–1918 (Frontispiece to *Dare We Be Christians*, 1914)

while there: its message "left an indelible imprint on my thinking by giving me a theological basis for the social concern which had already grown up in me."[15] The church, as Rauschenbusch presented it, was committed to whole persons in their social circumstances. In this and eight other books Rauschenbusch drew on his experience with poor members of his church in Hell's Kitchen in New York City, allowing him to speak with the compassion of a pastor and with the incisive mind of a scholar.

Born in Rochester, New York, to a seminary professor as father, he was educated in Germany and returned to minister in New York City. There, leading a German-speaking Baptist congregation for eleven years, he encountered the human effects of poverty, unemployment, insecurity, malnutrition, disease, and crime. He gathered national notice for his condemnations of the way social evil caused individual and collective misery. In books like the best-selling *Christianity and the Social Crisis* (1907) and *Christianizing the Social Order* (1912), he promoted the progressive spirit of the times, insisting that human life really could be made "more Christian" by eliminating child labor, requiring children to stay in school until age 16, and adopting an 8-hour workday and a 40-hour workweek for the sake of laborers. Social gospel advocates and political progressives could agree on this much, and they would accomplish a few sterling reforms during the presidencies of Theodore Roosevelt and Woodrow Wilson. But one of the social gospel's weaknesses was that it was not a unified worldview as much as a sentiment that society should be more Christian, which could take on a variety of actual, even opposing positions.

Rauschenbusch saw the limitations of the social gospel as a mere position without abiding principles and sought to address it more thoroughly in his later work after he had moved to Rochester to be a professor at Colgate Rochester Divinity School. In 1917, just a year away from his early death of tuberculosis, he delivered the book the waning movement most needed, *A Theology for the Social Gospel.* Rauschenbusch explained the need for such a work on the opening page: The social gospel needed "a theology to make it effective," he wrote, and "theology needs the social gospel to vitalize it." Theologically, Rauschenbusch was innovative at several points. He sought to return the church to a vital sense of the kingdom of God, a preoccupation of the followers of Jesus that had been, in his view, supplanted by the church. The kingdom of God could serve as a future-oriented, ethical, and godly corrective to the business-as-usual orientation of life in the church, Rauschenbusch believed. He also spent considerable time tackling the problem of evil in ways that prefigured the analyses of Reinhold Niebuhr and Martin Luther King Jr., viewing sin as much more than individual acts of resisting God. This led directly to a restatement of the causes of Jesus' death:

> Religious bigotry, the combination of graft and political power, the corruption of justice, the mob spirit [being "the social group gone mad"] and mob action, militarism, and class contempt—every student

of history will recognize that these sum up constitutional forces in the Kingdom of Evil. Jesus bore these sins in no legal or artificial sense, but in their impact on his own body and soul. He had not contributed to them, as we have, and yet they were laid on him. They were not only the sins of Caiaphas, Pilate, or Judas, but the social sin of all [hu]mankind, to which all who ever lived have contributed, and under which all who ever lived have suffered.[16]

The meaning of Christ's atonement, therefore, required "no legal fiction of imputation to explain that 'he was wounded for our transgressions, he was bruised for our iniquities.' Solidarity explains it." Christianity had to see social sin as devastating as individual sin, Rauschenbusch believed, or Christianity would continue in its failed attempts to engage society. He wrote, "It has not evoked faith in the will and power of God to redeem the permanent institutions of human society from their inherited guilt of oppression and extortion." With the death of Rauschenbusch, African American religious leaders, not white social gospel leaders, were the ones who best embodied the faith that it was God's will to redeem institutions of oppression.

Black Religious Life in the Nadir

During the Gilded Age the lives of African Americans were subject to all the ups and downs felt by other Americans, plus the heavy new burden of Jim Crow laws enacted especially yet not exclusively in the South, to segregate and disenfranchise black citizens under the law. The name Jim Crow itself stems from a long-running minstrel act staged by an English entertainer, Tim Rice, which ran from the 1830s forward. Rice amused white audiences by mocking the poverty, language, and customs of a stereotyped enslaved man in blackface and rags. These modes of entertainment lasted more than a century.

Jim Crow laws began to be enacted by Southern state legislatures as soon as the states were removed from Reconstruction's federal supervision in the Compromise of 1877. The first assault was on black voting rights through the use of poll taxes and literacy tests to qualify to vote (unless your grandfather was eligible to vote, in which case you were "grandfathered" from having to so qualify). In this way states disenfranchised their black citizens without writing racial qualifications into the law. Next came the segregation of schools and transportation. Black children were forced to go to different (always inferior) schools from those of white children. Finally, trains and trolleys, the principal public transportation of the day, were segregated by car or section. Each of these practices was challenged all the way to the U.S. Supreme Court, which every time ruled against black plaintiffs and for segregation. The most famous of these cases, and in some ways the most exemplary, was *Plessy v. Ferguson* (1896).

Homer Plessy allowed himself to be a test case to challenge Louisiana's segregation of train cars. Plessy himself was seven-eighths white and one-eighth black and relatively prosperous in New Orleans, a city with a much more fluid color line and more dynamic race relations than Louisiana sought to impose on its citizens. In spite of his upstanding character, or locally privileged status, the Supreme Court ruled definitively that as long as "separate, but equal" accommodations were provided, the races could be legally separated. And so they were, and more and more viciously so as time went by. Only a single justice, John Harlan, dissented. The Kentuckian reflected the racist presuppositions of his time, but also signaled how things were supposed to change. Harlan wrote:

> The white race deems itself to be the dominant race in this country. And so it is, in prestige, in achievements, in education, in wealth, and in power. So, I doubt not, it will continue to be for all time, if it remains true to its great heritage and holds fast to the principles of constitutional liberty. But in the view of the Constitution, in the eye of the law, there is in this country no superior, dominant, ruling class of citizens. There is no caste here. Our Constitution is color-blind and neither knows nor tolerates classes among citizens. In respect of civil rights, all citizens are equal before the law.[17]

The series of court decisions emboldened other racist actions. Sharecroppers were forced to work on lands they had once worked as slaves yet now for less support. This led to a mass exodus to northern cities—Detroit, Chicago, Pittsburgh, Philadelphia, Cleveland, Baltimore—for jobs on the bottom rungs of industrial America. There, too, segregation prevailed, especially in housing and jobs. Then, where the state did not govern, "lynch law" terrorized black citizens who were seen by white racists as needing to be "taught a lesson" by extrajudicial mob executions. Nearly half of the more than 4,700 lynchings occurred in the 1890s and 1900s. Hangings, tortures, and burnings continued in large numbers during the presidency of Woodrow Wilson, a racist Southerner who turned a deaf ear to the complaints of race and faith leaders. These lynchings continued all the way up to 1968. Through the long reign of terror, the Tuskegee Institute tracked every lynching in every state of the United States, publishing annual statistics, and a cumulative map of the blight on the nation (see figure 13-4).

In the black community, therefore, this period is remembered as "the nadir," the lowest point. After freedom from slavery and a brief taste of real freedoms during Reconstruction, black Americans were beset by oppression on every side—except in their churches, schools, and colleges and among the leaders who had come of age in those institutions. The response of America's black religious leaders to the precipitous circumstances facing their people during this period constitutes an outstanding chapter in American religious history.

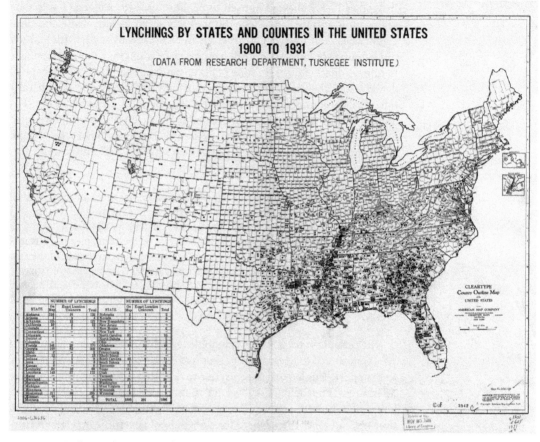

FIGURE 13-4. Tuskegee Institute Map of Lynchings, 1900–1931 (Library of Congress loc.gov/resource/g3701e.ct002012/).

Booker T. Washington and the Atlanta Compromise of 1895

Given white aversion to participation in any way in the social and political rise of African Americans during Jim Crow, a division occurred within black leadership regarding the best way to move forward. Some leaders advocated black economic development in a separate sphere, while others saw this strategy as a capitulation to white racism, a surrender of constitutional and human rights. The debate was sharpened to a fine point by a speech made at the 1895 Cotton States Exposition in Atlanta by Booker T. Washington, a speech that would thereafter come to be known "the Atlanta Compromise."

Booker T. Washington (1856–1915), president of the Tuskegee Institute, was one of the most respected leaders of black America in the late nineteenth and early twentieth centuries. His autobiography, *Up from Slavery*, was widely read and admired across race lines. So too was his educational work at Tuskegee in Alabama, where the education focused on job-training skills for the formerly enslaved and their offspring. The Atlanta Compromise, though never written down, was an agreement between white Southerners and black leaders like Washington who wished to continue to offer vocational training so that black families might improve their economic prospects. Essential elements of the agreement were that blacks would not ask for the right to vote; they would not retaliate against racist behavior; they would tolerate segregation and discrimination; they would receive free basic education, education that would be limited to vocational or industrial training (for instance, as teachers or nurses), but liberal arts education would be prohibited (for instance, college education in the classics, humanities, art, or literature). Washington himself spoke publicly for this accommodationist position at the Exposition:

> The wisest among my race understand that the agitation of questions of social equality is the extremist folly, and that progress in the enjoyment of all the privileges that will come to us must be the result of severe and constant struggle, rather than of artificial forcing. No race that has anything to contribute to the markets of the world is long in any degree ostracized. It is important and right that all privileges of the law be ours, but it is vastly more important that we be prepared for the exercise of these privileges. The opportunity to earn a dollar in a factory just now is worth infinitely more than the opportunity to spend a dollar in an opera house. In conclusion, may I repeat, that nothing in thirty years has given us more hope and encouragement and drawn

FIGURE 13-5. Booker T. Washington, 1856–1915 (Library of Congress LC-J694-255)

us so near to you of the white race as the opportunity offered by this Exposition; here bending, as it were, over the altar that represents the results of the struggles of your race and mine, both starting practically empty-handed three decades ago, I pledge that, in your effort to work out the great and intricate problem which God has laid at the doors of the South, you shall have at all times the patient, sympathetic help of my race.[18]

Though Washington was not alone in being willing to get along in racist America, other prominent African American leaders were offended. Washington Gladden had attended the Exposition and initially came away thinking Booker T. Washington was the greatest statesmen and educator of his race. He met a young black Harvard-educated academic by the name of W. E. B. Du Bois (1868–1963) on the train ride back north, and Du Bois's lively and extended explanation of all that Washington had traded away persuaded Gladden to join the early civil rights struggle. It was Du Bois who coined the term "Atlanta Compromise," by which the agreement would be known and seen as a forfeiture of rights. Atlanta Baptist professor (later Morehouse College's president) John Hope responded to Washington directly in writing:

> If we are not striving for equality, in heaven's name for what are we living? I regard it as cowardly and dishonest for any of our colored men to tell white people that we are not struggling for equality. If money, education, and honesty will not bring to me as much privilege, as much equality as they bring to any American citizen, then they are to me a curse, and not a blessing. God forbid that we should get the implements with which to fashion our freedom, and then be too lazy or pusillanimous to fashion it. Let us not fool ourselves nor be fooled by others. If we cannot do what other free men do, then we are not free. Yes, my friends, I want equality. Nothing less. I want all that my God-given powers will enable me to get, then why not equality?[19]

As word of the Compromise spread, the African American pulpit began to respond. In Washington, D.C., Francis J. Grimké, pastor of the Fifteenth Avenue Presbyterian Church, formerly enslaved himself, told his congregation that

> the saddest aspect of it all is that there are members of our race and not the ignorant, unthinking masses, who have had no advantages, and who might be excused for any seeming insensibility to their rights, but the intelligent, the educated who are found condoning such offenses, justifying or excusing such a condition of things on the ground that in view of the great disparity in the condition of the two races, anything different from that could not reasonably be expected. Any Negro who takes that position is a traitor to his race, and shows that he is deficient in manhood, in true self respect.

Grimké noted the growing lawlessness of the South in which 33 years after the passage of the 13th, 14th, and 15th Amendments, the goal of the

FIGURE 13-6. Francis J. Grimké, 1850–1937 (digital.history.pcusa.org)

white Southerner was to negate their effect and render the Negro servile or administer him "the shotgun policy." Fortunately, Grimké said, with as much encouragement as he could muster, such weak compromise "is not the sentiment of this black race. No, and never will be." As lynching became more frequent, Grimké laid responsibility at the feet of white clergy. "This is the charge which I make against the Anglo American pulpit today; its silence has been interpreted as an approval of these horrible outrages."

FRANCIS GRIMKÉ: THE SILENCE OF THE WHITE CHURCH

"The pulpits of the land are silent on these great wrongs. The ministers fear to offend those to whom they minister. We hear a great deal from their pulpits about suppressing the liquor traffic, about gambling, about Sabbath desecration, and about the suffering Armenians, and about polygamy in Utah when that question was up, and the Louisiana lottery. They are eloquent in their appeals to wipe out these great wrongs, but when it comes to Southern brutality, to the killing of Negroes and despoiling them of their civil and political rights, they are, to borrow an expression from Isaiah [56:10], 'dumb dogs that cannot bark.' Had the pulpit done its duty, the Southern savages, who have been sinking lower and lower during these years in barbarism, would by this time have become somewhat civilized, and the poor Negro, instead of being hunted down like a wild beast, terrorized by a pack of brutes, would be living amicably by the side of his white fellow citizen, if not in the full enjoyment of all his rights, with a fair prospect, at least of having them all recognized."*

*Francis J. Grimké, "The Negro Will Never Acquiesce as Long as He Lives [Sermon]," November 20, 1898, printed in the *Richmond (Va.) Planet*, a black weekly, www .blackpast.org/african-american-history/1898-reverend-francis-j-grimke-negro-will -never-acquiesce-long-he-lives/.

The Talented Tenth, Black Arts and Letters, and Civil Rights

After the turn of the twentieth century, other black leaders, most notably W. E. B. Du Bois and William Monroe Trotter (1872–1934), took issue with the Atlanta Compromise, believing instead that African Americans should engage in a struggle for civil rights. It was Du Bois who characterized Washington and others like him as "accomodationists." As a forceful alternative, Du Bois and Trotter first founded the Niagara Movement as a radical alternative to the program offered by the "Bookerites." Its declared aims included "particularly the increase of intelligence, the buy-in of property, the checking of crime, the uplift in home life, the advance in literature and art, and the demonstration of constructive and executive ability in the conduct of great religious, economic and educational institutions."[20] In Du Bois's address at the July 1905 movement's first meeting, he noted that black Americans were not more criminal, but were more likely to be arrested, and called for an end to the convict lease system in the South, under which men accused of crimes as small as vagrancy could be imprisoned for years and then leased out to farms and factory in conditions much like slavery for years at a time. The movement took other strong positions, such as opposition to the way labor unions excluded black workers. The movement fizzled after Trotter abandoned the group, but in 1910 many of the same activists, including Du Bois, founded a lasting organization, the National Association for the Advancement of Colored People (NAACP), on the site of a 1908 Springfield race riot and in honor of Abraham Lincoln. After Washington's death in 1915, supporters of the Atlanta Compromise gradually shifted their support to civil rights activism, until the modern civil rights movement commenced in the 1950s.

W. E. B. Du Bois coined a term for people like himself that came to be misunderstood over time: "The Talented Tenth." The point of calling out the privilege of education, respectable status, and relatively secure positions in business, or a prominent pulpit, or an institution of education was to stress the need to use the talents that the "10th" possessed for the benefit of African Americans who were not so fortunate. To twenty-first-century ears, "Talented Tenth" sounds like a not-so-humble brag, but the attempts of the Tenth (probably more like the Talented 3 percent in actuality) to raise up the race need to be seen in light of the risks its leaders were willing to take for the sake of black dignity and freedom. In Du Bois's case, his academic writing was closely related to his protest activities. As a historian and sociologist, he wrote books to describe the inner life of the black community. A pathbreaking statistical study of one black community, *The Philadelphia Negro* (1899), was followed by *The Souls of Black Folk* (1903), where he challenged white readers on its opening page to stick with him and thereby learn: "Herein lie buried many things which if read with patience may show the strange meaning of being black at the dawn of The Twentieth Century. This meaning is not without interest to you, Gentle Reader; for the problem of the Twentieth Century is the problem of the color-line."

FIGURE 13-7. William Edward Burghardt Du Bois,1868–1963 (Library of Congress LC-DIG-ppmsca-38818)

This work also contained a strong defense of education. Du Bois wrote, "The South believed an educated Negro to be a dangerous Negro. And the South was not wholly wrong; for education among all kinds of men always has had, and always will have, an element of danger and revolution, of dissatisfaction and discontent. Nevertheless, men strive to know." One idea concerning African American self-understanding from *Souls* would last for the ages: the notion of "double-consciousness." Du Bois explained what he meant:

W. E. B. DU BOIS: "DOUBLE CONSCIOUSNESS"

"It is a peculiar sensation, this double-consciousness, this sense of always looking at one's self through the eyes of others, of measuring one's soul by the tape of a world that looks on in amused contempt and pity. One ever feels his two-ness, an American, a Negro; two souls, two thoughts, two unreconciled strivings; two warring ideals in one dark body, whose dogged strength alone keeps it from being torn asunder. The history of the American Negro is the history of this strife—this longing to attain self-conscious manhood, to merge his double self into a better and truer self. In this merging he wishes neither of the older selves to be lost. He does not wish to Africanize America, for America has too much to teach the world and Africa. He wouldn't bleach his Negro blood in a flood of white Americanism, for he knows that Negro blood has a message for the world. He simply wishes to make it possible for a man to be both a Negro and an American without being cursed and spit upon by his fellows, without having the doors of opportunity closed roughly in his face."*

*W. E. B. Du Bois, *The Souls of Black Folk* (Chicago: A. C. McClurg & Co., 1903), 2–3.

Du Bois first voiced the concept of double-consciousness in an *Atlantic Monthly* article in 1897. He also wrote of black people going through life because of this behind a "veil." The metaphor of veil may have come from another member of the Talented Tenth, poet Paul Laurence Dunbar (1872–1906), whose 1896 poem "The Mask" likewise spoke from and to the black interior experience of living in America:

We wear the mask that grins and lies,
It hides our cheeks and shades our eyes,—
This debt we pay to human guile;
With torn and bleeding hearts we smile,
And mouth with myriad subtleties.

Why should the world be overwise,
In counting all our tears and sighs?
Nay, let them only see us, while
We wear the mask.

We smile, but, O great Christ, our cries
To thee from tortured souls arise.
We sing, but oh the clay is vile
Beneath our feet, and long the mile;
But let the world dream otherwise,
We wear the mask!

Paul Laurence Dunbar was just one of a group of outstanding writers and artists who were being recognized in the American Negro Academy founded by the Rev. Alexander Crummell (1819–98). If there was to be an Academy recognizing African American artists, poets, and writers, then they would need to start their own, just as doctors and lawyers of color had founded their own National Bar and National Medical associations. Similar American organizations across the spectrum banned black Americans from membership. Perhaps Crummell's founding of the organization bore some weight from the way he was routinely treated in his own Episcopal Church, where he reported this painful incident:

I entered, sometime ago, the parlor of a distinguished southern clergyman. A kinsman was standing at his mantel, writing. The clergyman spoke to his relative, "Cousin, let me introduce to you the Rev. C., a clergyman of our Church." His cousin turned and looked down at me; but as soon as he saw my black face, he turned away with disgust, and paid no more attention to me than if I were a dog. Now, this porcine gentleman, would have been perfectly courteous, if I had gone into this parlor as a cook, or a waiter, or a bootblack. But my profession, as a clergyman, suggested the idea of letters and cultivation; and the contemptible snob at once forgot his manners, and put aside the common decency of his class.[21]

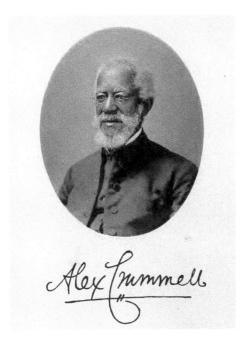

FIGURE 13-8. Alexander Crummell, 1819–98. (In his work *The Greatness of Christ: And Other Sermons* [New York: Thomas Whittaker, 1882])

Crummell reported this incident in his 1897 address to the American Negro Academy, which he had led in founding the preceding year in Washington, D.C. His purpose, he made plain, was to counter the so-called scientific racism of the age by demonstrating the achievements of people of color in intellectual pursuits. He also took on detractors more directly, telling the Philadelphia minister and editor H. L. Wayland that he was wrong when he said African Americans should be educated for industry, not Greek, Latin, or the liberal arts. Crummell's retort was rather "That the Negro has no need to go to a manual labor school. He has been for two hundred years and more, the greatest laborer in the land." Civilization was what was needed for "man was made by his Maker to traverse the whole circle of existence, above as well as below; and that universality is the kernel of all true civilization, of all race elevation."[22] Crummell's religion had a high role for artistic and intellectual achievement, a passion equaled and surpassed by anti-lynching advocate Ida B. Wells-Barnett.

Ida B. Wells-Barnett (1862–1931) was one of the bravest writers of the post-Reconstruction generation. Born a slave and raised in Mississippi, she attended Rust College in Memphis, Tennessee. After graduation, she taught school in Memphis and became the part owner of the *Memphis Free-Speech*, a newspaper. A devout Christian, she believed in the power of black churches and black schools even when they disappointed or avoided her outspoken views. Wells-Barnett was a suffragist, advocating women's voting. She also was a founder of the NAACP and used her pen for causes she believed in and against those—including black ministers and other

FIGURE 13-9. Ida B. Wells, 1862–1931 (Library of Congress LC-USZ62-107756 DLC)

movement leaders—who were less committed than she to justice for black and female persons.

Wells first became well known in 1883 for refusing to be removed from a whites-only train car to a segregated car in Tennessee, and then suing—and winning her case. Though the Tennessee Supreme Court would later overturn her victory, the schoolteacher emerged as a fighter for justice. In 1885 she joined other "club women" (women in local literary clubs who were turning to advocate change in public policies) in the Memphis Lyceum and was soon reporting in newspapers on the literary affairs of her group under the pen name "Iola." Iola's fame grew as she took on the problems and solutions, as she saw them, of the black community. When she was approached about writing for the *Free Speech and Headlight* in 1889, she agreed only on the condition that she be a one-third owner. In 1891 she was dismissed as a teacher for articles she wrote critical of black schooling in Memphis. In March of the next year she covered a fight between two children that with police help escalated into the lynching of a black grocer. She never looked back, taking anti-lynching journalism as her life's work. In May of 1892 she wrote an editorial repudiating "that old threadbare lie that Negro men rape white women. If Southern men are not careful, a conclusion might be reached which will be very damaging to the moral reputation of their women." Her newspaper was burned to the ground, her life threatened, and Wells departed for the North to continue her publishing about Southern lynching from a geographical distance. Eventually Wells married

African-American civil rights advocate Ferdinand Barnett, and together they published the Chicago *Conservator*. Wells-Barnett wrote for other periodicals, too, as in this blistering excerpt from *The Arena* in 1900:

IDA B. WELLS-BARNETT: AMERICA'S NATIONAL CRIME

"Our country's national crime is lynching. It is not the creature of an hour, the sudden outburst of uncontrolled fury, or the unspeakable brutality of an insane mob. It represents the cool, calculating deliberation of intelligent people who openly avow that there is an 'unwritten law' that justifies them in putting human beings to death without complaint under oath, without trial by jury, without opportunity to make defense, and without right of appeal.

"The alleged menace of universal suffrage having been avoided by the absolute suppression of the negro vote, the spirit of mob murder should have been satisfied and the butchery of negroes should have ceased. But men, women, and children were the victims of murder by individuals and murder by mobs, just as they had been when killed at the demands of the 'unwritten law' to prevent 'negro domination.' Negroes were killed for disputing over terms of contracts with their employers. If a few barns were burned, some colored man was killed to stop it. If a colored man resented the imposition of a white man and the two came to blows, the colored man had to die, either at the hands of the white man then and there or later at the hands of a mob that speedily gathered. If he showed a spirit of courageous manhood, he was hanged for his pains, and the killing was justified by the declaration that he was a 'saucy nigger.' Colored women have been murdered because they refused to tell the mobs where relatives could be found for 'lynching bees.' Boys of fourteen years have been lynched by white representatives of American civilization. In fact, for all kinds of offenses—and for no offenses—from murders to misdemeanors, men and women are put to death without judge or jury; so that, although the political excuse was no longer necessary, the wholesale murder of human beings went on just the same. A new name was given to the killings and a new excuse was invented for so doing."*

*Ida B. Wells-Barnett, "Lynch Law in America," *The Arena* 23 (January 1900): 15–24.

Alongside Wells-Barnett some six million other African Americans left the South in the Great Migration, so that the South itself went from containing 90 percent of all black Americans in 1900 to just 53 percent in 1970. With the migration came a great increase in new churches for African American

Methodists and black Baptists, but also some new opportunities for freedom. New religious movements not so closely tied to traditional Christianity also attracted Northern black adherents. The Ethiopian Hebrews viewed black people as the true biblical Hebrews. The Nation of Islam and the Moorish Science Temple provided their members with an identity tied to Asia, not Europe. Father Divine's Peace Mission located its members' identities in a vision of raceless children of God and economic uplift, while Charles Manuel "Sweet Daddy" Grace, who founded the United House of Prayer for All People, created a charismatic nondenominational church that would succeed as a model for countless other churches in the century after its founding in 1927. Just as the cities of the North changed and challenged every other group, the alterations of life facing African Americans in the first decades of the twentieth century were just beginning.[23]

14. The Birth of the American Century and the Fundamentalist-Modernist Battles

It is fair to say that for America, the twentieth century was born in 1898, when the United States became an imperial, expansionist global power by going to war with Spain over Cuba, setting off a martial spirit that has waxed and waned but never since ended. In an age of war, everything in a culture becomes a battle. So it was even in the dominant religious setting of evangelical Protestantism, which would go from a big tent of many persuasions to divided and warring camps in just a quarter century. To see how the consensus collapsed, we need to see both what was lost and the cultural and religious innovations that contributed to religious strife on the home front.

A Big Tent and the Big Stick

Though John D. Rockefeller Jr. was the only son of the richest man in America, Sundays with the Rockefellers were austere affairs. John and his sisters spent the afternoon reading the Bible and were encouraged to "choose a besetting sin" and to pray to the Lord with their mother for help in "combatting the sin." At one point Laura Spelman Rockefeller confessed to her neighbor, "I am so glad my son has told me what he wants for Christmas, so now it can be denied him."[1] This pattern of child rearing was not considered cruel, but rather fitting children to value the things of the Spirit and their home in heaven. Two states away, in Western New York, a young Harry Emerson Fosdick experienced religion as both omnipresent and oppressive:

> I was a serious boy, deeply religious, and, as I see it now, morbidly conscientious, and the effect upon me of hell-fire-and-brimstone preaching was deplorable. I vividly recall weeping at night for fear [of] going to hell, with my mystified and baffled mother trying to comfort me. Once, when I was nine years old, my father found me so pale that he thought me ill. The fact was that I was in agony for fear that I had committed the unpardonable Sin, and reading that day in the book of Revelation about the horrors of hell, I was sick with terror.[2]

Fosdick later turned against the kind of literalist Christianity that preoccupied him as child and was exemplified in Rockefeller as a child. Millions of other turn-of-the-century Americans similarly experienced the evangelical piety of American Protestantism.

The election of 1896 pitted William Jennings Bryan, a Presbyterian, against William McKinley, a Methodist—two pious evangelicals separated by their party affiliations and economic plans, but little else. This broad religious and political-cultural consensus might well have continued, but for a conflict between America and Spain over the fate of Cuba. Cuba was then embroiled in a war of independence against Spain, which simultaneously threatened American business interests and brought to public attention the atrocities conducted under Spanish General Valeriano "the Butcher" Weyler—including imprisoning a large proportion of the civilian population in concentration camps.

Most students who have taken an American history class in high school learn that a press war between William Randolph Hearst and Joseph Pulitzer, engaging in "yellow journalism," baited Americans into the so-called Spanish-American War (1898). Diplomatic historians have disproved this interpretation by showing that the press coverage followed President McKinley's decision to let the Congress appear to force his hand to intervene in Cuba's war for independence from Spain—a course of action he had already decided upon (but did not want to get blamed for politically). What the press surely did besides sell papers, however, was to stoke a martial spirit among Americans. This spirit was one that cast the United States as a disinterested savior among the avaricious world powers. Only America would fight to liberate Cuba from Spain, to empty its concentration camps, and not create an empire for itself. Religious leaders joined the chorus of voices calling this a moral duty. This self-perception followed the congressional action to preclude taking Cuba as a U.S. possession. It conveniently overlooked what happened to Spain's other captured lands (Puerto Rico, Guam, and the Philippines), and to Hawaii and Wake Island—all of which became U.S. possessions as a result of this war. Despite refraining from taking Cuba, the United States had become an overnight world power with far-flung possessions, all without sullying its self-image.

Religious leaders grabbed on to the humanitarian justifications for intervention offered by William McKinley and the U.S. Congress—screening out calls for revenge (for the mysterious explosion on the USS *Maine* in Havana harbor) or gain. While some politicians and newspapers argued for possible gains for party and nation in a war with Spain, sermons and religious periodicals featured titles like "Worthy and Unworthy Motives," the title of an April 21, 1898, *Watchman* editorial making the case that base motives alone could not account for Americans' desire to confront Spain in the Caribbean. Instead, the true cause of passion was American "hatred of oppression and injustice that has aroused the hearts of the people." The Boston Baptists of the *Watchman* had anticipated by just a week the editorial opinions in the *Congregationalist*, also of Boston, opining that "Remember the Maine" might be "the only word that can spur on men of limited mental capacity and low moral ideas." Then with great hopes for something better of both its readers and "this Christian nineteenth century," it ended ominously by stating that the "only possible justification for this war on our part is that it is a holy war."[3]

Almost two decades before Woodrow Wilson, the son of a Presbyterian minister, would lead America into a "war to end all wars," American clergy were already talking about American war as a humanitarian act and a holy war. In their view, the congressional pledge not to annex Cuba just underlined the height of the nation's moral standing. Charles Albertson, one of the leading Methodists of the day, claimed that if war with Spain came, it would be neither for vengeance nor conquest, but instead a "war of freedom," and something new, a "war of merciful intervention." Once the war had begun in late April, these kinds of distinctions continued to be employed, as when the African American Congregationalist minister H. H. Proctor addressed the sufferings of the Cuban people: "This state of things has become a stench in the nostrils of the American people." He told the assembled "Colored Military Companies of Atlanta" that what was happening was "not a war of passion against the Spaniard, but of compassion for the Cuban."[4] Americans took to heart two misleading lessons from their experience of war with Spain. From their preachers they learned that they were selfless and noble in war. From the rapidity of victory, they gleaned that fighting their (presumed) moral and military inferiors was easy. Both lessons would prove to have ill consequences over time.

The next presidency, that of Theodore Roosevelt, continued the martial spirit. Even before William McKinley's assassination (September 14, 1901), Roosevelt came to public notice by his masculine exploits of killing buffalo in the West, and above all in leading his "Rough Riders" in some of the fiercest fighting of the war in Cuba. Riding this fame to the vice presidency in 1901, Roosevelt was both a devout member of the Reformed Church and could be said to represent another important faith of the age: "muscular Christianity." Roosevelt often conflated virile effort with goodness, telling an 1899 audience in Chicago, "We do not admire the man of timid peace. We admire the man who embodies victorious effort; the man who never wrongs his neighbor, who is prompt to help a friend, but who has those virile qualities necessary to win in the stern strife of actual life." What was good for a man was also good for a nation, Roosevelt believed, and so he ended his speech with a further call to greatness: "Above all, let us shrink from no strife, moral or physical, within or without the nation, provided we are certain that the strife is justified, for it is only through strife, through hard and dangerous endeavor, that we shall ultimately win the goal of true national greatness."[5] No mandate for an American Century could be clearer. It would be one achieved through strife and a strong sense of moral justification.

As President 1901–9, Theodore Roosevelt led much as he spoke—with big plans and decisive actions, be they assuring food safety, busting monopoly trusts, or pacifying the Philippines and confronting China. Roosevelt became identified with an aphorism he attributed to West Africa, but may have coined himself, "Speak softly and carry a big stick; you will go far." Practically, for the purposes of statecraft, this meant being prepared to send the Navy in to get what diplomats or the President had asked for, notably in Panama to build a canal and in China for access to markets. All this was from a man who never missed church and frequently extolled the Bible and its wisdom.

Roosevelt's successor as President (1909–13), William Howard Taft, was religiously something of an odd man out. He was a Cincinnati Unitarian lawyer and a hero of sorts for his success in acting as the appointed civil governor of the Philippines during the first of many cross-cultural guerrilla uprisings that the newly international United States would face in the twentieth century. Taft was remarkably open for the time to Roman Catholics, at home and abroad. He also allowed that, as much as he believed in God, he rejected the divinity of Christ. Taft came home from the Philippines to become Roosevelt's Secretary of War, closest adviser, and chosen successor. Taft served only one term after Roosevelt split his support by heading the Bull Moose Party in the election of 1912, leading directly to the election of a Democrat, Woodrow Wilson, the first Southern President after the Civil War. During these early years of the twentieth century, we can see the elements of explosive religious conflict gathering steam, which would later blow up the evangelical big-tent consensus.

Preparing the Way for Fundamentalism

George Marsden, American fundamentalism's greatest historian, defines the movement as "militantly anti-modernist, Protestant evangelicalism." This definition contains within it a critical insight that the early fundamentalists themselves did not possess. They believed they were just standing inside the old received religion, doing things just as they had always been done, while in fact their experience and religious witness was shaped by reaction to modernists, people working to update Christianity to keep pace with modern society and science. In the end each of these groups was responding to the challenges of modernity. Their activities would bring them to blows eventually, but it is well to see fundamentalism as the product of several contributing movements and ideas.

The oldest element in what became the fundamentalist movement was, of course, revivalist evangelicalism, which displayed a concern to maintain evangelical dominance in U.S. culture at a time when religious diversity, by virtue of immigration and religious experimentation, was growing as never before. This kind of evangelicalism, earlier associated with Dwight L. Moody, was carried into the twentieth century by a barnstorming, colorful former baseball player turned evangelist named Billy Sunday. He and others like him did not have much use for theological niceties, or the social gospel, unless it was the kind that got people sober: what he called "The sober gospel." This was also the faith expressed by the "Great Commoner" and three-time Democratic presidential candidate William Jennings Bryan. They and most evangelical Christians were pragmatic and sought to avoid intellectual disputes within the faith or about the faith. As Bryan told a gathering at Winona Lake, Indiana, even though he was a Presbyterian, he never had studied the differences in doctrine between Baptists, Methodists, and his own group (at the time these were the biggest three). This conveyed a common trust characteristic of most evangelical Christians in one another's goodwill. And instead of explaining everything in the Bible, Bryan said (to great applause): "If we try to live up to that which we can understand, we will be kept so busy doing good that we will not have time to worry about the things that we do not understand."[6]

The second element contributing to fundamentalism was dispensational premillennialism. This was the teaching that divided biblical history into seven dispensations given by God, or eras experienced in time. John Nelson Darby (1800–82) first popularized the idea that each dispensation included a covenant between God and humanity and ended with judgment. The premillennial part of Nelson's teaching emphasized Christ's physical future return to Earth, with a rapture of saints in the clouds, a seven-year "tribulation" including the rise of antichrist, the conversion of many Jews to Christianity, the battle of Armageddon, ending with a thousand-year reign of Christ, a millennial kingdom. The dispensationalists read the book of Revelation *predictively*: it was less about Christians oppressed by Rome in the first century CE, under Emperor Nero Claudius (64–68), than it was about a future yet (and soon) to come.

Darby promoted dispensational premillennialism in conferences and speaking engagements for decades in the United Kingdom and in the United States. The ideas got a huge boost in 1909 with the publication of the *Scofield Reference Bible* by Oxford University Press. The book contained the entirety of the King James Version of the Bible, together with a system of marginal notes and links devised by Kansas attorney Cyrus I. Scofield (1843–1921) that "demonstrated the truth of" dispensational views throughout the Old and New Testaments. The book became an immediate bestseller. Alongside this new less-than-commonsense reading of the Bible (a system of secrets Christians had to know), the Keswick, or Victorious Christian Life, movement was teaching people through Charles Trumbull's popular *Sunday School Times* that complete surrender of sin, followed by filling with the Holy Spirit, was possible. Though the claims that "Pentecost Has Come" emanating from Los Angeles starting in 1906 in the Azusa Street Revival were not accepted as orthodox by all those who became fundamentalist, the revival's leader, William J. Stewart (1870–1922), taught something remarkably similar to the Keswick movement: that baptism with the Holy Spirit was the third work of grace, following new birth (a first work of grace) and entire sanctification (a second work of grace). The great difference that separated these early Pentecostals from proto-fundamentalists was speaking in tongues, healing, and their interracial worship.

One can see the beginnings of fundamentalism as commitment to a short list of propositions to which Christians—or at least their ministers—should subscribe in a controversy in the Presbytery of New York City in 1910. In that year this presbytery struggled with some of its candidates for ministry who had attended Union Theological Seminary, the same seminary served by Prof. Charles A. Briggs, who had been charged with heresy in 1892 and later defrocked. These ministerial candidates did not affirm belief in the virgin birth of Jesus, among other things. Church rules in place since 1729 allowed candidates for ordination to express their "scruples [in other words, uncertainties or doubts] about doctrine, worship, or government," so long as these did not include essential articles of belief. But scruples about the virgin birth and the divinity of Christ led directly to others asking, "What beliefs are essential?" This in turn led to articulating a short list of points of essential belief that the Presbyterian Church's General Assembly, the denomination's annual national meeting, adopted in May 1910 and reaffirmed in 1916, to try to keep this from happening again. Though reasons were given for each at length, the list in summary reads:

THE FIVE POINTS OF FUNDAMENTALISM

1. Inerrancy of Scripture
2. Virgin Birth of Christ
3. Christ's substitutionary atonement
4. Christ's bodily resurrection
5. Authenticity of miracles in the Bible*

*Minutes of the General Assembly, Presbyterian Church (U.S.A.), May 28, 1910 (Philadelphia: Office of the General Assembly, 1910), 272–74.

That list was to come, in various forms, to stand for the "five points of fundamentalism" and to divide some church bodies, especially Presbyterians and Northern Baptists, but for now, in the period 1910 to 1915, the term "The Fundamentals" was doubtlessly more closely associated with a series of twelve books published privately under that name by the wealthy Union Oil Company founders, brothers Lyman and Milton Stewart. Lyman Stewart, a Presbyterian and a dispensationalist, had conceived the idea of edging out liberal Protestantism, evolutionists, Roman Catholicism, and new religious movements and their ideas by publishing the best of a broad swath of sixty-four well-known Christian theologians and pastors of the day with the help of Moody-associated editors A. C. Dixon and Reuben A. Torrey. The set of books was mailed free of charge to ministers, missionaries, professors of theology, YMCA and YWCA secretaries, Sunday school superintendents, and other Protestant religious workers in the United States and other English-speaking countries. Over three million volumes (in 250,000 sets) were mailed out. The tone of each book typically ranged from affirmation of a doctrine like the atonement or the deity of Christ, to refutations of higher criticism and non-evangelical religions, with personal testimonies and guides to effective evangelism. The volumes also demonstrated the unity of Methodists, Baptists, Presbyterians, and Congregationalists across broad theological lines from biblical institutes, establishment seminaries, and tall steeples across the land up until the eve of the First World War.

A final element in setting the stage for fundamentalism was the rise of the "new woman" in society, and ironically, the perception inside worshiping communities that churches had become overly feminized spaces. Male backlash to these developments drove some preachers, Billy Sunday not the

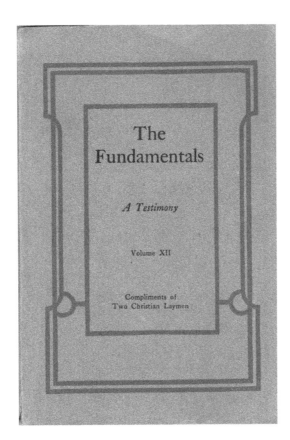

FIGURE 14-1. Volume 12 of *The Fundamentals: A Testimony to the Truth* (12 vols. [Chicago: Testimony Publishing Company of Chicago, 1910–15])

least, to use their pulpits to put women back in their places with purported biblical sanction. Christianity, he told audiences, "was not a "pale, effeminate proposition"—implying that it had become so. He also proclaimed, "Jesus was no ascetic," but rather, like the former Chicago White Stockings player himself, "a robust, red-blooded man" who knew how to live life to the fullest. The men who became Sunday's converts loved this, perhaps as much as his line "Going to church doesn't make you a Christian any more than going to a garage makes you an automobile."[7] When he was not telling men to be masculine like Jesus, Sunday was valorizing motherhood and insulting single women: "The home is on a level with the women; the town is on a level with the homes." The never-married missions executive Robert E. Speer told women at a Moody conference that they should make their homes "a little church. I do not know a more sacred institution than the home, nor any priesthood higher than that of the Christian father as he sits at the head of the table."[8] Christian patriarchy needed women to be home and pure. Secular magazines promoting the "new woman" were particularly anathema, as can be seen in the cartoon drawn by E. J. Pace for the *Sunday School Times* to show that a woman's attention to cosmetics and appearance came directly at the neglect of her holiness before God.

FIGURE 14-2. "Her First Love." (Cartoon by E. J. Pace for *The Sunday School Times*, 1920, Digital Commons @ Biola)

Fighting for Faith

The simmering conflict between a liberal Christianity updated to fit modern society and more conservative evangelicals might have continued for some time but for the acceleration of their differences by the events and temper of World War I and its aftermath. Woodrow Wilson (1856–1924) was elected President in 1912 and brought with him a tendency to see international conflict in moral terms, as good and evil. This meshed well with the notions of American moral and social superiority stoked in and since the war with Spain. Wilson's first term was full of domestic reforms that remade U.S. government capabilities in far-reaching ways, most of them salutary. But he brought Southern prejudices with him when it came to race, resulting in the destruction of the black managerial class in the federal Civil Service. Though the U.S. did not enter World War I until 1917, just one year after Wilson was reelected to the presidency on the promise to "keep us out of the war," Americans were developing strong impressions about the villains and heroes of the European conflict. One of the principal American witnesses to the atrocities in Cuba under Spanish General Valeriano "the Butcher" Weyler had been Richard Harding Davis. Davis also reported on the entry of a vast German army into neutral Belgium on its way to attack France:

> All through the night, like a tumult of a river when it races between the cliffs of a canyon, in my sleep I could hear the steady roar of the passing army. And when early in the morning I went to the window[,] the chain of steel was still unbroken. It was like the torrent that swept down the Conemaugh Valley and destroyed Johnstown. This was a machine, endless, tireless, with the delicate organization of a watch and the brute power of a steam roller. . . .
> For three days and three nights the column of gray, with hundreds of thousands of bayonets and hundreds of thousands of lances, with gray transport wagons, gray ammunition carts, gray ambulances, gray cannon, like a river of steel, cut Brussels in two.[9]

Reports like these conveyed "the rape of Belgium" by German soldiers in the most graphic terms possible. American pulpits from August 1914 forward were full of sermons decrying the inhuman "Hun." These intensified considerably with the sinking of the steamship *Lusitania* on May 7, 1915, by a German U-boat. With a loss of 1,195 passengers, 123 of them American, remaining U.S. opinion turned against Germany. For two years, as Wilson tried to maintain official neutrality and seek peace between the belligerents on an equal footing, clergy built the case against Germany in their pulpits and press. In January 1917, upon hearing that Wilson was working to end the war in Europe on essentially neutral terms, 65 of the most prominent clergymen in the country—among them were Lyman Abbott, Harry Emerson Fosdick, John Timothy Stone, William Moody, and Billy Sunday—signed a public letter urging the war not to end before the true aggressors could be punished. They used religious words to frame their willingness to spend American lives on this pursuit: "The just God who withheld not His son from the cross, would not look with favor upon the people who put their fear of pain and death, their dread of suffering and loss, their concern for conquest in these above the holy claims of righteousness and justice, and freedom, and mercy and truth. . . . The memory of all the saints and martyrs cries out against such but backsliding of mankind. Sad is our lot if we have forgotten how to die for a holy cause."[10]

After the entry of the U.S. into the war on April 16, 1917, the religious partisanship on behalf of the Allies and war only grew. Billy Sunday left no one in doubt where he stood, saying, "If hell were turned upside down, it would say 'Made in Germany.'" Lyman Abbott, the most visible moderate Protestant of the age, wrote that it was Christian to hate, just as Christ hated evil and said woe unto the Pharisees. "I do not hate the Predatory Potsdam gang," he wrote, "because it is my enemy. I do not hate it for any evil which it has done to me. I hate it for what it has done to my defenseless neighbor across the sea. I hate it for what it is. I hate it because it is a robber, a murderer, a destroyer of homes, a pillager of churches, a violator of women. I do well to hate it."[11] But it was Henry Ward Beecher's popular successor at Brooklyn's Plymouth Congregational Church, N. D. Hillis, who went the furthest, proposing that at the conclusion of the war, German men should be exterminated to prevent a recurrence of war:

> A singular revulsion of sentiment as to what must be done with the German army after the war, is now sweeping over the civilized world. Men who once were pacifists, men of chivalry and kindness, men whose life has been devoted to philanthropy and reform, scholars and statesmen, whose very atmosphere is compassion and magnanimity towards the poor and weak, are now uttering sentiments that four years ago would have been astounding beyond compare. These men feel there is no longer any room in the world for the German. Society has organized itself against the rattlesnake and the yellow fever. Shepherds have entered into a conspiracy to exterminate the wolves. The Boards of Health are planning to wipe out typhoid, cholera, and the Black Plague. Not otherwise, lovers of their fellow man have finally become perfectly hopeless with reference to the German people. They have no more relations to the civilization of 1918 than to an orang-outang, a gorilla, a Judas, a hyena, thumbscrew, scalping knife in the hands of a savage. These brutes must be cast out of society.[12]

Of the major Christian figures of the day, William Jennings Bryan alone stayed true to his pacifist principles, resigning as Wilson's Secretary of State when the President chose the course of war. The overall effect of the belligerent rhetoric that religious leaders used was to amplify the subsequent fundamentalist-modernist controversy, but the war had other effects on American religious life as well.

The war effort mobilized religious groups as never before: most notably, it brought portions of the American society into the national effort that had been peripheral heretofore. World War I was the first major conflict in which black Americans fought in large numbers as organized units. American Catholics, who could be expected to be reluctant to engage in the European war, not only fought in proportionate numbers to their fellow citizens, but also organized a National Catholic War Council to coordinate the responses of Catholics to the war. Legendary priest Monsignor John A. Ryan (1869–1945) provided a blueprint for reconstruction along social-justice principles to the organization as, after the war, it morphed into the National Catholic Welfare Council and a National Conference of Catholic Bishops. While Rome and some American archbishops were suspicious of too much national organization, Ryan, and Paulist Father and *Catholic World* editor John J. Burke, together with patriotic archbishops such as James Cardinal Gibbons and George Cardinal Mundelein, used the exigencies of war to serve Catholic soldiers and sailors and promote Catholic acceptance and social teachings on the home front.

In addition to the Catholic effort, the Salvation Army—previously seen as a bit too confrontational for Victorian society, with its loud bands and public preaching on city streets—endeared itself forever to doughboys and Americans more generally with its "doughnut lassies" serving doughnuts, hot coffee, and cheer to soldiers coming off the line in France. The Salvation Army's magazine *The War Cry* celebrated this service as the new model of the organization's identity, as did a popular song, "Don't Forget the Salvation Army," from New York's Tin Pan Alley (see figure 14–3).

FIGURE 14-3. Popular Song Celebrating Salvation Army's "Doughnut Girls," https://lccn.loc. gov/2014562095 (Library of Congress)

Not to be outdone by the newcomers, John D. Rockefeller Jr. headed a funds drive for the United War Work Campaign, under the combined auspices of the Young Men's Christian Association, the Young Women's Christian Association, the National Catholic War Council, the Jewish Welfare Board, the War Camp Community Service, the American Library Association, and the Salvation Army. These organizations were authorized by the Secretary of War and the Secretary of the Navy to work for the soldiers and sailors in and near the camps. These groups set up sanitary camps and clean fun for the troops being mobilized at home and abroad. All these religious groups were critical to the war effort, and especially the well-being of service personnel, since the United States government's rapid mobilization of men far outpaced its own capacities to care for the people rapidly gathered into improvised camps. Indeed, more U.S. armed personnel were to die of diseases (especially the influenza) than be killed or wounded in battle. Aiming for $170 million, the fund raised more than $200 million. Rockefeller put the case to potential givers in a speech:

> Do you want to see the flower of the manhood of this country, which has brought everlasting glory to our nation, neglected in the hour of its greatest need, and afraid to face temptation? Then withhold your contribution to this fund.
>
> Or do you want to see a chapter of moral victory and prowess as superb and as glorious as that of the victories of arms which have already been achieved, added to the annals of the history of this country, and high standards of morality maintained and perpetuated by our sons and brothers in the days to come?[13]

Not only did World War I mark the first time Jews, Catholics, and Protestants had raised money for common philanthropic work; it was also the first time that military chaplains worked to minister across faith lines. Protestants, Catholics, and Jews met one another in the service of their country as nowhere before and on an equal footing. Their chaplains found themselves struggling with the preconceptions of mostly Protestant commanders, but practicing America's first successful interfaith experiment on the field of battle as Jewish chaplains buried Protestant boys, and a whole machine gun unit decided to a man they were Catholic for the duration so their fine priest would not be taken from them. Chaplain Chelis V. Smith claimed of his experience, "Nowhere else on earth have clergymen worked so well together as in the army."[14]

Before and after the war, an organization and picture news magazine—*The Christian Herald*, now largely forgotten—raised and spent more money than the American Red Cross for relief of Belgians, Armenians, Greeks, and other refugees of the war and its aftermath.[15] *Christian Herald's* form of American religious philanthropy from the grassroots prompted by skillful use of modern media was the model of American religious internationalism to come: a mostly genuinely altruistic and helpful by-product of Americans'

FIGURE 14-4. Poster for the United War Work Campaign of 1917–19 (Library of Congress loc. gov/item/2002699394/)

compulsion to help others the world over. The purposes of mission philanthropy, however, were to be debated repeatedly in the years to come. Were missions to save souls, help the downtrodden, bring Christian civilization, or some combination of all three of these? These too became vexed topics in the years after the war.

The Battle Comes Home—Intensified Faith Controversies

At the close of the World War I on November 11, 1918, America and its religious groups were notably unified. Victory against Germany and the Central Powers had been achieved, and it had been done by Americans working together. Yet once the focus shifted from the conflict abroad, Americans rapidly turned their attention to troubles at home. The 1918 influenza pandemic spread first by the war's troop movements continued to pop up in communities throughout the world in four waves through 1920, killing an estimated 850,000 people in America and perhaps fifty million worldwide. Churches and synagogues, like other entities, responded with alternating concerned action and pandemic fatigue. Some canceled activities, even religious services, for months on end. Others resisted even masking to stop the spread. Because young adults were among the hardest hit, inflenza mortality had a lasting effect on the forming of families and job participation. The economy was in tatters, with three years of high inflation and difficulties in reabsorbing demobilized men, creating massive unemployment. Anarchists sent bombs to famous individuals all over the nation throughout 1919, and the following September a bomb exploded on Wall Street in New York City, killing 38. Attorney General A. Mitchell Palmer began the so-called Palmer raids during the resulting 1919–20 Red Scare. America's problems were not just in Europe; there were enemies also at home. Even the 1919 enactment prohibiting beverage alcohol can be seen as Protestantism's attempt to socially control the perceived deviance of others. This action would be followed in 1924 by a law restricting nearly all immigration from south, central, and eastern Europe, together with Asia.

There were also frustrations with the peace process. America's allies in the prolonged peace conference leading to the Treaty of Versailles treated with disdain not only Woodrow Wilson, but every other person who believed in a "war to end all wars." The League of Nations, the Treaty's principal mechanism to prevent future wars, was not approved by the U.S. Senate. Moreover, the more the very clergy who called for the war found out about its cost in human lives (17 million), the atrocities committed by both sides, and the needless sacrifice in blood and treasure thoughtlessly perpetrated by the military leadership of both sides—the more horrified they became. These clergy, who had preached war, were now determined that to be pacifists the rest of their lives was the only Christian thing to do. In Chicago, the Federation of Churches, representing fifteen denominations, declared itself "unalterably opposed to war." A later national poll of twenty thousand clergy found 54 percent opposed to any future war, with nearly half vowing not to serve as wartime military chaplains either.[16] Harry Emerson Fosdick, Reinhold Niebuhr, and his brother H. Richard Niebuhr were prominent among those who believed they had become less than faithful during the war by supporting it.

Postwar America was anxious; its religious rhetoric had become more strident, as especially noticeable from liberal Christians. Two professors at the University of Chicago's Divinity School singled out nearby Moody Bible Institute for special abuse. The Divinity School's dean for more than twenty-five years, Shailer Mathews (1863–1941), was a popular proponent of modernizing received Christian ideas and doctrine, working in this stronghold of progressive academic Baptist theology. As Moody's James Orr became more and more famous for his premillennial prophecies, from 1917 onward the University of Chicago theologians became increasingly exercised. While the war was still on, Mathews and his colleague Shirley Jackson Case (1872–1947) charged that, with its otherworldly concern, premillennialism bred a distinct lack of patriotism. This attack was as much on the cultural as on the doctrinal plane. Questioning a lack of patriotism during wartime marked a dangerous shift in the controversy. As for the question "Will Jesus Come Again?" Mathews answered at learned length in a work of the same name a firm "No." Then Case, a church historian, reduced Moody Institute's brand of theology to a psychological phenomenon, as per the title of his 1918 book, *The Millennial Hope: A Phase of War-Time Thinking*. This thinking, however, was not benign; Case believed its growth to be caused by a sinister conspiracy funded by spending two thousand dollars a week to spread it. He went further, saying, "Where the money comes for is unknown, but there is a strong suspicion that it emanates from German sources. In my belief the fund would be a profitable field for governmental investigation."[17] These kinds of charges continued well after the war, and the Chicago theologians then also associated the premillennialists with the International Workers of the World and domestic Bolshevism. The conservatives did not take this lying down. In the journals *The King's Business* and *Our Hope*, they countercharged: although the idea that the funding for premillennialism came from German sources was ludicrous, there could be no doubt where liberal academics got their ideas: Germany. And where had those ideas led the Germans?[18] This set the stage for the most vicious phase of the intra-Protestant conflict; it no longer was just a theological debate over doctrines, but over civilization itself. Only these stakes can explain how Darwinism and fundamentalism became linked and a preoccupation of the first half of the 1920s.

The doctrinal issues reemerged in annual denominational meetings to the point where Harry Emerson Fosdick, a popular Baptist preacher then serving as stated supply of the First Presbyterian Church of New York City, mounted his pulpit on May 21, 1922, with a salvo of his own. Just before the Northern Baptist Convention was to meet, Fosdick's sermon, titled "Will the Fundamentalists Win?," spoke for moderates like himself with his answer: most of the things that fundamentalists ascribed to miracles could be credited to God working through normal historical processes. This did not make modernist Christians less faithful than their fundamentalist counterparts, Fosdick argued:

> There is nothing new about the situation. It has happened again and again in history, as, for example, when the stationary earth suddenly began to move, and the universe that had been centered in this planet was centered in the sun around which the planets whirled. Whenever such a situation has arisen, there has been only one way out: the new knowledge and the old faith had to be blended in a new combination. Now the people in this generation who are trying to do this are the liberals, and the Fundamentalists are out on a campaign to shut against them the doors of the Christian fellowship. Shall they be allowed to succeed?[19]

The sermon went over so well that Ivy Lee, one of Fosdick's parishioners and the father of modern public relations, had 24,000 copies printed up and sent all over the country. Inside the denominations, both sides were thus struggling for position and worried that they might be driven out of their own churches. Outside, the battle was being waged over an unlikely symbol of primacy in the culture: teaching evolution in the public schools.

The Scopes Trial

In Tennessee, the state legislature had passed a bill barring the teaching of evolution in public schools. The governor was persuaded to sign the bill into law on the promise that it would be only for show; the law would not be enforced. Civil libertarians opposing the new law sought to test it in court almost immediately and found a young substitute high school teacher, John Scopes, in Dayton, Tennessee, who agreed to be arrested for the crime of teaching evolution, even though he could not remember ever teaching it in the first place (he did, however, remember having thought about it). What ensued came to be called the trial of the century as lawyers William Jennings Bryan and Clarence Darrow squared off in court. The nation followed on radio and newspaper for eight days in steamy July 1925 as the two lions argued law and religion. Barred from allowing most of his own witnesses to testify, Darrow called Bryan to the stand and made him defend biblical accounts of miracles and creation that made fundamentalism look ridiculous—at least as it was reported by the cynical columnist H. L. Mencken for the *Baltimore Sun* and dozens of other papers. John Scopes was convicted and fined $100, though even this conviction was later overturned on appeal. But the real losers were Bryan, who died just five days after the trial amid the derision heaped on him afterward; and the fundamentalists, who suffered humiliation in the court of public opinion.

FIGURE 14-5. Outdoor Court Proceedings in Tennessee v. John T. Scopes, 1925. Smithsonian Institution

After 1925 the action moved back inside the churches. An increasing number of Baptists, congregationalists when it came to polity, formed bonds with others of fundamentalist leanings, thus nudging their way of religion away from the Northern Baptist Convention. For Presbyterians, the fight was not yet over. Two dilemmas vexed Presbyterians well into the 1930s. The first had to do with foreign missionaries. Were they converting the heathen? Or were missionaries neglecting their evangelistic responsibilities while providing medicine and education to people in foreign lands, yet without asking them to give their lives to Christ? Closely related to that, the second issue asked, Is liberal Christianity actually Christianity at all, or is it something else entirely? Both of these problems were forcefully addressed by J. Gresham Machen (1881–1937), one of the most influential professors at Princeton Theological Seminary. In 1922 he wrote an essay titled "Liberalism or Christianity," later expanded into a book that reversed the nouns but made the same argument.

J. GRESHAM MACHEN: LIBERALISM OR CHRISTIANITY?

"The chief modern rival of Christianity is 'liberalism.' An examination of the teachings of liberalism will show that at every point the liberal movement is in opposition to the Christian message. . . .

"In the Christian view of God as set forth in the Bible, there are many elements. But one attribute of God is absolutely fundamental in the Bible; one attribute is absolutely necessary in order to render intelligible all the rest. That attribute is the awful transcendence of God. From beginning to end the Bible is concerned to set forth the awful gulf that separates the creature from the Creator. It is true, indeed, that according to the Bible God is immanent in the world. Not a sparrow falls to the ground with Him, but he is immanent in the world not because He is identified with the world, but because He is the free Creator and Upholder of it. Between the creature and the Creator a great gulf is fixed.

"In modern liberalism, on the other hand, this sharp distinction between God and the world is broken down, and the name 'God' is applied to the mighty world process itself. We find ourselves in the midst of a mighty process, which manifests itself in the indefinitely small and in the indefinitely great—in the infinitesimal life which is revealed through the microscope and in the vast movements of the heavenly spheres. To this world-process, of which we ourselves form a part, we apply the dread name of 'God.' God, therefore, it is said in effect, is not a person distinct from ourselves; on the contrary our life is a part of His. Thus the Gospel story of the Incarnation, according to modern liberalism, is sometimes thought of as a symbol of the general truth that man at his best is one with God."*

Minutes of the General Assembly, Presbyterian Church (U.S.A.), May 28, 1910 (Philadelphia: Office of the General Assembly, 1910), 272–74.

After publishing *Christianity and Liberalism* (1923), Machen went to war with the Presbyterian Church's liberal wing. Their attempts to settle him were met, first, with his involvement in founding Westminster Theological Seminary, an alternative to Princeton Theological Seminary; and then starting a mission agency that would only support the "right kind" of missionaries in direct competition with the church's own such board. Finally, in 1936 Machen and some of his former students began a new denomination, the Orthodox Presbyterian Church.

Reactions and Legacy

As fundamentalists withdrew from public scrutiny and major denominational fights to more quiet enclaves where their faith could be pursued in the privacy of churches, colleges, seminaries, and missionary efforts of their own design, the fundamentalist-modernist controversy began to wane. This did not, however, betoken a triumph of liberal Christianity. World War I itself was a judgment on too much faith in civilized people to advance humanity. H. Richard Niebuhr (1894–1962) looked back on the liberal Christianity, and even the social gospel popular in his younger years, and cast its aims as hopelessly naive: "A God without wrath brought men without sin into a kingdom without judgment through the ministrations of a Christ without a cross."[20]

In Germany, the Swiss-born theologian and pastor Karl Barth (1886–1968) turned away from his own prior liberalism after encountering the apostle Paul's Letter to the Romans and composing a pathbreaking theological commentary on it. His discoveries that God is totally other, coming from outside human experience—in the threefold revealed form of the Word of God in Christ revealed in the incarnation, announced in Scripture, and proclaimed in the sermon in a word of grace—was something old and something new. It was fit to the human crises of postwar Germans and postwar disasters across the Atlantic world. In Germany, the Pauline-inflected theology became known as Crisis Theology. In the United States, where Germany's Paul Tillich (1886–1965) soon joined Reinhold Niebuhr (1892–1971) on the faculty of Union Theological Seminary, the new and less liberal theology, more confident in God and less hopeful in human beings left to their own devices, was called neo-orthodoxy. Liberalism was chastened.

Fundamentalism, meanwhile, was rebuilding underground. And Americans were moving into a season of economic depression, with totalitarianism in Europe and another war on the horizon. Perhaps sin was not such an old-fashioned concept after all.

15. A World in Crisis and an American Religious High

The years from the mid-1920s through the 1950s featured immense challenge, change, and finally opportunity for religion in America. While the nation prospered in the later 1920s, organized religion slumped. The Great Depression gave rise to new figures of hate associated with religion even as charitable organizations increased yet were outmatched by need. When worldwide war broke out again (1939), religious groups coalesced around fighting fascism. After the Second World War ended in 1945, Americans were simultaneously terrified by the atomic bomb and by communism, yet experienced unparalled prosperity. As never before, they turned to religion—the Protestant, Catholic, and Jewish faiths—to find belonging and hope.

Religion in the Roaring Twenties and the Great Depression

Popular depictions of the 1920s are suffused with images of the Jazz Age, in which people are wealthy, well-dressed, and dancing at all hours of the night in speakeasies, or at lawn parties by the water, reminiscent of F. Scott Fitzgerald's *The Great Gatsby* (1921). Indeed, religion is far from the mind in these depictions, and some scholars have suggested that religion underwent its own depression of activity and enthusiasm during the years 1925–35. While churches were having difficulty sustaining memberships and their budgets, there was much activity outside houses of worship that interests us in American religious history. First, Protestant anxiety about other people and groups, such as anarchists and communists, led to the passage of the Immigration Act of 1924, including the Asian Exclusion Act and National Origins Act. The law effectively restricted the flow of central and south European immigrants to a mere trickle. Second, a revived Ku Klux Klan pitted white Anglo-Saxon Protestants against everyone else. And third, Catholicism was divided from most other Americans in holding to its antipathy toward communism.

In addition to the religiously inflected conflicts of the age, not everyone was as rich and famous as movies and popular depictions would lead one to believe. Much of the celebrated wealth of the 1920s was in fact levied at the expense of industrial workers, whose unions slipped in power and membership in the 1920s. In the 1930s organized labor would become famous for the length and number of their strikes and the violence rained down upon them by industrialists. President Warren G. Harding (1865–1923) had campaigned on a return to normalcy, dying in office during a major scandal over near-giveaway leases of government oil deposits in the Teapot Dome scandal. He was succeeded by his vice president, Calvin Coolidge (1872–1933), an austere New Englander, best remembered for the slogan "The business of America is business." It was his view that, to promote prosperity, the best policy was for government to be passive, get out of the way, and allow businesses to pursue their aims—a goal that the three Republican presidents after Woodrow Wilson were pleased to champion. Eventually a passive federal government, or one that did too little and too late under President Herbert Hoover, did not suffice after the stock-market crash of Black Friday, October 29, 1929, brought the economy to its knees. But first, Hoover faced a Catholic opponent, a contest that brought out the worst in American's attitudes toward Catholics.

One of the primary influences of the 1920s on both politics and religious life was the extraordinary popularity of a reconstituted Ku Klux Klan. In 1915 a small group of men, led by a former Methodist minister, William Joseph Simmons, gathered on Georgia's Stone Mountain outside Atlanta, burned a cross, and declared a new fraternal order. The new Klansmen were heavily influenced by D. W. Griffith's *Birth of a Nation*, a 1915 silent drama film that glorified the first KKK based on Thomas Dixon's romantic and violent novel and play *The Clansman* (1905). Simmons, a great joiner of fraternal orders (he belonged to 12 and used his membership in men's groups to attract more men to the Klan cause, selling them memberships and the distinctive hooded robe he personally designed), premised the new Klan on white racial purity and Protestant superiority. This second Klan was remarkable for its vocal, sometimes violent hatred of Catholic, Jewish, black, Asian, and Hispanic Americans, together with immigrants. It likewise supported prohibition, white female purity, and restriction of immigration, wrapping itself in the mantle of Christian civilization. The Klan grew rapidly, particularly among the "respectable" middle class. Indeed, foremost among its five million members nationwide were ministers, doctors, judges, and businessmen. In his 1927 novel *Elmer Gantry*, Sinclair Lewis observed that the Klan was simply "an organization of the fathers, younger brothers and employees of the men who had succeeded and become Rotarians."

Although the first Klan was confined to the rural South, over half of the new Klan's members were in the burgeoning industrial cities of the North with high growth rates, like Detroit, Dayton, Indianapolis, Philadelphia, Denver, and Portland, Oregon. The Klan was likewise strong in the new cities of the South: Atlanta, Dallas, Memphis, and Houston. Though never a majority of citizens, the group used its clout politically to achieve its exclusionary ends. So, in Oregon, the Klan helped elect the Democratic governor, then pressed him for a law that succeeded in wiping out Catholic schools by requiring parents to send all children between the ages of eight and sixteen to public schools. In Indiana, Grand Dragon David Stephenson effectively controlled the state's political system until he was brought down in a sex-and-poisoning scandal and sentenced to life in prison.

Klan members were more likely to persecute white women who crossed the color line and white Protestant men who did not support prohibition or the Klan's idea of family values than they were to actively engage in overt acts of hate against other groups. While Klansmen mostly policed their culture's social, gender, and religious boundaries, their leaders employed increasingly derogatory rhetoric about Catholics, Jews, and every racial minority. Though the Klan began to decline in the 1930s, especially after the Stephenson scandal, it left two key legacies. The first was the creation of a modern right-wing political hate group clothed in the self-righteousness of defending Christian civilization. The second Klan also preached "One-Hundred Percent Americanism," a doctrine that would survive the Klan itself down to the present day, shaping isolationist and white supremacist tendencies in the political sphere long beyond its demise in the later 1930s. Before it moved off the scene as a mass force, however, the Klan's members engaged in a vicious nationwide attack on the candidacy of Al Smith in the 1928 presidential election.

New York's governor Alfred E. Smith (1873–1944) was the first Catholic nominee of a major party for President. Though Smith was wildly popular in New York, having won four terms as its governor, the Klan and other

FIGURE 15-1. Ku Klux Klan members parade down Pennsylvania Avenue in Washington, D.C., 1928. (National Archives 306-NT-650-4)

so-called "concerned citizens" groups attacked his Catholicism. They staged protest parades all over the country and engaged in dirty-tricks electioneering. In Daytona Beach, Florida, the school board instructed that a note be placed in every child's lunch pail that read: "We must prevent the election of Alfred E. Smith to the presidency. If he is chosen president, you will not be allowed to read or have a Bible." Protestant ministers told their congregations that if Smith became President, all non-Catholic marriages would be annulled, and all children of these marriages would be declared illegitimate. The Klan set up burning crosses to meet Smith's campaign all across the Midwest. Herbert Hoover won in a landslide that included five states from the usually Democratic South, beating Smith 21,437,227 votes to 15,007,698. So many allegations were made against Smith as a Catholic that a joke went around New York City that on the day after the election, Smith wired the pope a one-word telegram: "Unpack!"

Herbert Hoover was no sooner inaugurated in March 1929 than the stock market first overheated and then crashed. Because of the extremely limited government views of Hoover and his predecessors, the early setbacks of the Great Depression met with no effective government action. Hoover had run on a promise of prosperity, and now that promise had evaporated. Millions of people were laid off their jobs, businesses found it impossible to borrow money to keep their operations afloat, tariffs—a favorite conservative economic tactic meant to preserve American jobs and industries—led to further contraction of the economy and the spread of economic depression to other countries. Men and women who had held steady jobs only days

FIGURE 15-2. Unemployed queued outside a Great Depression soup kitchen opened in Chicago by Al Capone in February 1931. (National Archives, 306-NT-165.319c)

before in American cities found themselves on the streets begging, or in bread lines, or at church-run soup kitchens. Tents and shacks sprung up throughout major American cities to house the homeless. These encampments were given the name "Hoovervilles." Ultimately 11,000 of the nation's 25,000 banks would fail. Some $140 billion of Americans' deposits simply disappeared. Unemployment peaked at 24.9 percent in 1933.

After Hoover was soundly defeated for a second term by Franklin Delano Roosevelt in the election of 1932, the federal government began experimenting with new social programs to provide jobs, prop up the banking system to save people's savings, and even provide old-age and disability pensions under a new program called Social Security. Americans had entered the Great Depression expecting their churches to provide a social safety net, as they had in other times. The depression, however, threw so many people out of work and lasted so long that churches and synagogues were not up to the task, though they continued to help feed as many people as they could in soup kitchens. Instead, Americans began to look to the government to take care of their needs for food, work, and relief. Roosevelt also addressed the fears of the nation throughout the Great Depression, beginning with his inaugural address, which began with this memorable opening paragraph:

> I am certain that my fellow Americans expect that on my induction into the Presidency I will address them with a candor and a decision which the present situation of our Nation impels. This is preeminently the time to speak the truth, the whole truth, frankly and boldly. Nor need we shrink from honestly facing conditions in our country today. This great Nation will endure as it has endured, will revive and will prosper. So, first of all, let me assert my firm belief that the only thing we have to fear is fear itself—nameless, unreasoning, unjustified terror which paralyzes needed efforts to convert retreat into advance. In every dark hour of our national life a leadership of frankness and vigor has met with that understanding and support of the people themselves which is essential to victory. I am convinced that you will again give that support to leadership in these critical days.[1]

While Roosevelt promised to lead the nation to combat "fear itself," other nations were falling into dictatorships and open warfare. Of all these conflicts, the one that most divided Americans was the Spanish Civil War (1936–39). In the United States, Protestant sympathies flowed toward the Spanish Republic. Some Americans joined the "Abraham Lincoln brigade" to fight in solidarity with Republican forces against Franco's Nationalists. American Catholics, however, were in sympathy with Franco and the Nationalists because of the suppression of the church, its convents, and schools under the Republic. Since communists were in the Spanish Republican coalition, and the Soviet Union was the only major power to come to its aid, Catholics were predisposed to support the Nationalists because they knew what happened in revolutions and under communists: the church was dissolved. They were still smarting from the anticlericalism of the Mexican and Russian revolutions, where churches were shuttered and priests killed.

Throughout the 1930s American Catholic anti-communist sentiment grew with intensity. Labor unions, which had strong socialist and communist elements, were particularly concerned. The Catholic fraternal order, the Knights of Columbus, and American priests pushed Catholics to oppose leftists in their unions. Parish literature racks were filled with booklets with titles like "The Socialist Conspiracy against Religion." These pamphlets showed how socialists were against Catholicism by quoting the words of the socialists themselves. In 1935, Jesuits at St. Joseph's College in Philadelphia initiated the School of Social Sciences, where more than a thousand Catholics each year were trained to promote the rights of workers without giving an inch to socialists in their trade unions. Catholics made progress in part because, unlike in Europe, the Catholic working class and even union workers identified with Catholicism. In European countries, with their landed gentry and aristocracies, the Catholic Church was identified with the wealthy. As historian Richard Gid Powers writes, "The extreme nature of American Catholic anticommunism made it almost inevitable that the Catholic community sooner or later would produce anticommunist extremists. And it did, both sooner and later, in Father Charles Coughlin and Senator Joseph McCarthy."[2]

The first of these figures, Father Charles E. Coughlin (1891–1979), started as an enthusiastic supporter of FDR, popularizing the slogan "Roosevelt or Ruin" in 1933 and 1934. His chief platform was a radio show originating at WJR in Detroit and carried by radio stations coast-to-coast. It is nearly impossible for us today to comprehend the power of radio from the 1920s through the late 1950s. Coughlin was the first nationally successful religious political commentator and the first right-wing media star. Coughlin claimed the term "social justice" for his own ideology, but he consistently preached an anti-communist message. He particularly displayed great animus for banks and bankers; the way he talked about the latter made it clear that he thought Jewish bankers were to blame for the country's ills. As Roosevelt continued to innovate government responses, Coughlin turned his ire on Roosevelt, alleging that the President too was a misguided socialist and "anti-God." This proved to be the beginning of the end for Coughlin. His *New York Times* obituary noted that, as he moved further to the right, "Units of the Christian Front organization, which he supported, made raids on Jewish institutions and businesses. The mere mention of his name at rallies of the pro-Nazi German American Bund touched off wild cheering." Coughlin declared in 1936, "I take the road of Fascism." Only with the entry of the United States into the Second World War in 1941 (an action Coughlin opposed) was Coughlin silenced by a combined effort of the U.S. Catholic hierarchy and the federal government itself.[3]

Father Coughlin was only one figure to sense the power of radio and to use to it to maximum effect. President Roosevelt himself made successful use of the medium in intimate "fireside chats" with American citizens. The radio also inspired religious leaders to try to reach new audiences over the airwaves. Just two months into its history as America's first radio station in 1921, KDKA in Pittsburgh aired its first religious service. Pittsburgh's Calvary Episcopal Church was chosen for this "remote" because one of the engineers belonged to the choir. Calvary's senior minister demurred from going on radio, and an assistant pastor preached in his place. For the broadcast, KDKA's technicians, one Jewish and one Catholic, were put into choir robes in order to minimize congregational distractions. The program was a hit, and the senior member of Calvary's staff was persuaded to preach in subsequent services.

Soon other churches and clergy in other cities were preaching over the radio, too. Evangelical and fundamentalist broadcasters were the quickest to see the possibilities and scale up their radio ministries. Pentecostal Aimee Semple McPherson was the first woman ever to preach a sermon on the radio, and her station KFSG (for "Kalling Four Square Gospel") became the first radio station wholly owned and operated by a religious body. Evangelists like William Ward Ayer, Paul Rader, Donald Grey Barnhouse, Walter Maier, and Charles Fuller built radio audiences in the millions as they were proclaiming the gospel. By 1942, *The Lutheran Hour* was receiving more fan mail than the popular commercial *Amos 'n' Andy* program. Charles Fuller's *Old Fashioned Revival Hour* was the largest program on the Mutual Broadcasting System, purchasing more radio time on that network than any secular content producer. The radio evangelists were so successful filling the airwaves that in 1943 the Federal Council of Churches, representing the largest Protestant denominations, proposed regulations that would take the independent evangelicals off all national radio networks. Instead the FCC wanted religious broadcasting to be aired as a public service during free or "sustaining" time donated by the radio networks—and for the religious programs to come from approved organizations like the Federal Council or local councils of churches. This led to the prominence of some preachers like Harry Emerson Fosdick preaching every Sunday afternoon on the National Broadcasting Corporation's radio network. But it forced the evangelistic pioneers off the national networks and onto low-power stations. Still, it was estimated that more than 1,400 such religious broadcasters were on the radio at this time, and an increasing number of these owned their own stations. Decades before there were televangelists producing paid programs and asking for support, evangelical entrepreneurs honed their media practices on radio.[4]

The Crisis of Totalitarianism

The Great Depression in the United States was paralleled by worldwide economic depression. Perhaps nowhere were the effects felt as dramatically as in the countries of Western and Central Europe, where the economic distress allowed the rise of totalitarian regimes promising prosperity on the one hand, yet on the other hand dealing harshly with their various opponents while establishing effective authoritarian regimes. Both monarchy and democracy were on the defensive. In the Soviet Union, Joseph Stalin was in firm control of a planned economy guided by successive show trials, Gulag prisons, and five-year economic plans, replete with executions to enforce commitment to the Soviet state and to Stalin himself. In Italy, Benito Mussolini came to power at the head of a new party and movement, the Fascisti, or fascists, distinguished by their black shirts. Unlike the communist government of the Soviet Union, Mussolini sought and received the blessing of the Vatican, which was desperately afraid of Italy and other European countries falling into communism. The experience of religious persecution after revolutions in Russia and Mexico meant that Roman Catholics worldwide were opposed to leftist and socialist states, both out of principle since the 1890s, and in practice born of sad familiarity.

After the economy of the liberal Weimar Republic in Germany collapsed into runaway deflation (1930–33), for which millions of marks were needed to buy a loaf of bread and life savings were reduced to nil, a minor party of brown-shirted fascists from Bavaria, led by Adolf Hitler, came to power in 1933 in a democratic vote. Then the Nazis, as they were called, bullied and terrorized other German parties into their support, first blaming the Communist Party for the burning of the Reichstag (Germany's national statehouse in Berlin) and soon enacting a series of racial laws and seeking to remilitarize. The Nazi state effected a concordat, an agreement to allow the Catholic Church to go about its business so long as the church agreed not to involve itself in matters of the state. Similar efforts were undertaken to neutralize German Protestant church efforts to oppose the state, including the German Christian movement, which co-opted some of Germany's greatest theologians to portray Jesus as an Aryan, not a Jew, and replace the worship of Christ with Hitler himself in an effort to establish a new church based upon German pagan ideals, not dependent on the weak and suffering Christ of Christianity.

Finally, in East Asia and Japan wars were already waged from the early 1930s. In 1931, Japan invaded the part of Manchuria in northeastern China and occupied the resource-rich portion of China from the area just north of Beijing all the way to the Russian and Mongolian borders. The occupation was deadly, a foretaste of the aims of Imperial Japan to come. The republican government brought to power in 1931 in Spain (as mentioned above) consisted of a popular front combining those of liberal, socialist, and communist orientations in opposition to wealthy interests allied with the monarchy and the church. The government oriented itself to basic needs such as education for even the poorest children but made a strong enemy of the Catholic Church. When Francisco Franco led the nationalist faction in the Spanish Civil War, he did so with the firm support of the Catholic Church hierarchy in Spain and abroad, including in the United States.

In America the combination of the Great Depression at home and totalitarian governments abroad destroyed nearly all the people's confidence in the progress of humanity, on which liberal modernist theology had counted. In a 1933 article titled "After Liberalism—What?," theological ethicist John C. Bennett wrote:

JOHN C. BENNETT: THE DISINTEGRATION OF LIBERALISM

"The most important fact about contemporary American theology is the disintegration of liberalism. *Disintegration* may seem too strong word; I'm using it quite literally. It means that as a structure with a high degree of unity[,] theological liberalism is coming to pieces. The liberal preacher has had a coherent pattern of theological assumptions in the background of his message. He is often had the kind of self-confidence which goes with the preaching of an orthodoxy, for liberalism has been a new orthodoxy in many circles. It is that coherent pattern of assumptions, that self-confidence, which are going. Now many of us are left with the feeling of theological homelessness."*

*John C. Bennett, "After Liberalism—What?," *Christian Century* 50 (1933): 1403.

By 1939 this feeling of theological homelessness had intensified. The mainline *Christian Century* magazine ran a series on "How My Mind Has Changed," including E. G. Homrighausen's reflection that he "saw evidences of man's lostness: the depression, the constant threat of war, the return to brutality on so vast a scale, the loss of the spiritual substance of life that alone gives society structure, the uncertainty and insecurity of life."[5] Even Harry Emerson Fosdick changed his mind about modernism, arguing, "We cannot harmonize Christ himself with modern culture. What Christ does to modern culture is to challenge it."[6]

In 1932 Reinhold Niebuhr published *Moral Man and Immoral Society: A Study in Ethics and Politics*, a book that looked back to the First World War, explained much of the depression, and foresaw the rise of fascism. In it he argued that people were more likely to sin, and sin badly in groups, rather than as individuals. Even so, he depicted human beings, both individually and collectively, as prone to the characteristic sin of selfish pride. This revival of a doctrine of "original sin" for the twentieth century fit the facts of both the inability of democratic societies to provide for their people and the evils committed under totalitarianism. People were just not as good as liberal Protestantism had hoped.

The depression years also weakened Protestantism's hold on American culture, as was made clear by the repeal of prohibition in the 21st Amendment. Passed by Congress in February 1933, repeal was ratified by the states on December 5, 1933. Meanwhile American Jews and Catholics exercised an increasing role in public affairs, even as Protestants suffered somewhat of a cultural dethronement.

As most students of American history know, the Great Depression only really ended when the U.S. entered World War II after the attack on Pearl Harbor on December 7, 1941. President Roosevelt, already an extraordinary communicator, again took to the airwaves to articulate hope amid worry, just as he had in 1933 at his first inaugural address, when he told Americans they had "nothing to fear but fear itself." Now on January 6, 1941, less than a month after he declared the Japanese attack "a day which shall live in infamy," Roosevelt made an even more crucial speech before the U.S. Congress, articulating "the four freedoms" to which all Americans, indeed all the citizens of the world, were entitled as human beings. He told Congress and millions of American listening by radio: "As men do not live by bread alone, they do not fight by armaments alone. Those who man our defenses, and those behind them who build our defenses, must have the stamina and the courage which come from unshakable belief in the manner of life which they are defending." Even now, at the beginning of American participation in the war, Roosevelt articulated what kind of world he hoped would emerge from war's ashes:

> In the future days, which we seek to make secure, we look forward to a world founded upon four essential human freedoms.
>
> The first is freedom of speech and expression—everywhere in the world.
>
> The second is freedom of every person to worship God in his own way—everywhere in the world.
>
> The third is freedom from want—which, translated into world terms, means economic understandings which will secure to every nation a healthy peacetime life for its inhabitants—everywhere in the world.
>
> The fourth is freedom from fear—which, translated into world terms, means a world-wide reduction of armaments to such a point and in such a thorough fashion that no nation will be in a position to commit an act of physical aggression against any neighbor—anywhere in the world.[7]

These four freedoms, claimed Roosevelt, projected "no vision of a distant millennium." Instead, he proclaimed that this new world order characterized by freedom was attainable now, and moreover, the very opposite of the tyranny that the dictators sought to create by violence the world over.[8]

Something very similar to the ideas of the "Four Freedoms" speech was represented in the thinking of the Federal Council of Churches' Commission to Study the Bases of a Just and Durable Peace, led by John Foster Dulles. Unlike many pronouncements of church bodies designed to improve the world, this one, adopted in 1943 while the war was still going on in both Europe and the Pacific, became the framework of the United Nations organization (1945–), which was designed to unite the world in a system of just relations, to promote peaceful resolution of differences.

THE FEDERAL COUNCIL OF CHURCHES: SIX PILLARS OF PEACE

"The peace must provide the political framework for a continuing collaboration of the United Nations and, in due course, of neutral and enemy nations.

"The peace must make provision for bringing within the scope of international agreement those economic and financial acts of national governments which have widespread international repercussions.

"The peace must make provision for an organization to adapt the treaty structure of the world to changing underlying conditions.

"The peace must proclaim the goal of autonomy for subject peoples, and it must establish international organization to assure and to supervise the realization of that end.

"The peace must establish procedures for controlling military establishments everywhere.

"The peace must establish in principle, and seek to achieve in practice, the right of individuals everywhere to religious and intellectual liberty."*

*"Churchmen Detail 'Pillars of Peace': Six Political Principles Aimed at Meeting Post-War Needs," New York Times, March 19, 1943, 1.

The support of the nation's churches at this crucial juncture helped to assure that the future would be one of decolonization. It further helped establish an appetite for American foreign aid to free African, Latin American, and Asian nations and people. In this, America joined in the aspirations of people living in the empires created by Europeans and by the Japanese over people of color the world over. From 1923 to 1945, Britain alone held sway over roughly 23 percent of the world's human population in colonies and proctectorates. These colonies, in thrall to colonizers for as much as four hundred years, experienced immense excitement over independence as more than eighty countries attained their own sovereignty between 1943 and 1965. Still, many of these "new nations," as they were called, struggled with the rapid change and even more with the baggage of having been colonized for so long in a dependency that brought on a long period of reckoning with what it meant to be in a postcolonial state of affairs. But before any of that could begin, the war against the Axis nations needed to end for the United Nations leading the fight against the Axis nations so that the United Nations postwar institution could begin on October 24, 1945.

Franklin Roosevelt himself drew great strength from his Episcopalian faith, which showed at moments when he evidenced hope that others did not possess even in the face of dictators. During the war there was once again remarkable cooperation between the major faith groups, and Roosevelt did not stint from talking in religious terms that he trusted would span the faiths. A key example of this is the prayer he wrote to be read to all the soldiers, sailors, and marines about to participate in the D-Day invasion of France in June 1944. The prayer ended with these words:

> And, O Lord, give us faith. Give us faith in Thee; faith in our sons; faith in each other; faith in our united crusade. Let not the keenness of our spirit ever be dulled. Let not the impacts of temporary events, of temporal matters of but fleeting moment—let not these deter us in our unconquerable purpose.
>
> With Thy blessing, we shall prevail over the unholy forces of our enemy. Help us to conquer the apostles of greed and racial arrogances. Lead us to the saving of our country, and with our sister nations into a world unity that will spell a sure peace—a peace invulnerable to the schemings of unworthy men. And a peace that will let all of men live in freedom, reaping the just rewards of their honest toil.
>
> Thy will be done, Almighty God.
>
> Amen.

Not even Abraham Lincoln had spoken so directly to the Deity on behalf of the nation, yet this particular war was conducted against dictators who had committed such evil acts that it tended to cloak American war efforts in apparent unsullied grace. In fact, the war effort led Americans to their own acts of hubris and misplaced motives. Under a Presidential Executive Order, American citizens of Japanese descent were rounded up into camps in the western U.S. for the duration of the war—even while some of their sons and fathers fought for America in Europe. Americans saved far fewer European Jews from Nazi death camps than they could have because Roosevelt's own anti-Semitic State Department blocked immigration to the U.S. of Jews at every turn. Roosevelt himself elected not to divert bombers in order to destroy the railways to camps like Auschwitz, believing that the best solution for Europe's Jews was to win the war as quickly as possible. American bombers not only were used to drop atomic bombs on Hiroshima and Nagasaki, Japan, but also killed at least 25,000 civilians in Dresden, Germany, where firebombing sucked away all available oxygen.

THE FOUR CHAPLAINS

In spite of its many moral compromises, the war was remembered in American minds as a "good war." The nobility of the four chaplains of the SS *Dorchester* reflected American cooperation and honor as did perhaps no other story from the war. The chaplains—a Methodist minister, a Catholic priest, a Jewish rabbi, and a Reformed Church minister—had all met at Harvard's Army Chaplain School. They were reunited six months later when they were assigned to accompany troops sailing for Europe on the SS *Dorchester*, a civilian liner converted for military service. On February 3, 1943, a German submarine torpedoed the *Dorchester* near Newfoundland. As the ship sank, the chaplains worked to calm the soldiers and orchestrate the transfer of the wounded to lifeboats. When life vests ran out, each of the chaplains took off his own vest and gave it to a man without one. As the ship went down, survivors reported hearing the chaplains' voices, praying in English, Hebrew, and Latin for the almost seven hundred dying and drowning men. The story of the chaplains' bravery and courage circulated and became the subject of a 1948 postage stamp.

FIGURE 15-3. Four Chaplains United States Postage Stamp, 1948

Protestant, Catholic, Jew in Postwar America

The story of the four chaplains' giving their lives on the SS *Dorchester* possessed a life beyond the war itself: it demonstrated a truth that America was trying to embrace. The war had brought people from all three major faiths together in common cause as never before. In 1955 the sociologist Will Herberg (1906–77) wrote a book simply titled *Protestant, Catholic, Jew*. In it he announced the new status quo: "America is a three-religion country." One could be distinctively American by identifying with one of these three faiths. "The newcomer is expected to change many things about him as he becomes an American—nationality, language, culture. One thing, however, he is not expected to change—and that is religion." Religious identity among white Americans had trumped ethnic identity. Now in America, marriages joined German Jew with Russian Jew, Scottish with Swedish Protestants, and Irish with Italian Roman Catholics. Indeed, the hyphenated Americanism of the past had almost entirely disappeared, but this was not without its own problems. First, the identification with Americanism was so strong as to vie, in Herberg's view, with any other traditional religious belief. Second, the color line between white and black Americans was so defined as to call into question Americans' claims to be committed above all to freedom for all.

American life in the postwar era was defined by three central facts: a Cold War fight against "godless communism," especially from Russia and China; unparalleled domestic prosperity; and the problem of racial segregation. The fifteen years following the end of World War II featured a remarkable resurgence in religion's cultural popularity, yet the resurgence was both a sign of and a challenge to these three central determinants.

Wartime cooperation between the allied forces, including the United States and the Soviet Union, came to a crashing halt with the end of the war. The Soviet Union scrambled to occupy Eastern Europe as Winston Churchill warned of a lowering of an Iron Curtain in a 1946 speech in Fulton, Missouri:

> From Stettin in the Baltic to Trieste in the Adriatic, an iron curtain has descended across the Continent. Behind that line lie all the capitals of the ancient states of Central and Eastern Europe. Warsaw, Berlin, Prague, Vienna, Budapest, Belgrade, Bucharest and Sofia; all these famous cities and the populations around them lie in what I must call the Soviet sphere, and all are subject, in one form or another, not only to Soviet influence but [also] to a very high and in some cases increasing measure of control from Moscow.[9]

In very short order, the Soviets went from being allies to enemies of the West, and a Cold War ensued. The landmarks of this change came in quick succession: Berlin was cut off by the Soviets, resulting in the Berlin Airlift of 1948–49; mainland China was "lost" to the Communists led by Mao Zedong in 1949; the Soviets successfully tested an atomic bomb in 1949; they also supported North Korea in the Korean War in 1950. These would be followed by the Hungary Crisis of 1956 and the Cuban revolution (1953–58) under Fidel Castro, culminating in the Cuban Missile Crisis in October 1962. America, it seemed, had a new implacable enemy: communism. The fear of communism, and of "enemies within" the United States who might be giving aid and comfort to Soviet Russia, inspired the House Un-American Activities Committee led by Representative Richard Nixon and staff attorney Bobby Kennedy to attack personnel in the Truman State Department who had past socialist and communist memberships. After Klaus Fuchs and Julius and Ethel Rosenberg, among others, were caught giving atomic secrets to the Soviets, a full-fledged witch hunt began for communists in all parts of American life: movie writers and directors, college professors, government workers, and scientists. Senator Joseph R. McCarthy of Wisconsin led infamous attacks against suspected communist conspirators. Hollywood writers and directors were "blacklisted" for refusing to "name names" after they were asked the question of the hour: "Are you now, or have you ever been, a member of the Communist Party?"

Amid all this fear, Americans clung to their religion all the more tightly; there was no greater contrast than that between "godless communism" and America's love of God. President Harry Truman recognized the new State of Israel in 1948 as much for his own Christian sentiments as to make up for American inaction to save European Jews during the war. Under President Dwight D. Eisenhower, Americans added "In God We Trust" to all American currency. It was adopted by the U.S. Congress in 1956 as the nation's official motto, supplanting *E pluribus unum*, in use since the 1776 design of the Great Seal of the United States. Two years earlier, on the Sunday before Lincoln's birthday, Eisenhower listened as his pastor, Presbyterian George Docherty, argued in a sermon, "To omit the words 'under God' in the Pledge of Allegiance is to omit the definitive factor in the American way of life." From the pulpit, Docherty said he felt that "under God" was broad enough to include Jews and Muslims but to exclude atheists. "An atheistic American is a contradiction in terms," Docherty preached. "If you deny the Christian ethic, you fall short of the American ideal of life." Docherty himself was picking up an idea that had been advanced since 1948. The Catholic Knights of Columbus had been adding "under God" to the pledge whenever they said it from 1951 onward. On Flag Day, June 14, 1954, at Eisenhower's initiative, Congress officially added "under God" to the Pledge, so the words said by all schoolchildren now read, "I pledge Allegiance to the flag of the United States of America and to the Republic for which it stands, one nation under God, indivisible, with Liberty and Justice for all."

At another time in American history, adding God into the official signifiers of American life—money and patriotic speech—might have faced major opposition. But in the 1950s God not only differentiated good Americans from bad communists but was also culturally popular. President Eisenhower himself memorably framed the words of the Declaration of Independence religiously: "In other words, our form of government has no sense unless it is founded in a deeply felt religious faith, and I don't care what it is. With us, of course, it is the Judeo-Christian concept, but it must be a religion that all men are created equal."[10] The sentence is typically off-the-cuff Eisenhower, but its meaning conveys great respect for all religions that recognize God as creator. The consensus in the 1950s was that theistic religions (at least Judaism, Catholicism, and Mormonism) had come to be seen on an equal footing with traditional Protestantism, but that this did not represent an equal endorsement of all religions. At this point, full religious diversity and pluralism still lay in the future. Some other popular depictions of the time went further in promoting a common American nonspecific theism. Songs on the radio spoke of God as "The Big Man in the Sky," and New York City hosted a Dial-a-Prayer line, where people who needed a prayer could telephone in for one.

Prosperity and Popular Religiosity

During this time, Gallup surveyed Americans every year to see if they professed a belief in God. In all, 96 percent of the population claimed belief in God. Magazines were unusually full of articles about how scientists could validate the existence of God. These periodicals were also interested in the topic of prayer: how to pray and how to know God answered prayer. Even unlikely magazines like *Mademoiselle* ran religious-interest stories, including one on "Religion's Root Meaning." Popular interest in religion also propelled some religious leaders into celebrity status. Rabbi Joshua Loth Liebman published a 1946 book that spent over a year as number one on the bestseller list. This self-help book combined psychoanalysis with Liebman's rabbinic insights about how to stop hating oneself and others and change for the better. Here is one sample of his counsel: "Many people are miserable because they think that occasional destructive feelings necessarily make them terrible persons. But just as Aristotle maintained, 'One swallow does not make a spring,' we must understand that one or two or even a dozen unadmirable traits does not make an unadmirable person."[11]

In 1952, Norman Vincent Peale, pastor of Marble Collegiate Church in New York, published his own bestseller, *The Power of Positive Thinking*. Peale claimed to have "written with the sole objective of helping the reader achieve a happy, satisfying, and worthwhile life." Many found Peale theologically shallow, but the book still sells well today. Meanwhile a Roman Catholic priest and later bishop, Fulton Sheen, became a television star while teaching staunch morality, the dangers of communism, and Roman Catholic theology, all the while drawing an audience from all faiths that exceeded even the audience for the comedian Milton Berle, who had a popular show on at the same time.

Even taking into account a postwar baby boom, congregational membership increased considerably more than the rate of population increase. By 1961, membership in all religious groups had increased 30.94 percent from a decade before. This was on top of huge gains in the late 1940s. Out of a nation of 179 million people in 1961, some 116 million belonged to a congregation, or 64 percent of the country. This figure considerably underestimated total church affiliation since most churches did not count children and youth as members. When the Gallup organization asked adults which religious tradition they identified with, 98 percent claimed an affiliation. During the same time the percentage of people who claimed no religious affiliation dropped by two-thirds. For the religious denominations, these years featured tremendous growth; while every group experienced enlargement, some more evangelistic pentecostal bodies grew more dramatically. The Church of God in Christ grew 1,025 percent; the Assemblies of God grew 474 percent from 1926 to 1949 and added even more in the 1950s and 1960s.[12]

Much of the numerical growth of the churches came along with the move of the American white population to the suburbs in large numbers. The suburbs not only housed a burgeoning population in a nation that had not built many houses during the depression and war; they were also especially geared toward families with children. The Sunday school had moved out from a dank basement under an urban sanctuary, into a wing of its own with bright light. The child-sized tables, chairs, and even toilets reinforced the impression that the culture revolved around children. So did the other activities at religious congregations and Jewish centers: Boy Scout and Girl Scout troops, teen clubs, dances, B'nai B'rith, meetings of the temple sisterhood, pancake dinners, potluck suppers, and choirs for every age. And for adults, a sea of coffee was served at "fellowship hours," allowing religious participants to socialize in addition to worshiping.

Domestic prosperity in the postwar years led to use of the repeated slogan "We've never had it so good." Some observers, however, asked the moral question: "Affluence for what?" Social thinkers who focused on the failure of the system to clothe and feed people back in the 1930s were now concerned that American life was being undermined by its attachment to prosperity. Books like C. Wright Mills's *White Collar*, William H. Whyte's *The Organization Man*, and David Riesman's *The Lonely Crowd* saw big corporations that exchanged stable middle-class jobs (for men) for total loyalty as undermining authentic living and even the freedom that Americans thought they had fought to preserve. Religious critics of the American dream continued in this vein. Writers like Will Herberg, Gibson Winter, Peter Berton, and Peter Berger thought that the numerical success of churches and synagogues masked faith compromises with mammon. The pews were too comfortable since believers were rarely challenged, and the move to the suburbs had actually made things worse. Suburbanization had moved faith communities from the public sphere, near where people worked and suffered, and out to a domestic sphere of children, schools, and the family home. Who and what had the churches left behind in the city? The poor, the immigrant, black Americans, and the chance to make life in the urban core better. Above all, there was a suspicion that Americans were sometimes going to religious services because everyone around them did. As the practical theologian Georgia Harkness (1891–1974) observed, "One can be coerced to church, but not to worship. Prayer is the opening of the soul to God so that he may speak to us. The perpetual danger which besets religion is that it may substitute gentility and aestheticism for prophetic insight and power."

Not every religious development in the postwar years was as mixed as suburban prosperity appeared to be. The more biblical neo-orthodox Protestantism associated with Reinhold Niebuhr, Karl Barth, and Paul Tillich thrived. Niebuhr (1892–1971) wrote *The Irony of American History*, in which he argued that American foreign policy's tendency to urge other nations to emulate the United States was ignorant about the amazing advantages Americans had experienced in resources and security with which to build their democracy. This view helped positively inform American reception of the "new nations" created by massive decolonialization in the 1950s and early 1960s. Karl Barth (1886–1968) influenced a generation of preachers to spend their time "proclaiming" the Word of God found in Scripture and consequently helped fund a kind of golden age for biblical interpretation in seminaries and universities, supporting interest in staying closer to the biblical witness. Perhaps the most surprising voice from the religious academy to achieve celebrity was that of Paul Tillich (1886–1965). Tillich combined existential thought with Christian theology in coining terms like "ultimate concern" to explain why not everyone valued or worshiped the same things. He also spoke to anxiety-fixated people in popular sermons with repackaged Pauline themes, such as "You Are Accepted." Another scholar who, like Tillich, escaped Nazism in Europe to have an extraordinary impact in the U.S. was Abraham Joshua Heschel (1907–72). In books like *Man Is Not Alone* (1951) and *God in Search of Man* (1950), Heschel probed human existential loneliness and assured Jews and Christians alike that God was active in the world in the past and present, seeking relationship with God's creatures.

New Voices, New Movements

Religiously, the 1950s featured more than just suburban conformity. Some dissenting voices were coming out of Catholicism and Judaism that gathered widespread attention. Also, two new movements would reshape American life—neo-evangelicalism and the civil rights movement, each led by a charismatic minister—Billy Graham and Martin Luther King Jr., respectively. It is common to see the 1960s as constituting a sharp break with the religion and culture that came before. Instead, we should see the roots of diversity and change beginning in the supposedly calm 1950s.

Among the figures to achieve widespread literary success from outside the white Protestant mainstream were Abraham Joshua Heschel, Thomas Merton, Dorothy Day, Jack Kerouac, D. T. Suzuki, Gary Snyder, and Martin Luther King Jr. As authors, all shared an emphasis on a religious path that broke from conformity for safety's sake. Each seemed radical from the perspective of 1950s America, but each actually was about the rediscovery of some more ancient form of religious wisdom and above that a recommended practice. For Rabbi Heschel, the new path was a way of responsive deeds that acknowledged the human's proper place before God. In the face of possible nuclear annihilation, he reminded readers that while human beings could now indeed destroy all of life, no one but God could create a single life. He depicted Jewish life as about making the world better by deeds done, rather than worse by neglect.

Thomas Merton (1915–68) held up contemplation as a way that opens human beings to the "real," to God, and to others, not a neglect of life. His bestselling autobiography, *The Seven Storey Mountain* (1948), tells the story of how a disillusioned Columbia University graduate working in Manhattan turned to God and found a way to peace and out of daily purgatory (the "seven storey mountain" is a reference to Dante) by becoming a Trappist monk. Lots of young men followed Merton's footsteps to the monastery. Millions more found their way into a more contemplative life. Dorothy Day (1897–1980) told the story of her conversion from atheism to Catholicism in her autobiography, *The Long Loneliness* (1952). She explained the establishment of the *Catholic Worker* magazine and the Houses of Hospitality, depicting ministries of urban solidarity that did not make life pretty, but made poor neighbors into real neighbors for readers unfamiliar with Catholicism but inspired by Day's saintly activities.

Some of the new voices explored beyond the Christian and Jewish boundaries of most of American religiosity. Jack Kerouac (1922–69) introduced readers to Zen Buddhism in *On the Road* (1957) and *Dharma Bums* (1958). His inspiration was his friendship with the Berkeley wunderkind Gary Snyder (1930–). Snyder, the only major Beat with a rural upbringing, inspired his fellow writers and poets to turn toward nature. They and millions of others learned about Zen Buddhism from its key popularizer, D. T. Suzuki (1870–1966). Suzuki taught and published widely, including as a professor at Columbia University from 1952 to 1957. At a time when there were fewer than 80,000 Buddhists in America, D. T. Suzuki's representation of the faith became Buddhism for Americans. The popular embrace of Buddhism by Americans of non-Asian descent began at this time. Finally, with Martin Luther King Jr. (1929–68) and his book *Stride Toward Freedom: The Story of the Montgomery Bus Boycott*, Americans became interested in a rising religious star and received a glimpse of the power of nonviolent resistance for confronting segregation.

As King was just coming into broader notice, another religious figure, Billy Graham (1918–2018) was at the zenith of his long popularity. William

Franklin "Billy" Graham was born in North Carolina and attended Bob Jones College, followed by the Florida Bible Institute, followed by Wheaton College in Illinois. That educational trajectory demonstrated his movement from a rigid fundamentalism to something broader, which was coming to be called neo-evangelicalism. After college, Graham became a traveling evangelist for a new group, Youth for Christ, founded in 1944 to foster Christian commitments on the part of young people in the midst of war. Graham was YFC's first full-time evangelist beginning in 1946. The movement was an expression of an evangelicalism that was breaking away from the strictures of fundamentalism. It also took shape during World War II as leaders representing conservative Protestantism who were willing to work together formed a national organization in 1943, the National Association of Evangelicals. The group drew together Pentecostals, holiness leaders, Baptists, Reformed, Wesleyan, and nondenominational Christians who were prepared not to fight over the theology that divided them in favor of promoting Christ together. Graham fit into this model insofar as he had himself abandoned his fundamentalist roots and now addressed audiences in a sportscoat (to look more modern) and with a simple message of the possibility of turning one's life over to Christ. Every sermon contained a pitch for marriage and a condemnation of communism. Most brought home the urgency of making a decision for Christ by using the specter of life ending with an atomic mushroom cloud. Graham also made savvy use of radio, featuring his own syndicated show, *The Hour of Decision*, beginning in 1950. Graham became a household name soon after he began a Los Angeles revival in 1949. Graham's revival was foundering in this secular city when publisher William Randolph Hearst ordered his editors all over the country to "Puff Graham." Whether Hearst was more impressed with Graham's enthusiastic sermons or his condemnation of communism, no one knows, but overnight the revival was extended, and word about how Hollywood celebrities were turning their lives over to Christ traveled far. Soon Graham reached out to new cities, including London, England, Atlanta, and New York. Everywhere he went, Graham achieved notable success. Graham later remembered the change that accounted for his success: "During the crusade I discovered the secret that changed my ministry. I stopped trying to prove that the Bible was true. I had settled in my own mind that it was, and this faith was conveyed to the audience. Over and over again I found myself saying 'The Bible says.' I felt as though I were merely a voice through which the Holy Spirit was speaking."[13]

Billy Graham was both a symbol of 1950s evangelicalism and a sign of how far things had come since the Scopes "monkey trial" of 1925. Graham was the product of an evangelical subculture that had been gathering steam. Historian Joel Carpenter describes how a network of colleges (Wheaton, Whitworth, Grove City, Calvin College, Hope College, Houghton College, Luther Rice College, Lincoln Christian University, Abilene Christian, Baylor

FIGURE 15-4. Martin Luther King Jr. and Billy Graham, shown here in 1962, first met during the Madison Square Garden Revival, New York, 1957 (From *Chicago Tribune.* © 1962. Chicago Tribune. All rights reserved. Used under license.)

University, Trevecca Nazarene University, Gordon College, Westmont College) supplemented by seminaries (Fuller, Westminster, Gordon-Conwell, Asbury, Luther Rice, Calvin) were preparing evangelical leaders of the future in a conducive environment. The colleges and seminaries relied on a set of publishers (Baker, Zondervan, Thomas Nelson) that kept evangelicals informed, while these institutions' professors published with the same presses. Billy Graham even started a new magazine, *Christianity Today* (1956), that soon eclipsed the mainline standard, *Christian Century*. All these institutions helped break down the fundamentalist ecclesiastical tendency to "separate from unholiness" in favor of fellowshiping in the face of a common enemy and for a common Savior. Leaders like Harold John Ockenga (1905–80) and Carl F. H. Henry (1913–2003) began to claim a new name for the movement, distinguishing "neo-evangelicalism" from liberalism, neo-orthodoxy, and fundamentalism.

It was Carl F. H. Henry who penned a book in 1947, *The Uneasy Conscience of Modern Fundamentalism*, in which he decried the lack of social involvement by fundamentalists. "If the Bible believing Christian is on the wrong side of social problems such as war, race, class, labor, liquor, imperialism, etc., it is time to get over the fence to the right side. The church needs a progressive Fundamentalist with a social message." He went even further: "Fundamentalism is the modern priest and Levite, by-passing suffering and humanity. . . . By and large, the Fundamentalist opposition to societal ills has been more vocal than actual."[14] In time, Henry and Graham would come to be known as the head and heart of neo-evangelicalism, a movement that would be more socially engaged than fundamentalism.

The South from which Graham emerged was changing—as much from outside as from within. In 1954 the Supreme Court decision in *Brown v. Board of Education* invalidated the long-standing principle of "separate but equal" in American public education. The leading national denominations (though not the Southern Baptist Convention) adopted positions against racial segregation. Still, a Supreme Court decision did not change segregationist hearts; school boards and white citizens continued to resist desegregation at every turn for the next twenty years. Graham, though a southern moderate at best, nevertheless began integrating his revivals even before the *Brown* decision. In 1953 he personally took down the rope that divided black from white seating at his Chattanooga revival. Though other venues later found ways to try to racially divide revival seating, by 1956 he was public in his opposition to segregation on religious grounds. In 1956 Graham published articles in *Life* and *Ebony*, the widest general and black circulation periodicals of the day, declaring, "There's no color-line in heaven," and imploring Americans to act accordingly on earth as well.[15]

Also in 1956, the Montgomery Bus Boycott caught Americans' attention. The boycott began after Rosa Parks was arrested for refusing to give up her seat to a white bus passenger. From December 5, 1955, to December 20, 1956, African Americans refused to ride city buses in Montgomery, Alabama, to protest segregated seating. Parks's actions were planned in advance by the local NAACP and propelled a young minister, Rev. Dr. Martin Luther King Jr., the pastor of Dexter Avenue Baptist Church in Montgomery, to national attention as its leader. Montgomery constituted the first large-scale U.S. demonstration against segregation. King's leadership of forty thousand boycotters in nonviolent resistance in the face of the bombings of four churches and boycott leaders' homes, plus terroristic activities by a resurrected third Ku Klux Klan, galvanized black hopes. The boycott only ended when the Supreme Court sided with a district federal court in ruling that segregated bus seating violated the equal protection clause of the 14th Amendment to the Constitution. Mass protest was enlisting the courts to dismantle segregation.

After Montgomery, Martin Luther King Jr. established a new organization, the Southern Christian Leadership Conference (SCLC), to continue to press nonviolently for civil rights. On July 18, 1957, Martin Luther King gave a public invocation at Madison Square Garden as part of the long-running Billy Graham evangelistic campaign. Graham praised King for leading "a great social revolution." For this crusade, Graham also invited the black gospel stars Mahalia Jackson and Ethel Waters to sing, backed by a mixed-race volunteer choir from churches all over the New York metropolitan area.

MARTIN LUTHER KING JR. PRAYS
AT BILLY GRAHAM'S CRUSADE

"We stand amid the compelling urgency of the Lord of the earth as exemplified in the life Jesus Christ yet we live our lives so often in the dungeons of hate. For all of these sins, Oh God, forgive. And in these days of emotional tension when the problems of the world are dynamic in extent and chaotic in detail give us penetrating vision, broad understanding, the power of endurance and abiding faith and save us from the paralysis of crippling fear. Oh God, we ask you to help us to work with renewed vigor for a warless world and for the brotherhood that transcends race or color."*

*"Dr. Martin Luther King, Jr.—1957 New York Crusade," https://billygrahamlibrary.org /dr-martin-luther-king-jr-1957-new-york-crusade/.

America's pastor, Graham, had met and affirmed America's prophet, Martin Luther King Jr., and been blessed in return. Yet more changes, surprises, and challenges were on the way. The year 1960 ended with the previously unthinkable election of a Roman Catholic, John F. Kennedy, as President. Yet underneath this American high, the cancer of racial segregation persisted, and black Christians would take the leading role in moving the issue forward in the 1960s.

16. A Catholic President, the Civil Rights Movement, and the Ferment of the 1960s

The year 1960 ended with the previously unthinkable election of a Roman Catholic, John F. Kennedy, as President. Yet underneath this American high, the cancer of racial segregation festered, and black Christians took the leading role in moving the issue forward into public consciousness. Many religious participants involved with the civil rights movement and opposition to the war in Vietnam remember the time as faith's finest hour—an experience when religion was relevant as never before and perhaps never again. At the same time, as the struggle for equality before the law turned toward a concern for reparations for past wrongs, and youth turned against their parents on the morality of the war, moral questions became more vexed. Then leaders of clarity—Malcolm X, Martin Luther King Jr., and Robert F. Kennedy—were removed from the conversation by assassination. In the midst of it all, a modification in immigration policy, the 1965 Hart-Celler Act, opened up future immigration to the first significant numbers of Muslims, Hindus, and Buddhists, who would change what religious diversity meant for the future of American life.

A Catholic President and Vatican II

Catholics had come a long way in America since Al Smith lost the race for the presidency in 1928. They had served with honor in World War II, Bishop Fulton Sheen's television show had helped demystify some Catholic teachings for millions of non-Catholics, and Catholicism in the U.S. had thrown off most tinges of its immigrant past. But was America ready for John F. Kennedy (1917–63) to become President? Not all Protestants thought so. In August of 1960, Protestant organizations in Michigan and Kentucky voiced their opposition to a Catholic President. Next, twenty-five Baptist, Methodist, and pentecostal ministers vowed to "oppose with all powers at our command, the election of a Catholic to the Presidency of the United States." Soon other Protestant leaders and groups declared similar anti-Catholic opposition to Kennedy. On September 7, 1960, some 150 prominent Protestants, led by Dr. Norman Vincent Peale and including Billy Graham, went public with accusing the Catholic Church of being a "political as well as religious organization [that has] specifically repudiated, on many occasions, the principle sacred to us that every man shall be free to follow the dictates of his conscience in religious matters." On the same day the organization Protestants and Other Americans United for Separation of Church and State released a statement arguing a similar point: "We cannot avoid recognition of the fact that one church in the U.S., the largest church operating on American soil, officially supports a world-wide policy of partial union of church and state wherever it has the power to enforce such a policy. In the U.S. the bishops of this church have specifically rejected the Supreme Court's interpretation of the separation of church and state."

At this point, then, John F. Kennedy was on his back foot politically in the campaign. He knew that he needed to win Democrats in the South, a very Protestant region. One of the places where Southern Baptists were most against his candidacy was Texas, so it was arranged for him to go and speak to the overwhelmingly Baptist Greater Houston Ministerial Association. In a speech written for him by Ted Sorensen, Kennedy told the assembled clergy:

> I believe in an America where the separation of church and state is absolute—where no Catholic prelate would tell the President (should he be Catholic) how to act, and no Protestant minister would tell his parishioners for whom to vote—where no church or church school is granted any public funds or political preference—and where no man is denied public office merely because his religion differs from the President who might appoint him or the people who might elect him. . . . I believe in a President whose views on religion are his own private affair, neither imposed upon him by the nation or imposed by the nation upon him as a condition to holding that office. . . .
>
> Whatever issues may come before me as President, if I should be elected—on birth control, divorce, censorship, gambling, or any other subject—I will make my decision in accordance with these views, in accordance with what my conscience tells me to be in the national interest, and without regard to outside religious pressure or dictate. And no power or threat of punishment could cause me to decide otherwise.[1]

While the press and Kennedy's supporters celebrated the success of his speech, his statements on the relation of church and state displeased others. Key members of the Catholic hierarchy, especially New York's Francis Cardinal Spellman, believed that the candidate had given away federal issues important to the Roman Catholic Church, such as the aid to parochial schools that the hierarchy sought. John Courtney Murray (1904–67), the influential editor of the Jesuit magazine, *America*, and himself an advocate for a robustly free church under conditions of officially secular governments, thought that Kennedy had gone too far, saying, "To make religion merely a private matter, was idiocy." Ted Sorensen had consulted Murray while preparing the speech. Father Murray was upset that Sorensen ignored his advice to add that while church leaders should never coerce a public official, they should always be free to instruct Catholics from the pulpit as to the Catholic Church's teachings on moral issues debated in the public square. The devotional magazine for families—*The Ave Maria*, coming out of Notre Dame—expressed its disappointment too, featuring an editorial arguing, "To relegate your conscience to your 'private life' is not only unrealistic, but dangerous as well."[2] Historian William Lee Miller reflected, "The joke was that he turned out to be, in effect, our first Baptist president, one, that is, who defended a thoroughgoing separation more characteristic of that group than of his own church."[3] However much Kennedy's fellow Catholics might have wished he had spoken differently as a Catholic, they voted for him overwhelmingly, and more importantly, he won over enough formerly suspicious Protestants to be elected.

Even as Kennedy was running for the presidency, changes were underway in the structures of worldwide Catholicism led by a new pontiff, Angelo Giuseppe Roncalli (1881–1963), who chose the name John XXIII. Remembered just a few years later, at the time of his death in 1963, as "the good Pope," Pope John XXIII issued several memorable encyclicals. Unlike many men who rose to the papacy, Roncalli was the son of sharecroppers, one of thirteen children, and exhibited a gift for connecting with common people. He liked to remind the public and church leaders, "We were all made in God's image, and thus we are all godly alike." Long before he became pope, he put this theology into practice during World War II while serving in Eastern Europe to save refugees, most of them Jews, during the Holocaust. His early relationships with Jews and Eastern Europeans resulted in his support for the founding of the State of Israel, outreach to persons living under communism, and efforts to improve relations with Orthodox Christians. Interfaith and ecumenical outreach became hallmarks of his papacy and of the Second Vatican Council, which he called for in 1959. His encyclical *Mater et Magistra* (1961) embraced the dignity of human work and the social role of the church. His last, *Pacem in Terris* (1963), advocated establishing worldwide peace on the grounds of justice, liberty, and charity; it was especially notable for advocating the rights of women.

In various discussions before the Second Vatican Council actually convened, John XXIII often said that it was time to open the windows of the church to let in some fresh air. Announcing his plan to convoke Vatican II just three months after his election as pope, various handlers among the Vatican's cardinals and bishops told him he could not do it. John XXIII responded that the church of the Trent and Vatican I councils was due for updating, so the timeless faith of the gospel could be communicated. "Aggiornamento"—literally, "updating" in Italian—became the expression for what Vatican II was about.

John XXIII was not alone in thinking the Catholic Church was due for an update: throughout the 1950s theologians, notably Karl Rahner, SJ; Michael

Herbert; and John Courtney Murray, SJ, had been pulling away from the prevailing Scholastic Thomism and constructing Catholic theology on new premises, using modern scientific understandings of life and society and a fresh approach to the work and person of Jesus Christ. At the same time historical theologians and biblical scholars—Yves Congar, Joseph Ratzinger, and Henri de Lubac—in their work were trying to secure an accurate understanding of Scripture and the early church fathers as a source of renewal. Finally, the world wars had left a medieval church trying to make its way uncertainly through the structures of modern, secular, and less friendly societies in ways that called for an updating, as the Kennedy election and problems for the church in communist countries demonstrated.

Vatican II, which lasted from 1961 to 1965, remade the largest Christian church the world over, internally and in its relationship with non-Catholics. At the opening session of the council, which included delegated observers from other Christian churches and even Jewish and Muslim leaders, John XXIII told the assembly what was required:

POPE JOHN XXIII AT THE SECOND VATICAN COUNCIL

"What is needed at the present time is a new enthusiasm, a new joy and serenity of mind in the unreserved acceptance by all of the entire Christian faith, without forfeiting that accuracy and precision in its presentation which characterized the proceedings of the Council of Trent and the First Vatican Council. What is needed, and what everyone imbued with a truly Christian, Catholic and apostolic spirit craves today, is that this doctrine shall be more widely known, more deeply understood, and more penetrating in its effects on men's moral lives. What is needed is that this certain and immutable doctrine, to which the faithful owe obedience, be studied afresh and reformulated in contemporary terms. For this deposit of faith, or truths which are contained in our time-honored teaching[,] is one thing; the manner in which these truths are set forth (with their meaning preserved intact) is something else."*

*John XXIII, opening address of Vatican II, *"Gaudet Mater Ecclesia"* (October 11, 1962), in *The Documents of Vatican II*, ed. Walter M. Abbott (New York: Guild Press, 1966), 773.

The Second Vatican Council produced sixteen long documents addressing a wide variety of issues, including apologies for the way the Catholic Church had victimized Jews and reaching out to Protestant believers as "separate brethren" who one day might be reconciled with Catholics but whose faith could be respected as Christians in the meantime. For Americans, the Council brought rapid visible changes. The mass could now be offered in the vernacular language of the people, which in America meant English in most settings, instead of Latin. The pastoral vocation of priests and bishops was stressed, and the laity were recognized as an important class of the faithful, helping to constitute with clergy and the religious "the people of God." Consequently, altars came away from the wall, and priests now faced congregations when celebrating the Mass. Laypeople were encouraged to bring their gifts for ministry and soon were leading folk songs with guitars during the mass service. Nuns were offered the opportunity to adopt dress that was less formal and facilitated their work in the world. Many orders gave up or simplified their ornate habits. Religious sisters had been the ubiquitous teachers in Catholic K–12 education; now there were opportunities for lay Catholics to take up vocations in teaching and youth work. The changes demystified Catholicism to a degree for Protestants and other Americans who were now able to attend ecumenical services involving their own congregation and a Catholic parish. Finally, the Council's Declaration on Religious Liberty, introduced by John Courtney Murray, promoted the view that Catholics were free to exercise their religious rights in secular societies, like the United States, that recognized religious liberty. This eliminated the more restrictive unitary view of church and state that had created the backlash to Kennedy's election in the first place.

By the end of 1963, both John F. Kennedy and John XXIII were dead, but the way they had lived and led had revolutionized the place of Catholics in American society. On a personal level, many of the people who had not voted for Kennedy against Nixon in 1960 went to their own churches on the day of his funeral to mourn a man with a young family they had come to recognize as not so different from their own. John XXIII had inaugurated changes in the church that made Catholicism more modern and intelligible to Protestants, who were soon adopting parts of the ancient liturgy that Catholicism had preserved together with an interest in the lectionary, the regular reading of biblical texts to read through the most important parts of the Bible every three years.

The Civil Rights Movement

The early to middle years of the 1960s proved to be the most consequential years of the movement for the freedom and rights of black Americans. The Southern Christian Leadership Conference (SCLC) was joined in 1960 by new allies: African American students, inspired by the Montgomery Bus Boycott, began to use direct nonviolent resistance to desegregate lunch counters, public accommodations, and interstate buses.

The student phase of the movement began on February 1, 1960, when four North Carolina A&T students in Greensboro, North Carolina, sat down at a Woolworth lunch counter and asked to be served. By February 4, hundreds of students from A&T, Bennett College, and Dudley High School had joined the sit-in. Although a few students had tried to be served earlier, in the 1950s, the Greensboro sit-in marked the first time that a mass, sustained movement ensued. Soon there were similar such movements in other cities, including Nashville and Atlanta. The Nashville sit-ins, which lasted from February 13 to May 10, 1960, were led by James Lawson, a 29-year-old divinity student, who had studied nonviolent social change with Mahatma Gandhi in India. To the students he trained in resisting violence—people like John Lewis, Diane Nash, Bernard Lafeyette, and Bob Moses—Lawson became known as "the teacher." Nashville students had the first and most wide-ranging success in the decade when Jim Crow was routed. They stayed at it with such resolve that the Rev. Martin Luther King Jr., on a visit to Fisk University during the students' efforts, said he came not to inspire but to be inspired. Atlanta, with its seven Historically Black Colleges and Universities (HBCUs), was also an early and successful case of a February movement achieving success in its sit-ins by October of the same year. In all, some 55 student movements in 13 states began in the winter and spring of 1960.

In April 1960, Ella Baker, a veteran civil rights organizer and an SCLC official, invited black college students who had participated in earlier sit-ins to an April 1960 gathering at Shaw University in Raleigh, North Carolina. Baker helped the students found their own organization, the Student Nonviolent Coordinating Committee (SNCC). SNCC was independent and student-run, not a student auxiliary to the minister-led SCLC. This did not mean, however, that religion did not play a role in the movement. James Lawson drafted the new organization's statement of purpose: "We affirm the philosophical or religious ideal of nonviolence as the foundation of our purpose, the presupposition of our faith, and the manner of our action. Nonviolence as it grows from Judaic-Christian traditions seeks a social order of justice permeated by love." This mass movement also drew on black spirituals and popular song to create "freedom songs"; thus "I woke up with my mind focused on Jesus" became "I woke up with my mind focused on freedom."[4]

Student enthusiasm for an end to segregation was also channeled by another group, the Congress of Racial Equality (CORE), which organized "Freedom Rides" into the South to test new Interstate Commerce Commission regulations and court orders barring segregation in interstate transportation in 1961. The Freedom riders were mixed-race teams of students trying to test whether the law would be enforced. CORE's riders were beaten by mobs in several places, including the Alabama cities of Anniston, Birmingham, and Montgomery. When CORE abandoned the rides, SNCC took up the cause and saw the Riders through to Jackson, Mississippi, where many were jailed. Soon SNCC was mounting other actions on its own, including a voter registration drive in McComb, Mississippi, and an attempt to desegregate the city of Albany, Georgia.

Letter from Birmingham Jail

For both SCLC and SNCC, early victories in the upper- and mid-South were hard to repeat when the action moved to the Deep South. In 1963 the SCLC came to the aid of the Rev. Fred Shuttlesworth, who had endured years of bombings and violence from the Klan and at the hands of police led by Birmingham Police Chief Theophilus Eugene "Bull" Connor. When Martin Luther King Jr. came to town in the spring of 1963, he and Ralph David Abernathy were soon arrested and charged with parading without a permit. While King was jailed for eleven days in solitary confinement, eight moderate white clergy wrote an open letter to King in the local paper. The statement expressed concern that "honest convictions in racial matters could properly be pursued in the courts, but urged that decisions of those courts should in the meantime be peacefully obeyed." This determination to resolve racial matters only under conditions of "law and order" led these clergymen to note: "However, we are now confronted by a series of demonstrations by some of our Negro citizens, directed and led in part by outsiders. We recognize the natural impatience of people who feel that their hopes are slow in being realized. But we are convinced that these demonstrations are unwise and untimely."[5]

This paragraph of the letter was a direct rebuke of King, the SCLC, and the demonstrations themselves. It prompted King to write the "Letter from a Birmingham Jail," a twenty-page (in typed format) treatise on the morality of and need for the civil rights movement. The letter, addressed to "My Fellow Clergymen," started by seeking to address why King was in Birmingham: "since you have been influenced by the view which argues against 'outsiders coming in.'" After noting that the SCLC was there at the invitation of a local movement, the Alabama Christian Movement for Human Rights, King wrote,

> But more basically, I am in Birmingham because injustice is here. Just as the prophets of the eighth century B.C. left their villages and carried their "thus saith the LORD" far beyond the boundaries of their home towns, and just as the Apostle Paul left his village of Tarsus and carried the gospel of Jesus Christ to the far corners of the Greco-Roman world, so am I compelled to carry the gospel of freedom beyond my own home town. Like Paul, I must constantly respond to the Macedonian call for aid.[6]

King went on to eloquently cite a wide variety of Christian and Jewish sources of morality, including saints Paul, Augustine of Hippo, and Thomas Aquinas. He enlisted some of the central figures of America's civil religion, including Abraham Lincoln and Thomas Jefferson. King also quoted the most respected religious thinkers of the day—Martin Buber, Paul Tillich, and Reinhold Niebuhr—all to show where the balance of justice stood.

MARTIN LUTHER KING JR.: JUST VERSUS UNJUST LAWS

"One may well ask: 'How can you advocate breaking some laws and obeying others?' The answer lies in the fact that there are two types of laws: just and unjust. I would be the first to advocate obeying just laws. One has not only a legal but a moral responsibility to obey just laws. Conversely, one has a moral responsibility to disobey unjust laws. I would agree with St. Augustine that 'an unjust law is no law at all.'

"Now, what is the difference between the two? How does one determine whether a law is just or unjust? A just law is a man made code that squares with the moral law or the law of God. An unjust law is a code that is out of harmony with the moral law. To put it in the terms of St. Thomas Aquinas: An unjust law is a human law that is not rooted in eternal law and natural law. Any law that uplifts human personality is just. Any law that degrades human personality is unjust. All segregation statutes are unjust because segregation distorts the soul and damages the personality."*

*Martin Luther King Jr., "Letter from a Birmingham Jail," The Martin Luther King, Jr. Research and Education Institute, https://kinginstitute.stanford.edu/king-papers/documents/letter-birmingham-jail.

Once King was released, a new strategy was mounted in Birmingham that would come to be known as the Birmingham Children's Crusade of May 2–5, 1963. As the nation watched on live television, Birmingham's police turned firehoses against demonstrating children and youth; they even released German shepherd dogs to attack them. So many young people were arrested that the jails could not hold them, and the national mood changed decisively against the segregationists.

FIGURE 16-1. Martin Luther King Jr. addresses a crowd from the steps of the Lincoln Memorial during the Aug. 28, 1963, March on Washington, D.C. (U.S. Information Agency National Archives 542014)

There seemed to be a strong national consensus forming over civil rights that summer when more than a quarter of a million people participated in the March on Washington on August 28, 1963, and heard Martin Luther King Jr. deliver his "I Have a Dream" speech. Yet less than a month later, Fred Shuttlesworth's Sixteenth Street Baptist Church in Birmingham was bombed on September 15, killing four African American girls attending Sunday school: Denise McNair, age 11; and Cynthia Wesley, Carole Robertson, and Adie Mae Collins, each 14 years old. The 1963 events in Birmingham, and civil rights worker killings in Mississippi, topped off by John F. Kennedy's assassination, led directly to the 1964 Civil Rights Act in response.

Even though there was a Civil Rights Act in place, that did not assure compliance when it came to local law in the most southern states; voting rights in the Deep South were a particular problem. Indeed, only an estimated 2 percent of black adults eligible to register in Selma, Alabama, had managed to do so. This became the basis for the Selma March. On "Bloody Sunday," March 7, 1965, some 600 civil rights marchers headed east out of Selma on U.S. Route 80. They got only as far as the Edmund Pettus Bridge, six blocks away, when state and local lawmen attacked them with billy clubs and tear gas, driving protestors back into Selma. President Lyndon Johnson (1908–73) later compared the assault to Lexington and Concord, a turning point in American history, because it touched the conscience of the nation and accelerated the passage of the historic Voting Rights Act.

Next, 2,000 marchers were again turned back at the bridge. Their ranks had swelled with the addition of religious leaders from beyond the South, determined to stand with Dr. King, who had the prior year been awarded the Nobel Peace Prize. Not even in these numbers were marchers safe. One, a young white Unitarian minister, James Reeb, was beaten to death. After these events, on the night of March 15, President Johnson appeared on

FIGURE 16-3. Dr. Martin Luther King Jr., arm in arm with Reverend Ralph Abernathy, leads marchers as they begin the Selma to Montgomery civil rights march from Brown's Chapel Church in Selma, Alabama, US, March 21, 1965; (L–R) an unidentified priest and man, John Lewis, an unidentified nun, Ralph Abernathy (1926–90), Martin Luther King Jr. (1929–68), Ralph Bunche (1904–71) (partially visible), Abraham Joshua Heschel (1907–72), Fred Shuttlesworth (1922–2011). (Photo by William Lovelace/ Daily Express/Hulton Archive/Getty Images).

national television, pledging his support to the Selma marchers and calling for the passage of a new voting rights bill that he was introducing in Congress: "There is no Negro problem. There is no Southern problem. There is no Northern problem. There is only an American problem. . . . Their cause must be our cause too. Because it is not just Negroes, but really it is all of us, who must overcome the crippling legacy of bigotry and injustice. And we shall overcome."[7]

Rabbis, ministers, and nuns kept coming to Selma to join John Lewis, C. T. Vivian, Hosea Williams, King, and others. A total of 3,600 persons began the third attempt to march from Selma to Montgomery (March 21–25, 1965). The numbers marching grew each day.

Though there were tensions inside the civil rights coalition, particularly among young activists who resented the attention given by television and other media to King, the crowd clamored for King to speak upon their arrival. "How long must justice be crucified and truth buried?" King asked, "How long? Not long because no lie can live forever. How long? Not long, because you still reap what you sow. How long? Not long because the arc of the moral universe is long, but it bends toward justice. How long? Not long, 'cause mine eyes have seen the coming of the Lord." The crowd knew that he was referring to the "Battle Hymn of the Republic." Some joined in with the rest of the verse:

Mine eyes have seen the glory of the coming of the Lord;
He is trampling out the vintage where the grapes of wrath are stored;
He has loosed the fateful lightning of his terrible swift sword;
His truth is marching on.

Glory, glory, hallelujah!
Glory, glory, hallelujah!
Glory, glory, hallelujah!
His truth is marching on.

He has sounded forth the trumpet that shall never call retreat;
He is sifting out the hearts of men before His judgment seat.
O, be swift, my soul, to answer Him! Be jubilant, my feet!
Our God is marching on.

Then marchers sang, "We Shall Overcome," bringing the Selma March to an end. A smaller delegation presented a list of grievances and demands to Governor George Wallace, who reacted with predictable disdain. Nevertheless, Congress responded more positively, passing the 1965 Voting Rights Act.

Ferment and Division

When people remember the 1960s, they often divide it into the good early sixties, in which a Catholic was elected President to lead a "New Frontier," Vatican II brought amazing changes to the Catholic Church, the Beatles invaded, astronauts traveled into space, and the civil rights movement achieved many of its aims to eliminate legal segregation; and later the "second sixties," where things fell apart. The second sixties in this account features violence in the streets, assassinations, an explosion of drug use, and a generation gap dividing families and society about the war in Vietnam. The problem with this version of history is that, chronologically, many of the events that people remember less positively were already underway in the early 1960s. It is therefore useful to see these years as another side of the same coin of the rapid social change of the 1960s. Once again, we see religion amid things even propelling change. By the end of the long sixties (a historical term to recognize that the years beginning with the Montgomery bus boycott and ending with the end of the war in Vietnam belong together), we can see American religion itself being changed by diversification, the choices made in conflicts, and the rise of theologies of liberation.

One of the reasons not to separate the sixties chronologically, but to see them as opposite sides of the same transformative years, is the rise of Malcolm X (1925–65) in the early 1960s. Malcolm X became a hero to many younger black Americans because he said what they had concluded from events like the Mississippi "Freedom Summer" of 1964: that the respectable nonviolent resistance advocated by Martin Luther King Jr. and the SCLC was no match for the nighttime violence of armed white supremacists, who murdered without consequence. Leaders of SNCC like Stokely Carmichael left Freedom Summer determined to pursue a new philosophy they called "Black Power." Involved in the black freedom movement since the Freedom

Rides of 1961, Carmichael drew his inspiration from Malcolm X, a black Muslim, who did not believe in asking or begging for rights, but in demanding them.

Malcolm X, part of the Nation of Islam and one of its leading public figures from 1952, eventually grew famous for saying quotable things to the American public through the media. One example: "We declare our right on this earth to be a human being, to be respected as a human being, to be given the rights of a human being in this society on this earth in this day, which we intend to bring into existence by any means necessary."

"By any means necessary" became a scary prospect for white Americans, for by it Malcolm meant that black Americans would not confine themselves to nonviolent resistance, but would utilize violence if necessary to obtain their human rights. Malcolm said, "I don't call it violence when it's in self defense. I call it intelligence." Malcolm X was so prominent in the early 1960s that Martin Luther King (MLK) used his views and reputation as leverage in his "Letter from a Birmingham Jail": "I am further convinced that if our white brothers dismiss as 'rabble rousers' and 'outside agitators' those of us who employ nonviolent direct action, and if they refuse to support our nonviolent efforts, millions of Negroes will, out of frustration and despair, seek solace and security in black nationalist ideologies—a development that would inevitably lead to a frightening racial nightmare." King reacted to being called an extremist by pointing to the alternative. In his many television appearances, Malcolm X was constantly asked, especially by white television personalities, "Are you a racist?" His replies to these queries

FIGURE 16-4. Malcolm X after returning from Mecca, 1964. (Photo by Herman Miller, Library of Congress, New York World-Telegram & Sun Collection)

went like this: "I'm not a racist. I'm against every form of racism and segregation, every form of discrimination. I believe in human beings, and that all human beings should be respected as such, regardless of their color." In this respect, Malcolm was not antithetical to MLK. Both were religious leaders seeking mediating positions for social change, but Malcolm X employed a forceful rhetoric.

By the point where Malcolm became a popular guest on television news and public affairs programs and become a rival to the Nation of Islam's Wallace Muhammad, he had traveled to Mecca. There he experienced international Islam, where Africans, Asians, South Asians, Indonesians, Arabs, and even white European Muslims were one community. He then began to argue that America needed to understand Islam because, he said, "Islam is the one religion that erases the race problem from its society." While Malcolm X had come to reject the black separatism of the Nation of Islam, he still advocated that force be met with force. He would be remembered for speeches like the one he gave at Ford Auditorium in Detroit in 1965 the night after his family was bombed out of their home:

MALCOLM X: THE LANGUAGE THEY UNDERSTAND

"Brothers and sisters, if you and I would just realize that once we learn to talk the language that they understand, they will then get the point. You can't ever reach a man if you don't speak his language. If a man speaks the language of brute force, you can't come to him with peace. Why, good night! He'll break you in two, as he has been doing all along. If a man speaks French, you can't speak to him in German. If he speaks Swahili, you can't communicate with him in Chinese. You have to find out what does this man speak. And once you know his language, learn how to speak his language, and he'll get the point. There'll be some dialogue, some communication, and some understanding will be developed.

"You've been in this country long enough to know the language the Klan speaks. They only know one language. And what you and I have to start doing in 1965—I mean that's what you have to do, because most of us [have] already been doing it—is start learning a new language. Learn the language that they understand. And then when they come up on our doorstep to talk, we can talk. And they will get the point. There'll be a dialogue, there'll be some communication, and I'm quite certain there will then be some understanding. Why? Because the Klan is a cowardly outfit. They have perfected the art of making Negroes be afraid. As long as the Negro's afraid, the Klan is safe. But the Klan itself is cowardly. One of them will never come after one of you. They all come together. Sure, and they're scared of you."*

*Malcolm X, "Speech at Ford Auditorium" in Detroit, February 14, 1965, www.blackpast .org/african-american-history/1965-malcolm-x-speech-ford-auditorium/.

Malcolm went on to offer an implied critique of the black Christians in the audience who, as ropes were being placed around their necks, would say like Jesus, "Forgive them, Lord; they know not what they do." Instead, he pointed out, "As long as they've been doing it, they're experts at it; they know what they're doing!" Just one week after giving this speech, Malcolm X was assassinated at the Aududon Ballroom in Harlem. He was thirty-nine years old, the same age Martin Luther King Jr. would be when he was killed three years later in Memphis.

With these assassinations and those of John F. Kennedy (JFK) and his brother Robert Kennedy, America was in uncharted territory. Lyndon B. Johnson (LBJ), the President who had succeeded JFK, envisioned himself as continuing the New Deal and Fair Deal liberalism of Franklin D. Roosevelt and Harry S. Truman. He called his social proposals the Great Society, and it included a War on Poverty, Medicare, Medicaid, and the creation of a new department, Housing and Urban Development (HUD). Thus LBJ saw himself as a champion of poor and disenfranchised Americans, but his support for civil rights and his escalation of the conflict in Vietnam into a major undeclared war contributed to American society becoming more divided than at any time since the Civil War a century earlier. Southern white Democrats like George Wallace of Alabama and Republicans from that party's right wing, like Barry Goldwater, dissented on civil rights; both Wallace and Goldwater made strong runs against LBJ in 1964. Though Johnson won his own term as President in November 1964, another decision he made that year undercut his long-term success: the expansion of the war in Vietnam. After the French had lost the First Indochina War in 1954 at Dien Bien Phu, Vietnam was deemed one of those places that might fall to communist rule in what was called the "domino theory," where one country's political upheaval would spread to its neighbors like dominoes in a line knocking down subsequent dominoes. Despite this fear, President Eisenhower, wary of another Korea, had refused to come to the aid of the French or to replace them with American troops. During JFK's presidency, military advisers were sent to support South Vietnam in its fight against the Viet (Việt) Minh and Viet Cong, who were trying to unify Vietnam under communist rule. Though Kennedy was cautious about further involvement, his defense and security advisers were more enthusiastic. It was these advisers whom Johnson as President inherited. Using an alleged attack on two U.S. destroyers in the Gulf of Tonkin of North Vietnam (on August 5, 1964), advisers like Secretary of Defense Robert McNarmara and National Security Adviser McGeorge Bundy recommended an escalation of the war. Johnson obtained a congressional resolution in August of 1964 enabling him to take any action he deemed necessary to respond. In 1964, LBJ sent 23,300 American troops to war. In 1966, the number of soldiers in Vietnam had risen to 185,000. By 1969, at the peak of involvement, 543,400 armed service members were in Vietnam.[8]

Malcolm X and Martin Luther King Jr. both decried the disproportionate impact Vietnam was having on black men early in the war: they constituted over 20 percent of the combat deaths in 1965 and 1966.[9] A former Olympian turned professional champion boxer named Muhammad Ali announced his refusal to report for induction into the Army:

> Why should they ask me to put on a uniform and go ten thousand miles from home and drop bombs and bullets on brown people in Vietnam while so-called Negro people in Louisville are treated like dogs and denied simple human rights?
>
> No, I am not going ten thousand miles from home to help murder and burn another poor nation simply to continue the domination of white slave masters of the darker people the world over. This is the day when such evils must come to an end. I have been warned that to take such a stand would put my prestige in jeopardy and could cause me to lose millions of dollars which should accrue to me as the champion. But I have said it once and I will say it again. The real enemy of my people is right here.
>
> I will not disgrace my religion, my people or myself by becoming a tool to enslave those who are fighting for their own justice, freedom, and equality.
>
> If I thought the war was going to bring freedom and equality to 22 million of my people, they wouldn't have to draft me; I'd join tomorrow. But I either have to obey the laws of the land or the laws of Allah. I have nothing to lose by standing up for my beliefs. So I'll go to jail. We've been in jail for four hundred years.[10]

Ali's stand was unpopular with older white Americans but was more understandable to draft-age Americans of all backgrounds. Vietnam was the first war to be broadcast nightly on network news into homes. And neither hawks who supported the war nor doves who opposed it liked what they saw. An unprecedented number of young men dodged the draft by seeking medical and educational deferments, or by declaring conscientious objector status, which required attestation by one's religious leader and alternative service for a period of years. Perhaps as many as 125,000 young Americans fled to Canada during the Vietnam War, with 20,000 to 30,000 becoming permanent residents and citizens. At the heart of the extraordinary opposition to the war was the morality of the war itself. For antiwar youth, the question was whether they could trust the politicians and generals. A saying went about that exemplified the gulf of understanding: "Never trust anyone over thirty!" LBJ himself was daily taunted by protesters outside the fence of the White House, "Hey, hey, LBJ, how many kids do you kill today?"

The war became an issue throughout the religious leadership of America. Conservative Protestants tended to support the war well into the 1970s. For an extraordinary array of other leaders, however, the war violated just-war principles as to both the means and ends of the war's conduct. On January

11, 1966, John C. Bennett, William Sloane Coffin Jr., Abraham Heschel, Daniel Berrigan, Richard John Neuhaus, Martin Luther King Jr., and others organized the National Emergency Committee of Clergy Concerned About Vietnam. This committee soon developed a national organization of Roman Catholic, Jewish, and Protestant clergy and laity, known as Clergy and Laymen Concerned About Vietnam, later shortened and gender-balanced to Clergy and Laity Concerned (CALC). Nearly all the early members had been part of the civil rights struggle, though King was one of the few black members and the only Southerner. Elected as co-chairs were a Protestant, a Catholic, and a Jew: Neuhaus, Berrigan, and Heschel. Many members of this growing new interfaith anti-Vietnam movement considered Heschel to be "its prophetic voice." Ever since releasing his 1962 book, *The Prophets*, Heschel seemed not only an expert on the Hebrew prophets, but also to spiritually and socially communicate their voice on current issues. When it came to Vietnam, Heschel early on said, "In regard to the cruelties committed in the name of a free society, some are guilty, all are responsible."[11] In a 1967 book, *Vietnam: Crisis of Conscience*, Heschel's essay titled "The Moral Outrage of Vietnam" began by observing, "It is weird to wake up one morning and find that we have been placed in an insane asylum. It is even more weird to wake up and find that we have been involved in slaughter and destruction without knowing it." He made the case that all Americans were implicated in evil, no matter their personal views or actions. "The thought that I live a life of peace and nonviolence turns out to be an illusion," wrote Heschel. He argued that he and most Americans had been "decent in tiny matters on a tiny scale, but [we] have become vicious on a large scale." This made him seem upright in his conduct to himself, but a "nightmare" to victims, like those of the Vietnamese suffering in the war.

ABRAHAM JOSHUA HESCHEL: "GOD'S PRESENCE UNITES US"

"The encounter of man and God is an encounter within the world. We meet within a situation of shared suffering, of shared responsibility.

"This is implied in believing in One God in whose eyes there is no dichotomy of here and there, of me and them. They and I are one; here is there, and there is here. What goes on over there happens even here. Oceans divide us, God's presence unites us, and God is present wherever man is afflicted, and all of humanity is embroiled in every agony wherever it may be.

"Though not a native of Vietnam, ignorant of its language and traditions, I am involved in the plight of the Vietnamese. To be human means not to be immune to other people's suffering. People in Vietnam, North and South, have suffered, and all of us are hurt."*

*Robert McAfee Brown, Abraham Joshua Heschel, and Michael Novak, *Vietnam: Crisis of Conscience* (New York: Association Press, 1967), 48–60.

Martin Luther King Jr. offered his views at an event organized by CALC at the Riverside Church on April 4, 1967, one year to the day before he was murdered. King had been moving in an increasingly radical direction since 1965, linking civil rights, Vietnam, poverty, and racism in Northern cities as struggles evidencing common causes. That night he came out forcefully against the war. King told his listeners, "I come to this magnificent house of worship tonight because my conscience leaves me no other choice." He called their attention to his agreement with the CALC statement "A time comes when silence is betrayal." Then he added, "That time has come for us in relation to Vietnam." King spoke of his own transformation on the war:

> Over the past two years, as I have moved to break the betrayal of my own silences and to speak from the burnings of my own heart, as I have called for radical departures from the destruction of Vietnam, many persons have questioned me about the wisdom of my path. At the heart of their concerns this query has often loomed large and loud: Why are you speaking about war, Dr. King? Why are you joining the voices of dissent? Peace and civil rights don't mix, they say. Aren't you hurting the cause of your people? they ask. And when I hear them, though I often understand the source of their concern, I am nevertheless greatly saddened, for such questions mean that the inquirers have not really known me, my commitment, or my calling. Indeed, their questions suggest that they do not know the world in which they live.[12]

While religious leaders were making the case for American moral culpability, the point was driven home in an even more graphic way in March of 1968 when U.S. soldiers massacred between 347 and 504 unarmed women, men, children, and infants in the village of My Lai, South Vietnam. Soon there were women in mothers' marches carrying signs reading, "Don't turn our sons into killers!" The war raged on for five more years.

New Forms of Religious Diversity

Even as the war tore America apart, fresh movements and events were occurring that brought far-reaching consequences for religion. America entered the sixties with a fairly small set of religious options, "Protestant, Catholic, Jew," in the memorable formulation of Will Herberg. By 1968 the options had exploded. In places like Berkeley, California; Ann Arbor, Michigan; and Haight-Ashbury, San Francisco, protest and youth culture produced a genuine counterculture. Young people there listened to and made their own music, talked in a vocabulary all their own, with hippies, yippies, the 1967 Summer of Love, and the Monterey Pop festival all constituting a decisive break from "straight" culture. During this time psychedelic art, psychedelic music, and the subculture that went with it formed around people who used psychedelic drugs such as LSD, mescaline (peyote), and psilocybin (magic mushrooms). The art and music mirrored the experience of altered consciousness brought on by such drugs, and advocates compared the result to a religious experience. Eventually it would even produce a religious movement, the Jesus People, who would testify to "getting high on Jesus."

Simultaneously Americans, especially college students, were discovering Eastern religions and reading books about Zen Buddhism. Religious studies and philosophy departments taught books by D. T. Suzuki, *The Analects* by Confucius, the Tao Te Ching, the Upanishads, and the Qur'an. Young Americans were also meditating and taking yogic instruction. Alan Watts, an Episcopal priest, and Gary Snyder, a poet and ecologist, were popularizing Buddhism. Father Thomas Merton even met the Dalai Lama in exile in Dharamsala, India. Merton was on a quest to find what all serious religions and contemplative spiritualities held in common. The Lama would remember him as a "spiritual brother."[13]

Meanwhile, in 1963 the National Association of Biblical Instructors adopted a new name, the American Academy of Religion, placing Buddhism, Hinduism, Islam, Judaism, and Christianity as subjects of study on essentially an equal footing.

Not only were Americans studying non-Western religions; more adherents of these religions were becoming Americans. The Hart-Celler Immigration Act of 1965 abolished the 1924 National Origins Formula restrictions on who could immigrate to the United States legally. This produced profound

FIGURE 16-5. Photograph of Thomas Merton and the Dalai Lama (Used with permission of the Merton Legacy Trust and the Thomas Merton Center, Bellarmine University.)

consequences over succeeding years. Between 1870 and 1965, for instance, a total of 16,000 immigrated from India to the United States. In the first decade after the 1965 law was passed, the number was almost 100,000 people from the nation of India immigrating; for the most part, these new Indian immigrants entered under the needed-skills preference of the 1965 law. Subsequently, then, they thrived. Recent immigrants brought family members, while other new immigrants continued to arrive. The United States began to notice more people practicing the religions they brought with them from Asia and from Africa. More and more came and brought their families, and so did Arab, Indonesian, and South Asian Muslims; Koreans, Vietnamese, and people from forty other countries of Asia; and Africans from all over that continent. All this immigration would have lasting effects on religious diversity and pluralism in America.

The story of Muslim immigration was long in coming. Some of the Syrian, Lebanese, and Turkish Muslims who came at end of the nineteenth century stayed, but others (particularly darker-skinned Arabs) found themselves treated badly because of their appearance during the era of Jim Crow segregation. Muslims from places like Albania and Bosnia fared better and blended in with the southern and eastern European immigration. The oldest continuous Muslim community in America was begun in 1895, when brothers Musa, Ali, and Abbas Hahbab arrived in Cedar Rapids, Iowa. By 1920 almost 60 Muslims were living in Cedar Rapids; on June 16, 1934, this community dedicated the so-called "mother mosque," North America's first purpose-built Islamic house of worship. Other communities in the Midwest, such as Chicago; Michigan City, Indiana; Dearborn and Detroit, Michigan; and Pittsburgh, Pennsylvania, also were early hosts to both Muslim and Christian immigrants from the faltering Ottoman Empire. Many of these communities worshiped in adapted buildings at first. All of these places, centers of industrial employment, developed in time to be major Muslim communities. European Muslims in the 1920s—in Maine, Connecticut, and New York State—founded neighborhood mosques in converted buildings. Likewise, Muslims from the Punjab region of India gravitated toward the Western states of California, Oregon, and Washington. In total, scholars estimate that all Muslims living in the United States prior to World War II totaled a few thousand individuals. Another wave of refugee immigrants after World War II pushed the number up to roughly a quarter of a million Muslims.[14]

As of 1965, the largest number of people of the Islamic faith were African Americans who had joined the Nation of Islam or Noble Drew Ali's Moorish Science Temple. These converts away from white-dominated Christianity were drawn to a faith that affirmed their inestimable and equal dignity. During the 1960s this Islam of converts would become increasingly more like the rest of the world's Islam, with the exception of Louis Farrakhan's black nationalist offshoot of the Nation of Islam. After the 1965 change in immigration laws, the Muslim families of the early 1960s were joined by Muslim college students and skilled workers from abroad. Already waiting for them was an infrastructure built over time by the pioneering genera- tions: Muslim student associations on college campuses and the Islamic Society of North America (ISNA), which grew out of the collective student associations in 1963.

Most of the new immigrants gravitated to centers where there were already groups of Muslims, like southeastern Michigan and the Chicago area. Those who came in this wave were fluent in English and highly edu- cated before their arrival. Because these Muslims came from all over the world, all three main forms of Islam (Sunni, Shi'ite, and Sufi) were practiced by later immigrants from the 1970s and 1980s forward. After the Iranian Revolution and wars between Iraq and Iran brought substantial numbers of Shi'ite Muslims to the United States, they accounted for one-fifth of the American Muslim population, yet only 10 percent of worldwide Islam.

Because Muslims range from the Far East in the Philippines to Indonesia, Sudan, Somalia, sub-Saharan Africa, Europe, South Asia, and the Middle East, it is not readily apparent who might be Muslim. Only at America's Islamic centers, which function both as mosques and as community centers, or in college campus groups is this diverse population readily identified as bonded by religion.

The 1965 change in immigration law also opened up opportunities for Indian Hindus, Sikhs, Japanese Buddhists, and Middle Eastern Christians and Jews to come in ever larger numbers. Each of these communities mostly contributed their best-educated members to the American scene. Engineers, physicians, scientists, and their families quickly assimilated into the work- force because of their skills. Since these immigrants achieved moderate or even high incomes, it was not long until houses of worship arose in cities and suburbs in order to celebrate and transmit the old faith in a new place. Among these, the Hindu temples arising in the Midwest, Houston, and Los Angeles areas were not designed as a platform for charismatic yogis to attract other Americans, but for Indian immigrants to observe ritual devotions, fes- tivals, and rites of passage. These temples also served a secondary function as ambassadors to their neighborhoods. Still, misconceptions arose for the mostly Christian neighbors who did not see the worship of an ultimate God behind the devotion to, for instance, Ganesh, the elephant-headed Hindu god of beginnings, who is traditionally worshiped before any major enter- prise and who is the patron of intellectuals, bankers, scribes, and authors. America was becoming more religiously diverse, but misconceptions about other people's religions were also increasing.[15]

Amid immigration and the study of diverse religions in college, another sign of religious alternatives came in 1966, the year that Gene Rodden- berry created a universe portrayed in a movie called *Star Trek*, seeing space as the "final frontier," in which he pictured future people as having outgrown religion and the problems it caused. Still in space, but in real time, on December 24, 1968, on one of the most watched broadcast programs to date in television history, the crew of Apollo 8 read from the book of Genesis as they orbited the moon. Astronauts Bill Anders, Jim Lovell, and Frank Borman took turns reading the first ten verses of Genesis in the King James Version, in what they hoped would unite all of humanity; a story where God creates the earth, the heavens, and all creatures and calls it "very good."

Theologies of Liberation and the End of Universal Truth

In some ways America was coming apart in the 1960s. Viewed in another light, people earlier without public voices, who possessed legitimate grievances, were seizing opportunities to offer their perspectives in an America emerging as a multicultural society. Thus 1968 was a hard year. MLK and RFK were assassinated just weeks apart. The Democratic National Committee's convention in Chicago erupted into a riot between youthful protesters and the Chicago police. In a three-way presidential election—George Wallace running on white aggrievement, Richard Nixon talking of law and order, and Hubert Humphrey stuck holding LBJ's Vietnam record—Nixon emerged as the victor, a standard bearer of "silent Americans." The year 1968 was hard, yet it was the shape of things to come, a foretaste of the American religion and American culture experienced to this day.

In 1969 James Forman, a civil rights and Black Power leader of SNCC fame, and later of the Black Panthers, marched into Manhattan's Riverside Church to present the Black Manifesto, which called for the nation's white churches and synagogues to pay reparations because of their historical involvement in slavery and discrimination.

In the next few months, Forman and his associates broke into other meetings to present their demands and went to the headquarters of many majority-white denominations and to the National Council of Churches. Many of these same churches, which had supported the civil rights movement, now found themselves accused of complicity in racism. White clergy did not appreciate the accusation. They were apt to reply with some version of "Don't you know that I marched with Dr. King in Selma?" Meanwhile, black clergy in these denominations supported Forman's demands. Leaders like Gayraud Wilmore tried to interpret for mostly white denominations how whites had benefited from slavery and racism down to the present time. A few denominations did seriously consider the moral force behind the Black Manifesto. In response, the Presbyterian Church (U.S.A.) and the Episcopal Church made some multimillion-dollar contributions to help black Americans rise economically—but they retained control of where the money went.

In view of the real but limited success of the civil rights movement, black clergy were beginning to be inspired by the Black Power philosophy more associated with Malcolm X than with the earlier integrationist ideals of MLK. In the late 1960s, black clergy created or reorganized black caucuses in many majority white denominations. They also moved to make common cause with their brothers and sisters in the historically black denominations. And then a young theologian named James Cone (1938–2018) came on the scene. Cone's rise was rapid. In 1968 he was sitting in a rented space in his minister brother's parish in Arkansas, writing what would become his dissertation. Two years later he published his breakthrough book, *A Black Theology of Liberation*, in which he sought to reconcile King's emphasis on divine love with Malcolm's stress on divine justice. Cone said the black theologian must reject any conception of God that stifled black self-determination by picturing God as a God of all peoples. He expressed himself in strong words.

JAMES CONE: THE BLACKNESS OF GOD

"Either God is identified with the oppressed to the point that their experience becomes God's experience, or God is a God of racism.

"The blackness of God means that God has made the oppressed condition God's own condition. This is the essence of the biblical revelation. By electing Israelite slaves as the people of God and by becoming the Oppressed One in Jesus Christ, the human race is made to understand that God is known where human beings experience humiliation and suffering. It is not that God feels sorry and takes pity on them (the condescending attitude of those racists who need their guilt assuaged for getting fat on the starvation of others); quite the contrary, God's election of Israel and incarnation in Christ reveal that the *liberation* of the oppressed is a part of the innermost nature of God. Liberation is not an afterthought, but the very essence of divine activity."*

"There is no use for a God who loves white oppressors the same as oppressed blacks. We have had too much of white love, the love that tells blacks to turn the other cheek and go the second mile. What we need is the divine love as expressed in black power, which is the power of blacks to destroy their oppressors, here and now, by any means at their disposal. Unless God is participating in this holy activity, we must reject God's love."†

*James H. Cone, *A Black Theology of Liberation*, 1st ed., C. Eric Lincoln Series in Black Religion (Philadelphia: Lippincott, 1970), 67. †James H. Cone, *A Black Theology of Liberation*, 40th anniversary ed. (Orbis Books, 2010), 74.

Cone, like Malcolm X, attacked the white mainstream religious community for its racist interpretation of Christianity, but he also reproached the black Christian community, as had Martin Luther King, for accepting white racist interpretations and for not thinking more critically about Christianity in their lives. Mainstream theologians vilified Cone as a racist, but his theory ignited a re-examination of the role of Christianity in the lives and struggles of black people. A year earlier, Cone had argued, "To be black in America has little to do with skin color. To be black means that your heart, your soul, your mind, and your body are where the dispossessed are. Being reconciled to God does not mean that one's skin is physically black. It essentially depends on the color of your heart, soul, and mind."[16]

Cone's was the first of the so-called liberation theologies. The Peruvian theologian Gustavo Gutiérrez (1928–) published *Teología de la liberación* in 1971 [*A Theology of Liberation* in 1973]. A Theology of Liberation in 1971, popularized the name, and provided a lasting slogan, "God's preferential option for the poor." In his book Gutiérrez drew from the Gospels to argue that God is with the poor of the world. Those are the people whom God loves.

> But the poor person does not exist as an inescapable fact of destiny. His or her existence is not politically neutral, and it is not ethically innocent. . . .
> The poor are a by-product of the system in which we live and for which we are responsible. They are marginalized by our social and cultural world. They are the oppressed, exploited proletariat, robbed of the fruit of their labor and despoiled of their humanity. Hence the poverty of the poor is not a call to generous relief action, but a demand that we go and build a different social order.[17]

The Catholic Church saw such words as a combination of the Christian gospel and Marxism. The poor are a by-product of the system in which we live and for which we are responsible. Though the Vatican would initially denounce this theology because of its critique of the way the church in Latin America had sided with the wealthy against the poor, whom Jesus loved, Pope John Paul II would eventually embrace the "preferential option for the poor" as his own social theology. Putting this theology into practice, Jorge Mario Bergoglio, an Argentinian priest and bishop, would be elected pope in 2013 and choose the name Francis, in honor of Francis of Assisi, a saint known for his work to help the poor.

In the Catholic community at the end of the sixties, the post-Vatican-II church became divided by sex and by the role of women in the life of the church. A 1965 Gallup poll asked Catholic Americans if they believed their church would approve the use of birth control. "Yes," said 61 percent of Catholics. After all, "the Pill" had been available then for five years without an official word from the church. Some grounded their hope in the fact that the pill was not a barrier and only regulated what was natural. Then on July 25, 1968, Pope Paul VI issued his sixth encyclical, *Humanae Vitae*. In it he sought to apply natural-law teaching to the innovation of artificial birth control while promoting a traditional appreciation for the role of mothers and families. The use of the Pill, moreover, constituted a mortal sin. The letter landed poorly in the United States: many clergy found themselves on the defensive, and lay Catholics largely responded by ignoring the pope's guidance, going ahead and using birth control. One bishop, the rising star James Shannon of Minnesota, was outraged to the point of asking to be laicized (being officially released from the priesthood to return to lay status). In America the Catholic Church's immense moral authority was in trouble: laypeople were picking and choosing what moral teachings to obey, while some of the hierarchy valiantly tried to uphold traditional teachings.[18]

Catholic women theologians were incensed that they were still being treated as "the Second Sex," as Simone de Beauvoir had observed. The French de Beauvoir used this distinction to help explain why she had no use for the church. Mary Daly (1928–2010), then a theologian at Boston College, wrote a series of books—starting with *The Church and the Second Sex* (1968) and *Beyond God the Father: Toward a Philosophy of Women's Liberation* (1973)— to take on the gendered theology of the Catholic Church from inside one of its leading institutions. In the latter work she posed a memorable syllogism: "If God is male, then male is God." Daly went on to say, "The divine patriarchy castrates women as long as he is allowed to live on in the human imagination."[19] She and Rosemary Radford Ruether were writing on the Catholic side of feminist theology at the same time as women like Valerie Saiving on the Protestant side and Judith Plasgow as a Jewish theologian were initiating feminist theology as a community of discourse and as a lasting challenge to the way men had done theology for two millennia.

For a time white male theologians would try to write off black, liberation, and feminist theology as merely "contextual theologies." Yet more theologians recognized the emerging truth: every theology was written from a context. After the early 1970s it was increasingly difficult to do theology from a universal (God's-eye) position after so many diverse voices had asserted themselves. What for many was welcome multiplicity in American religion and theology became a threat as the years unfolded in the 1970s. No new voice was ever extinguished, but a backlash to the religious spirit of the 1960s soon followed.

17. The Culture Wars, Pentecostalization, and American Religion after 9/11

The rise of the religious right as a political force in American life in the 1970s and 1980s was countered in other religious quarters by the growing acceptance of gay and lesbian people and interfaith tolerance. Far from a site of universal welcome, however, religious identity became a marker in long-running culture wars. At the same time, beliefs in the gifts and nearness of the Holy Spirit grew well beyond traditional pentecostal-holiness denominations to constitute a broad consensus among practicing Christians in America. After the turn of the twenty-first century, Americans experienced the terrorist attacks on 9/11 and awoke both to the diversity of religious life around them and to religion's capacity to stimulate violence—including, for the Christian majority, their own faith's darker side.

Religious Realignment on Political Lines

The presidential election of 1972 constituted a decisive realignment of American politics and of culture with it, including religious life. Republicans were no longer interested much in African Americans, appealing instead to the rapidly growing Sunbelt and its white evangelicals and to working-class Catholics. Democrats, meanwhile, aligned themselves to large cities on the East and West coasts, African Americans, intellectuals, and liberals. Up until 1968 the Democratic Party had—except for the fusion candidate Eisenhower, who appealed to voters of all parties—held the presidency and usually the Congress from 1934 until 1968. Even after 1968 the House of Representatives remained in Democratic hands until 1994; the Senate's first switch to Republican control was in 1980. A book by the Nixon and Republican strategist Kevin Phillips, *The Emerging Republican Majority*, seemed like a pipe dream when he wrote it in 1970, but later it proved prescient.[1] From 1968 to 2020, Republicans operating from Phillips's playbook (peel off Southern Democrats, abandon civil rights, stress law and order) occupied the White House 36 of the 52 years. The Democratic presidents who managed to win majorities were in some manner fusion candidates themselves. Jimmy Carter and Bill Clinton were both from the Sunbelt and

Baptists. Barack Obama, perhaps the one exception to the rightward drift of America's political culture and presidents, achieved success over both liberal consensus candidates (Hillary Clinton and Joe Biden) by fusing Kennedyesque idealism about America with a reverence for the reconciliation politics of his own presidential hero, Abraham Lincoln. Obama, therefore, represented the exception that proved the rule. Moreover, as a 2008 candidate he was lucky enough to be running against the sitting party amid an economic crisis.

Through 1965 the ecumenical denominations, plus the Catholic Church, and a small number of historically African American denominations dominated the American religious landscape. But starting during the mid-1960s the white ecumenical Protestant denominations began to experience actual membership losses, which in terms of their representation within the culture boded something even more dire, given a growing population. They were losing their market share of the American religious populace. Theories abound as to what happened to make these churches, strong since the colonial period, falter. Dean M. Kelley argued that conservative churches were growing in America because they represented something more than secular American white culture at prayer. By contrast, Kelley thought, conservative churches made strong demands of their would-be members: do not drink, observe sex only within marriage, do not dance, do not listen to secular music, read the Bible, and come to church twice a week.[2] Another theory as to what happened was advanced by scholars such as Dean Hoge and Graham Reside. They argued that differential birth rates explained much of the membership losses of the establishment churches. People inside so-called mainline Protestant churches were having fewer offspring, thanks to the Pill, and even fewer of those children grew up claiming the church's membership for themselves. This was to establish a pattern by which every generation, across religious groups, was less institutionally religious than the prior cohort.[3] David Hollinger advanced his own reasons for what was going on among those he first called ecumenical Protestants: these churches had largely achieved their purposes in American life and culture, he claimed. The civil rights movement, anti-Vietnam War activity, and even the promotion of women's rights in church and society, many of the things that indeed constituted the ecumenical Protestants' religious social agenda, were already achieved. Because they had largely abandoned belief in the sanctions of hell and damnation, these churches offered no negative reinforcement against leaving the fold. More positively, the children of ecumenical Protestants could find the peace-and-justice agenda (ecumenical Protestantism's most compelling legacy) outside the church itself. An increasing number of Americans did just that: looked to practice their spirituality outside the confines of a conventional congregation.[4]

In the 1970s participants and observers alike spoke of a "consciousness revolution," in which younger adults (in particular) sought fulfillment, not salvation. These seekers could be found in a variety of groups. Werner Ehrhardt's est and L. Ron Hubbard's Scientology were among the new movements with a more ostensibly secular bent. Krishna Consciousness, Rev. Sun Myung Moon's Unification Church, Transcendental Meditation, and Jewish people practicing Buddhist meditation—all constituted examples of Americans from Christian and Jewish backgrounds turning east after 1970 for a religious authenticity they found lacking at home. There was also substantial interest in practices of healing like Reiki, the use of crystals and copper, or doing wellness activities like yoga. These practices could be used by people involved in other religions, but they also were grounded in Eastern religions, or pagan beliefs, and appealed to Americans distrustful of conventional church-type religion.

Not everyone was leaving traditional forms of American religiosity, however. The widespread introduction of air-conditioning made the South and the Sunbelt extending westward to southern California newly attractive places for Americans to migrate; Southern Baptists, other evangelicals, and pentecostal denominations were building new churches at a record pace. The same was true of Midwestern evangelicals in suburban areas. At the very time the formerly mainline churches virtually abandoned church planting, evangelicals in the South, Sunbelt, and Midwest were building churches in the strategic places of suburban growth. They believed in heaven and hell, a system of eternal rewards and punishments for the faithful and sinners, and taught this doctrine to their children. Perhaps most crucially, they increasingly accepted the moral case against contemporary American culture.

One of the key leaders in the conservative movement was the Catholic lawyer, antifeminist, and anti-abortion activist Phyllis Schlafly (1924–2016). Spurned for the presidency of the National Federation of Republican Women after her vociferous 1964 support of Barry Goldwater for President against Nelson Rockefeller, she campaigned against everything the Rockefeller wing of the party stood for. Feminism was on the rise in the late 1960s and early 1970s, leading to a proposed Equal Rights Amendment to the Constitution, supported overwhelmingly by both political parties and passed by 28 of the required 38 states by 1972. That was when Schlafly stepped into the fray with a movement called "STOP ERA." Schlafly became an outspoken opponent of the Equal Rights Amendment (ERA) during the 1970s as the organizer of the "STOP ERA" campaign. STOP was an acronym for "Stop Taking Our Privileges." Schlafly argued that the ERA would take away gender-specific privileges then enjoyed by women, including "dependent wife" benefits under Social Security, separate restrooms for men and women, and exemption from the Selective Service (the agency running the military draft). These scare tactics eventually stopped the ERA in its tracks, with Indiana being the last state to narrowly approve the ERA in 1977, still short of the states required for adoption. Many historians think the ERA would have passed easily without Schlafly's movement.

FIGURE 17-1. Activist Phyllis Schlafly wearing a "Stop ERA" badge, demonstrating with other women against the Equal Rights Amendment in front of the White House, Washington, D.C., February 4, 1977 (Photo by Warren K. Leffler, LC-DIG-ds-00757, Library of Congress)

Conservative women's victories led feminists and other women to flee the Republican Party, formerly the home of most college-educated women, for the Democrats. Republicans meanwhile became increasingly the party of "family values" and the causes that activists like Schlafly embraced, none more strongly than opposition to legalized abortion. Abortion had been legal in some states and illegal in others prior to *Roe v. Wade* (1973) in which the U.S. Supreme Court held that all women had a right to abortion under the Constitution's "penumbra of privacy" and the right to control their own bodies. Richard Vigueri, a fellow Goldwater Republican, would eventually use the issue of abortion to unite Catholics, like Schlafly, and evangelicals, like Pat Robertson and Jerry Falwell, into a single "right to life" movement that would support candidates dedicated to their cause.

In 1976 the *Newsweek* magazine printed a cover story proclaiming "1976: The Year of the Evangelical." The story was occasioned by the rise of a self-proclaimed born-again Christian, Jimmy Carter, to the U.S. presidency. Evangelicals had, of course, been around for a while, but while non-evangelical Americans were asking one another what "born again" even meant, followers of Christ determined to share the gospel with all and to enact godly principles into the life of the nation were becoming a prominent cultural and political force. Though Carter taught Sunday school and freely shared his views on his faith, he was abandoned by even his own fellow Southern Baptists in the election of 1980. His religious biography, *Redeemer: The Life of Jimmy Carter*, begins with an epigraph from John 1:11, "He came unto his own, and his own received him not." What happened? Carter's political rise and fall coincided with the eclipse of Christian progressivism and the emergence of the religious right. His version of bringing a moral emphasis to the presidency was to guide foreign relations by a policy of promoting human rights, and to promote peace between world leaders like Egypt's Anwar Sadat and Israel's Menachem Begin. Carter sought to lead Americans to save energy for geopolitical and ecological reasons. Progressives like Senator Ted Kennedy found Carter too pious and conservative. Leaders in the burgeoning religious right thought he cared about the wrong moral issues.[5]

The religious beliefs of the religious right were those of resurgent fundamentalism. Biblical inerrancy was a key marker distinguishing many evangelicals from ecumenical Protestants. This could be especially seen in the rightward shift of the Southern Baptist Convention, beginning in the late 1970s. Dispensational premillennialism, involving the idea that world is getting worse, not better, also played a role in the social worldview of the religious right; the theology made some evangelicals unwilling to get on board with efforts for social reform, civil rights, anti-poverty, and the like; they were critical of churches and politicians who tried to do such. Yet one scholar of the movement, Matthew Sutton, argues that such apocalyptic theology also helped give contemporary politics its urgency, absolute morals, and refusal to compromise. The soul-winning impulse of evangelicalism played a strong role in the way the religious right went about trying to win political battles as though the nation's soul was at stake. Movement leaders also had no doubt that America was God's chosen nation: after the 1960s and 1970s, they needed to reclaim America, save the nation, and bring it back to God.[6]

Historian Bill J. Leonard characterized politicized fundamentalism in this way: "Premillennialism made them hesitant to change the world; evangelical conversionism compelled them to try." Jerry Falwell (1933–2007) stood as the classic example of this paradox. He was both quite premillenialist, thinking that the world and particularly American society was always getting worse. Yet Falwell was also quite committed to political transformation. This was the impetus for the Moral Majority organization he founded. Starting in 1976, Falwell toured the nation, hosting "I Love America" rallies. In 1979 he founded the Moral Majority organization to tap the political potential of conservative Christians for the Republican Party and reform. The decade that Falwell's organization existed saw a massive uptick of people willing to see their faith in terms of political ends, including Baptists like himself, who had historically advocated the complete separation of church from state and religion from politics. Falwell and the Moral Majority portrayed issues such as abortion, divorce, feminism, gay and lesbian rights, and the Equal Rights Amendment as attacks on the value of the traditional American family. They also campaigned for the inclusion of prayer in schools and for the right of religious groups, including racially exclusive religious schools, to be free of government interference, even if their students received federal grants and loans. Falwell wrote a book in 1980, *Listen America!*, detailing his core message.

JERRY FALWELL: BACK TO MORALITY

"I believe that Americans want to see this country come back to basics, back to values, back to biblical morality, back to sensibility, and back to patriotism. Americans are looking for leadership and guidance. It is fair to ask the question, 'If 84 percent of the American people still believe in morality, why is America having such internal problems?' We must look for the answer to the highest places in every level of government. We have a lack of leadership in America. But Americans have been lax in voting in and out of office the right and the wrong people.

"My responsibility as a preacher of the Gospel is one of influence, not of control, and that is the responsibility of each individual citizen. Through the ballot box Americans must provide for strong moral leadership at every level. If our country will get back on the track in sensibility and moral sanity, the crises that I have herein mentioned will work out in the course of time and with God's blessings.

"It is now time to take a stand on certain moral issues, and we can only stand if we have leaders. We must stand against the Equal Rights Amendment, the feminist revolution, and the homosexual revolution. We must have a revival in this country."*

*Jerry Falwell, *Listen, America!*, 1st ed. (Garden City, NY: Doubleday, 1980), 17–23.

Falwell was not alone in his advocacy of these backward-looking positions. Other prominent religious-right leaders and their organizations included James Dobson's Family Research Council and his nationally syndicated radio show, *Focus on the Family*; Pat Robertson's Christian Coalition and American Center for Law and Justice; Donald Wildmon's American Family Association; and Michael Farris's Home School Legal Defense Association. Together they became a sustained political force in American life during the presidency of Ronald Reagan and continued well into the early twenty-first century.

Former actor and California Governor Ronald Reagan played hard for evangelical Christians as a voting bloc and supporters for his presidency. In 1980, evangelicals turned against one of their own, sitting President and born-again Christian Jimmy Carter, electing instead the previously divorced Reagan as their standard bearer. In one respect above all others, Reagan and the evangelicals were on the same page: fear of the U.S. government itself, coupled with a determination not to be weak in the face of the Soviet Union. In a March 1983 speech to the National Association of Evangelicals (NAE), Reagan demonstrated his outreach to his religious base:

> I'll tell you there are a great many God-fearing, dedicated, noble men and women in public life, present company included. And, yes, we need your help to keep us ever mindful of the ideas and the principles that brought us into the public arena in the first place. The basis of

those ideals and principles is a commitment to freedom and personal liberty that, itself, is grounded in the much deeper realization that freedom prospers only where the blessings of God are avidly sought and humbly accepted.[7]

After establishing his bona fides as a Christian President before the NAE, Reagan went on trying to enlist evangelicals in his crusade for maintaining military superiority against communist Russia, calling it the "evil empire." He also asked the clergy present to stand up to other religious voices calling for a nuclear freeze:

> So, in your discussions of the nuclear freeze proposals, I urge you to beware the temptation of pride—the temptation of blithely declaring yourselves above it all and label both sides equally at fault, to ignore the facts of history and the aggressive impulses of an evil empire, to simply call the arms race a giant misunderstanding and thereby remove yourself from the struggle between right and wrong and good and evil.

The sociologist James Davidson Hunter analyzed what was happening at the religion/politics nexus in a 1992 book, *Culture Wars: The Struggle to Define America*. In it, he described the battle between what he called "progressives," who value reason and equality, versus a group he deemed the "orthodox," who value the transcendent and liberty. Though Hunter was careful not to simply match these cultural combatants to the two major parties, it was hard to deny that the nation had become divided.

For many Christian conservatives, the culture and even mainstream Protestants had gone too far in embracing the values of individual expression and especially sexuality beyond marital fidelity, one man with one woman. The Southern Baptist Convention responded to its sense of a culture adrift by recommending that its members boycott Disney shows, film productions, and even theme parks because some of its shows featured lesbians in a positive light. Like many churches of the 1990s, the Southern Baptist Convention defined marriage as being between one man and one woman, but in 1998 it went further and expressed these commitments in the Baptist Faith and Message, the closest the Convention comes to having a binding confession of faith:

> God has ordained the family as the foundational institution of human society. It is composed of persons related to one another by marriage, blood, or adoption.
>
> Marriage is the uniting of one man and one woman in covenant commitment for a lifetime. It is God's unique gift to reveal the union between Christ and His church, and to provide for the man and the woman in marriage the framework for intimate companionship, the channel for sexual expression according to biblical standards, and the means for procreation of the human race.[8]

The Convention went on to declare that "the husband and wife are of equal worth before God, since both are created in God's image. The marriage relationship models the way God relates to His people." But nevertheless, it said, "A wife is to submit herself graciously to the servant leadership of her husband even as the church willingly submits to the headship of Christ." So wives were both equal to their husbands spiritually, but subordinate to them in "managing the household and nurturing the next generation."

Meanwhile American Catholicism experienced a crisis of vocations, with few young people choosing to become priests or nuns. The number of priests held steady at about 59,000 from 1965 to 1975, but the Catholic population was still growing. After that the number of priests fell steadily with retirements and deaths until there were just 37,000 priests in 2012, with the Catholic population continuing to grow. From 1981 to 2012 the ratio of Catholic laypeople to a priest soared from 875:1 to 2,000:1, leaving 3,496 parishes without a resident priest of their own.[9] Over the period 1968 to 2016, Catholics lost large numbers of non-Hispanic whites, but gained in the number of Hispanic Catholics, maintaining Catholicism's status as America's largest faith expression, while still losing overall market share of a growing population. Moreover, the bishops appointed by Popes John Paul II and Benedict were overwhelmingly from the conservative wing of the church with respect to positions taken in Vatican II. As a result of the rightward drift of the Catholic hierarchy, official positions of the church increasingly lined up with the Republican Party, even though lay Catholics were split fairly evenly between the parties.

Though distrustful of Southern Baptists, Catholics made common cause with them on issues like vouchers for private education, opposition to abortion, and opposing required employer provision of contraception to employees. Catholics embraced a consistent "culture of life," a way of life based upon the belief that human life at all stages from conception through natural death is sacred, which led them to oppose both abortion and the death penalty. Yet their conservative evangelical allies were among the strongest advocates for capital punishment. Indeed, the same states where Baptists predominated over Catholics proved to be the most likely to have the death penalty, while the reverse was also true. The northern tier of states did not adopt (or repealed) the death penalty after the Supreme Court ruled it again permissible in 1977 (after ruling against the death penalty in 1972). The southern band of states hosted nearly all the nation's death row prisoners. Yet, ironically, it was the evangelical churches that were most likely to have prison ministries. This apparent conundrum was resolved in evangelical minds by their belief in an eternal system of rewards and punishments that needed to be replicated in this world at the same time as prisoners needed the opportunity to turn to Jesus before it was too late. And, of course, evangelical Christians were just the people to bring prisoners to Christ.

American Catholic bishops in the 1980s and 1990s worked together in the U.S. Conference of Catholic Bishops to offer moral guidance to the society at large as well as to the Catholic faithful. The bishops' letter on "The Challenge of Peace" in 1983 opposed the use of nuclear weapons as irreconcilable with just-war principles of discrimination, proportionality, and avoiding attacks on noncombatants. The bishops wrote in the context of an escalation of the arms race between the USSR and the United States, led by Ronald Reagan. The bishops declared:

> Both the just-war teaching and nonviolence are confronted with a unique challenge by nuclear warfare. This must be the starting point of any further moral reflection: nuclear weapons, particularly, and nuclear warfare as it is planned today, raise new moral questions.
>
> In the nuclear arsenals of the United States or the Soviet Union alone, there exists a capacity to do something no other age could imagine: We can threaten the entire planet. For people of faith this means we read the Book of Genesis with a new awareness. Today the destructive potential of the nuclear powers threatens the human person, the civilization we have slowly constructed, and even the created order itself.

The Catholic Bishops went on to declare that people needed to "refuse to legitimate the idea of nuclear war" and that such a refusal would require a "conversion of the heart." The chief problem with the reliance on nuclear weapons, even if never used, was its violation of the very just-war principles that constituted several religions' greatest contribution to justice in statecraft: "The political paradox of deterrence has also strained our moral conception. May a nation threaten what it may never do? May it possess what it may never use? Who is involved in the threat each superpower makes: government officials? or military personnel? or the citizenry in whose 'defense' the threat is made?"[10]

The bishops' letter was hailed as a major contribution to the cause of antinuclear resistance and peace. Four years later the Catholic Bishops addressd faith and society again, this time on "Catholic Social Teaching in the U.S. Economy." This letter criticized America's reliance on market capitalism, saying it abused those least able to defend themselves. Moreover, the bishops also decried modern maladies like the workaholic lifestyle, even for those who succeeded in the market. This time the bishops had gone too far, believed some prominent Catholics such as former Treasury Secretary William Simon, Clare Booth Luce, Michael Novak, Peter Grace, and Michael Joyce, who preempted the bishops with their own letter and alternative organization called "The Lay Commission on Catholic Social Teaching and the U.S. Economy." These Catholic industrialists, philanthropists, and intellectuals believed Catholic Bishops should stick to the care of souls and appreciate democratic capitalism as the freest, most productive economic system ever devised. This action coming from the right wing of lay Catholicism, featuring the laity speaking back to the teachings of their church, resembled nothing so much as liberal Catholics choosing their own position on matters of contraception. The authority of bishops was not what it used to be.

During the 1980s and for the next four decades, the authority of the Catholic hierarchy was also undermined from inside by one priestly sexual abuse scandal after another. Although Catholic priests were not the only clergy to abuse their office and parishioners, it was Catholic bishops who, in many cases, knew about alleged abuses and covered them up, often by reassigning accused priests to other parishes, only to have the abuse occur again. While there were bishops like Joseph Cardinal Bernardin who dealt with the issue early and publicly, many other bishops tried to protect the church by denying the problem, like Boston's Archbishop Bernard Cardinal Law. In case after case, dioceses paid dearly for the damage to souls, compounded by their cover-up conspiracies.

One Catholic who epitomized the right wing of the Republican Party was Pat Buchanan (1938–). In 1992, the former Nixon aide and conservative columnist ran against sitting President George H. W. Bush. He lost the fight for the nomination, but the speech he gave at that summer's convention was memorable for how he framed what he called a religious war in describing where Republicans stood on the issues:

> Yes, we disagreed with President Bush, but we stand with him for the freedom to choose religious schools, and we stand with him against the amoral idea that gay and lesbian couples should have the same standing in law as married men and women.
>
> We stand with President Bush for right-to-life, and for voluntary prayer in the public schools, and we stand against putting our wives and daughter and sisters into combat units of the United States Army. And we stand with President Bush in favor of the right of small towns and communities to control the raw sewage of pornography that so terribly pollutes our popular culture.
>
> We stand with President Bush in favor of federal judges who interpret the law as written, and against would-be Supreme Court justices like Mario Cuomo who think they have a mandate to rewrite the Constitution.
>
> My friends, this election is about more than who gets what. It is about who we are. It is about what we believe, and what we stand for as Americans. There is a religious war going on in this country. It is a cultural war, as critical to the kind of nation we shall be as was the Cold War itself, for this war is for the soul of America. And in that struggle for the soul of America, Clinton & Clinton are on the other side, and George Bush is on our side. And so, to the Buchanan Brigades out there, we have to come home and stand beside George Bush.[11]

In the years after Israel's 1967 Six-Day War with its Arab neighbors, American Jews turned somewhat away from the goal of assimilation in

American society that had preoccupied earlier generations. Israel's victory in 1967, and a repeat engagement in 1973, caused Jewish Americans to be proud of their victorious fellow Jews in Israel, yet also concerned that attacks on the State of Israel represented the first major threat to Jews since the Holocaust. Jews from America began to travel to Israel more, to send their young people on "birthright" trips, and to pay close attention to the United States' military and foreign aid support for Israel.

Another issue that captured attention was the plight of Soviet Jews, many of whom had asked to emigrate to the U.S. or to Israel, only to be denied. These "Refuseniks," as they became known, would struggle with anti-Semitism and the inability to get work once they had filed a request to leave the country. Only 150,000 Jews could leave the USSR during the 1970s. Their plight became a cause shared by American Jews and politicians alike. Because of the support raised, eventually 1.6 million Jews left the Soviet Union and post-Soviet Russia between 1989 and 2006. Of these, about 979,000, or 61 percent, migrated to Israel. Another 325,000, or 20 percent, migrated to the United States, followed by 219,000, or 14 percent, who migrated to Germany. The success of Jewish Americans in achieving this freedom for former Soviet Jews was deeply empowering and fostered further attention to the needs of the Jewish community, at home and abroad.[12]

The Consciousness Revolution and New Religious Identities

Not everyone from the 1970s forward moved in a conservative direction. As we have seen, Catholics and Jews were mostly responsive to internal issues. The more ecumenical Protestant churches embraced more cultural change, ordaining women, supporting choice in the abortion issue, and eventually becoming open to the full participation of LGBT persons and same-sex marriage. Before that, however, experiments in new religious movements accelerated during the 1970s. In addition to the turn toward religions and practices from the East, American Christian-based groups also established new movements where participants sought to live together in peace. The new communitarian groups were a popular alternative to the middle-class nuclear family for a time, but few lasted long. Perhaps the longest lasting major group was the Jesus People, who looked like hippies (even calling themselves "Jesus Freaks") and mostly represented an evangelical response to secular American culture. Two religious communities, however, became especially notorious: Jim Jones's People's Temple and David Koresh's Branch Davidians. Both groups came to violent ends. The People's Temple was founded as a countercultural experiment in racial harmony and social justice. Jones began the movement as an extension of his ministry as a Disciples of Christ pastor. Even before Jones (1931–78) moved his flock of roughly 1,000 followers to Jonestown, Guyana, some People's Temple refugees came to the Berkeley, California, Freedom Center to escape physical and emotional abuse. On November 18, 1978, everything came to a crashing halt when Jones ordered over 900 followers to drink Kool-Aid laced with cyanide. Jones had been engaging in suicide drills all the way back in San Francisco, testing members' loyalty by saying the wine was poison. He had also systematically degraded members in various ways to render them despicable in their own minds—as unfit to live in any other kind of society than the one he had created. As for the deaths, Jones preached they would be regarded as heroes, "a symbolic protest against the evils of mankind," as a later analyst described it.[13]

Fifteen years after Jonestown another religious movement went up in flames just outside Waco, Texas. Led by a man who had renamed himself David Koresh (1959–93), the Branch Davidians waited in their compound for the end of days. They also attracted the attention of neighbors who reported stockpiling of weapons and alleged child abuse. Because the subsequent standoff between the Davidians and the Bureau for Alcohol, Tobacco, and Firearms (ATF) and the Federal Bureau of Investigation (FBI) extended from an initial raid for another two months, the eventual conflagration of April 9, 1993, was televised, covered by the broadcast networks and the relatively new 24-hour cable news network CNN. Later in the same year, Michael Barkun wrote about what happened as a fundamental problem in religion-state relations:

> The single most damaging mistake on the part of federal officials was their failure to take the Branch Davidians' religious beliefs seriously. Instead, David Koresh and his followers were viewed as being in the grip of delusions that prevented them from grasping reality. As bizarre and misguided as their beliefs might have seemed, it was necessary to grasp the role these beliefs played in their lives; these beliefs were the basis of their reality. The Branch Davidians clearly possessed an encompassing worldview to which they attached ultimate significance. That they did so carried three implications. First, they could entertain no other set of beliefs. Indeed, all other views of the world, including those held by government negotiators, could only be regarded as erroneous. The lengthy and fruitless conversations between the two sides were, in effect, an interchange between different cultures—they talked past one another.[14]

Instead of taking the Branch Davidians' religion seriously, government officials, Barkun wrote, assimilated "the Waco situation to more familiar and less threatening stereotypes, treating the Branch Davidians as they would hijackers and hostage takers."[15] The armed millenarians, meanwhile, possessed a script of what would happen at the end of time, and government law enforcement attacks played right into that script. Religion was demonstrating a capacity to foment violence in the late twentieth century that did not fit with mainstream America's understanding of the role of faith, but which was a sign of things to come. Two years later Timothy McVeigh's Oklahoma

City bombing was a direct retribution for the ATF's and FBI's actions in Waco. The World Trade Center bombing of 1993 and the 9/11 attacks in 2001 were, likewise, premised on something the United States government, and by extension the American people, had done to offend strong religious commitments. In the latter cases, bombers and hijackers attacked America because Americans had, in their view, violated the religion of Islam by stationing U.S. troops in Saudi Arabia, the holy land of Mecca and Medina.

New Roles for Women in Religious Leadership

In the years after 1970, increasing numbers of women were first ordained to ministry in the ecumenical Protestant churches. The issue of women's ordination proved to be perhaps most divisive in the Episcopal Church (U.S.A.). The Episcopalians were caught between their social progressivism and their view of the priesthood that (similar to Roman Catholicism) believed priests represented Christ, thus requiring they be male. Women's ordination to the priesthood only came in 1974, when eleven women were irregularly ordained in Philadelphia by a retired bishop, one not even from the Philadelphia diocese. One of the first women to be ordained soon afterward was lawyer, civil rights activist, and feminist Pauli Murray (1919–85). Later Murray remembered how much the weight of church history bore down upon this otherwise brave pioneer in so many fields.

PAULI MURRAY: THE ORDINATION OF WOMEN

"Several days before ordination, I was suddenly seized by an agony of indecision, as though I had been assaulted by an army of demons. The thought that the opponents of women's ordination might be right and that I might be participating in a monstrous wrong terrified me. As a sister priest put it later, speaking of herself, 'I felt that God might strike me dead before it happened.' I have since been told by other priests, male and female, that they faced a similar ordeal just before their ordination, but at the time I thought this ambivalence was peculiar to me, so personal that I dared not speak to anyone about it. I prayed fervently for some sign that I was doing God's will."*

*Pauli Murray, *Song in a Weary Throat: Memoir of an American Pilgrimage* (Harper & Row, 1987), 435.

Murray went through with receiving ordination, reporting later that just as the bishop placed his hands upon her forehead, the sun broke through and sent strong shafts of rainbow-colored light down through the stained-glass windows, causing people in the congregation to gasp. She took this as the sign of God's will she had prayed for. The meaning of her ordination was even more striking, as Murray later wrote: "All the strands of my life had come together. Descendant of slave and of slave owner, I had already been called poet, lawyer, teacher, and friend. Now I was empowered to minister the sacrament of One in whom there is no north or south, no black or white, no male or female—only the spirit of love and reconciliation drawing us all toward the goal of human wholeness."[16] By 1980 an estimated 3 percent of clergy in the ecumenical traditions were female. By 2000 that number would rise to 30 percent, and the number of women in seminaries and divinity schools of these traditions often exceeded 50 percent. Still, female-headed congregations numbered just 21 percent in 1998.[17]

When it came to lesbian and gay persons, the ecumenical Protestant churches were of a divided mind. They usually advocated for social acceptance of LGBT people in society, arguing for decriminalization of homosexual acts in the 1970s, for nondiscrimination in employment, and for acceptance of persons living with HIV or AIDS from the early 1980s. The gay activists who turned June into Pride Month, after the Stonewall Riot of June 1969, often held their meetings in the basements of sympathetic churches.[18] Despite these social positions, the churches largely blocked LGBT persons from positions of ministerial leadership and officially held (in the words of the Episcopal Church in 1977) that "it is not appropriate for this Church to ordain a practicing homosexual." The United Church of Christ was the first to break this barrier, making the Rev. William R. Johnson the first openly gay man to be ordained in 1972. The Episcopal Church followed in 1994, while several denominations with congregational polities, including the American Baptist Churches and the Disciples of Christ, did not take a national position, allowing congregations to ordain whomever they would. The Presbyterian Church (U.S.A.) and the Evangelical Lutheran Church in America allowed gay ordination as of 2010; the United Methodist and Reformed churches, the other large ecumenical traditions, were still debating the issue in 2020. Remarkably, as same-sex marriage became lawful first in selected states and nationwide after 2015, the traditions that ordained LGBT persons were quick to allow ministers to perform marriage ceremonies. Though these denominations, the oldest American Protestant churches, read the same Bible as the religious right, they read it in a markedly different way when it came to so-called family matters and issues of inclusion.

Private Religion, Pentecostalization, and the Prosperity Gospel

In 1989, the World Wide Web (www) was invented by a British scientist working at CERN (Conseil Européen pour la Recherche Nucléaire). Like the Internet itself, the Web was intended to serve the technical needs of scientists to share and look up information. It soon became much, much more as ordinary people and companies the world over began to create content and look up information, first using rudimentary search engines starting in

1993, and "Googling" results by 1997. In the meantime, a variety of general- and focused-interest Internet forums were operating at CompuServe and America Online. A surprising amount of Internet content and queries were religious in nature. A *New York Times* examination found that "searches related to the Bible, God, Jesus Christ, church, and prayer are all highly concentrated in the Bible Belt. They rise on Sunday everywhere." Additionally, there were lots of questions that expressed doubt or wonder, questions that perhaps people were uncomfortable asking their priests, ministers, and rabbis, if they had them: "Who created God? Why does God allow suffering? Why does God hate me? Why does God want us to worship him? Why doesn't God answer my prayers? Why does God not show himself?" People in retirement communities asked for visuals of hell and heaven.[19]

The Web also became a place where mainstream and alternative religious groups and individuals offered their perspectives on religious matters. There is a saying that "on the internet, no one knows you are a dog." While there was curated content from encyclopedias, religious bodies, and scholars, an extraordinary amount of religious content was produced by people no one had ever heard of in public, ranging from premillennial dispensationalism, to modern paganism, and studies of the meaning of jihad in the Qur'an. The Internet became a place for expressive religiosity; no editors, publishers, or peer reviewers weighed in on the validity of religious content (or anti-religious content, for that matter).

Older forms of religious expression also continued, of course. Religious novels that asked and answered some of the same questions as Google searches became enormously popular. The *Left Behind* series of sixteen books (1995–2007) written by Tim LaHaye and Jerry Jenkins dramatized the rapture, the antichrist, and events associated with the biblical book of Revelation; they ended with a glorious second coming of a warrior Christ. The books sold millions to adults and especially young adults. Though premillennial dispensationalist Christians recognized the apocalyptic framework of rapture and end-times they were taught in church, many more teens found themselves starting the books for the adventure or because their friends were reading them and ending up thinking about life, death, good, and evil in radically different terms. Not every evangelical liked *Left Behind*, to be sure. Sojourners founder Jim Wallis, a significant leader in progressive evangelicalism, offered this reflection about the new millennium and expectations for a "Second Coming": "As far as progressive Christians are concerned, we've generally held to the theology that says you should live by the values of the kingdom of God right now, rather than worrying about when and how it's all finally going to be implemented. In fact, that's the best way to implement it. So, not much Second Coming discussions going on during or after church."[20]

After 9/11, two other multimillion bestsellers conveyed popular theologies about these matters. Mitch Albom's *The Five People You Meet in Heaven* (2003) conveyed a secularized American idea of heaven as a place where the meaning of your life is explained to you. William Young's *The Shack* (2007), meanwhile, became an evangelical Christian favorite with its tale of an abduction and killing of a young daughter, a father's pain and depression, and going to the shack alone, where he encounters the three persons of the Trinity: God the Father takes the form of an African American woman who calls herself Elousia and Papa; Jesus is a Middle Eastern carpenter; and the Holy Spirit physically manifests as an Asian woman named Sarayu. The novel resolves with the trial of the serial killer, found through God's direct revelation. These novels answered a need to find a meaning in life at the turn of the millennium, but they also portrayed a much more personally involved and active God than had traditionally been portrayed in most American religious life. This was changing, however, thanks to the suffusion of pentecostal and charismatic theology in American culture.

The pentecostal movement that began at the beginning of the twentieth century both produced specific denominations—the Church of God in Christ, the Assemblies of God, the Church of God (Cleveland, Tennessee), the Foursquare Church, the United Pentecostal Holiness Church International, and many others—and created a new understanding of how the Holy Spirit worked that influenced other churches and believers the world over. In the United States, the term *pentecostal* came to mean specific denominations and churches receiving and exercising the gifts of the Spirit. Though by the 1990s only a minority of American pentecostal churches regularly observed speaking in tongues, the conviction that the Spirit of God was available for healing, prophecy, and ecstatic worship characterized the entire movement. These beliefs were also to be found in other Protestant and Catholic churches, as part of what is called the charismatic movement.

Charismatic Christians began to be found in Catholicism as the result of a 1966 spiritual encounter when Duquesne University young theology professors Ralph Kiefer and William Storey attended a meeting of the Cursillo movement (a three-day short course on Christianity meant to strengthen faith and discipleship). There they encountered the book *They Speak with Other Tongues*, which emphasizes the Holy Spirit and the Spirit's gifts, or "charisms." The following February, Storey and Kiefer attended an Episcopalian prayer meeting and were baptized in the Holy Spirit. They brought the experience back to Duquesne the next week, when Kiefer laid hands on other professors, and they too experienced the Spirit. This experience of the "infilling of the Spirit" became the basis for what is known as "Charismatic Renewal."

Traditional Catholics were suspicious insofar as they believed that the presence of Christ in the Eucharist was the sufficient basis of Catholic faith. The movement, however, fit into Catholicism's active view of spiritual sodalities (religious guilds or brotherhoods) and the role of prayer, miracles, and healing. By 1985, the movement received pontifical recognition and grew as a worldwide movement of more that 150 million members committed to seeking a personal relationship with Jesus Christ. The movement was cautiously supported by the Vatican in early years, before being embraced, especially by Popes John Paul II and Francis. In 2019, Pope Francis inaugurated a new umbrella organization, CHARIS (Catholic Charismatic Renewal International Service). When asked what he expected of "the spiritists," as he jokingly called them, Francis said he expected them to share baptism of the Holy Spirit with everyone in the church, to serve the unity of the body of Christ, and "to serve the poor and those in greatest need, physical or spiritual."[21] Despite this support for charismatics in Catholicism, a quiet exodus among Latinx people to pentecostal churches, led by Hispanic pastors, occurred. Nearly 25 percent of American Hispanics who were raised Catholic had left, according to a Pew Forum survey, mostly for pentecostal and evangelical churches.[22]

Not only Catholics were becoming charismatic, but thanks to the Full Gospel Businessmen's Fellowship, more than 300,000 people from other Protestant traditions were also being exposed to charismatic practices by the year 1972. During the 1970s and 1980s the movement, led by California businessman Demos Shakarian, more than doubled in size, sponsored television shows promoting becoming "The Happiest People on Earth," and generally extolled the values of success, Christian prosperity, and spiritual business-growth principles. Meetings of chapters often included testimonies of how the Lord had prospered members after they became better Christians, together with prayers for healing, and speaking in tongues. Businessmen members often promoted church growth principles in their own congregations. The fellowship was not a church, but its teaching became popular in many evangelical churches beyond the pentecostal orbit. Shakarian himself helped support evangelistic campaigns like those of Oral Roberts and William Branham. He also helped Paul Crouch begin the Trinity Broadcasting Network (TBN) and John Osteen, father of Joel Osteen (whose preaching and publishing ministries would later eclipse those of his father), to start his own pentecostal ministry.[23]

Shakarian's work and lay ministry marks a turning point in modern Pentecostalism insofar as the movement was broadening beyond pentecostal denominations, to include more and more independent evangelists, congregations that described themselves as nondenominational, and charismatic believers from Methodism, Episcopalianism, and Presbyterianism who were forming their own charismatic fellowships within their denominations. As the twenty-first century dawned, the ideas and practices of the once despised Pentecostals were being absorbed into evangelical and ecumenical churches—quite apart from membership in a pentecostal church or charismatic fellowship. A 2008 survey of mainline Protestants found large percentages identifying themselves as born again, believing that God answers prayer, and praying for healing for themselves or someone else.[24]

Another way contemporary Pentecostalism was extending its reach was the rise of "Bapticostal" churches. These African American Baptist churches were characterized by practices that intersected with the "Word of Faith" movement among pentecostal evangelists like A. A. Allen (1907–70), Kathryn Kuhlman (1907–76), and especially Kenneth Hagin (1917–2003). Allen and Kuhlman led traveling revivals that offered "healing miracles" and later were among the first to do the same on television. Hagin did the same; borrowing from Oral Roberts (1918–2009), he preached what he termed the "Word of faith" or "faith in God's Word," based on his reading of Mark 11:23–24:

> For verily I say unto you, That whosoever shall say unto this mountain, be thou removed, and be thou cast into the sea, and shall not doubt in his heart, but shall believe that those things which he saith shall come to pass, he shall have whatsoever he saith. Therefore I say unto you, What things soever ye desire, when ye pray, believe that ye receive them, and ye shall have them.

In 1974 Hagin founded the Rhema Bible Training Center to spread his message internationally. He taught that God wanted to give faithful believers whatsoever they desired. The Word of Faith movement is, therefore, also known as the Prosperity Gospel movement, associated with evangelists like Kenneth and Gloria Copeland, Benny Hinn, Eddie Long, Joyce Meyers, T. D. Jakes, Creflo Dollar, and Joel Osteen. According to this "health and wealth" gospel, no true Christian should be sick or impoverished. These Christians are encouraged to demonstrate their faith by trusting in the promises of God, tithing 10 percent of their income, giving "love offerings" to the preacher, and then making a "seed offering" that God will bless and return a hundredfold. Then after "naming" their desire or need for health or wealth, the believer can "claim it." In addition to these "hard prosperity" preachers, many Bapticostal leaders, like Dwight McKissic, practice, believe in, and exhibit the charismatic gifts of the Spirit that are evident in Pentecostalism, such as speaking in tongues and being slain in the Spirit in their worship services. Most of these same churches also worship via consistently high-tempo traditional black gospel and Christian contemporary music.

American Religion after 9/11

On the morning of September 11, 2001, the United States suffered a coordinated terrorist attack by suicide hijackers from the Islamic terrorist group al-Qaeda. Two passenger planes flew into the twin towers of the World Trade Center in New York City, one plane crashed into the Pentagon in Washington, D.C., and a fourth plane intended for the White House was brought down in a field in Stonycreek Township, Pennsylvania, by the plane's passengers. The initial fatalities totaled 2,977, including citizens of 80 countries, with an additional 25,000 injured. Over time, first responders and construction workers clearing the destruction also suffered lung ailments and cancer. Religiously, 9/11 was a reckoning on two levels: people turned to their faith to plumb the depths of evil and to seek secure moorings; many Americans also came to realize the growing, sometimes hidden, diversity of America's religious groups, and many responded in fear.

Across the religious spectrum, people attended their houses of worship in high numbers for weeks. Religious leaders also joined forces against hatred and for the love of neighbors. A key example of the latter was a massive memorial service held in Yankee Stadium that was streamed by the major cable networks. Billed as "Prayer for America," the event was hosted by Oprah Winfrey. Police officers, firefighters, and opera stars sang patriotic anthems and hymns, and religious leaders from every conceivable body and branch of New York's religious life spoke, prayed, chanted, or read from their traditions' sacred scriptures. Muslim imams, Jewish rabbis, Buddhist and Catholic priests, Hindu clerics, bishops, archbishops, and ministers of many traditions all pointed to the unity of humanity. Bette Midler sang "Wind beneath My Wings," and Lee Greenwood sang "God Bless the U.S.A."

In these same early days, however, some Americans began violently attacking American Muslims and their places of worship. Even in this, their ignorance of other religions was on display, as when a Sikh man, Balbir Singh Sodhi, was mistaken for a Muslim and fatally shot on September 15, 2001, in Mesa, Arizona. President George W. Bush made an early public appearance at Washington's largest Islamic center to call for all American Muslims to be accorded respect. American Muslim groups were quick to condemn the attacks and join in raising funds for victims' families. Bush memorably also included these words in his joint address to Congress:

> I also want to speak tonight directly to Muslims throughout the world. We respect your faith. It's practiced freely by many millions of Americans and by millions more in countries that America counts as friends. Its teachings are good and peaceful, and those who commit evil in the name of Allah blaspheme the name of Allah.
>
> The terrorists are traitors to their own faith, trying, in effect, to hijack Islam itself.
>
> The enemy of America is not our many Muslim friends. It is not our many Arab friends. Our enemy is a radical network of terrorists and every government that supports them.[25]

Maintaining the distinction that Bush tried to make became difficult in practice. While Americans supported a response to al-Qaeda, the expansion of the "War on Terror" to Iraq on questionable premises divided public opinion and led to atrocious behaviors by American service personnel against Muslim prisoners under their control, most notably at the Abu Ghraib prison. President Bush had received the overwhelming support of people who attended church weekly. Yet now, if Christians condoned torture and indiscriminate drone strikes, many members of the younger generations did not want to be associated with the name "Christian."

In the summer of 2001, a Harvard Divinity School professor, Diana C. Eck, was promoting the work of her long-running research venture The Pluralism Project, which was documenting the growing presence of the Muslim, Buddhist, Hindu, pagan, Sikh, Jain, and Zoroastrian communities in the U.S. and their encounter with American Christian, Jewish, and secular traditions. A book, *A New Religious America: How a "Christian Country" Has Become the World's Most Religiously Diverse Nation*, detailed her findings and hit bookstores that year, just in time to be more immediately newsworthy. Many Americans had little or no idea that in particular areas there were high concentrations of people of faith beyond the usual Christians and Jews.

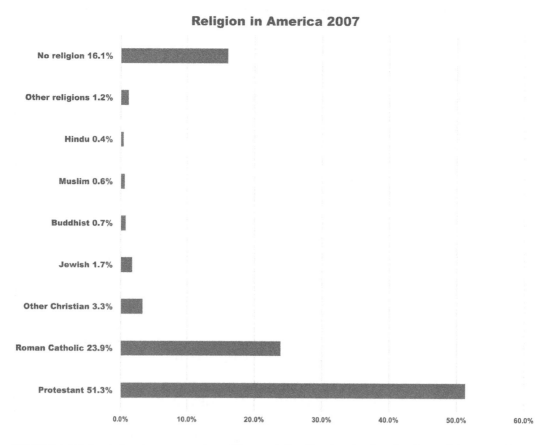

FIGURE 17-2. Religions in America as a percentage of the population. (Based on data from Pew Forum, Religious Landscape Survey, Summary of Findings, 2007)

In places like Dearborn, Michigan, and Toledo, Ohio, large populations of Muslims were focused. Indian immigrants and their families were numerous enough to build Hindu centers in New Jersey, Illinois, California, and Georgia.[26] Eck's book promoted interfaith understanding and acceptance, but even progressive Muslims like Feisal Abdul Rauf found themselves lumped together with terrorists. Rauf's liberal Cordoba Initiative became negatively rebranded by opponents as "the Mosque at Ground Zero." Though these overreactions would continue over the next decades, they would also lead to movements like the Interfaith Youth Core, founded by Eboo Patel, based on the belief that religion should be a bridge of cooperation rather than a barrier of division.

The adherents of the world's many religions in America were both more and less visible as the years progressed. Most schoolchildren in the twenty-first century, especially in more urban and suburban areas, went to school with children from Muslim, Hindu, and Buddhist families (and others) as each generation was more culturally diverse than the last. Greater emphasis was placed upon children learning facts about other religions' and cultures' holidays like Deepavali (a festival of lights celebrated by Hindus, Sikhs, and Jains), Chinese New Year, Eid al-Fitr (the end of the Muslim holy month of Ramadan), and the Jewish festival of dedication, Hanukkah. Predictably, some conservative Christian parents took exception to these innovations or asked why schools were not celebrating Christmas. Most children, however, appreciated the additional festivity.

At the same time, some important forms of religious diversity went unmarked. While the number of Buddhists grew beyond two million in America (0.7 percent of the population), more than half of these were white (53 percent) and only a third were Asian and South Asian (32 percent). Moreover, 74 percent of all American Buddhists had converted to the religion, rather than being born into it. While the nearly two million Hindus, Sikhs, and Jains were of South Asian descent, a given Asian or South Asian person in America is also likely to be counted among the Christians, Muslims, or those professing no religion. There are also Hispanic, black, Asian, and white followers of Islam among the three-plus million Muslims in America. All of this is to say that while Americans often judge things by appearance, that appearance is a misleading indication of religious identification.[27]

As President, Barack Obama signaled the value of religious pluralism. Gary Scott Smith observed, "No other president has so effusively praised the work of so many diverse religious communions or hosted such a wide variety of religious groups." Obama's religious advisers included Christians of a wide variety, together with Jews and Muslims. He was often fond of saying that America was "one nation under God," but was quick to add that each religion's "path to grace" needed to be respected, "as much as our own."[28] As much as Obama, the pluralist, preached the unity of each tradition's reverence for life and the dignity of every human being, conservative evangelical

FIGURE 17-3. President
Barack Obama delivers the
eulogy at the funeral of Rev.
Clementa Pinckney at the
College of Charleston, in
Charleston, South Carolina,
June 26, 2015 (Official White
House Photo by Lawrence
Jackson)

Christians were not buying the value of pluralism with its stated equivalence between the faiths. They consumed a vast amount of alternative history, such as promulgated in Glenn Beck's television program and David Baron's books retelling American history, which asserted that America was founded as a "Christian nation" and recast the founders as Christian gentlemen, one and all. As for Obama himself, he was written off by these groups as a "Muslim" instead of the Reinhold Niebuhr-loving black Protestant he in fact was.

Barack Obama's faith became especially clear during moments of tragedy, when he spoke as effectively as any minister. One especially significant moment was when he gave a eulogy for Rev. Clementa Pinckney just days after he and eight of his parishioners were killed (June 17, 2015) by white nationalist Dylann Roof. At the memorial service, a tearful Obama broke into singing "Amazing Grace," a song of lament and hope. For a few days, at least, tragedy was met with national unity.

Underneath these divisions in American society, a fragmentation was taking place. Conservative evangelical Christians were becoming more reliably identified with the Republican Party, even to the extent of supporting Donald J. Trump, the most morally flawed candidate in contemporary American politics, for President in 2016 and again in 2020. Meanwhile, each generation of Americans was less likely to claim a religious identity for themselves. Millennials and members of Generation Z were far more likely to embrace a "spiritual but not religious" identity than the Baby Boomers, who themselves were less religiously identified than the so-called Silent and Greatest generations. As it turns out, this did not mean that the so-called

FIGURE 17-4. Aggregated data from surveys conducted by the Pew Research Center for the People & the Press, January–July 2012 (Based on data from Pew Research Center)

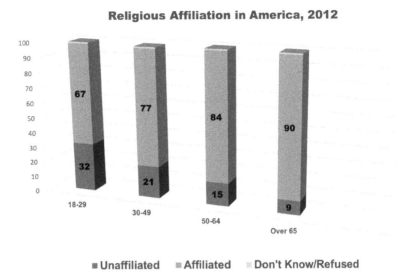

Nones (for claiming "none" when asked their religion) and the Spiritual but Not Religious (SBNRs) had no religious interests, but rather that the Christian tradition (still America's largest identification) was losing its institutional grip on them. If, in the course of events after 9/11, Christians condoned torture, the exclusion of LGBT people, the oppression of immigrants, and withholding food stamps from the hungry, they simply did not want to be known as Christian. Some few were truly atheist, but many more of the 16–20 percent of American adult Nones counted in 2012 and 2014 were privately interested in heaven, leading a good life, prayer, yoga, and meditation, what Jesus or the Buddha taught, and often all these things. Religion in America was still institutional, but for many the spiritual path was eclectic and very personal. In addition to the roughly 5 percent of Americans who claimed to be agnostic (3 percent) or atheist (2 percent), nearly 15 percent categorized their religion as "nothing in particular."[29]

During the Covid-19 pandemic beginning in 2020, most houses of worship were closed for months. But questions of life and death, meaning, and purpose continued to be explored virtually. Americans experienced Lent, Easter, Passover, Ramadan, and Eid al-Fitr through the Internet and in intimate family gatherings. Some religious groups, especially conservative evangelicals, claimed their First Amendment rights to open the churches no matter what. Still other faith groups staged food drives for their hungry neighbors and distributed help in "no contact" drive-by events. Many also expressed their faith by taking to the streets against police killings and to overcome the long American history of racism after the murder of George Floyd in Minneapolis (May 25, 2020). Protest, fear, and faith combined in ways predictable and novel. As the United States looked ahead to 2026, the 250th anniversary of its establishment as a new nation, religion was still at its cultural heart and more diverse in its expressions than ever before.

Notes

Introduction

1. "Letter to King Ferdinand of Spain, describing the results of the first voyage," Christopher Columbus, in 1493, http://xroads.virginia.edu/~hyper/hns/garden/columbus.html.
2. *The* Diario *of Christopher Columbus's First Voyage to America, 1492–1493*, abstracted by Fray Bartolomé de las Casas, trans. Oliver Dunn and James E. Kelly Jr. (Norman: University of Oklahoma Press, 1989), 291.
3. CNN, "Prayer Service at Yankee Stadium Aired September 23, 2001—14:30 ET," http://transcripts.cnn.com/TRANSCRIPTS/0109/23/se.03.html.
4. "Lutheran Panel Reinstates Pastor after Post-9/11 Interfaith Service," Associated Press, May 13, 2003, www.nytimes.com/2003/05/13/nyregion/lutheran-panel-reinstates-pastor-after-post-9-11-interfaith-service.html.
5. David Treuer, in *The Heartbeat of Wounded Knee: Native America from 1890 to the Present* (New York: Riverhead Books, 2019), Kindle edition, 512, offers these varied terms as ones that reflect particular people's preferences, noting, "My own choices of usage are governed by a desire for economy, speed, flow, and verisimilitude. A good rule of thumb for outsiders: Ask the Native people you're talking to what they prefer."

Chapter 1: Catholic Missions, European Conquests

1. David Treuer, *The Heartbeat of Wounded Knee: Native America from 1890 to the Present* (New York: Riverhead Books, 2019), 26–27; Thomas S. Kidd, *American Colonial History: Clashing Cultures and Faiths* (New Haven: Yale University Press, 2016), 1–3.
2. Catherine L. Albanese, *America: Religions and Religion*, 2nd ed. (Belmont, CA: Wadsworth Publishing, 1992), 25–26.
3. Albanese, *America: Religions,* 31, 34.
4. Albanese, *America: Religions*, 36–38.
5. "For White Mountain Apaches," Joel W. Martin writes, "religion means nothing without dirt; morality comes from the earth." Martin, *Native American Religion* (New York: Oxford University Press, 1999), 16. See also Joel W. Martin, *The Land Looks After Us: A History of Native American Religion* (New York: Oxford University Press, 1999, 2000), 8; Albanese, *America: Religions*, 26.
6. Lisa Poirier, "Native American Religions," in *Encyclopedia of Religion in America*, ed. Charles H. Lippy and Peter W. Williams, 4 vols. (Washington, DC: CQ Press, 2010), 3:1503. This reference work is henceforth abbreviated *ERA*.
7. Poirier, "Native American Religions," in *ERA* 3:1503–5.
8. Poirier, "Native American Religions," in *ERA* 3:1503–5.
9. Poirier, "Native American Religions," in *ERA* 3:1505–7.
10. Poirier, "Native American Religions," in *ERA* 3:1506.
11. Quotations and commentary in Martin, *Native American Religion*, 39–43.
12. Kidd, *American Colonial History*, 11.
13. Jon Butler, Grant Wacker, and Randall Balmer, *Religion in American Life: A Short History*, 2nd ed. (New York: Oxford University Press, 2011), 5.
14. As quoted in Kidd, *American Colonial History*, 11.
15. Kidd, *American Colonial History*, 11–12.
16. Columbus, as quoted in Mark Noll, *A History of Christianity in the United States and Canada* (Grand Rapids: Wm. B. Eerdmans Publishing Co., 1992), 12.

17. Kidd, *American Colonial History*, 13–14.
18. As quoted in Kidd, *American Colonial History*, 8.
19. Kidd, *American Colonial History*, 25.
20. Francis Augustus MacNutt, ed. and trans., *The Five Letters of Relation from Fernando Cortes to the Emperor Charles V*, vol. 1 (New York: Putnam, 1908), 207.
21. MacNutt, *Five Letters*, 201–2.
22. Kidd, *American Colonial History*, 25.
23. J. H. Elliott, *Empires of the Atlantic World: Britain and Spain in America, 1492–1830* (New Haven: Yale University Press, 2006), 5.
24. Kidd, *American Colonial History*, 26.
25. Kidd, *American Colonial History*, 27.
26. Kidd, *American Colonial History*, 28.
27. Kidd, *American Colonial History*, 28–29; Noll, *History of Christianity*, 13.
28. "*Sublimus Dei*: On the Enslavement and Evangelization of Indians, Pope Paul III—1537," in *Papal Encyclicals Online*, www.papalencyclicals.net/paul03/p3subli.htm. Kidd, *American Colonial History*, 29.
29. David J. Weber, *The Spanish Frontier in North America* (New Haven: Yale University Press, 1994), 100–101.
30. Weber, *Spanish Frontier*, 101–2.
31. Weber, *Spanish Frontier*, 104; Kidd, *American Colonial History*, 35.
32. Ramón A. Gutiérrez, *When Jesus Came the Corn Mothers Went Away: Marriage, Sexuality and Power in New Mexico, 1500–1846* (Stanford, CA: Stanford University Press, 1991), 157–60; Kidd, *American Colonial History*, 35.
33. Kidd, *American Colonial History*, 35–36.
34. Noll, *History of Christianity*, 15. "Saint Junípero Serra," *Britannica Academic, Encyclopædia Britannica*, September 23, 2015, www.britannica.com/biography/Saint-Junipero-Serra.
35. Noll, *History of Christianity*, 16–17; "Pope Canonizes 18th-Century Missionary; Not Everyone Happy," www.pbs.org/newshour/politics/pope-canonizes-18th-century-missionary-everyone-happy.
36. Pekka Hamalainen, *The Comanche Empire*, Lamar Series in Western History (New Haven: Yale University Press, 2008).
37. Kidd, *American Colonial History*, 43–44.
38. Kidd, *American Colonial History*, 46–47.
39. Quotations in Noll, *History of Christianity*, 19. See also Jean de Brébeuf, "Instructions for the Fathers of Our Society Who Shall Be Sent to the Humans," in *Shaped By the West: A History of North America to 1877*, by William Deverell and Anne Hyde (Oakland: University of California Press, 2018), 34.
40. Noll, *History of Christianity*, 19–20.
41. Quoted in Daniel K. Richter, "War and Culture: the Iroquois Experience," in *Religion and American Culture: A Reader*, ed. David G. Hackett (New York: Routledge, 2003), 55.
42. Richter, "War and Culture," 57–58.
43. Noll, *History of Christianity*, 20.
44. Emma Anderson, "Blood, Fire, and 'Baptism': Three Perspectives on the Death of Jean De Brébeuf, Seventeenth-Century Jesuit 'Martyr,'" in *Native Americans, Christianity, and the Reshaping of the American Religious Landscape*, ed. Joel Martin and Mark A. Nicholas (Chapel Hill: University of North Carolina Press, 2010), 126.

Chapter 2. Puritanism in New England

1. Mark Noll, *A History of Christianity in the United States and Canada* (Grand Rapids: Wm. B. Eerdmans Publishing Co., 1992), 31.
2. Noll, *History of Christianity*, 31–32.
3. Noll, *History of Christianity*, 31–35.
4. William Bradford, as quoted in Noll, *History of Christianity*, 38.
5. *Britannica Academic*, s.v. "Mayflower Compact," https://academic-eb-com.proxy.library.vanderbilt.edu/levels/collegiate/article/Mayflower-Compact/51595; cf. www.britannica.com/topic/Mayflower-Compact.
6. Noll, *History of Christianity*, 35.

7. John Winthrop, "Model of Christian Charity," in *American Religions: A Documentary History*, ed. R. Marie Griffith (New York: Oxford University Press, 2008), 18–19.

8. Noll, *History of Christianity*, 33.

9. Quotations in E. Brooks Holifield, *Theology in America: Christian Thought from the Age of the Puritans to the Civil War* (New Haven: Yale University Press, 2003), 29. For the definitive work on this topic, see the outstanding book by Theodore Dwight Bozeman, *To Live Ancient Lives: The Primitivist Dimension in Puritanism* (Chapel Hill: University of North Carolina Press, 1988).

10. Noll, *History of Christianity*, 43–44.

11. As quoted in Holifield, *Theology in America*, 39.

12. Holifield, *Theology in America*, 39–42.

13. Holifield, *Theology in America*, 38.

14. Holifield, *Theology in America*, 38.

15. Holifield, *Theology in America*, 38–39.

16. James P. Byrd, *The Challenges of Roger Williams* (Macon, GA: Mercer University Press, 2002), "Introduction," 1–20.

17. Roger Williams, *Mr. Cottons Letter Lately Printed, Examined and Answered*, in vol. 1 of *The Complete Writings of Roger Williams* (Providence, RI: Narragansett Club Publications, 1874; repr., New York: Russell & Russell, 1963), 41.

18. Roger Williams, *A Key into the Language of America*, ed. James Hammond Trumbull, in vol. 1 of *The Complete Writings of Roger Williams* (Providence: Narragansett Club Publications, 1866; repr., New York: Russell & Russell, 1963).

19. Roger Williams, *Christenings Make Not Christians* (London: Iane Coe, 1645); repr. in *Rhode Island Historical Tracts*, no. 14, ed. Henry Martyn Dexter (Providence, RI: Sidney S. Rider, 1881), 10–11, https://babel .hathitrust.org/cgi/pt?id=coo.31924108200308&view=1up&seq=34.

20. Williams, *Christenings Make Not Christians*, 1–2.

21. Williams, *Christenings Make Not Christians*, 3, 9–10.

22. Noll, *History of Christianity*, 33.

23. Noll, *History of Christianity*, 33.

24. Holifield, *Theology in America*, 42–43; Thomas Shepard is quoted on p. 43.

25. Noll, *History of Christianity*, 60–61.

26. Michael P. Winship, *Making Heretics: Militant Protestantism and Free Grace in Massachusetts, 1636–1641* (Princeton: Princeton University Press, 2002), 228. See also Mark A. Peterson's helpful review of Winship, *Making Heretics*, in *The American Historical Review* 108, no. 1 (February 2003): 184–85.

27. For the authoritative documentary history, including trial transcripts, see David D. Hall, *The Antinomian Controversy, 1636–1638: A Documentary History* (Durham, NC: Duke University Press, 1990). This is a reprint edition of the volume published in 1968.

28. Thomas S. Kidd, *American Colonial History: Clashing Cultures and Faiths* (New Haven: Yale University Press, 2016), 92–93.

29. Jill Lepore, *The Name of War: King Philip's War and the Origins of American Identity* (New York: Vintage Books, 1998), xi, xv, 7.

30. Lepore, *Name of War*, xiv.

31. Lepore, *Name of War*, xvi–xvii, 107–13.

32. Noll, *History of Christianity*, 48–49.

33. Emerson W. Baker, *A Storm of Witchcraft: The Salem Trials and the American Experience* (New York: Oxford University Press, 2015), 4–5.

34. Baker, *Storm of Witchcraft*, 5. For data on witchcraft accusation and executions, see p. 7.

35. Jon Butler, Grant Wacker, and Randall Balmer, *Religion in American Life: A Short History*, 2nd ed. (New York: Oxford University Press, 2011), 61–62.

36. Butler, Wacker, and Balmer, *Religion in American Life*, 61; Carol F. Karlsen, *The Devil in the Shape of a Woman: Witchcraft in Colonial New England* (New York: W. W. Norton, 1998), xi–xvii; Paul S. Boyer and Stephen Nissenbaum, *Salem Possessed: The Social Origins of Witchcraft* (Cambridge: Harvard University Press, 1974).

37. Amanda Porterfield, *American Religious History*, Blackwell Readers in American Social and Cultural History series (Malden, MA: Blackwell, 2002), 5.

38. Porterfield, *American Religious History*, 5–6.

39. A main source for this and the preceding two paragraphs is Porterfield, *American Religious History*, 5–8.

Chapter 3. Early American Religious Diversity

1. John Corrigan and Winthrop S. Hudson, *Religion in America*, 9th ed. (New York: Routledge, Taylor & Francis Group, 2018), 72–73.

2. Charles Deane, ed., *A Discourse concerning Western Planting, Written in the Year 1584 by Richard Hakluyt* (Cambridge: John Wilson & Son, 1877); Peter C. Mancall, *Hakluyt's Promise: An Elizabethan's Obsession for an English America* (New Haven: Yale University Press, 2007), 3–5, 237; Thomas S. Kidd, *American Colonial History: Clashing Cultures and Faiths* (New Haven: Yale University Press, 2016), 64–65.

3. Mancall, *Hakluyt's Promise*, 3–5, 237; Kidd, *American Colonial History*, 64–65.

4. Deane, *Discourse*, 8, 10–11 (with spelling modernized).

5. Deane, *Discourse*, 71, 75–76; Kidd, *American Colonial History*, 64–65.

6. Kidd, *American Colonial History*, 65–66.

7. Kidd, *American Colonial History*, 65–66.

8. Jill Lepore, "Our Town: Four Centuries On, the Battles over John Smith and Jamestown Still Rage," *The New Yorker*, April 26, 2007, www.newyorker.com/magazine/2007/04/02/our-town.

9. Jill Lepore, *The Story of America: Essays on Origins* (Princeton: Princeton University Press, 2012), 19.

10. Edmund Morgan, one of the most renowned American historians of the twentieth century, called Jamestown a "fiasco." "Measured by any of the objectives announced for it," Morgan said, "the colony failed." From the moment they arrived, the colonists spent the first decade making "nearly every possible mistake and some that seem almost impossible." Morgan quotes are in Lepore, *Story of America*, 20.

11. As quoted in Lepore, *Story of America*, 20–21.

12. "The Reverend Robert Hunt: The First Chaplain at Jamestown," *Historic Jamestowne*, National Parks Service, www.nps.gov/jame/learn/historyculture/the-reverend-robert-hunt-the-first-chaplain-at-jamestown.htm.

13. Theo Emery, "Jamestown Thought to Yield Ruins of Oldest U.S. Protestant Church," *The New York Times*, November 13, 2011, www.nytimes.com/2011/11/14/us/ruins-of-oldest-us-protestant-church-may-be-at-jamestown.html; Kidd, *American Colonial History*, 63, 68.

14. Edwin S. Gaustad and Mark A. Noll, *A Documentary History of Religion in America*, vol. 1, 3rd ed. (Grand Rapids: Wm. B. Eerdmans Publishing Co., 2003), 54–56 (spelling modernized).

15. Gaustad and Noll, *Documentary History*, 1:54–56 (spelling modernized).

16. As quoted in Jon Butler, Grant Wacker, and Randall Balmer, *Religion in American Life: A Short History*, 2nd ed. (New York: Oxford University Press, 2011), Kindle ed., 49–50.

17. Kidd, *American Colonial History*, 69–71.

18. Kidd, *American Colonial History*, 69–71.

19. Butler, Wacker, and Balmer, *Religion in American Life*, Kindle ed., 63.

20. Corrigan and Hudson, *Religion in America*, 67–68.

21. John D. Krugler, *English and Catholic: The Lords Baltimore in the Seventeenth Century* (Baltimore: Johns Hopkins University Press, 2004), 1.

22. Edwin S. Gaustad and Leigh E. Schmidt, *The Religious History of America*, rev. ed. (New York: HarperSanFrancisco, 2002), 96.

23. Gaustad and Schmidt, *Religious History*, 95–96.

24. Kidd, *American Colonial History*, 183–205.

25. Gaustad and Schmidt, *Religious History*, 97–100.

26. Russell Shorto, *The Island at the Center of the World* (New York: Vintage Books, 2005), 2–3.

27. Gaustad and Noll, *Documentary History*, 1:43.

28. Gaustad and Noll, *Documentary History*, 1:43–44.

29. Gaustad and Schmidt, *Religious History*, 75–76.
30. Gaustad and Noll, *Documentary History*, 1:47; Gaustad and Schmidt, *Religious History*, 75–76.
31. Gaustad and Noll, *Documentary History*, 1:47; Gaustad and Schmidt, *Religious History*, 75–76.
32. Kidd, *American Colonial History*, 119.
33. Kidd, *American Colonial History*, 119.
34. Gaustad and Schmidt, *Religious History*, 84–85.
35. William Penn, *The Political Writings of William Penn*, introduction and annotations by Andrew R. Murphy (Indianapolis: Liberty Fund, 2002), https://oll.libertyfund.org/titles/893, §84; Mark Noll, *A History of Christianity in the United States and Canada* (Grand Rapids: Wm. B. Eerdmans Publishing Co., 1992), 65–66.
36. Gaustad and Schmidt, *Religious History*, 84–85.
37. Gaustad and Schmidt, *Religious History*, 85–86.
38. Corrigan and Hudson, *Religion in America*, 70–71.
39. Katharine Gerbner, "The Ultimate Sin: Christianising Slaves in Barbados in the Seventeenth Century," in *Slavery and Abolition* 31, no. 1 (March 2010): 57–73, esp. 59–61.
40. Gerbner, "Ultimate Sin," 61.
41. Gerbner, "Ultimate Sin," 62–63.
42. Gerbner, "Ultimate Sin," 66–70.
43. Virginia Bernhard, "Religion, Politics, and Witchcraft in Bermuda, 1651–55," in *The William and Mary Quarterly* 3/67, no. 4 (October 2010): 679–80. See also Kidd, *American Colonial History*, 139–40.
44. Bernhard, "Religion, Politics," 680–82.
45. Bernhard, "Religion, Politics," 684–85.
46. Bernhard, "Religion, Politics," 686, 690–91.
47. Bernhard, "Religion, Politics," 686, 690–91, 693, 696–700.
48. Karen Ordahl Kupperman, "Errand to the Indies: Puritan Colonization from Providence Island through the Western Design," in *The William and Mary Quarterly* 3/45, no. 1 (January 1988): 72–73.
49. Kupperman, "Errand to the Indies," 81–82, 84–86.
50. Kupperman, "Errand to the Indies," 81–82, 84–86.
51. Richard S. Dunn, *Sugar and Slaves: The Rise of the Planter Class in the English West Indies, 1624–1713* (Chapel Hill: University of North Carolina Press, 2000), 149.
52. Dunn, *Sugar and Slaves*, 150, 156–57, 165.
53. Dunn, *Sugar and Slaves*, 183–84.
54. Dunn, *Sugar and Slaves*, 186–87.
55. Kidd, *American Colonial History*, 136–37.
56. Patricia Bonomi, *Under the Cope of Heaven: Religion, Society, and Politics in Colonial America*, updated ed. (New York: Oxford University Press, 2003), 31–32; Gaustad and Schmidt, *Religious History*, 103.
57. "The Fundamental Constitutions of Carolina: March 1, 1669," *The Avalon Project*, Lillian Goldman Law Library, Yale Law School, https://avalon.law.yale.edu/17th_century/nc05.asp.
58. Bonomi, *Under the Cope*, 31–32.
59. "Fundamental Constitutions of Carolina: March 1, 1669."
60. Ryan A. Quintana, *Making a Slave State: Political Development in Early South Carolina* (Chapel Hill: University of North Carolina Press, 2018), 1, 16–17.
61. Bonomi, *Under the Cope*, 32–33; Gaustad and Schmidt, *Religious History*, 98–99, 111.
62. Bonomi, *Under the Cope*, 32–33.
63. Bonomi, *Under the Cope*, 32–33.
64. Richard P. Heitzenrater, *Wesley and the People Called Methodists* (Nashville: Abingdon Press, 1995), 58.
65. Heitzenrater, *Wesley and the People*, 58–59.
66. Heitzenrater, *Wesley and the People*, 61–69.
67. Heitzenrater, *Wesley and the People*, 69–71.
68. Butler, Wacker, and Balmer, *Religion in American Life*, 73–74.

Chapter 4. The Great Awakening

1. Thomas S. Kidd, *The Great Awakening: A Brief History with Documents*, The Bedford Series in History and Culture (Boston: Bedford/St. Martin's, 2008), 3–4; Leigh Eric Schmidt, *Holy Fairs: Scotland and the Making of American Revivalism*, 2nd ed. (Grand Rapids: Wm. B. Eerdmans Publishing Co., 1989).

2. Kidd, *Great Awakening: A Brief History*, 2.

3. Cole as quoted in Kidd, *Great Awakening: A Brief History*, 61–62; Douglas Winiarski, *Darkness Falls on the Land of Light: Experiencing Religious Awakenings in Eighteenth-Century New England* (Chapel Hill: University of North Carolina Press, 2017), 133.

4. Cole as quoted in Kidd, *Great Awakening: A Brief History*, 60–62.

5. Kidd, *Great Awakening: A Brief History*, 60, 62–63.

6. Kidd, *Great Awakening: A Brief History*, 63.

7. As historian Douglas Winiarski wrote, "New converts like Nathan Cole rejected the inherited traditions of the godly walk and raced to blow up the foundations of their former religious lives." Winiarski, *Darkness Falls*, 134–35, 137.

8. Thomas S. Kidd, *George Whitefield: America's Spiritual Founding Father* (New Haven: Yale University Press, 2014), 1–2.

9. Wesley, as quoted in Richard P. Heitzenrater, *Wesley and the People Called Methodists*, 2nd ed. (Nashville: Abingdon, 2013), 109. Wesley refers to 2 Samuel 6:22.

10. Benjamin Franklin, *The Autobiography of Benjamin Franklin*, ed. Peter Conn (Philadelphia: University of Pennsylvania Press, 2005), 83.

11. Thomas S. Kidd, *The Great Awakening: The Roots of Evangelical Christianity in Colonial America* (New Haven: Yale University Press, 2007), 48–49; Kidd, *Great Awakening: A Brief History*, 4.

12. Thomas S. Kidd, *Benjamin Franklin: The Religious Life of a Founding Father* (New Haven: Yale University Press, 2017), Kindle ed., 106.

13. Frank Lambert, "'Pedlar in Divinity': George Whitefield and the Great Awakening, 1737–1745," in *The Journal of American History* 77, no. 3 (December 1990): 812–14.

14. George Marsden, *Jonathan Edwards: A Life* (New Haven: Yale University Press, 2003), 73; Mark Noll, *A History of Christianity in the United States and Canada* (Grand Rapids: Wm. B. Eerdmans Publishing Co., 1992), 86–87.

15. James P. Byrd, *Jonathan Edwards for Armchair Theologians* (Louisville, KY: Westminster John Knox Press, 2008), chap. 3; Jonathan Edwards, *Faithful Narrative*, in *Works of Jonathan Edwards*, vol. 4, *Great Awakening*, ed. C. C. Goen (New Haven: Yale University Press, 1970), 146, 150, 158–59. All volumes of *The Works of Jonathan Edwards* are available online: *The Works of Jonathan Edwards*, vols. 1–26 (New Haven: Yale University Press, 1957–2008), http://edwards.yale.edu. All further citations are abbreviated *WJE*, with volume and page numbers.

16. *WJE* 4:194–99. See Job 21:26; 24:20.

17. *WJE* 4:199–204; Byrd, *Jonathan Edwards*, 41–43.

18. Harry S. Stout, "Edwards as Revivalist," in *The Cambridge Companion to Jonathan Edwards*, ed. Stephen Stein (Cambridge: Cambridge University Press, 2007), 140.

19. Jonathan Edwards, "Sinners in the Hands of an Angry God [1739]," in *WJE* 22:406–7, 410–12.

20. *WJE* 22:414.

21. *WJE* 22:410–12; Byrd, *Jonathan Edwards*, 36–37.

22. *WJE* 4:194–207.

23. Gilbert Tennent, "Danger of an Unconverted Ministry," in Kidd, *Great Awakening: A Brief History*, 14, 58–59.

24. Charles Chauncy, *Seasonable Thoughts on the State of Religion in New England: A Treatise in Five Parts* (Boston: Rogers & Fowle, 1743), v–vi.

25. Kidd, *Great Awakening: A Brief History*, 2.

26. Charles Goen, "Introduction," *WJE* 4:52–53; see also *WJE* 4:213–88.

27. *WJE* 2:84.

28. *WJE* 2:120.
29. *WJE* 2:95–99; Byrd, *Jonathan Edwards*, 50–51.
30. *WJE* 2:383–411.
31. Winiarsky, *Darkness Falls*, 9, 378.
32. Isaac Backus, "Reasons for Separation," in Kidd, *Great Awakening: A Brief History*, 133–35; Kidd, *Great Awakening: The Roots*, 181–83.
33. Kidd, *The Great Awakening: The Roots*, 183–84.
34. Mark A. Noll, *America's God: From Jonathan Edwards to Abraham Lincoln* (Oxford: Oxford University Press, 2002), 149; William Gerald McLoughlin, *Isaac Backus and the American Pietistic Tradition*, The Library of American Biography (Boston: Little, Brown, 1967), 4.
35. Kidd, *Great Awakening: A Brief History*, 13–14.
36. Catherine A. Brekus, *Strangers and Pilgrims: Female Preaching in America, 1740-1845* (Chapel Hill: University of North Carolina Press, 1998), 23–26, esp. 25.
37. Brekus, *Strangers and Pilgrims*, 26.
38. Brekus, *Strangers and Pilgrims*, 28.
39. Brekus, *Strangers and Pilgrims*, 36–37.
40. Brekus, *Strangers and Pilgrims*, 38.
41. Brekus, *Strangers and Pilgrims*, 43–45.
42. Brekus, *Strangers and Pilgrims*, 43–44, 48.
43. Brekus, *Strangers and Pilgrims*, 43–44, 48–50.
44. Brekus, *Strangers and Pilgrims*, 58–59.
45. Brekus, *Strangers and Pilgrims*, 61.
46. James P. Byrd, "Baptist Tradition and Heritage," *ERA* 1:255–68.
47. Brekus, *Strangers and Pilgrims*, 65–66.
48. Chauncy, *Seasonable Thoughts on the State of Religion in New-England*, 226; Kidd, *Great Awakening: The Roots*, 213.
49. For an excellent overview of slavery and African Americans in the Great Awakening, see Kidd, *The Great Awakening: The Roots*, chap. 14.
50. Edwards's quotes and commentary in Kidd, *The Great Awakening: The Roots*, 216–17.
51. Kidd, *The Great Awakening: The Roots*, 217–19.
52. Jon Butler, "Enthusiasm Described and Decried: The Great Awakening as Interpretative Fiction," *The Journal of American History* 69, no. 2 (September 1982): 305–7; Frank Lambert, "The First Great Awakening: Whose Interpretive Fiction?," *The New England Quarterly* 68, no. 4 (December 1995): 650–59; Thomas S. Kidd, *The Great Awakening: The Roots*, xvii–xix.
53. Winiarski, *Darkness Falls*, 8–9, 15.
54. As Thomas Kidd argues, "The Great Awakening was the greatest upheaval in the American colonies prior to the Revolutionary War of the 1770s and 1780s." Kidd, *Great Awakening: A Brief History*, 2–3.

Chapter 5. The Enlightenment in America

1. See David Jan Sorkin, *The Religious Enlightenment: Protestants, Jews, and Catholics from London to Vienna* (Princeton: Princeton University Press, 2008).
2. Kerry Walters, "Enlightenment," *Encyclopedia of Religion in America*, edited by Charles H. Lippy and Peter W. Williams (Washington, DC: CQ Press, 2010), 693–94, http://dx.doi.org.proxy.library.vanderbilt.edu/10.4135/9781608712427.n110.
3. Walters, "Enlightenment," 694.
4. Walters, "Enlightenment," 694–96.
5. Alexander Pope, *The Works of Alexander Pope, Esq.: In Verse and Prose*, ed. William L. Bowles (London: J. Johnson, 1806), 3:63.
6. John Locke, *The Reasonableness of Christianity*, in *The Works of John Locke, Esq.* (London: S. Birt, 1751), 2:512.

7. Walters, "Enlightenment," 695.
8. Gordon Wood, *Revolutionary Characters: What Made the Founders Different* (New York: Penguin Books, 2006), 3–4.
9. Walters, "Enlightenment," 697.
10. Wood, *Revolutionary Characters,* 69–70.
11. Robert Middlekauff, "Franklin, Benjamin." In *Encyclopedia of the Enlightenment* (New York: Oxford University Press, 2002), www.oxfordreference.com/view/10.1093/acref/9780195104301.001.0001/acref-9780195104301-e-238.
12. Thomas S. Kidd, *Benjamin Franklin: The Religious Life of a Founding Father* (New Haven: Yale University Press, 2017), Kindle ed., 2.
13. Jill Lepore, *The Story of America: Essays on Origins* (Princeton: Princeton University Press, 2012), Kindle ed., 51.
14. Gordon Wood comments on Franklin's profound thoughts on human nature. Wood, *Revolutionary Characters,* 72.
15. Wood, *Revolutionary Characters,* 72.
16. Lepore, *Story of America,* Kindle ed., 45, 55.
17. Lepore, *Story of America,* Kindle ed., 45.
18. Kidd, *Benjamin Franklin,* Kindle ed., 2, 6–8.
19. "To Josiah and Abiah Franklin Thu, Apr 13, 1738," *The Papers of Benjamin Franklin: Sponsored by The American Philosophical Society and Yale University,* vol. 2, *January 1, 1735, through December 31, 1744,* digital ed. (New Haven: Yale University Press, 1960), 202; Kerry Walters, "Franklin and the Question of Religion," in *The Cambridge Companion to Benjamin Franklin,* ed. Carla Mulford, Cambridge Companions to American Studies (Cambridge: Cambridge University Press, 2009), 91–92.
20. So argues Thomas Kidd, *Benjamin Franklin,* Kindle ed., 4–5.
21. D. Mayer, "Jefferson, Thomas" (2002), in *Encyclopedia of the Enlightenment,* www.oxfordreference.com/view/10.1093/acref/9780195104301.001.0001/acref-9780195104301-e-350.
22. Jefferson as quoted in Richard Samuelson, "Jefferson and Religion: Private Belief, Public Policy," in *The Cambridge Companion to Thomas Jefferson,* ed. Frank Shuffelton, Cambridge Companions to American Studies (Cambridge: Cambridge University Press, 2009), 143–54, esp. 143, doi:10.1017/CCOL9780521867313.011.
23. "From Thomas Jefferson to Peter Carr, with Enclosure, 10 August 1787" *Founders Online,* National Archives, https://founders.archives.gov/documents/Jefferson/01-12-02-0021. See also Samuelson, "Jefferson and Religion," 144–45.
24. Samuelson, "Jefferson and Religion," 145–46.
25. Samuelson, "Jefferson and Religion," 146–47.
26. Samuelson, "Jefferson and Religion," 147.
27. "Declaration of Independence: A Transcription," America's Founding Documents, National Archives, www.archives.gov/founding-docs/declaration-transcript; Thomas Jefferson, *Notes on the State of Virginia* (Philadelphia: Prichard & Hall, 1788), 173, https://docsouth.unc.edu/southlit/jefferson/jefferson.html; Samuelson, "Jefferson and Religion," 149–50.
28. Jefferson, *Notes on the State,* 169.
29. Robert Louis Wilken, *Liberty in the Things of God: The Christian Origins of Religious Freedom* (New Haven: Yale University Press, 2019), 189–90.
30. "Declaration of Independence: A Transcription," America's Founding Documents, National Archives, www.archives.gov/founding-docs/declaration-transcript; many have referred to "America's foundational contradiction." See, e.g., Lucia C. Stanton, *"Those Who Labor for My Happiness": Slavery at Thomas Jefferson's Monticello* (Charlottesville: University of Virginia Press, 2012), vii.
31. For a review of the history and historiography of Jefferson's relationship with Sally Hemings, see Francis D. Cogliano, *Thomas Jefferson: Reputation and Legacy* (Edinburgh: Edinburgh University Press, 2006), chap. 6. The groundbreaking historical study is by Annette Gordon Reed, *Thomas Jefferson and Sally Hemings: An American Controversy* (Charlottesville: University Press of Virginia, 1998). The DNA results appeared in E.

A. Foster et al., "Jefferson Fathered Slave's Last Child," *Nature* 5 (November 5, 1998): 27–28. See also Annette Gordon Reed, *The Hemingses of Monticello: An American Family* (New York: W.W. Norton & Company, 2008).

32. "Jefferson's 'Original Rough Draught' of the Declaration of Independence," in *The Papers of Thomas Jefferson*, vol. 1, *1760–1776* (Princeton: Princeton University Press, 1950), 423–28, https://jeffersonpapers.princeton .edu/selected-documents/jefferson's-"original-rough-draught"-declaration-independence.

33. Douglas R. Egerton, "Race and Slavery in the Era of Jefferson," in *The Cambridge Companion to Thomas Jefferson*, ed. Frank Shuffelton (Cambridge: Cambridge University Press, 2009), 73.

34. Jefferson, *Notes on the State*, 147; Egerton, "Race and Slavery," 74–75.

35. Jefferson, *Notes on the State*, 149–50.

36. Benjamin Rush, *The Letters of Benjamin Rush*, vol. 2, *1793–1813*, ed. L. H. Butterfield (Princeton: Princeton University Press, 1951), 758; Egerton, "Race and Slavery," 79.

37. Aaron Garrett and Silvia Sebastiani, "David Hume on Race," in *The Oxford Handbook of Philosophy and Race* (New York: Oxford University Press, 2017), 34, 39–41.

38. Quotations and commentary in Catherine A. Brekus, *Sarah Osborn's World: The Rise of Evangelical Christianity in Early America* (New Haven: Yale University Press, 2013), 9 (with original italics). See also p. 4.

39. Brekus, *Sarah Osborn's World*, 1–2, 5, 9.

40. Walters, "Enlightenment," 697; Mark Noll, "Common Sense Traditions and American Evangelical Thought," *American Quarterly* 37, no. 2 (Summer 1985): 220–23, 229–31.

41. Brekus, *Sarah Osborn's World*, 9–10; D. W. Bebbington, *Evangelicalism in Modern Britain: A History from the 1730s to the 1980s* (London: Routledge, Taylor & Francis e-Library, 2004), 142–43.

Chapter 6. The American Revolution

1. Harry S. Stout, "Review Essay: Religion, War, and the Meaning of America," *Religion and American Culture: A Journal of Interpretation* 19, no. 2 (Summer 2009): 275. Parts of this chapter first appeared in a different form in James P. Byrd, *Sacred Scripture, Sacred War: The Bible and the American Revolution* (New York: Oxford University Press, 2013).

2. For an examination and critique of this phenomenon, see Thomas S. Kidd, *Who Is an Evangelical?* (New Haven: Yale University Press, 2019).

3. Harry S. Stout, "Religion, Communications, and the Ideological Origins of the American Revolution," *The William and Mary Quarterly* 3/34, no. 4 (October 1977): 519–41, here 536–37. On the debate among historians, see Philip Goff, "Revivals and Revolution: Historiographic Turns since Alan Heimert's *Religion and the American Mind*," *Church History* 67, no. 4 (1998): 695–721. Another helpful overview is in Thomas S. Kidd, *God of Liberty: A Religious History of the American Revolution* (Philadelphia: Basic Books, 2010), 77.

4. Charles Royster, *A Revolutionary People at War: The Continental Army and American Character* (Chapel Hill: University of North Carolina Press, 1979), 24; J. T. Headley, *Chaplains and Clergy of the American Revolution* (New York: Charles Scribner, 1864), 92–93, 105. For an argument that recognizes Whitefield's influence on the Revolution, see Jerome Dean Mahaffey, *The Accidental Revolutionary: George Whitefield and the Creation of America* (Waco, TX: Baylor University Press, 2011).

5. Fred Anderson, *Crucible of War: The Seven Years' War and the Fate of Empire in British North America, 1754–1766* (New York: Alfred A. Knopf, 2000), 11–32; Fred Anderson, *The War That Made America: A Short History of the French and Indian War* (New York: Viking, 2005), Kindle ed.

6. Mark A. Noll, *America's God: From Jonathan Edwards to Abraham Lincoln* (Oxford: Oxford University Press, 2002), 78–80. See also Nathan O. Hatch, *The Sacred Cause of Liberty: Republican Thought and the Millennium in Revolutionary New England* (New Haven: Yale University Press, 1977). For background on this section, see James P. Byrd, *Sacred Scripture, Sacred War*, chap. 1.

7. Harry S. Stout, *The New England Soul: Preaching and Religious Culture in Colonial New England* (New York: Oxford University Press, 1986), 261–62.

8. Stout, *New England Soul*, 271–75.

9. For a good description, see "Boston Tea Party," www.history.com/topics/american-revolution/boston-tea -party; Kidd, *God of Liberty*, 66–67.

10. John Adams, "Letter to Dr. J. Morse, 2 December 1815," in John Adams, *The Works of John Adams, Second President of the United States: With a Life of the Author, Notes and Illustrations, by His Grandson Charles Francis Adams* (Boston: Little, Brown & Co., 1856), 10:185, https://oll.libertyfund.org/titles/2127.

11. Stout, *New England Soul*, 303, 6–7.

12. Samuel Sherwood, "The Church's Flight into the Wilderness: An Address on the Times," in *Political Sermons of the American Founding Era, 1730–1805*, ed. Ellis Sandoz, 2nd ed. (Indianapolis: Liberty Fund, 1998), 523.

13. Gordon S. Wood, *The Radicalism of the American Revolution* (New York: A. A. Knopf, 1992), 1:104–5.

14. See Francis J. Bremer, "Foxe in the Wilderness: The Book of Martyrs in Seventeenth-Century New England," in *John Foxe at Home and Abroad*, ed. David Loades (Burlington, VT: Ashgate Publishing, 2004), 105–16.

15. Thomas Brockway, *America Saved, or Divine Glory Displayed, in the Late War with Great Britain* (Hartford, CT: Hudson & Goodwin, 1784), 19–20.

16. See John Wesley, "A Calm Address to Our American Colonies," in *Political Sermons of the American Founding Era*, vol. 1, *1730–1788*, ed. Ellis Sandoz (Indianapolis: Liberty Fund, 1998), 409–20; cf. www.consource.org/document/a-calm-address-to-our-american-colonies-by-john-wesley-1775.

17. See Nathan R. Perl-Rosenthal, "The 'divine right of republics': Hebraic Republicanism and the Debate over Kingless Government in Revolutionary America," *William and Mary Quarterly* 3/66, no. 3 (July 2009): 535–64; Robert Middlekauff, *The Glorious Cause: The American Revolution, 1763–1789*, rev. ed. (New York: Oxford University Press, 2005), 3. On the use of Scripture among the founders, see Daniel L. Dreisbach, *Reading the Bible with the Founding Fathers* (Oxford: Oxford University Press, 2017); Byrd, *Sacred Scripture, Sacred War*, introduction.

18. Quotations and commentary in Jill Lepore, *The Story of America: Essays on Origins*, Kindle ed. (Princeton: Princeton University Press, 2012), 59–60.

19. Lepore, *Story of America*, 60.

20. Quotes and commentary in Lepore, *Story of America*, 61–62.

21. Thomas Paine, *Common Sense*, in *The Writings of Thomas Paine, Collected and Edited by Moncure Daniel Conway* (New York: G. P. Putnam's Sons, 1894), vol. 1, Online Library of Liberty, Liberty Fund, https://oll.libertyfund.org/pages/1776-paine-common-sense-pamphlet.

22. Paine, *Common Sense*.

23. Paine, *Common Sense*.

24. John Adams, *Diary and Autobiography of John Adams*, vol. 3, *Diary, 1782–1804 and Autobiography, Part One to October 1776*, in *The Adams Papers*, ed. C. James Taylor, digital ed. (Charlottesville: University of Virginia Press, Rotunda, 2008), 333; Byrd, *Sacred Scripture, Sacred War*, introduction.

25. Thomas Paine, *The Age of Reason* (New York: G. N. Devries, 1827), 17–18.

26. On "Hebraic republicanism," see Perl-Rosenthal, "The 'divine right of republics.'"

27. See Joyce Appleby, "The American Heritage: The Heirs and the Disinherited," *Journal of American History* 74, no. 3 (December 1, 1987): 809; John Adams to Benjamin Rush, February 2, 1807, in *The Founders on Religion: A Book of Quotations*, ed. James H. Hutson (Princeton: Princeton University Press, 2005), 23.

28. Noll, *America's God*, 56.

29. Declaration of Independence, The Avalon Project, Lillian Goldman Law Library, Yale Law School, https://avalon.law.yale.edu/18th_century/declare.asp.

30. Thomas Jefferson, *Summary View of the Rights of British America*, The Avalon Project, Lillian Goldman Law Library, Yale Law School, https://avalon.law.yale.edu/18th_century/jeffsumm.asp.

31. Samuel Johnson, *Taxation No Tyranny: An Answer to the Resolutions and Address of the American Congress* (London: T. Cadell, 1775), 89.

32. Ruth Bogin, "'Liberty Further Extended': A 1776 Antislavery Manuscript by Lemuel Haynes," *The William and Mary Quarterly* 3/40, no. 1 (January 1, 1983): 94–96, 104. See also Kidd, *God of Liberty*, 148.

33. Jonathan Edwards [Jr.], *The Injustice and Impolicy of the Slave Trade, and of the Slavery of the Africans: Illustrated in a Sermon . . . in New-Haven, Sept. 15, 1791* (Boston: Wells & Lilly, 1822), 4 (punctuation adjusted in the quote).

34. Gordon S. Wood, *Empire of Liberty: A History of the Early Republic, 1789–1815*, Oxford History of the United States, book 4, Kindle ed. (Oxford: Oxford University Press, 2009), chap. 14, "Between Slavery and Freedom."

Chapter 7. The New Nation

1. As Gordon Wood notes, "By 1815 America had become the most evangelically Christian nation in the world." Gordon S. Wood, *Empire of Liberty: A History of the Early Republic, 1789–1815*, The Oxford History of the United States (Oxford: Oxford University Press, 2009), 3.
2. Wood, *Empire of Liberty*, 10–11.
3. Madison, as quoted in Wood, *Empire of Liberty*, 9.
4. Thomas S. Kidd, *God of Liberty: A Religious History of the American Revolution* (Philadelphia: Basic Books, 2010), 216–18.
5. Kidd, *God of Liberty*, 218.
6. Thomas Paine, *The Writings of Thomas Paine, Collected and Edited by Moncure Daniel Conway* (New York: G. P. Putnam's Sons, 1894), vol. 1, https://oll.libertyfund.org/pages/1776-paine-common-sense-pamphlet.
7. Kidd, *God of Liberty*, 218.
8. For Franklin quotes in this, the next, and preceding paragraphs, see Benjamin Franklin, "From Benjamin Franklin: Convention Speech Proposing Prayers (unpublished), June 28, 1787," in *The Papers of Benjamin Franklin*, digital ed. (New Haven: Yale University Press, 2020), https://franklinpapers.org.
9. Franklin, "From Benjamin Franklin: Convention Speech."
10. Kidd, *God of Liberty*, 212.
11. Constitution of the United States, article VI, National Archives, www.archives.gov/founding-docs/constitution-transcript.
12. Wood, *Empire of Liberty*, 7–8.
13. As quoted in Wood, *Empire of Liberty*, 20.
14. George Washington, "Washington's Farewell Address 1796," The Avalon Project, Lillian Goldman Law Library, Yale Law School, https://avalon.law.yale.edu/18th_century/washing.asp.
15. Washington, "Washington's Farewell Address."
16. Kidd, *God of Liberty*, 167, 183; "Transcript For: A Bill Establishing A Provision For Teachers Of The Christian Religion," Monticello Digital Classroom, https://classroom.monticello.org/view/72279/.
17. "Memorial and Remonstrance Against Religious Assessments," National Archives, https://founders.archives.gov/documents/Madison/01-08-02-0163.
18. "Memorial and Remonstrance."
19. "Virginia Statute for Religious Freedom," in *The Thomas Jefferson Encyclopedia*, www.monticello.org/site/research-and-collections/virginia-statute-religious-freedom.
20. "82. A Bill for Establishing Religious Freedom, 18 June 1779," National Archives, https://founders.archives.gov/documents/Jefferson/01-02-02-0132-0004-0082.
21. "82. A Bill for Establishing Religious Freedom."
22. See Isaac Backus, *An Appeal to the Public for Religious Liberty against the Oppressions of the Present Day* (Boston: John Boyle, 1773).
23. Nathan O. Hatch, *The Democratization of American Christianity* (New Haven: Yale University Press, 1989), 95–96; "To James Madison from Joseph Spencer, 28 February 1788," *Founders Online*, National Archives, https://founders.archives.gov/documents/Madison/01-10-02-0310.
24. "To James Madison from John Leland, [ca. 15 February] 1789," *Founders Online*, National Archives, https://founders.archives.gov/documents/Madison/01-11-02-0322. Original source: *The Papers of James Madison*, vol. 11, *7 March 1788–1 March 1789*, ed. Robert A. Rutland and Charles F. Hobson (Charlottesville: University of Virginia Press, 1977), 442–43; Lyman H. Butterfield, "Elder John Leland, Jeffersonian Itinerant," *Proceedings of the American Antiquarian Society* 62 (1953): 190–91.
25. John Leland and L. F. Greene, *The Writings of the Late Elder John Leland: Including Some Events in His Life* (New York: Printed by G. W. Wood, 1845), 181.

26. Kidd, *God of Liberty*, 168–70.
27. See Robert Mitchell, "An Edible Token of Esteem: The 1,325–Pound Cheese Given to Thomas Jefferson," *The Washington Post*, July 14, 2019.
28. Quotations in Hatch, *Democratization of American Christianity*, 96. Some of this discussion of Leland draws on Hatch, *Democratization of American Christianity*, 93–101.
29. Leland and Greene, *Writings of the Late Elder*, 373.
30. Leland and Greene, *Writings of the Late Elder*, 193–94.
31. Leland and Greene, *Writings of the Late Elder*, 185.
32. Phoebe Palmer, "Witness of the Spirit," *Guide to Holiness* 47 (June 1865): 137, as quoted in Mark A. Noll, *The Civil War as a Theological Crisis* (Chapel Hill: University of North Carolina Press, 2006), 20.
33. Leland and Greene, *Writings of the Late Elder*, 193–94.
34. Leland and Greene, *Writings of the Late Elder*, 571.
35. Quotes and commentary in Jill Lepore, *The Story of America: Essays on Origins*, Kindle ed. (Princeton: Princeton University Press, 2012), 62.
36. Lepore, *Story of America*, 65.
37. Lepore, *Story of America*, 65.
38. Thomas Paine, *The Age of Reason: In Two Parts* (New York: G. N. Devries, 1827), 5–6.
39. Paine, *Age of Reason*, 6–7.
40. Paine, *Age of Reason*, 7–8, 11, 18, 170, 174.
41. Lepore, *Story of America*, 68–69.
42. Amanda Porterfield, *Conceived in Doubt: Religion and Politics in the New American Nation* (Chicago: University of Chicago Press, 2012), Kindle ed., chap. 1; Lepore, *Story of America*, 66.
43. See Robert Bellah, "Civil Religion in America," *Daedalus* 96, no. 1 (1967): 1–21.
44. Wood, *Empire of Liberty*, 50–52.

Chapter 8. New Revivals and New Faiths

1. For an analysis of this theme, see Gordon S. Wood, *Empire of Liberty: A History of the Early Republic, 1789–1815*, The Oxford History of the United States (Oxford: Oxford University Press, 2009), 1–4, "Rip Van Winkle's America."
2. Washington Irving, *The Sketch-Book of Geoffrey Crayon, Gent* (Philadelphia: Carey & Lea, 1835), 1:46.
3. Irving, *Sketch-Book*, 1:60–61, 63. Wood, *Empire of Liberty*, 1–4, "Rip Van Winkle's America."
4. Wood, *Empire of Liberty*, 315–16.
5. Wood, *Empire of Liberty*, 315–16.
6. Daniel Walker Howe, *What Hath God Wrought: The Transformation of America, 1815–1848*, The Oxford History of the United States (New York: Oxford University Press, 2007), Kindle ed., 33–34, 37, 40; James M. McPherson, *Battle Cry of Freedom: The Civil War Era*, The Oxford History of the United States (New York: Oxford University Press, 1988), 11.
7. Howe, *What Hath God Wrought*, 32.
8. Wood, *Empire of Liberty*, 320–21.
9. Bret E. Carroll, *The Routledge Historical Atlas of Religion in America*, Kindle ed. (New York: Routledge, 2000), 60.
10. Douglas A. Sweeney, "Evangelical Tradition in America," *Cambridge Companion to Jonathan Edwards*, ed. Stephen J. Stein (Cambridge: Cambridge University Press, 2007), 226; Harry S. Stout, Kenneth P. Minkema, and Adriaan C. Neele, eds., *The Jonathan Edwards Encyclopedia* (Grand Rapids: Wm. B. Eerdmans Publishing Co., 2017), 558.
11. Howe, *What Hath God Wrought*, 170–71.
12. Charles G. Finney, *Lectures on Revivals of Religion*, 6th ed. (New York: Leavitt, Lord & Co., 1835), 12.
13. Finney, *Lectures*, 257.
14. John Williamson Nevin, *The Anxious Bench* (Chambersburg, PA: Office of the Weekly Messenger, 1843), 3, 19, 29.

15. Howe, *What Hath God Wrought*, 172.
16. See Joseph Tracy, *The Great Awakening* (Boston: Charles Tappan, 1845), iii.
17. Wood, *Empire of Liberty*, 327; H. W. Brands, *Andrew Jackson: His Life and Times* (New York: Anchor Books, 2005), 135–37. The date was May 30, 1806: "Future president Andrew Jackson kills Charles Dickinson in a duel," *History Channel*, www.history.com/this-day-in-history/andrew-jackson-kills-charles-dickinson-in-duel.
18. Wood, *Empire of Liberty*, 327–28.
19. Wood, *Empire of Liberty*, 339–40.
20. Howe, *What Hath God Wrought*, 168; Carroll, *Routledge Historical Atlas*, 60.
21. Howe, *What Hath God Wrought*, 166.
22. Mark A. Noll, *America's God: From Jonathan Edwards to Abraham Lincoln* (Oxford : Oxford University Press, 2002), 427. See also Howe, *What Hath God Wrought*, 168.
23. Howe, *What Hath God Wrought*, 164–65.
24. Lyman Beecher, *A Plea for the West* (Cincinnati: Truman & Smith, 1835), 142; Edward Beecher, *The Papal Conspiracy Exposed and Protestantism Defended in the Light of Reason, History, and Scripture* (Boston: Stearns, 1855). See Susan M. Griffin, *Anti-Catholicism and Nineteenth-Century Fiction* (Cambridge: Cambridge University Press, 2004), 224 n. 20.
25. Peter Cartwright, *Autobiography of Peter Cartwright, the Backwoods Preacher*, ed. W. P. Strickland (New York: Carlton & Porter, 1857), 243.
26. Cartwright, *Autobiography*, 79–80; E. Brooks Holifield, *Theology in America: Christian Thought from the Age of the Puritans to the Civil War* (New Haven: Yale University Press, 2003), 256; Howe, *What Hath God Wrought*, 176.
27. Howe, *What Hath God Wrought*, 176–77.
28. Howe, *What Hath God Wrought*, 176; John Wigger, "Francis Asbury and American Methodism," in *The Oxford Handbook of Methodist Studies*, ed. James E. Kirby and William J. Abraham (New York: Oxford University Press, 2011), 53–62; Carroll, *Routledge Historical Atlas*, 64.
29. Estimates on Baptist membership vary. This 600,000 number is from Carroll, *Routledge Historical Atlas*, 65.
30. James P. Byrd, "Baptist Tradition and Heritage," in *ERA* 1:254–68.
31. See James Robinson Graves, *Old Landmarkism: What Is It?* (Memphis, TN: Baptist Book House, 1880).
32. James Robinson Graves, *Great Iron Wheel: or, Republicanism Backwards and Christianity Reversed* (Nashville: Graves & Marks, 1855), Dedication page, table of contents, 160, 169; Noll, *America's God*, 244–46.
33. William Gannaway Brownlow, *The Great Iron Wheel Examined: Or, Its False Spokes Extracted, and an Exhibition of Elder Graves, Its Builder* (Nashville: For the author, 1856), 108.
34. Theodore Dwight Bozeman, *To Live Ancient Lives: The Primitivist Dimension in Puritanism* (Chapel Hill: University of North Carolina Press, 1988).
35. Carroll, *Routledge Historical Atlas*, 69–72.
36. Monica Reed, "African Traditional Religions," *ERA* 1:52–58.
37. Reed, "African Traditional Religions," *ERA* 1:52–58.
38. Reed, "African Traditional Religions," *ERA* 1:52–58.
39. Albert J. Raboteau, *Slave Religion: The "Invisible Institution" in the Antebellum South* (New York: Oxford University Press, 1978), 132–33.
40. Raboteau, *Slave Religion*, 133.
41. Reed, "African Traditional Religions," *ERA* 1:57–58.
42. Raboteau, *Slave Religion*, 139–40.
43. Raboteau, *Slave Religion*, 140–43.
44. William B. Gravely, "African American Methodism," in *The Oxford Handbook of Methodist Studies*, ed. William J. Abraham and James E. Kirby (Oxford: Oxford University Press, 2009), 123.
45. Richard Allen, *The Life, Experience, and Gospel Labours of the Rt. Rev. Richard Allen* (Philadelphia: Martin & Boden, 1833), 6.
46. Allen, *Life, Experience*, 17.

47. Allen, *Life, Experience*, 10–11; Dennis C. Dickerson, "Richard Allen: A Quintessential Wesleyan," *Evangelical Journal* 18 (2000): 56–57.
48. Allen, *Life, Experience*, 13.
49. Allen, *Life, Experience*, 16.
50. Dickerson, "Richard Allen," 59.
51. Dickerson, "Richard Allen," 59–60.
52. Catherine A. Brekus counts "more than twenty female evangelists whose stories were told in print during the first decades of the nineteenth century." Brekus, *Strangers and Pilgrims: Female Preaching in America, 1740–1845* (Chapel Hill: University of North Carolina Press, 1998), 167.
53. Brekus, *Strangers and Pilgrims*, 168.
54. Brekus, *Strangers and Pilgrims*, 172.
55. Jarena Lee, *Religious Experience and Journal of Mrs. Jarena Lee, Giving An Account of Her Call to Preach the Gospel* (Philadelphia: Published for the Author, 1849), 4–5.
56. Brekus, *Strangers and Pilgrims*, 119–20.
57. Brekus, *Strangers and Pilgrims*, 138.
58. Wood, *Empire of Liberty*, Kindle ed., chap. 13, "Republican Reforms"; Brekus, *Strangers and Pilgrims*, 146–47; Ruth H. Bloch, "The Gendered Meanings of Virtue in Revolutionary America," *Signs: Journal of Women in Culture and Society* 13, no. 1 (1987): 37–58.
59. Brekus, *Strangers and Pilgrims*, 120, 144.
60. Brekus, *Strangers and Pilgrims*, 125–26.
61. Jeremy Rapport, "New Religious Movements: Nineteenth Century," *ERA* 3:1576–77.
62. See Whitney R. Cross, *The Burned-Over District: The Social and Intellectual History of Enthusiastic Religion in Western New York, 1800–1850* (Ithaca, NY: Cornell University Press, 1950).
63. Paul Gutjahr, *The Book of Mormon: A Biography*, Lives of Great Religious Books (Princeton: Princeton University Press, 2012), Kindle ed., "Prologue"; Howe, *What Hath God Wrought*, 317.
64. Book of Mormon, 3 Nephi 11–14, www.churchofjesuschrist.org/study/scriptures/bofm/3-ne/11?lang=eng. See also 3 Nephi 12–15; Gutjahr, *Book of Mormon*, "Prologue."
65. Howe, *What Hath God Wrought*, 314.
66. Howe, *What Hath God Wrought*, 30, 313.
67. Alexander Campbell, *Delusions: An Analysis of the Book of Mormon* (Boston: Benjamin H. Green, 1832), 11–13.
68. Howe, *What Hath God Wrought*, 314–16.
69. Doctrine and Covenants, 132:52–54, www.churchofjesuschrist.org/study/scriptures/dc-testament/dc/132.52?lang=eng&clang=eng#p52. See also Terryl L. Givens and Reid L. Neilson, eds., *The Columbia Sourcebook of Mormons in the United States* (New York: Columbia University Press, 2014), 279–87.
70. Kathleen Flake, "Latter-day Saints," in *ERA* 3:1216.
71. Jeremy Rapport, "New Religious Movements: Nineteenth Century," *ERA* 3:1577.
72. Rapport, "New Religious Movements," *ERA* 3:1577.
73. See John Humphrey Noyes, *Male Continence* (Oneida, NY: Oneida Office, 1872), 6; Rapport, "New Religious Movements," *ERA* 3:1577–78.
74. Noyes, *Male Continence*, 17.
75. Rapport, "New Religious Movements," *ERA* 3:1577–78.
76. Rapport, "New Religious Movements," *ERA* 3:1579–80. Howard Markel, "The Secret Ingredient in Kellogg's Corn Flakes Is Seventh-Day Adventism: America's favorite processed breakfast was once the pinnacle of healthfulness—and spiritual purity," *Smithsonian Magazine*, July 28, 2017, www.smithsonianmag.com/history/secret-ingredient-kelloggs-corn-flakes-seventh-day-adventism-180964247/.

Chapter 9. Slavery and the Civil War

1. Abraham Lincoln, "Second Inaugural Address," The Avalon Project, Lillian Goldman Law Library, Yale Law School, https://avalon.law.yale.edu/19th_century/lincoln2.asp (emphasis added). Some information from this chapter is published in a different form in James P. Byrd, *A Holy Baptism of Fire and Blood: The Bible and the American Civil War* (New York: Oxford University Press, 2021).

2. The Constitution of the United States: A Transcription, www.archives.gov/founding-docs/constitution
-transcript; Gordon S. Wood, *Empire of Liberty: A History of the Early Republic, 1789–1815*, The Oxford History of the United States (Oxford: Oxford University Press, 2009), 523–24.

3. This scene is well described in Joseph J. Ellis, *Founding Brothers: The Revolutionary Generation* (New York: Random House, 2000), 81–82.

4. "Benjamin Franklin's Anti-Slavery Petitions to Congress," National Archives, www.archives.gov/legislative
/features/franklin; "Memorial of the Pennsylvania Abolition Society, 3 February 1790," https://www2.gwu
.edu/~ffcp/exhibit/p11/p11_5text.html.

5. Ellis, *Founding Brothers*, 82–83.

6. Ellis, *Founding Brothers*, 84–88.

7. Benjamin Franklin, *The Works of Benjamin Franklin*, ed. Jared Sparks (Boston: Hilliard, Gray, & Co., 1836), 2:517–21; Ellis, *Founding Brothers*, 111.

8. Ellis, *Founding Brothers*, 114.

9. Wood, *Empire of Liberty*, 528, 530–32.

10. Heather Andrea Williams, *American Slavery: A Very Short Introduction* (New York: Oxford University Press, 2014), 55.

11. David Walker, *Walker's Appeal, in Four Articles* (Boston: David Walker, 1830), 42–43.

12. Walker, *Walker's Appeal*, 20, 47, 66.

13. Walker, *Walker's Appeal*, 82.

14. Maria W. Stewart, *Meditations from the Pen of Mrs. Maria W. Stewart* (Washington, DC: n.p., 1879), 4. On Walker and Stewart, see Byrd, *Holy Baptism of Fire*, 21–25.

15. Daniel Walker Howe, *What Hath God Wrought: The Transformation of America, 1815–1848*, The Oxford History of the United States (New York: Oxford University Press, 2007), Kindle ed., 323–24.

16. Patrick H. Breen, *The Land Shall Be Deluged in Blood: A New History of the Nat Turner Revolt* (New York: Oxford University Press, 2015), 21.

17. Nat Turner and Thomas R. Gray, *The Confessions of Nat Turner* (Baltimore: Lucas & Dearer, 1831), 10–11, electronic ed. in *Documenting the American South*, University of North Carolina, Chapel Hill, https://docsouth
.unc.edu/neh/turner/turner.html.

18. Howe, *What Hath God Wrought*, 324–25; Turner and Gray, *Confessions*, 11; Byrd, *Holy Baptism of Fire*, 25–26.

19. C. C. Goen, *Broken Churches, Broken Nation: Denominational Schisms and the Coming of the American Civil War* (Macon, GA: Mercer University Press, 1985).

20. Richard Fuller and Francis Wayland, *Domestic Slavery Considered as a Scriptural Institution* (New York: L. Colby, 1845), 3–4; Byrd, *Holy Baptism of Fire*, 27–28.

21. Fuller and Wayland, *Domestic Slavery*, 76–77, 90.

22. Fuller and Wayland, *Domestic Slavery*, 29–30.

23. Fuller and Wayland, *Domestic Slavery*, 99–100.

24. Fuller and Wayland, *Domestic Slavery*, 4–5.

25. Fuller and Wayland, *Domestic Slavery*, 7–9.

26. Fuller and Wayland, *Domestic Slavery*, 23.

27. See Mark Noll, *The Civil War as a Theological Crisis* (Chapel Hill: University of North Carolina Press, 2006), chap. 3, "The Crisis over the Bible." On Fuller and Wayland, see pp. 36–38. Henceforth abbreviated as *CWTC*.

28. E. Brooks Holifield, *Theology in America: Christian Thought from the Age of the Puritans to the Civil War* (New Haven: Yale University Press, 2003), 494–95.

29. Louis P. Masur, *The Civil War: A Concise History* (Oxford: Oxford University Press, 2011), 10.

30. Andrew Delbanco, *The War before the War: Fugitive Slaves and the Struggle for America's Soul from the Revolution to the Civil War* (New York: Penguin Press, 2018), 5–6.

31. James M. McPherson, *Battle Cry of Freedom: The Civil War Era* (New York: Oxford University Press, 1988), 38. Henceforth abbreviated as *BCF*.

32. Douglass as quoted in David S. Reynolds, *Mightier Than the Sword: Uncle Tom's Cabin and the Battle for America* (New York: W. W. Norton, 2012), Kindle ed., 129.

33. David W. Blight, *Frederick Douglass: Prophet of Freedom* (New York: Simon & Schuster, 2018), xiv.
34. Frederick Douglass, *Narrative of the Life of Frederick Douglass* (Boston: Anti-Slavery Office, 1845), 118–19.
35. Abraham Lincoln, *The Collected Works of Abraham Lincoln*, ed. Roy P. Basler, 9 vols. (New Brunswick, NJ: Rutgers University Press, 1953), 4:147, https://quod.lib.umich.edu/l/lincoln/; McPherson, *BCF*, 179–80.
36. "Seeking Abraham: A Report of Furman University's Task Force on Slavery and Justice," 2nd ed., pp. 28 and 30, www.furman.edu/about/wp-content/uploads/sites/2/2019/10/Seeking-Abraham-UpdateAug2019 -Final.pdf.
37. Furman et. al., "Letter," 5; McPherson, *BCF*, 243.
38. Noll, *CWTC*, 14.
39. George C. Rable, *God's Almost Chosen Peoples: A Religious History of the American Civil War* (Chapel Hill: University of North Carolina Press, 2010), 18–19.
40. Rable, *Almost Chosen*, 1.
41. Nicholas Guyatt, *Providence and the Invention of the United States, 1607–1876* (New York: Cambridge University Press, 2007), 1–2, 6
42. McPherson, *BCF*, 544; Byrd, *Holy Baptism of Fire*, 160–62.
43. Abraham Lincoln, "Preliminary Emancipation Proclamation," *American Originals: National Archives and Records Administration*, www.archives.gov/exhibits/american_originals_iv/sections/preliminary_emancipation _proclamation.html#.
44. McPherson, *BCF*, 558.
45. McPherson, *BCF*, 502–4; Lincoln quotations on 503–4.
46. Frederick Douglass and John W. Blassingame, *The Frederick Douglass Papers: Series One, Speeches, Debates, and Interviews* (New Haven: Yale University Press, 1979–92), 3:549–551.
47. "Black Soldiers," in William L. Barney, *The Oxford Encyclopedia of the Civil War* (New York: Oxford University Press, 2011), 30.
48. P. K. Rose, "The Civil War: Black American Contributions to Union Intelligence," in *Black Dispatches: Black American Contributions to Union Intelligence During the Civil War*, Center for the Study of Intelligence, cia.gov, www.cia.gov/static/6f73b7277dc7315abd223891b8fa585d/Black-Dispatches.pdf; see also History Central, www.historycentral.com/CivilWar/intelliegence.html; see also James M. McPherson, *This Mighty Scourge: Perspectives on the Civil War* (Oxford: Oxford University Press, 2007), Kindle ed., 28; Byrd, *Holy Baptism of Fire*, 210.
49. Gabor Boritt, *The Gettysburg Gospel: The Lincoln Speech That Nobody Knows* (New York: Simon & Schuster, 2008), 99–100.
50. Abraham Lincoln, "Gettysburg Address," The Avalon Project, Lillian Goldman Law Library, Yale Law School, https://avalon.law.yale.edu/19th_century/gettyb.asp.
51. See: Robert Alter, *Pen of Iron: American Prose and the King James Bible* (Princeton: Princeton University Press, 2010), 13–14; Allen C. Guelzo, *Fateful Lightning: A New History of the Civil War and Reconstruction*, 1st ed. (Oxford: Oxford University Press, 2012), 407–8; Boritt, *Gettysburg Gospel*, 120–22; Byrd, *Holy Baptism of Fire*, chap. 13.
52. Mark A. Noll, *America's God: From Jonathan Edwards to Abraham Lincoln* (Oxford: Oxford University Press, 2002), 426–38; Douglass as quoted by Ronald C. White Jr., "Lincoln's Sermon on the Mount," in *Religion and the American Civil War*, ed. Randall M. Miller, Harry S. Stout, and Charles Reagan Wilson (New York: Oxford University Press, 1998), 223.
53. Lincoln, "Second Inaugural."
54. Lincoln, "Second Inaugural."
55. Lincoln, "Second Inaugural."
56. Noll, *America's God*, 431–34.
57. Jill Lepore, *The Story of America: Essays on Origins*, Kindle ed. (Princeton: Princeton University Press, 2012), 304.

58. Lincoln, *Works*, 8:356. See also John Burt, "Collective Guilt in Lincoln's Second Inaugural Address," *American Political Thought* 4 (Summer 2015): 467–68; Byrd, *Holy Baptism of Fire*, chap. 15.

59. See the outstanding book by David B. Chesebrough, *No Sorrow Like Our Sorrow: Northern Protestant Ministers and the Assassination of Lincoln* (Kent, OH: Kent State University Press, 1994). On the Bible and the assassination, see Byrd, *Holy Baptism of Fire*, chap. 16.

60. Harry S. Stout, *Upon the Altar of the Nation: A Moral History of the American Civil War* (New York: Viking, 2006), 459.

61. Jill Lepore, *The Name of War: King Philip's War and the Origins of American Identity*, 1st ed. (New York: Vintage Books, 1999), x; John Adger, "Northern and Southern Views of the Province of the Church," *Southern Presbyterian Review* 16 (March 1866): 390, 392–93.

Chapter 10. The Second American Revolution

1. "Full Text, preliminary and final, of the Emancipation Proclamation, issued by President Abraham Lincoln in 1863: Final Version," January 1, 1863, www.historynet.com/emancipation-proclamation-text.

2. Source: Table Bc793-797—Illiteracy rate, by race and nativity: 1870–1979 U.S. Department of Commerce, Bureau of the Census, *Historical Statistics of the United States, Colonial Times to 1970; and Current Population Reports*, Series P-23, Ancestry and Language in the United States: November 1979.

3. Paul Harvey, *Freedom's Coming: Religious Culture and the Shaping of the South from the Civil War through the Civil Rights Era* (Chapel Hill: University of North Carolina Press, 2005), 5.

4. William E. Montgomery, *Under Their Own Vine and Fig Tree: The African-American Church in the South, 1865–1900* (Baton Rouge: Louisiana State University Press, 1993), 343.

5. James T. Campbell, *Songs of Zion: The African Methodist Episcopal Church in the United States and South Africa* (New York: Oxford University Press, 1995), 53–54.

6. *The American Annual Cyclopædia and Register of Important Events of the Year* (New York: D. Appleton & Co., 1866, 1876).

7. Campbell, *Songs of Zion*, 54.

8. John C. Lester and D. L. Wilson, *Ku Klux Klan: Its Origin, Growth and Disbandment* (Nashville: Wheeler, Osborn & Duckworth Manufacturing Co., 1884).

9. Leslie M. Harris, *In the Shadow of Slavery: African Americans in New York City, 1626–1863* (Chicago: University of Chicago Press, 2003), 279–88.

10. Rena Mazyck Andrews, *Archbishop John Hughes and the Civil War*, PhD diss. (Chicago: University of Chicago Library, 1935), 4.

11. John Loughery, *Dagger John: Archbishop John Hughes and the Making of Irish America* (Ithaca, NY: Three Hills, Cornell University Press, 2018), 41–55.

12. William J. Stern, "How Dagger John Saved New York's Irish," *City Journal*, Spring 1997, www.city-journal.org/html/how-dagger-john-saved-new-york%E2%80%99s-irish-11934.html.

13. Walter G. Sharrow, "John Hughes and a Catholic Response to Slavery in Antebellum America," *The Journal of Negro History* 57, no. 3 (July 1972): 254–69.

14. Thomas T. McAvoy, *The Americanist Heresy in Roman Catholicism, 1895–1900* (Notre Dame, IN: University of Notre Dame Press, 1963); Gerald P. Fogarty, *The Vatican and the Americanist Crisis: Denis J. O'Connell, American Agent in Rome, 1885–1903*, Miscellanea historiae Pontificiae edita a facultate historiae ecclesiasticae in Pontificia Universitate gregoriana 36 (Rome: Università gregoriana, 1974).

15. William D. Jones, *Wales in America: Scranton and the Welsh, 1860–1920* (Scranton, PA: University of Scranton Press, 1993), xvi.

16. Thomas P. Christiansen, "Danish Settlement in Minnesota," *Minnesota History* 8 (December 1927): 363–85, here 367.

17. Sarah Richardson, "Interview with J. David Hacker: An Awful Tally Goes Higher," HistoryNet, July 31, 2017, www.historynet.com/interview-j-david-hacker-awful-tally-goes-higher.htm; from the *Civil War Times*, August 2012.

18. J. David Hacker, "A Census-Based Count of the Civil War Dead," *Civil War History* 57, no. 4 (December 2011): 307–48.

19. Jenny Goellnitz, compiler, "Statistics on the Civil War and Medicine," EHISTORY, https://ehistory.osu .edu/exhibitions/cwsurgeon/cwsurgeon/statistics; Jenny Goellnitz, compiler, "Civil War Battlefield Surgery," EHISTORY, https://ehistory.osu.edu/exhibitions/cwsurgeon/cwsurgeon/amputations.

20. Drew Gilpin Faust, *This Republic of Suffering: Death and the American Civil War*, 1st ed. (New York: Alfred A. Knopf, 2008).

21. Ann Braude, *Radical Spirits: Spiritualism and Women's Rights in Nineteenth-Century America* (Boston: Beacon Press, 1989), 24.

22. David K. Nartonis, "The Rise of 19th-Century American Spiritualism, 1854–1873," *Journal for the Scientific Study of Religion* 49, no. 2 (2010): 361–73.

23. Mary Baker Eddy, *Science and Health, with Key to the Scriptures* (Boston: A. V. Stewart, 1912), 304.

Chapter 11. The New Science and the Old-Time Religion

1. A. F. R. Wollaston, *Life of Alfred Newton: Professor of Comparative Anatomy, Cambridge University, 1866–1907, with a Preface by Sir Archibald Geikie, O.M.* (New York: Dutton, 1921), 118–20.

2. Henry Adams, *The Education of Henry Adams* (Boston: Houghton, Mifflin, 1918), 225.

3. Charles Hodge, *What Is Darwinism?* (New York: Scribner, Armstrong & Co., 1874), 48.

4. Bradley J. Gundlach, "McCosh and Hodge on Evolution: A Combined Legacy," *The Journal of Presbyterian History* 75, no. 2 (June 1997): 85–102.

5. James Miller, "Beyond Non-Contradiction: Lessons from the Case of James Woodrow," *The Presbyterian Outlook*, November 16, 2009, https://pres-outlook.org/2009/11/beyond-non-contradiction-lessons-from -the-case-of-james-woodrow/.

6. James Woodrow, *Evolution: An Address Delivered May 7th, 1884, Before the Alumni Association of the Columbia Theological Seminary* (Columbia, SC: Printed at the Presbyterian Publishing House, 1884), 9–11.

7. Woodrow, *Evolution*, 9–11.

8. Woodrow, *Evolution*, 12.

9. Miller, "Beyond Non-Contradiction."

10. Henry Ward Beecher, *Evolution and Religion* (New York: Fords, Howard & Hulbert, 1886), 1.

11. *Christian Union* 26 (September 21, 1882): 230–31.

12. Lyman Abbott, *Reminiscences* (Boston: Houghton, Mifflin, 1915), 4.

13. Lyman Abbott, *The Theology of an Evolutionist* (Boston: Houghton, Mifflin, 1897), 176.

14. Mark Twain, *The Innocents Abroad* (Hartford, CT: American Publishing Co., 1869), 567.

15. B. B. Warfield, "Inspiration," *The Presbyterian Review*, no. 6 (April 1881): 237.

16. Charles Augustus Briggs, "A Plea for the Higher Study of Theology," *The American Journal of Theology* 8, no. 3 (July 1904): 433–51.

17. Briggs, "Plea for the Higher Study."

18. Briggs, "Plea for the Higher Study."

19. Martyn McGeown, "The Life and Theology of D. L. Moody (with Particular Emphasis on His British Campaigns)," Covenant Protestant Reformed Church, https://cprc.co.uk/articles/moody.

20. Phoebe Palmer, "Witness of the Spirit," *Guide to Holiness* 47 (June 1865), 137.

Chapter 12. Mass Immigration and the Closing Western Frontier

1. Josiah Strong, *Our Country: Its Possible Future and Its Present Crisis* (New York: Baker & Taylor Co., 1885), 174–75.

2. Reform Judaism, "The Pittsburgh Platform," November 1885, www.jewishvirtuallibrary.org/the-pittsburgh -platform.

3. Lloyd P. Gartner, *History of the Jews in Modern Times* (Oxford: Oxford University Press, 2010), 163–90.

4. Mary Antin, *The Promised Land* (Boston: Houghton Mifflin, 1912), 29–30.

5. Antin, *Promised Land*, 249–50.

6. Antin, *Promised Land*, 250.
7. Jonathan D. Sarna, *American Judaism: A History* (New Haven: Yale University Press, 2004), 174.
8. Sarna, *American Judaism*, 176.
9. Cyrus Adler, *Jacob Henry Schiff: A Biographical Sketch* (Philadelphia: American Jewish Committee, 1921).
10. "The Stranger at Our Gate," *The Ram's Horn* [Social Gospel magazine] (Chicago), April 25, 1896.
11. Takao Ozawa v. United States: 260 U.S. 178 (1922), www.law.cornell.edu/supremecourt/text/260/178.
12. Richard Hughes Seager, *The World's Parliament of Religions: The East/West Encounter, Chicago, 1893*, Religion in North America (Bloomington: Indiana University Press, 1995).
13. Julian Miranda, in S. J. Lagumina, *The Immigrants Speak* (New York: Center for Migration Studies, 1979), 131–32 (with adjusted punctuation).
14. Avtokefal′naia Amerikanskaia pravoslavnaia tserkov′, *Orthodox America, 1794–1976: Development of the Orthodox Church in America*, ed. Constance J. Tarasar (Syosset, NY: Orthodox Church in America, Department of History and Archives, 1975), 66–67.
15. Matthew Namee, "Historical Census Data for Orthodoxy in America," *Orthodox History* (blog), October 11, 2010, https://orthodoxhistory.org/2010/10/11/historical-census-data-for-orthodoxy-in-america/.
16. In-mut-too-yah-lat-lat, "Speech at Lincoln Hall in Washington, D.C., 1879," in *North American Review* 128, no. 269 (April 1879): 412–34, www.jstor.org/stable/i25100738.
17. David Treuer, *The Heartbeat of Wounded Knee: Native America from 1890 to the Present* (New York: Riverhead Books, 2019), 133.
18. Louis S. Warren, *God's Red Son: The Ghost Dance Religion and the Making of Modern America* (New York: Basic Books, 2017), 55–56.
19. Treuer, *The Heartbeat of Wounded Knee*, 4.
20. Lt. Col. Guy Carlton, as quoted in Warren, *God's Red Son*, 275 (punctuation adjusted).
21. Frederick Jackson Turner, *The Frontier in American History* (New York: Dover Publications, 1996).

Chapter 13. A Social Gospel and Black Religious Life in the Nadir

1. "Mrs. Stuyvesant Fish—Vintage Powder Room," https://vintagepowderroom.com/?tag=mrs-stuyvesant-fish.
2. Eric Foner, John A. Garraty, and Society of American Historians, eds., *The Reader's Companion to American History* (Boston: Houghton-Mifflin, 1991).
3. Paul Avrich, *The Haymarket Tragedy* (Princeton: Princeton University Press, 1984).
4. George Hodges, *Henry Codman Potter, Seventh Bishop of New York* (New York: Macmillan, 1915), 92.
5. James Sheerin, *Henry Codman Potter, an American Metropolitan* (New York: Fleming H. H. Revell Co., 1933), 122–23.
6. Andrew Cameron, editorial, "Liberal Christianity," *Workingman's Advocate* 4, no. 17 (November 16, 1867): 2.
7. Henry George, *Social Problems* (London: Kegan Paul, Trench & Co., 1884), 9.
8. Richard Theodore Ely, *Social Aspects of Christianity: And Other Essays* (New York: T. Y. Crowell, 1889), 6–7.
9. W. T. (William Thomas) Stead, *If Christ Came to Chicago! A Plea for the Union of All Who Love in the Service of All Who Suffer* (London : Review of Reviews, 1894), http://archive.org/details/ifchristcametoc02steagoog.
10. Jacob A. Riis et al., *How the Other Half Lives: Studies among the Tenements of New York*, 2nd ed. (New York: Charles Scribner's Sons, 1890).
11. "The Project Gutenberg E-Text of *In His Steps*, by Charles M. Sheldon," www.gutenberg.org/files/4540/4540-h/4540-h.htm.
12. Robert T. Handy, *The Social Gospel in America, 1870–1920* (New York: Oxford University Press, 1966), 113.
13. Washington Gladden, "Mr. Rockefeller and the American Board," *Outlook* 79 (April 22, 1905): 988.
14. Russell Herman Conwell, *Acres of Diamonds: A Lecture* (Philadelphia: J. D. Morris & Co., 1901), http://archive.org/details/acresofdiamondsl00conw.
15. Martin Luther King Jr., *The Autobiography of Martin Luther King, Jr.*, ed. Clayborne Carson (New York: Intellectual Properties Management with Warner Books, 1998), chap. 3, "Crozer Seminary," http://mlk-kpp01.stanford.edu/kingweb/publications/autobiography/chp_3.htm.
16. Walter Rauschenbusch, *A Theology for the Social Gospel* (New York: Macmillan, 1919), 258.
17. Plessy v. Ferguson, 163 U.S. 537 (1896), https://supreme.justia.com/cases/federal/us/163/537/.

18. Ronald H. Bayor, *The Columbia Documentary History of Race and Ethnicity in America* (New York: Columbia University Press, 2004), 358.

19. Philip Sheldon Foner and Robert J. Branham, eds., *Lift Every Voice: African American Oratory, 1787–1900* (Tuscaloosa: University of Alabama Press, 1998), 833.

20. "The Niagara Movement's Declaration of Principles," *Black History Bulletin* 68, no. 1 (March 2005): 21–23.

21. Alexander Crummell, "The Attitude of the American Mind toward the Negro Intellect [1898]," Black-Past (blog, reference center), January 29, 2007, www.blackpast.org/african-american-history/1898-alexander-crummell-attitude-american-mind-toward-negro-intellect/.

22. Crummell, "Attitude of the American Mind."

23. Judith Weisenfeld, *New World A-Coming: Black Religion and Racial Identity during the Great Migration* (New York: New York University Press, 2016).

Chapter 14. The Birth of the American Century and the Fundamentalist-Modernist Battles

1. Ron Chernow, *Titan: The Life of John D. Rockefeller, Sr.* (New York: Vintage Books, 2004), 188.

2. Harry Emerson Fosdick, *The Living of These Days: An Autobiography*, 1st ed. (New York: Harper, 1956), 35.

3. Editorial, "Worthy and Unworthy Motives," *Watchman*, April 21, 1898; "Remember the Maine" critiqued in the *Congregationalist*, April 28, 1898.

4. Charles Albertson and H. H. Proctor, as quoted in Matthew McCullough, *The Cross of War: Christian Nationalism and U.S. Expansion in the Spanish American War* (Madison: University of Wisconsin Press, 2014), 24–25.

5. Theodore Roosevelt, "The Strenuous Life" (speech), April 10, 1899.

6. George M. Marsden, *Fundamentalism and American Culture: The Shaping of Twentieth Century Evangelicalism, 1870–1925* (New York: Oxford University Press, 1980), 134.

7. Margaret Lamberts Bendroth, *Fundamentalism and Gender, 1875 to the Present* (New Haven: Yale University Press, 1993), 24.

8. Betty A. DeBerg, *Ungodly Women: Gender and the First Wave of American Fundamentalism* (Minneapolis: Fortress Press, 1990), 65.

9. Richard Davis Harding, "The German Army Marches through Brussels, 1914," EyeWitness to History, www.eyewitnesstohistory.com/brussels.htm (2004).

10. Ray Hamilton Abrams, *Preachers Present Arms* (Philadelphia: Round Table Press, 1933), 41.

11. Lyman Abbott, "To Love Is to Hate," *Outlook* 19 (May 15, 1918): 99.

12. N. D. Hillis, *The Blot on the Kaiser's Scutcheon* (New York: Fleming H. Revell Co., 1918), 56.

13. American Rhetoric: Online Speech Bank, John D. Rockefeller Jr., "United War Work Campaign," www.americanrhetoric.com/speeches/johndrockefellerwarwork.htm.

14. David Mislin, "One Nation, Three Faiths: World War I and the Shaping of 'Protestant-Catholic-Jewish' America," *Church History* 84, no. 4 (December 2015): 828–62, https://doi.org/10.1017/S0009640715000943.

15. Heather D. Curtis, *Holy Humanitarians: American Evangelicals and Global Aid* (Cambridge, MA: Harvard University Press, 2018).

16. Joe Loconte, *The End of Illusions: Religious Leaders Confront Hitler's Gathering Storm* (Lanham, MD: Rowman & Littlefield, 2004), 7.

17. As quoted in Marsden, *Fundamentalism and American Culture*, 147.

18. Marsden, *Fundamentalism and American Culture*, 149.

19. Harry Emerson Fosdick, "Shall the Fundamentalists Win?," sermon, May 21, 1922, http://baptiststudiesonline.com/wp-content/uploads/2007/01/shall-the-fundamentalists-win.pdf.

20. H. Richard Niebuhr, *The Kingdom of God in America* (New York: Harper & Row, 1937), 193.

Chapter 15. A World in Crisis and an American Religious High

1. Franklin Delano Roosevelt, "First Inaugural Address," March 4, 1933, *The Avalon Project*, Lillian Goldman Law Library, Yale Law School, https://avalon.law.yale.edu/20th_century/froos1.asp.

2. Richard Gid Powers, "American Catholics and Catholic Americans: The Rise and Fall of Catholic Anticommunism," *U.S. Catholic Historian* 22, no. 4 (Fall 2004): 22.

3. Albin Krebs, "Charles Coughlin, 30's 'Radio Priest,'" *New York Times*, October 28, 1979, 44.

4. National Religious Broadcasters, "Our History," http://nrb.org/about/history.

5. E. G. Homrighausen, "Calm after Storm: Twelfth in the Series How My Mind Has Changed in This Decade," *Christian Century* 56, no. 1 (April 12, 1939): 477–79.

6. Harry Emerson Fosdick, "Beyond Modernism: A Sermon," *Christian Century* 52 (1935): 1552.

7. Franklin D. Roosevelt, "The Four Freedoms," 1941 State of the Union Address (January 6, 1941), www.ourdocuments.gov/doc.php?flash=false&doc=70&page=transcript.

8. Roosevelt, "The Four Freedoms."

9. Winston Churchill, "The Sinews of Peace ('Iron Curtain Speech')," Westminster College, Fulton, Missouri, March 5, 1946, https://winstonchurchill.org/resources/speeches/1946-1963-elder-statesman/the-sinews-of-peace/.

10. Patrick Henry, "'And I Don't Care What It Is': The Tradition-History of a Civil Religion Proof-Text," *Journal of the American Academy of Religion* 49, no. 1 (1981): 4 (punctuation adjusted).

11. Joshua Loth Liebman, *Peace of Mind* (New York: Simon & Schuster, 1946), 54.

12. James Hudnut-Beumler, *Looking for God in the Suburbs: The Religion of the American Dream and Its Critics, 1945–1965* (New Brunswick, NJ: Rutgers University Press, 1994), 31–37.

13. Robert S. Ellwood, *The Fifties Spiritual Marketplace: American Religion in a Decade of Conflict* (New Brunswick, NJ: Rutgers University Press, 1997), 135.

14. Carl F. H. Henry, *The Uneasy Conscience of Modern Fundamentalism* (Grand Rapids: Wm. B. Eerdmans Publishing Co., 1947), xx, 2–3.

15. Grant Wacker, *America's Pastor: Billy Graham and the Shaping of a Nation* (Cambridge, MA: The Belknap Press of Harvard University Press, 2014), 125–28.

Chapter 16. A Catholic President, the Civil Rights Movement, and the Ferment of the 1960s

1. John F. Kennedy, "Address to the Greater Houston Ministerial Association," September 12, 1960, www.jfklibrary.org/learn/about-jfk/historic-speeches/address-to-the-greater-houston-ministerial-association.

2. "JFK's Houston Speech at 50: Three Views," The Catholic Thing, September 10, 2010, www.thecatholicthing.org/2010/09/10/jfks-houston-speech-at-50-three-views/.

3. Richard G. Hutcheson, *God in the White House: How Religion Has Changed the Modern Presidency* (New York: Macmillan, 1988), 53.

4. Christopher Wilson, "Lessons Worth Learning from the Moment Four Students Sat Down to Take a Stand," *Smithsonian Magazine*, www.smithsonianmag.com/smithsonian-institution/lessons-worth-learning-moment-greensboro-four-sat-down-lunch-counter-180974087/; "Student Nonviolent Coordinating Committee (SNCC): Biography," The Martin Luther King, Jr., Research and Education Institute, https://kinginstitute.stanford.edu/encyclopedia/student-nonviolent-coordinating-committee-sncc; Paul Harvey, *Through the Storm, through the Night: A History of African American Christianity* (Lanham, MD: Rowman & Littlefield Publishers, 2011), 114–15.

5. "Statement by Alabama Clergymen," April 12, 1963, https://ibs.cru.org/files/1614/7870/5988/ALABAMA_CLERGYMENS_LETTER_TO_DR._MARTIN_LUTHER_KING_JR..pdf.

6. Martin Luther King Jr., "Letter from a Birmingham Jail," The Martin Luther King, Jr. Research and Education Institute, https://kinginstitute.stanford.edu/king-papers/documents/letter-birmingham-jail.

7. "President Johnson's Special Message to the Congress: The American Promise," March 15, 1965, www.lbjlibrary.org/lyndon-baines-johnson/speeches-films/president-johnsons-special-message-to-the-congress-the-american-promise.

8. Nell Irvin Painter, *Creating Black Americans: African-American History and Its Meanings, 1619 to the Present* (New York: Oxford University Press, 2006), 281.

9. "Vietnam War Deaths, by Race, Ethnicity and Nat[iona]l Origin," www.americanwarlibrary.com/vietnam/vwc10.htm.

10. Mike Marqusee, *Redemption Song: Muhammad Ali and the Spirit of the Sixties* (New York: Verso, 2005), 214.

11. Edward K. Kaplan, *Abraham Joshua Heschel: Mind, Heart, Soul* (Lincoln: University of Nebraska Press, 2019), 295.

12. Martin Luther King Jr., "Beyond Vietnam: A Time to Break Silence," April 4, 1967, www.americanrhetoric .com/speeches/mlkatimetobreaksilence.htm.

13. Morgan C. Atkinson, producer of the documentary *The Many Storeys, and Last Days of Thomas Merton*, contributes: "Dalai Lama Reminisces about Meeting Kindred Spirit Thomas Merton," December 6, 2017, HuffPost, www.huffpost.com/entry/dalai-lama-reminisces-about-meeting-kindred-spirit-thomas-merton_b_8481898.

14. Charles H. Lippy and Peter W. Williams, eds., *Encyclopedia of Religion in America* (Washington, DC: CQ Press, 2010), 1086.

15. Gurinder Singh Mann, Paul David Numrich, and Raymond Brady Williams, *Buddhists, Hindus, and Sikhs in America: A Short History* (New York: Oxford University Press, 2008).

16. James H. Cone, *Black Theology and Black Power* (New York: Seabury Press, 1969), 151–52.

17. Gustavo Gutiérrez, *A Theology of Liberation: History, Politics, and Salvation* (Maryknoll, NY: Orbis Books, 1973).

18. PBS: American Experience, "The Pope Issues *Humanae Vitae*," www.pbs.org/wgbh/americanexperience /features/pill-pope-issues-humanae-vitae-human-life/.

19. Mary Daly, *Beyond God the Father: Toward a Philosophy of Women's Liberation* (Boston: Beacon Press, 1973).

Chapter 17. The Culture Wars, Pentecostalization, and American Religion after 9/11

1. Kevin Phillips, *The Emerging Republican Majority* (Garden City, NY: Anchor Books, 1970).

2. Dean M. Kelley, *Why Conservative Churches Are Growing: A Study in Sociology of Religion*, 1st ed. (New York: Harper & Row, 1972).

3. Dean R. Hoge, *Vanishing Boundaries: The Religion of Mainline Protestant Baby Boomers*, 1st ed. (Louisville, KY: Westminster John Knox Press, 1994); James David Hudnut-Beumler, ed., *The Future of Mainline Protestantism in America*, The Future of Religion in America (New York: Columbia University Press, 2018).

4. David A. Hollinger, *After Cloven Tongues of Fire: Protestant Liberalism in Modern American History* (Princeton: Princeton University Press, 2013).

5. Randall Herbert Balmer, *Redeemer: The Life of Jimmy Carter* (New York: Basic Books, Perseus Books Group, 2014).

6. Matthew Avery Sutton, *American Apocalypse: A History of Modern Evangelicalism* (Cambridge, MA: Belknap Press of Harvard University Press, 2014).

7. Ronald Reagan, Remarks at the Annual Convention of the National Association of Evangelicals in Orlando, Florida, March 8, 1983, https://voicesofdemocracy.umd.edu/reagan-evil-empire-speech-text/.

8. The Baptist Faith and Message, Southern Baptist Convention, Article XVIII, first adopted 1998, https://bfm.sbc.net/bfm2000/#xviii-the-family.

9. "FAQ," https://cara.georgetown.edu/frequently-requested-church-statistics/; Richard A. Schoenherr and Lawrence A. Young, *Full Pews and Empty Altars: Demographics of the Priest Shortage in United States Catholic Dioceses* (Madison: University of Wisconsin Press, 1993), 6, http://archive.org/details/fullpewsemptyalt0000scho.

10. "Excerpts from U.S. Bishops' Pastoral Letter on War and Peace," *New York Times*, May 5, 1983, B16.

11. Patrick Buchanan, "Culture War Speech," Speech Text (August 17, 1992), *Voices of Democracy*, https://voicesofdemocracy.umd.edu/buchanan-culture-war-speech-speech-text/.

12. Judy Maltz, "One, Two, Three, Four—We Opened Up the Iron Door," www.haaretz.com/st/c/prod/eng/25yrs _russ_img; Jonathan D. Sarna, *American Judaism: A History* (New Haven: Yale University Press, 2004), 317–20.

13. Keith Harary, "The Truth about Jonestown," *Psychology Today* 25, no. 2 (1992): 62–67, 72, 88.

14. Michael Barkun, "Reflections after Waco: Millennialists and the State [Cover Story]," *The Christian Century* 110, no. 18 (1993): 596.

15. Barkun, "Reflections after Waco," 596.

16. Pauli Murray, *Song in a Weary Throat: An American Pilgrimage* (New York: Harper & Row, 1987), 434–35.

17. Karen O'Connor, *Gender and Women's Leadership: A Reference Handbook* (Thousand Oaks, CA: SAGE Publications, 2010), 546.

18. Heather R. White, *Reforming Sodom: Protestants and the Rise of Gay Rights* (Chapel Hill: University of North Carolina Press, 2015), 148.

19. Seth Stephens-Davidowitz, "Opinion: Googling for God," *The New York Times*, September 19, 2015, www.nytimes.com/2015/09/20/opinion/sunday/seth-stephens-davidowitz-googling-for-god.html.

20. Jim Wallis, "Light the Spark," *Tikkun* 15, no. 1 (2000): 33.

21. Pope Francis, "To Participants in the International Conference of Leaders of the Catholic Charismatic Renewal International Service—Charis," June 8, 2019, www.vatican.va/content/francesco/en/speeches/2019/june/documents/papa-francesco_20190608_charis.html.

22. "The Shifting Religious Identity of Latinos in the United States," *Pew Research Center's Religion & Public Life Project* (blog), May 7, 2014, www.pewforum.org/2014/05/07/the-shifting-religious-identity-of-latinos-in-the-united-states/.

23. Val Fotherby, *The Awakening Giant* (London: Marshall Pickering, 2000); "Demos Shakarian; Founded Religious Group," *Los Angeles Times*, July 30, 1993, www.latimes.com/archives/la-xpm-1993-07-30-mn-18417-story.html.

24. "ARIS [American Religious Identification Survey] 2008 Summary Report," https://commons.trincoll.edu/aris/publications/2008-2/aris-2008-summary-report/.

25. Washingtonpost.Com, "President Bush Addresses the Nation," September 20, 2001, www.washingtonpost.com/wp-srv/nation/specials/attacked/transcripts/bushaddress_092001.html.

26. Diana L. Eck, *A New Religious America: How a "Christian Country" Has Now Become the World's Most Religiously Diverse Nation*, 1st ed. (San Francisco: HarperSanFrancisco, 2001).

27. Jacob Neusner, ed., *World Religions in America: An Introduction*, 4th ed. (Louisville, KY: Westminster John Knox Press, 2009), 206.

28. Gary Scott Smith, *Religion in the Oval Office: The Religious Lives of American Presidents* (Oxford: Oxford University Press, 2015), 388–89.

29. Pew Research Center, Washington, DC, "'Nones' on the Rise," *Pew Research Center's Religion & Public Life Project* (blog), October 9, 2012, www.pewforum.org/2012/10/09/nones-on-the-rise/; B. A. Kosmin, A. Keysar, et al., "American Nones: The Profile of the No Religion Population, a Report Based on the American Religious Identification Survey 2008" (Hartford: Program on Public Values, Trinity College, 2009), https://digitalrepository.trincoll.edu/cgi/viewcontent.cgi?article=1013&context=facpub.

Index

f behind a page number indicates a figure or photograph on that page.

CPSIA information can be obtained
at www.ICGtesting.com
Printed in the USA
LVHW110436201121
703852LV00003BA/10